H. P. Lovecraft's
Dark Arcadia

H. P. Lovecraft's Dark Arcadia

The Satire, Symbology and Contradiction

GAVIN CALLAGHAN

McFarland & Company, Inc., Publishers
Jefferson, North Carolina, and London

Permission to quote from the works of H. P. Lovecraft granted by Robert C. Harrall, Administrator, The H. P. Lovecraft Literary Estate, Cranston, RI, Lovecraft Holdings, LLC.

Neumann, Erich; *The Great Mother*. © 1955 Bollingen, 1983 renewed. Reprinted by permission of Princeton University Press.

LIBRARY OF CONGRESS CATALOGUING-IN-PUBLICATION DATA

Callaghan, Gavin, 1974–
    H. P. Lovecraft's dark Arcadia : the satire, symbology and contradiction / Gavin Callaghan.
       p.   cm.
    Includes bibliographical references and index.

    ISBN 978-0-7864-7079-2
    softcover : acid free paper ∞

    1. Lovecraft, H. P. (Howard Phillips), 1890–1937 — Criticism and interpretation.   I. Title.
    PS3523.O833Z5657 2013
    813'.52 — dc23   2013012987

BRITISH LIBRARY CATALOGUING DATA ARE AVAILABLE

On the cover: Juho Hamalainen, *H.P. Lovecraft,* darkroom collage, 16½" × 22¾", 2011 (juhoham.deviantart.com)

Manufactured in the United States of America

McFarland & Company, Inc., Publishers
  Box 611, Jefferson, North Carolina 28640
  www.mcfarlandpub.com

To the memory of
my brother Brian
1968–2010

Acknowledgments

Special thanks to Robert Harrall, administrator of the Estate of H. P. Lovecraft, for his generous permission to quote from H. P. Lovecraft's literary works.

To Sophia Brothers, image executive, Science and Society Picture Library, for permission to use a photograph by Fred Holland Day.

To Liz Kurtulik, of *Art Resource*, for her aid in procuring a Palmyrene funerary image.

To Peggy L. Gough, University of Texas Press, and Chris Sutherns, editorial and account manager, British Museum, for their aid in procuring an image of Theseus and his mother.

To Claudia Acevedo, contracts copyright and permissions assistant, for her aid in securing permission to quote from Erich Neumann's *The Great Mother*.

To Vinny at the New York Public Library, Art and Architecture Department, Room 300, for aid above and beyond the call of duty in procuring an image.

To scholar S. T. Joshi for his timely assistance in providing information, procuring articles, and giving sound advice on aspects of publishing, despite the severe limitations upon his time.

To scholar David E. Schultz, for answering a question on H. P. Lovecraft and Otto Weininger.

To my parents and my brother Chris, for material aid and other support.

To Shane T. French, Robin Snyder, and the late Everett Winrow, for their friendship and advice over the years.

Table of Contents

Introduction: Sympathy for the Shoggoths

This book began innocently enough, with an article about werewolf stories that I read in *Scary Monsters* magazine.[1] In it, Allen A. Debus provided a short history of werewolf stories published in the early twentieth century, including Jessie Douglas Kerruich's *The Undying Monster* (1922) and Guy Endore's *The Werewolf of Paris* (1933), among others. I noticed, however, that Debus made no mention of the various werewolf stories written by H. Warner Munn that, inspired by a suggestion from famed horror writer H. P. Lovecraft, had been published in *Weird Tales* magazine. I therefore began a short course of reading both Munn's and Lovecraft's werewolf stories, in preparation for what I thought would be a brief article on the appearances of werewolves in *Weird Tales*. What it turned into, however, was a revealing journey into the mind and motivations of H. P. Lovecraft, one that altered many of the standard preconceptions that I had held about him and his writings.

There are several "received truths" about H. P. Lovecraft and his horror stories that are fairly common in commentaries about Lovecraft and in Lovecraftian scholarship: that Lovecraft did not represent women, or sex, or "standard" horror figures like werewolves or witches in his weird fiction. That Lovecraft eschewed the grotesque and the mundane in favor of more celestial, alien, and cosmic horrors. That Lovecraft himself was a racist, yes, but that his weird fiction was largely separate from such concerns.[2] And that, while Lovecraft was definitely a conservative in his early life, he became increasingly liberal (in both his life and in his fiction) as the years went on, eventually adopting a form of enlightened socialism, which was diametrically opposed to his earlier aristocratic views.

As I continued my reading of Lovecraft's original texts, however, I found that the reality was quite the opposite. Not because Lovecraft's critics and readers had intentionally obscured the truth, but rather because received ideas and secondary texts had come to obscure the primary sources. As Will Brooker observes in his study of Batman, "there is a danger ... of received ideas building on each other, constructing a myth from secondary texts."[3] And much like Brooker, who during his research found many of his received notions of Batman to be quite incorrect, I also found, contrary to my expectations (and my remembrances of H. P. Lovecraft's stories from my youth), that Lovecraft was a far more mundane author than is commonly assumed. And that, far from eschewing "traditional" monsters such as witches and werewolves, instead Lovecraft filled his works with them: whether in the form of actual werewolves, or in cognate forms, such as nondescript howlers, bestial or animalistic hybrids, or ghouls.

Lovecraft's vaunted cosmicism, too (i.e., his supposed eschewing of mundane human interests, in favor of a grander cosmic scheme) which has become something of a byword in Lovecraftian criticism, I soon found to be more akin to a veneer over — or part of an admixture with — a fundamental sadism, as evidenced by Lovecraft's recurring interest in cannibalism, lycanthropy, and necrophilia. Lovecraft bore a much closer resemblance in this respect to the later sadism of American horror writers such as Robert Bloch and Stephen King than to the more abstract and alien hauntings of William Hope Hodgson, A. Merritt, or M. R. James. Even more important, I found that, far from banning women from his writings as is commonly supposed, Lovecraft instead evinced a lifelong engagement with the Feminine and aspects of women throughout his horror stories, Lovecraft's vision of women being directly grounded in the archetypal depictions of the Feminine found in the pulp and science-fantasy fiction that he read as a youth, by writers such as Lee Robinet (pseud. for Robert Ames Bennet), George Allan England, Perley Poore Sheehan, and Edgar Rice Burroughs.

At the same time, I found an increasing conservatism, rather than a lessening, in Lovecraft's horror fiction as time went on, as the growing complexity of Lovecraft's creative powers enabled him to more intricately combine his fiercely held socio-political polemics within the fabric of his weird stories, eventually resulting in the paranoid and justifiably famous neo–Puritan apologetics of his later Cthulhu apocalypses. Whereas the young Lovecraft had been more than willing to admit that "The Beast in the Cave" had once been a man, the elder Lovecraft reserved this recognition for his aristocratic Old Ones alone, consigning his bestial shoggoths, quite literally, into the outer darkness. I noted, too, the numerous continuities between the authoritarianism of Lovecraft's youthful aristocratic outlook and the authoritarianism of his later and altruistic period of "fascistic socialism,"[4] Lovecraft's pro–Czarist

Table 1. The Mundane vs. the Cosmic in HPL's Weird Fiction

Purely Mundane

- "Facts Concerning the Late Arthur Jermyn and His Family"* (miscegenation, bestiality, sadism)
- "Pickman's Model" (sadism, cannibalism)
- "The Picture in the House" (sadism, cannibalism)
- "The Outsider" (ghouls)
- "The Rats in the Walls" (sadism, cannibalism)
- "Psychopompos" (lycanthropy, infanticide)
- "The Tomb" (necrophilia, bacchanalia)
- "The Moon-Bog" (bacchanalia)
- "Herbert West: Reanimator" (necrophilia, sadism, infanticide)
- "The Loved Dead" (necrophilia, sadism)
- "The Lurking Fear" (incest, sadism, cannibalism)
- "The Unnamable" (incest, bestiality)
- "The Festival" (witchcraft)
- "The Horror at Red Hook" (bacchanalia, paganism, sadism, cannibalism, infanticide, witchcraft)
- *The Case of Charles Dexter Ward* (necromancy, necrophilia, vampirism)
- "The Shadow Over Innsmouth" (basically a recapitulation of "The Horror at Red Hook")
- "The Call of Cthulhu" (bacchanalia, apocalypticism)

Mixed Mundane & Cosmicism

- "The Dunwich Horror" (basically a recapitulation of the rural sadism of "The Unnamable" with transdimensional elements added)
- "Beyond the Wall of Sleep" (sadism, cosmicism)
- "The Colour Out of Space" (cosmicism, familial decay)
- "The Whisperer in Darkness" (cosmicism, social critique)
- *At the Mountains of Madness* (cosmicism, social critique, apocalypticism)
- "The Poe-et's Nightmare" (sadism and cannibalism as prelude to cosmicism)

Pure Cosmicism

- "The Shadow Out of Time" (pure cosmicism)
- "The Haunter of the Dark" (a cosmic entity of pure darkness)
- "From Beyond" (cosmicism vs. the limits of human perception)
- "Hypnos" (cosmicism as a critique of decadence)
- "The Music of Erich Zann" (pure cosmicism with a hint of bacchanalia)

*referred to hereafter as "Arthur Jermyn"

and pro-royalist elitism merging imperceptibly with the modern-day despotism of fascism.

H. P. Lovecraft's famous monster, Cthulhu, too — although commonly associated by many readers with the advent of a greater sense of cosmicism in Lovecraft's works[5] — is revealed to have a rather more mundane etiology, in the form of the sadistic Pigafetta illustrations seen in Lovecraft's story of New England cannibalistic degeneration, "The Picture in the House": Lovecraft referred there to what he called "a fabulous creature of the artist, which one might describe as a sort of dragon with the head of an alligator."[6] Thomas Huxley, however — from whom Lovecraft's description of Pigafetta's illustrations derives[7] — adds two additional details regarding this picture that are seemingly absent in Lovecraft's later recension, describing the creature as a "*winged, two legged,* crocodile-headed dragon"[8] (italics mine), details that eventually appeared in Lovecraft's description of Cthulhu himself, who is similarly called a "human caricature"[9] with a "vaguely anthropoid outline,"[10] who possesses "long, narrow wings behind."[11] (Both Lovecraft and Huxley, too, describe their creatures as being akin to a *dragon.*) Indeed, so clearly does Lovecraft underline this basically caricatural relationship of Cthulhu to the human form that one wonders what some readers are seeing when they, like critic Lorenzo Mastropierro in a 2009 essay, later describe Cthulhu as "a fully grown cosmic horror, ... a form of horror entirely extraneous to human anthropocentrism."[12] Indeed, given Lovecraft's direct association of Cthulhu with "voodoo orgies"[13] and African religions,[14] it seems entirely appropriate that Cthulhu should have its birth, here, in this hybrid African plate in "The Picture in the House," although Cthulhu's place of nativity has remained for so long unrecognized.

Perhaps the most egregious example of the later mythologization of H. P. Lovecraft's original texts, however, is to be found with regard to Lovecraft's well-known (Lovecraft biographer S. T. Joshi calls the lines "canonical")[15] "*they were men!*" passage from *At the Mountains of Madness,* in which Dyer famously exclaims about the Old Ones:

> "Poor devils! After all, they were not evil things of their kind. They were men of another age and another order of being....
>
> "...Radiates, vegetables, monstrosities, star spawn — whatever they had been, they were men!"[16]

As L. Sprague de Camp observes, quoting the above, "Here Lovecraft, once the most egocentric and anthropocentric of men, turns over a new leaf. The Old Ones were hardly Anglo-Saxon Protestants; but, since they have qualities he respects, he welcomes them as fellow civilized beings."[17] Justin Taylor, meanwhile, cites this passage as containing "what I believe to be the kernel of where his philosophy was headed. It is a kernel of hope."[18] Lovecraft scholar Peter Cannon, too, calls this admission of humanity on the part of the alien Old Ones "a glimpse of Lovecraft at his most humane,"[19] and suggests that Lovecraft's sentiment here "anticipates if it does not actually coincide with Lovecraft's conversion to liberalism in the spring of that year."[20] All of this perhaps dates back to science fiction writer Fritz Leiber's incredibly naive reading of this text in his essay "Through Hyperspace with Brown Jenkin" (1966), in which he observes how Lovecraft's "shoggoths eventually evolved mental powers which made them extremely dangerous creatures. (Here we begin to see Lovecraft's own evolving sympathy for his monsters; by and large he is for the Old Ones and against the shoggoths.[21])

Lovecraft's Old Ones are men, however, only insofar as they are required to be such for the purposes of his apocalyptic parable or warning[22] about societal decay. And Lovecraft's sympathies lie with the Old Ones mainly because they are the *masters* in their relationship with the shoggoths, what the earlier Puritan writers similarly saw as "The Happiness of a People in the Wisdome of Their Rulers Directing and in the Obedience of Their Brethren Attending."[23] The real monsters of the story, however, Lovecraft's shoggoths — excremental creatures forming the ultimate embodiment of that thing that should not be — remain as unreconstructed as ever; and the ultimate horror of the shoggoths, for Lovecraft, is the mere fact that they are no longer slaves. Virtually nothing has changed between *At the Mountains of Madness* and Lovecraft's early pro-slavery poem "De Triumpho Naturae" (1905). And while it is true, as S. T. Joshi observes, that Lovecraft's shoggoths are "loathsome, primitive, virtually mindless"[24] creatures, one must also remember that they only possess these qualities because Lovecraft himself bred them so, in order to better embody his complex web of personal antagonisms and hatreds. Unlike werewolves or vampires, whose depiction entails adherence to certain traditional characteristics and objective rules, the only rules to which Lovecraft's shoggoths conform are rooted in dark psychological reasons all his own. The newfound humanity of Lovecraft's Old Ones thus comes at the expense of the creation of a disposable slave-class of irredeemably offensive creatures, whose mass eradication becomes a duty.

This may seem a minor point, but failure to grasp the polemical intent of Lovecraft's writings can lead to some odd errors; perhaps the oddest interpretation of this aspect of *At the Mountains of Madness* comes in the midst of an interview with noted fantasy filmmaker Guillermo del Toro, who likens the emancipation of the shoggoths to 1930s Germany:

> It's a very funny parallel to the world that was in place [in the 1930's] and allowed Hitler to rise to power. It's really interesting and I hope some shred of

that will stay in the movie [of *At the Mountains of Madness*]. Because you know,
the decadence and the complacency and the pride and blindness that allowed
Hitler to exist is the same thing that allowed the shoggoths to rise.[25]

Lovecraft doubtless intended many parallels in his story of the shoggoths: to
the emancipation of the slaves in the U.S. South (to which Lovecraft was
opposed); to the increasing rise of anti-colonialist movements across the world
and the break-up of the British Empire during the early 20th century; to the
rise of black, Jewish and feminine power in Western culture during this same
time; or even to the destruction of his beloved Roman Empire, millennia
before. But a parallel with the rise of Hitler is not one of them, especially
since Lovecraft's rhetoric regarding the imitative and Palmyrene aspects of
the shoggoths' rise occasionally mirrors that of the Nazis against the Jews
themselves. (Strangely enough, Lovecraft and Kenneth Sterling's collaborative
science fiction story "In the Walls of Eryx" [1936] is rarely cited as evidence
of Lovecraft's increasing liberalization during his later years, despite its strong
anti-imperialist message — although the tone of this story is so radically different from Lovecraft's own, that the sentiments are more directly attributable
to Sterling.)

This misreading of Lovecraft is partly due, I think, to an underestimating
of Lovecraft's literary and polemical powers, a failure to acknowledge the ease
and skill with which he could transform and embody his views within caricatural and satirical form. A Roman satirist to the last, Lovecraft's biting,
acerbic vision is as discernable in his weird fiction as it is in his earlier poetic
satires. Indeed, in such stories as *At the Mountains of Madness*, Lovecraft's
sociology eventually came to supplant his cosmicism, and this combination
of sociological polemics with macabre sadism and cosmicism arguably is a
defining characteristic of Lovecraftian weird fiction. The unfortunate tendency
to underestimate Lovecraft, however, results in some of his most crass and
acerbic tendencies going completely unnoticed.

An example of this is the apparent Irishman named "Kid O'Brien" in
Lovecraft's "Herbert West: Reanimator," who is described, however, as a
"youth with a most un–Hibernian hooked nose."[26] As S. T. Joshi suggests in
his notes to the Penguin edition of "Reanimator," this ostensibly Irish boxer
may "not in fact [be] Irish, but perhaps Jewish, and is attempting to capitalize
on the fame of the great Irish-American boxer of the 1880's, John L. Sulli-
van."[27] In Lovecraft's correspondence, however, we find various similar
instances of Lovecraft "humorously" combining Irish with Jewish surnames:
such as "Officer McGoldstein"[28] or "Patrick J. Cohen," not to mention Lovecraft's Irish-Jewish beauty "Bridget Goldstein"[29] in his satirical short story
"Sweet Ermengarde"—all emblematic, perhaps, of Lovecraft's collectivized

view of America's various ethnicities, and their shoggoth-like hybridization, within the corridors of his own mind, into a single, loathsome mass. (Oddly, Lovecraft never seems to have considered that oftentimes these groups were just as inimical to intermixing as Lovecraft was himself.)

As Maurice Levy observes (and Kevin Dole elsewhere suggests),[30] an intricate polemical superstructure underlies Lovecraft's nightmare conceptions. And while such early stories as "The Beast in the Cave" and "Dagon" display tolerant and even semi-liberal tendencies, all of this was later overcome and overlaid by the paranoid racial vituperations of "The Call of Cthulhu" and *At the Mountains of Madness*. At the same time, however, it *is* possible to rescue Lovecraft's weird fiction from a complete identification with the worst of Nazism, since his sympathy with civilization, as suggested by his anti-lycanthropic, anti-bacchanalian polemic, is diametrically opposed to the barbarous and unashamedly pro-lycanthropic Nazi ethos.

The various misreadings of Lovecraft's weird stories are also partly due, I think, to the increasing attention that has been granted to Lovecraft's nonfiction writings, particularly his essays, letters, and autobiographical writings, in which Lovecraft gives disproportionate lip-service to a cosmicism that is not found in the actual stories themselves, or else is diluted there with an incongruous admixture of sadism. This unconscious sympathy with regard to Lovecraft's self-constructed personal narrative has even led biographer S. T. Joshi to entitle his two-volume biography of Lovecraft *I Am Providence* (based upon a famous declaration from Lovecraft's letters[31] that was later engraved upon his gravestone), an identification that most residents of Providence, if given the chance, would probably wish to contest, and which also betrays a certain level of hero-worship of Lovecraft (here identified with "Providence," i.e., the deity.) "*Puritan Anachronism*" would have been a far more accurate, if admittedly not a better, title. An advocate of the South and the Confederacy, who hung pictures of Confederate leaders on his wall; an enemy of the emancipation of the slaves, and even of the American Revolution; a twentieth century writer whose views, for much of his life, were closer to the Puritan divines of the Massachusetts Bay Colony than to his own state's very liberal Roger Williams: H. P. Lovecraft is hardly the embodiment of Providence, although he may certainly have liked to pretend that this was so. Lovecraft loved the architecture of Providence, true, but architecture does not simply just "happen"; it is built by human beings, operating under the rules and dictates of commerce and the marketplace, none of which could claim Lovecraft's sympathy. And when Lovecraft's critics themselves refer to his two years in New York as an "exile,"[32] they have perhaps gone too far in unconsciously emulating his mind-set.

This hero-worship of Lovecraft has had a curious muting effect on aspects of Lovecraftian criticism. Lovecraft's friend Rheinhart Kleiner, for example, retrospectively described his argument with Jewish amateur Charles Isaacson as "some editorial drollery,"[33] as if such things as a concern for equal rights under the law are mere "drolleries." For Lovecraft's friend Wilfred Branch Talman, meanwhile, his racism was merely an outgrowth of his bizarre 18th century aristocratic pose — Talman declaring that it is only natural that anyone assuming such a pose should then adopt a racist viewpoint, and that "it was others' fault if they did not understand."[34] But was Lovecraft an imperialist *because* he liked the 18th century, or did he mentally live within the 18th century because he was *already* an imperialist? Certainly, such figures as Roger Williams prove that Lovecraft's extremist views were no necessary component of his atavistic persona.

Yet, despite Lovecraft's intellectual errors, and the need to maintain a critical perspective on them, his acuity cannot be dismissed. His early "yellow peril" fulminations, for instance, accurately prefigured the role of the Japanese during World War II, just as Lovecraft's anti–Bolshevist rantings accurately forecast the dynamics of the decades-long Cold War later in the century. Lovecraft's depiction of Third World unrest in India and Africa in "The Call of Cthulhu," accurately forecast the anti-colonialist unrest of the early 20th century — just as his ongoing anti-bacchanalian critique accurately predicted the worst excesses of the 1960s counterculture and the insanity of the sexual revolution. Like Lovecraft's hypersensitive sculptor Henry Wilcox, whose dreams registered the seismic shifts of a restless sub-oceanic Cthulhu, Lovecraft's conservative, aristocratic nightmares proved to be an accurate indicator of the socio-political shifts and tremors of the twentieth century.

In this book, I will delve deeper into the buried satirical and symbolic aspects of Lovecraft's weird fiction. I will try to understand why his horror stories eventually went on to compose a mythos. And in the process — and much like biblical scholar Robert Eisenman before me, who discerned the inverted Hellenic satires of Jewish texts that underlie the New Testament — so too will I dissect the inverted Roman satire of Greek and bacchanalian themes embedded within his weird fiction, the blissful Arcadia of Lovecraft's early pastoral poetry going on to form the basis for that dark Arcadia, or Arkham, of his later horror stories. At the same time, I will delve even further beneath the outward polemical aspects of Lovecraft's stories, and into his recurring nightmares, and the buried anxieties that fuelled them. I will show how Lovecraft's vaunted "Great Old Ones" — far from being the cosmic, or pre-human, or alien creatures that they are commonly taken to be — actually have an origin in Lovecraft's infantile view of his own domestic situation and in a sinister apotheosis of his own mother and father.

And it is here, in Lovecraft's strained relationship with his devouring, all-powerful, and "Terrible Mother," and with his diseased and absent father, that I finally found what I had originally sought: the origin for his incongruous (and seemingly contradictory) alliance between cosmicism on the one hand and sadism on the other, in an anxiety reaction to a cosmic blackness that Lovecraft identified with both the cosmic Feminine and with the deepest, most repressed desires (whether sadistic, cannibalistic, sexual, racial, or excremental) of the mind. It is here where Lovecraft's shoggoths — whose blackness is the blackness both of excrement and of outer space — were born. It was in his paternal anxieties, meanwhile, that we find the origin of Cthulhu himself, who despite his cosmic veneer is basically little more than a paternal revenant, rising from his grave; a grave that Lovecraft, dwarfed as he was in size and age by his all-powerful parents, made larger and older than humanity itself.

The reader may note what appear to be various contradictions between the essays in this volume. In one essay, for instance, Lovecraft's Outsider is taken to represent his father redivivus, syphilitic and adulterous; while in another, it is taken to represent Lovecraft himself, and his own feelings of alienation under his inherited paternal stigma. In one essay, Lovecraft's symbol of the gate or door represents the trapdoor of Theseus, which he feared he would forever be unable to lift; while in another, it represents the entrance to the womb of the Great Goddess. My intent, however, was not to give a single, definitive interpretation of Lovecraft's works (which would, as critic Maurice Levy says, fix Lovecraftian symbols "into an univocal signification"[35]), but rather simply to follow where Lovecraft led me in each individual instance, and in so doing create a picture as wide and varied as the fabric of the stories themselves. My ultimate goal was to suggest the numerous overlapping ideas and warring inspirations that perhaps figured within Lovecraft's mind at the moment that he was writing, and thus to capture, if possible, the instant of inspiration. And it may be that at such a moment, Lovecraft's idea of the Outsider as the father redivivus, and his idea of the Outsider as being a reflection of himself, became one.

At the same time, however, Lovecraft himself was never one to balk at contradictions in his own life, and any criticism of his life and works must necessarily follow suit. Indeed, to say that Lovecraft — who, as Maurice Levy points out, was both "sensitive to cold"[36] and "fond of ice cream" — was a man of contradictions would be the merest understatement.

ONE

Dark Arcadia

Arcadia, Arkham and H. P. Lovecraft's Process of Classical Inversion

And even the skies of spring and the flowers of
summer must ever afterward be poison to me.
—H. P. Lovecraft, "The Call of Cthulhu"[1]

I. Rome vs. Greece

Horror writer H. P. Lovecraft is perhaps unique in the annals of modern classicism in his lifelong adherence to classical Rome, rather than classical Greece. Unlike Oscar Wilde, for instance, who complained that ancient Rome had "'no art; no myths'"[2]; or classical art collector Edward P. Warren, who "'believed beauty to be a monopoly of the Greeks'"[3]; or poet W. H. Auden, who "by heredity and temperament" could only "think of the Romans with distaste"[4]; or gnostic Platonist Simone Weil, for whom the Roman empire was "'history's greatest disaster'"[5]; or the 1890s Vagabond poets, who were, as Bliss Carman writes, "Greek in the morning / And Gothic at night"[6]; or even Oswald Spengler, for whom ancient Rome was, and always had been, a representative of the dreaded East; for Lovecraft Rome was his intellectual and philosophical center, a representative of aristocratic values and a bastion of civilization, as opposed to what he saw as the decadent, effeminate, and foreign Greeks. As Lovecraft himself observed, contrasting his position with that of his friend, decadent poet and aesthete Samuel Loveman:

Greece [...] has not for me the direct kinship it has for Loveman.... I can understand the tinge of patronage in the contemptuous diminutive expression *Graeculus*. In a word, I have to think of the whole Grecian world from a *Roman*

11

angle—something connected with eastern wars and proconsuls and foreign travel and academic studies"[7] [Lovecraft's italics].

All this, despite the fact that ancient Rome, as scholar Theodor Mommsen once observed, "'cannot arouse ... the mysterious shiver the heart seeks out'"[8]— hardly a prerequisite for attracting the interest of any weird fiction writer.

It would be futile to attempt to unravel the numerous contradictions inherent in Lovecraft's position, just as it is futile to argue against anyone's subjective likes or dislikes. Suffice it to say, Lovecraft preferred ancient Rome — as superstitious, decadent, and cruel as it was — over the equally superstitious, decadent, and cruel ancient Greeks. Nor was Lovecraft himself unaware of the contradictions inherent in such a position[9]; Lovecraft eventually went on, later in life, to extol the genius of ancient Greece[10] and acknowledge "'that the Romans were an extremely prosaic race; given to all the practical & utilitarian precepts I detest, and without any of the genius of the Greek or glamour of the Northern barbarian.'"[11]

These peculiar contours of Lovecraft's classicism were thus more emotive than intellectual, and doubtlessly owe much to Lovecraft's older male relatives, particularly his grandfather, who was, as both Peter Cannon and S. T. Joshi observe,[12] basically a surrogate father figure, and who was also a classicist and world traveler, who taught Lovecraft the lore, the language, and the love of ancient Rome. In the same way, ancient Rome itself—much like the British Empire,[13] of which Lovecraft was also enamored—came to form a masculine and paternal ideal within his mind; and there was a close similarity in this regard between the fervently masculine language in his pro–Allied World War I writings, which associate pacifism with "th' unmanly State"[14] of the "effeminate idealist,"[15] and his panegyrics about "the virile, warlike days of the [Roman] republic, when the conquering eagles of our consuls were carrying the name and dominion of the Roman people to the uttermost confines of the known world. S.P.Q.R.!"[16] Interestingly, Lovecraft even organized the cats in his fantasy-story *The Dream-Quest of Unknown Kadath* into strictly regimented military groupings, depicting feline generals, phalanxes,[17] regiments,[18] and sub-lieutenants.[19] Tellingly, these same cats are also described in purely masculine and, indeed, strikingly paternal terms: Randolph Carter is aided by what Lovecraft calls the "grandfather of that very kitten" that he once aided elsewhere,[20] also described as "that austere patriarch."[21] Later, too, Carter will meet with "*the old* chief of the cats in Celephais"[22] (italics mine)—yet another variation on Lovecraft's omnipresent theme of the "Old Ones"—and Lovecraft idealized the close relationship between this "*old* general [cat] and his grandson"[23] (italics mine).

Indeed, in much the same way that Lovecraft, throughout his life, successively bought part and parcel into the various other propaganda systems to which he was exposed (such as Temperance rhetoric, segregationist rhetoric, World War I propaganda, and 18th century aristocratic bigotry), Lovecraft wholeheartedly accepted both the Roman worldview and the 18th century English worldview through which it was filtered. Lovecraft sounded very much like the Roman patriarch Cato, who was known for his opposition to "Greek luxury and refinement,"[24] as he observed, "I think of Greeks as cultivated but somewhat sycophantic aliens — good tutors of rhetoric and philosophy, but a little servile, unctuous, ratlike, sharp, and effeminate — in a word, not quite as much *men* as real ROMANS."[25] As we shall see, Lovecraft's feelings in this regard do much to illuminate his larger polemical opposition to decadence, as well as his related differences with Samuel Loveman, an opposition that did much to determine the characteristic form assumed by his later weird fiction. And while, as Lovecraft's closest friend Frank Belknap Long observes, "There can be no doubt that all of Howard's writing in later years was influenced by his early familiarity with the timeless tales of classical antiquity in which gods and human heroes often battled for supremacy,"[26] such a statement only skims the surface of the symbolic and polemical complexity of Lovecraft's weird fiction.[27]

It is here, in Lovecraft's tortured attempts to reconcile his conservative, pastoral classicism on the one hand with his innate anti–Grecian sentiments on the other, that we find the origin of Lovecraft's famed Mythos, in an inverted Roman caricature of Greek Arcadian and sylvan myths, through which he was able to embody his larger Puritan, anti-bacchanalian sociopolitical polemics. Throughout this essay, I will chart the gradual process by which Lovecraft slowly reversed and inverted those Greek and Arcadian myths that he had loved as a youth, transforming nymph-haunted Arcadia into witch-haunted Arkham,[28] with the piping Pan of Arcadia's meadows slowly becoming the cannibalistic ghoul of Arkham's cemeteries. Indeed, what Lovecraft, in his 1917 poem "To the Arcadian," lovingly calls "The untainted glamour of Arcadian lands"[29] became in his later weird fiction quite tainted. As Lovecraft's frightened narrator avers after the unsettling events in "The Colour Out of Space": "I do not think I shall visit the Arkham country hereafter."[30] His Arcadia was forever blighted, as much by the bacchanalian excesses of the fauns as by the Puritan lens of Lovecraft's vision.

Like any good conservative, however, Lovecraft had initially begun by seeing the Arcadian and pastoral vision of the Greeks as an ideal to be maintained and as a model that must be defended against anti-traditionalist and modernist encroachment. The fact that this pastoral ideal he followed also cloaked an inextricable fabric of bacchanalian and sylvan lasciviousness, however — all anathema to Lovecraft's Puritan imagination — although it may have subtly troubled the fastidious Lovecraft, was a contradiction that was easily sloughed off, at least at first. After all, this basic disjunction between Rome and Greece was a contradiction that Ancient Rome itself never completely solved and that the prudish forces within Victorian England (for whom the more lascivious aspects of Greek life and literature were equally unseemly) were still struggling with hundreds of years later. This struggle — between Greece as an ideal to be maintained and as a subversive force to be opposed — gives characteristic form to the Lovecraftian weird canon and is reflected in such things as Lovecraft's strangely ambivalent attitude toward the aquatic, basically Atlantean society of the Deep Ones in "The Shadow Over Innsmouth," and Dyer's equally ambivalent reaction to the vanished civilization of the Old Ones in *At the Mountains of Madness*.

Such a process was not swift, however; Lovecraft only gradually felt his way toward an inversion of the Greek Arcadian pantheon as he went along. The process eventually culminated in his later, lengthy, Cthulhu Cult apocalypses, in which Lovecraft, like a latter-day Roman orator, sought to conserve what he saw as the last vestiges of white elite civilization and to satirize those forces that were destroying it. The Rome of Lovecraft's imagination was a place of strict order, practicality, and realism. Even the Roman gods were, as French writer Gerald Messadie points out, ultimately little more than "a guarantor of order and, ultimately, of the state, neither of which was tolerant of such eccentricities as saying that men were born of a stone or a bird with a lizard's tail or from some cosmic copulation with monsters."[31] The latter example, of course, has numerous striking parallels with the alien horrors of Lovecraft's own weird fiction.[32]

This distressingly prosaic attitude would likewise, Messadie writes, "come to brand Roman portraiture, in which there is no interpretation, no idealization, nothing but pure realism — which, it could be argued, was a Roman invention."[33] This attitude likewise came to characterize the weird aesthetic of H. P. Lovecraft, who (much like painter Richard Upton Pickman), summons up "actual scenes from the spectral world he lives in" that display "the actual anatomy of the terrible."[34] Lovecraft's horror writing follows the ancient Romans, too, in what scholar J. W. Mackail, in his introduction to Virgil's *Aeneid*, calls the "rhetorical turn"[35] of Roman literature; and Lovecraft — in what writer Mark Schorer deprecatingly calls his "excessively Latinate prose"[36] — took very much to heart the notion that "magis oratoribus quam poetis imitandus"[37] (orators rather than poets ought to be followed).

Lovecraft's Roman tendencies, however, are perhaps most strikingly highlighted by his satirical gift. H. P. Lovecraft possessed a genius for satire. It is clearly displayed in the wit, liveliness, and verve of his satirical verses and in his often quite fearsome attacks upon his opponents during his polemical battles in the pulp magazines, in the amateur press, and in his personal circle. As his friend Rheinhart Kleiner observed, "As a poetical satirist, he [Lovecraft] had as robust a vocabulary as Dean Swift, after whom his longer efforts seemed obviously patterned. His prose essays may sometimes have had a slightly sharper edge than those of Addison and Steele."[38] Kleiner also opined, with more than a little justification, that as a young man "Lovecraft pulled an amount of heavy artillery into action against his rabbits which might have been adequate for larger game."[39] It would be foolish to presume that Lovecraft somehow dampened or ignored this satirical or caricatural impulse in his later weird fiction, or that he would not attempt, given the increasing complexity of his literary abilities over time, an increasing integration of his deeply held socio-political polemics within the context of his horror stories. In such later apocalypses as "The Call of Cthulhu," *At the Mountains of Madness*, "The Whisperer in Darkness," and "The Shadow Over Innsmouth," Lovecraft finally found, as Rheinhart Kleiner put it, his "larger game." As Lovecraft himself observed, "classicism is ever the moulder of effective rhetoric"[40] — and, it would seem, of effective horror stories.

Other readers, however, such as early critic Matthew Onderdonk, studying the structure of the Lovecraft Mythos, have suggested that Lovecraft intended his mythos as an attempt at a new and scientific cosmology for the modern age (an idea that has since been perversely recapitulated by various modern occultists, who promulgate Lovecraft's cosmology as a new theology for mankind!). Such ideas, however, present the difficulty of suggesting that Lovecraft's fictional pantheon was something pre-existing, which required his fiction merely as a means by which to embody it, and not something added to organically, as his stories required it, over time, and in accordance with the needs of Lovecraft's conservative polemic. The idea expressed by Frank Belknap Long, too, that for Lovecraft "the Cthulhu Mythos was an artistic construct and nothing else,"[41] also seems to ignore or eliminate the polemical basis of many of the anti–Arcadian and anti-decadent inversions that underlie his stories. If, however, Lovecraft's pantheon was partly a caricatural construct, embodying a Roman critique of Grecian and mystical ecstatic religions (and those numerous modern and decadent corruptions that they signify), then the form assumed by Lovecraft's later weird fiction is more readily, and realistically, explained: as a series of polemical expedients, reflecting the inextricably linked connections underlying Lovecraft's complex and never-ending intellectual antagonisms. Ultimately, of course, as Long suggests, the most basic function of Lovecraft's mythos was the artistic suggestion of a primordial mythic background, one that would allow Lovecraft to postulate the existence of an unknown and even more ancient substratum of primal cosmic myths anterior to Greece or Rome. As we shall see, however, no matter how ostensibly cosmic Lovecraft's conceptions, they still maintained an uneasy resemblance to, and an uneasy relationship with, the classical myths that gave them form.

Lovecraft himself was quick to admit the origin of his horror stories in a combination or synthesis of Greek imagery with the Gothic or macabre, describing himself very early on as "a Greek influenced by Grimm's fairy tales,"[42] whose discovery of the works of Edgar Allan Poe at age eight caused "'the blue of Argos and Sicily [to be] darkened by the miasmal exhalations of the tomb!'"[43] Nor was his inversion of the Greek myths in the form of horror stories at all unusual. Certainly, something of the sort had already been accomplished by Christianity itself and by such theologians as St. Augustine, who recast the gods of ancient Greece and Rome into the syncretic demons of Christian theology. And although critic Maurice Levy apparently feels constrained to point out, in his book *Lovecraft: A Study in the Fantastic*, that "Lovecraft is not St. Augustine,"[44] in truth there are a number of parallels between Lovecraft's anti-bacchanalian anxieties and the earlier fulminations of Christian divines, such as the 17th century Massachusetts Bay Puritan elites, for whom increasing secularization — perceived by them as societal decay — was linked with a rise in witchcraft and demonolatry.

Edgar Allan Poe himself, despite his innate and spasmodic romanticism, also displays some links with classicism, famously invoking in his poem "To Helen": "the glory that was Greece, / And the grandeur that was Rome"[45] — a connection that Lovecraft later reflected in his story "Hypnos," which was dedicated to both Poe[46] and the decadent classicist Samuel Loveman.[47] Lovecraft's description of the simultaneously Poe-like and classical countenance of the narrator's friend in that story, too, also seems to reflect an early attempt at a synthesis of the classical with the macabre. Even Lovecraft's idolatrous description of Poe in his letters as "my God of Fiction"[48] reflects (perhaps unconsciously) the classical Roman practice of personifying and deifying an abstract idea. In his essay "The Despised Pastoral" (1918), too, printed in his self-published periodical *The Conservative*, Lovecraft even goes so far as to cite Poe in defense of the classical English pastoral form, observing how "it was no starched classicist, but the exceedingly unconventional Edgar Allan Poe, who roundly denounced the melancholy metaphysicians and maintained that true poetry has for its first object 'pleasure, not truth,' and 'indefinite pleasure instead of definite pleasure.'"[49]

Ultimately, however, the tension between these two opposing ideas was insurmountable, and Lovecraft was only able to maintain his allegiance to both Poe and classicism by aligning Poe's macabre vision with those Arcadian forces that Lovecraft distrusted; an alignment entirely characteristic of the American Puritan imagination, from Nathaniel Hawthorne's depiction of the bestial and sylvan revelries at Merry Mount to D. W. Griffith's silent horror film, *The Avenging Conscience* (1914), in which the macabre is given a clearly sylvan complexion. And then, of course, there are the weird stories of horror writers such as Dion Fortune, Algernon Blackwood, and Arthur Machen, in which the pagan and the macabre are also eerily combined, although none of these authors ever went so far as Lovecraft did, and actually wrote as if they were an aristocratic Roman satirist of the late classical era. And although one can see an obvious antecedent for Lovecraft's sinister use of sylvan entities via the "Fauns and Satyrs and Aegipans"[50] mentioned in Arthur Machen's *The Great God Pan*, nowhere else do we find such a total utilization of anti–Arcadian imagery and anti-sylvan rhetoric as in Lovecraft's weird fiction.

Lovecraft's inverted caricature of Arcadian myths does not characterize all of his fiction, however; and we must takes pains to distinguish (as Lovecraft himself did) between his fantasies (i.e., his "Dunsanian" works) on the one hand, in which he largely conserved his earlier rustic or pastoral Arcadian vision, and his fictional nightmares (i.e., his weird fiction) on the other. The former reflect Lovecraft's aristocratic lament at lost traditions, while the latter reflect a sly caricature of the forces destroying those traditions. (Scholar Maurice Levy advances a complex theory involving differing dream-levels in order to attempt to account for the obvious differences between Lovecraft's weird fiction and his Dunsanian fantasies[51]; in all things, however, a simpler explanation is always preferable, and an easier answer is amply provided by Lovecraft's differing polemical stances with regard to these fictional genres: fantasy vs. the horror story.) As Lovecraft observes in a 1916 letter, in terms which suggest the *raison d'etre* underlying his later Dunsanian fantasies: "To the poet there is the ability and privilege *to fashion a little Arcadia in his fancy*, wherein he may withdraw from the sordid reality of mankind at large. In short, the world abounds with simple delusions which we may call 'happiness,' if we be but able to entertain them"[52] (italics mine). This language closely parallels Lovecraft's later description, in 1922, of Lord Dunsany's stories as "the *Dresden-china Arcadia* of an author who will play with old ideas, ... in a deft pictorial way"[53] (italics mine). Critic Peter Cannon, too, writes of what he calls the "quasi–Arcadian" settings[54] of Lovecraft's Dunsanian stories. And while, as Cannon further observes, S. T. Joshi will argue "vigorously that all the early Dunsanian tales occur in the earth's distant past,"[55] this past is not so much a tangible place as it is an idealized Arcadia, analogous to both the classical world and, by extension, to Lovecraft's (largely classical) childhood itself.

In Lovecraft's more characteristically Lovecraftian weird fiction, however — especially his later Cthulhu apocalypses, in which the Lovecraft Mythos achieves characteristic and autonomous form — Lovecraft's earlier pastoral Arcadia has finally turned rotten, the "wilder hymn"[56] of Pan finally descending into chaos, a world that the patrician Lovecraft is viewing through xenophobic Roman eyes.

II. Et in Arcadia Ego...

> Thy pow'rs, Arcadian Muse, dispel the woe,
> And thro' the gloom unnumbered beauties shew!
> — H. P. Lovecraft, "Autumn"[57]

H. P. Lovecraft's autobiographical writings are filled with numerous references to his youthful love for Greek and Arcadian beauty, a period when "all the world became ancient Greece to me," and when he "looked for Naiades in the fountain on the lawn, and forebore to break the shrubbery for fear of harming the Dryades."[58] (Nor was Lovecraft in any way unique or alone in this hobby, Victorian children being noted for perpetuating "shrines to Pan."[59]) As Lovecraft himself avers, it was akin to "a kind of 'religious experience'"[60] to him, and it is possible to see, in the wild, orgiastic rites of his later Cthulhu-worshippers, an embarrassed parody of his own youthful enthusiasm, and what Lovecraft, in his early weird story "The Tomb," calls Jervas Dudley's "religious zeal,"[61] a zeal characterized in that story by an autoerotic and Dionysian ecstasy, in which the sylvan wonders of the forest are confused with the necrophilic wonders of the grave.

Indeed, all of the characteristic elements of Lovecraft's youthful worship — "dryads and satyrs," "the woods and fields at dusk," the "dancing" of "sylvan creatures"[62] — are perpetuated, undisguised, in his later weird fiction. The greenery that the young Lovecraft forebore to disturb becomes the "lawless luxuriance of green"[63] in "The Picture in the House." Lovecraft's "faun-peopled meadows in the twilight"[64] reappear via those fields in "The Dunwich Horror" where Lovecraft's ostensibly cosmic Old Ones are still said to tread, while even the dusk or twilight setting, so common to his early, pastoral poems,[65] likewise recurs throughout the Lovecraftian weird canon, albeit in quite a more sinister context: the perpetual twilight of the woods in "The Dunwich Horror"[66] and "The Whisperer in Darkness,"[67] the Satanic twilight of Frank Marsh's painting in "Medusa's Coil," and the "twilit grotto"[68] in "The Rats in the Walls." Even the "dryads and satyrs" of Lovecraft's youthful reveries will find their inverted analogue in the numerous and malevolent married couples seen so often in Lovecraft's weird fiction (as discussed in the final chapter of this book).

The landscape of Lovecraft's weird stories, too, although typically represented as being situated somewhere in New England, closely mirrors the typography of ancient Greece, which was characterized, according to classical scholar Stringfellow Barr, by its "omnipresent sea,"[69] no point in Greece being more than sixty miles from the Mediterranean, and also by its "fresh and delicious springs."[70] Lovecraft refers throughout "The Whisperer in Darkness" to "the gurgling, insidious trickle of strange waters from numberless hidden fountains in the shadowy woods,"[71] and the sinister residence taken up by Wilbur Whately's invisible brother within the depths of Cold Spring Glen, according to locals, "'ain't no healthy nor decent place.'"[72] As Lovecraft's narrator observes in "The Colour Out of Space," there is something sinister about "the new city water of Arkham,"[73] freshly piped in, of course, from the sinister fields to Arkham's west, water that has its ultimate origin, however, in the fountains of Arcadia. Ancient Hellas was also, according to Barr, "a limestone country, full of subterranean cavities, and the rivers had a disconcerting way of disappearing underground."[74] These underground rivers and cavities likewise have numerous Lovecraftian parallels, from the subterranean "dark sticky water lapping at onyx piers"[75] in "The Horror at Red Hook" to the "oily underground river"[76] in "The Festival." And while it is true that Lovecraft often based much of the natural imagery in his later weird fiction upon his first-hand experiences in rural Vermont, this landscape so impressed him in the first place only because it was so Arcadian (Lovecraft even describing it as that "weirdly beautiful Arcadia"[77]).

The numerous islands and archipelagos of Hellas are likewise reflected in the various small and sinister islands found throughout the Lovecraftian weird canon, whether the risen isles of R'lyeh, "Dagon," or Ghatanothoa, or else those more local islands in the Miskatonic described in "The Colour Out of Space" and "The Dreams in the Witch House," "where the devil held court beside a curious stone altar older than the Indians."[78] Indeed, very often these islands are associated by Lovecraft with some sort of dark worship, as in "The Moon-Bog"[79] and "The Picture in the House," in which he speaks of "sinister monoliths on uninhabited islands,"[80] language that suggests a darker version of the numerous holy islands of the Greeks and the Romans: Kalauria, a small island located opposite Troezen, which "possessed a celebrated temple of Poseidon" and "which was regarded as an inviolable asylum"[81]; or the sacred isle of the sylvan god Faunus, located in the Tiber in Rome, for whom sacrifices were performed around the time of the ides of February.[82] And then there was the mysterious "floating island"[83] of Delos, said to have been "called out of the deep by the trident of Poseidon" and later fastened by Zeus with "adamantine chains to the bottom of the sea,"[84] an instability later perpetuated by the equally unstable and ultimately Atlantis-like island of R'lyeh.

One of the earliest expressions of Lovecraft's unalloyed pastoral or Arcadian vision is his collection *Poemata Minora*, prepared by him in 1902, and "affectionately" dedicated "to the Gods, Heroes, & Ideals of the Ancients" by "a Great Admirer."[85] As yet untouched by Lovecraft's later caricatural impulse, his polemical and socio-political conceits co-exist side by side with an as-yet unrepentant Arcadian classicism. Lovecraft continued in this vein into the early 1920s, writing interminable if clever poems replete with typically Arcadian elements such as the springtime imagery of "birds' returning flight"[86] and the rising of the "sap within the tree,"[87] praising "Ye sylvan dryads!" of "the Vernal scene," and the "Spring," when "buds deck ev'ry forest bough."[88] Autumn, too, is called by Lovecraft an "Arcadian goddess!"[89] whose song brings "Th' unbroken promise of returning Spring"[90]; and even as late as his 1918 poem "April," we still find Lovecraft praising Hertha, the Germanic earth goddess, along with "the gentle Dryads" and "the dews that drape the sprouting green."[91] In his poem "A Winter Wish" (1918), meanwhile, Lovecraft even petitions the gods for a Pantheon-sized glass dome in the middle of winter, beneath which could exist the "fond delights" and "sweet Arcadian grace"[92] of summer, including the expected "Fauns and Satyrs" and "reedy Pan"[93] (Lovecraft intensely disliked the cold). This idea, in its obverse form, is strikingly reproduced in "The Colour Out of Space," in which the blasted heath likewise exists dead and desolate, amidst a larger scene of tangled vernal luxuriousness, like "a great spot eaten by acid in the woods and fields."[94] (Interestingly, given Lovecraft's general abhorrence for the cold in both his early pagan poems and his later weird fiction, one could perhaps consider his perpetuation of anti-cold imagery throughout his weird fiction to be a partial conservation of his earlier vernal or sylvan imagery amid his later anti–Arcadian vision. Pan wasn't *all* bad.)

One must note, however, that even Lovecraft's early Arcadianism is already being projected through a pastoral, 18th century filter. Even as a youth, Lovecraft's vision of a sylvan utopia consisted not of the wilds of Pan but rather of a vernal or rustic scene under human (read aristocratic and royal) cultivation, what Lovecraft calls, in his essay "The Despised Pastoral," "engaging scenes of Arcadian simplicity, which not only transport the imagination through their intrinsic beauty, but recall to the scholarly mind the choicest remembrances of classical Greece and Rome."[95] Lovecraft could abide the breeding of plants, and the rustic, natural forms of forest, hill, and river, so long as such forms were suitably managed, and supervised within a royalistic, pastoral, and aristocratic hierarchy, with the peasant "tilling ancestral acres in the good old way."[96] But the pagan rites and revels in propitiation of this lush sylvan fertility (along with the orgiastic nudity, chanting, dancing, and fornication they involved) were something the Puritan Lovecraft could not abide or tolerate, even at the expense of eventually largely discarding his Arcadian vision. And when his earlier Arcadian vision finally is revived, as it is in "The Whisperer in Darkness"— into which large portions of his pro–Arcadian 1927 Vermont travelogue were incorporated — it is a wilderness tainted by the decadent rites of Pan and the satyrs, in which the immigrant cosmic aliens of the story assume the sinister Arcadian roles that Lovecraft, in his 1927 essay, had so wished to conserve.

Hence, too, the ungoverned primal wildness of Arkham Country as depicted in "The Colour Out of Space," in which, as Lovecraft writes, "there are valleys with deep woods that no axe has ever cut"[97] and where "weeds and briers reigned"[98] amid the deserted and vacant farms; in these scenes Lovecraft's pastoral paradise from his poem "Quinsnicket Park" has been reinvaded by a dominant and strangely sinister nature. Even the helpful old man Ammi Pierce, who (somewhat like Zadok Allen in "The Shadow Over Innsmouth") represents the last, if semi-deranged, vestige of Western civilization in the area, makes his home in what Lovecraft calls an "ancient tottering cottage where the trees first begin to get very thick"[99] (language that recalls the similarly tottering vestiges of Western civilization at the end of "The Call of Cthulhu"[100]).

As we have seen, joyous references to the nymphs and goddesses also prevail throughout Lovecraft's early pastoral poems (giving the lie to the common notion that Lovecraft never represented women in his writings): Lovecraft wrote fancifully of the "fays,"[101] of the "Shy Oreads," and of the "Corybantian glee" of the dancing "river-gods" in his poem "The Spirit of Summer" (1918), all language and imagery shortly to be inverted in his weird fiction, in which the goddesses and nymphs are subsumed beneath the sinister, overpowering figure of the all-devouring Terrible Mother. Even outside the weird fiction, in his satirical poetry, the term *nymph* will continue to be used by Lovecraft as a metaphor or synonym for young women, particularly sexually active ones, in such writings as "The Nymph's Reply to the Modern Businessman" (1917) and "The Pathetick History of Sir Wilful Wildrake" (ca. 1921). Indeed, as I further explore in the final chapter of this book, it seems that Lovecraft's inversion of Arcadian themes was rooted, at least partially, in his aversion to the Feminine, as represented by such figures as his mother and by such maternal substitutes as the poetess Winifred Jackson, who was, as Lovecraft himself points out, the author of several poems his mother knew "by heart, and frequently repeated; especially 'A Merchant from Arcady.'"[102] Did Winifred Jackson play the role of Eve within Lovecraft's ideal Arcadia, blighting it forevermore within his formidable imagination?

Perhaps the most important Arcadian figure to appear in Lovecraft's later writings, however, was the great god Pan, likewise a central figure in contemporary decadent poetry and occultism. As scholar William Smith observes, Pan "was originally only an Arcadian god; and Arcadia was always the principal seat of his worship."[103] The "god of forests, pastures, flocks, and shepherds," Smith goes on, Pan "dwelt in grottoes, wandered on the summits of mountains and rocks, and in valleys, either amusing himself with the chase, or leading the dances of the nymphs."[104] Pan was thus also a god of eroticism, bestiality, and phallicism (a fact Lovecraft slyly alludes to in his description of the "proboscidian Chaugnar Faugn"[105] in his collaborative story "The Horror in the Museum." This is an analogue, perhaps, to the pox'd and phallic "nose"[106] of Lovecraft's priapean "Sir Wilful Wildrake"), ever piping on his favorite instrument, the syrinx — an image that inspired both the decadent vagabond poets of the 1890s[107] and Lovecraft's own recurring image of the piping flutes of outer darkness. (Note here, too, the archetypal, ancestral symbolism of the phallic pipes and horns of various primitive peoples, which, according to anthropologist H. R. Hays, are often "taboo to women"[108] and which "are used in ceremonies in which they represent male ancestors, quite clearly as phallic symbols." Given the curiously primitive texture of so much of Lovecraft's weird fiction, it is tempting to view Lovecraft's piping flutes in a similar light: i.e., as direct, if unconscious, paternal or ancestral symbols.)

Pan was only one of a plethora of such bestial, sylvan male deities, however, including the fauns, the satyrs, the sileni, and many others, all of whom were regarded, like the feminine dryads, as protectors of and dwellers within the deep dark woods, what Lovecraft, in "The Picture in the House," calls "The haunted wood and the desolate mountain."[109] And although Robert M. Price, in his essay "Mythos Names and How to Say Them" (1987), will observe of the monster-name Chaugnar Faugn that "'Fawn' seems highly inappropriate for a horrific entity, whether one thinks of Bambi or of the fauns of classical myth,"[110] the truth is that the Arcadian sylvan deities had darker aspects, as well, which would have definitely recommended them to Lovecraft's notice. As William Smith observes, Pan was "dreaded by travellers," being known for startling people in forests and meadows with "sudden awe and terror." This feeling of "sudden fright without any visible cause" was "ascribed to Pan, and was called Panic Fear"[111] — a fear which Lovecraft, not uncoincidentally, will refer to throughout his weird fiction.[112] This fear, as scholar Alexander Murray observes, was most commonly associated with the characteristic "feeling of solitude and lonesomeness which weighs upon travelers in wild mountain scenes, when the weather is stormy, and no sound of human voice is to be heard."[113] Lovecraft, in "Dunwich Horror," calls them those "lonely places" where the Old Ones "walk unseen and foul."[114] Indeed, such wild mountain scenes prevail throughout his writings, from the thunder-haunted Catskills of "The Lurking Fear" to the desolate Antarctic environs of *At the Mountains of Madness*.

In Lovecraft's macabre poem "Nemesis" (1917), too, the poet suffers from an apparent attack of panic fear in a "hoary primordial grove," when he senses what he calls a "thing" that "leers thro' dead branches above," also described as a (Pan-like?) "presence that marches / And stalks on where no spirit dares rove."[115] This idea later reappears in "The Haunter of the Dark" with regard to the ostensibly cosmic entity in that story, called "some formless alien presence close to him [Robert Blake] and watching him with horrible intentness," which fills Blake with a "gnawing, indeterminate panic fear."[116] Lovecraft also reflects something of this sinister connotation of the Fauni and their cohorts in his letter to fellow amateur press writer E. A. Edkins, in which he writes of that "'odour of a goat' or some reptilian taint, detected (in the best of weird fiction) when some sinister character of faunesque or vampirish or werewolfish nature passes by.'"[117] This idea suggests something of Lovecraft's otherwise incongruous attribution of reptilian or saurian traits to the faunesque Wilbur Whately.[118]

The fact that Lovecraft, as Peter Cannon suggests, intended a "sardonic inversion"[119] of his own family life in his picture of Wilbur Whately and his diseased kin further illuminates his incorporation of faunesque or Pan-like traits in his portrait of Whately. Pan's odd appearance at birth causes his guardians such horror when they first see him that they jump into the sea and drown.[120] This idea suggests a certain similarity with Lovecraft's own lantern-jawed visage as a youth, which caused his mother so much discomfort.[121] A jutting lower jaw is also a feature of Lovecraft's necrophilic ghouls, whose cannibalistic aspects retain some of the more sadistic aspects of both Pan — who was said to pursue the dancing nymphs and Oreads "with violence"[122] — and the Arcadian region itself, which was the source of the sadistic and cannibalistic myth of the werewolf in ancient times.[123]

One also sees a resemblance to Pan in the various horned and cloven-hoofed monstrosities in Lovecraft's fiction, such as the sadistic creature in "The Unnamable" (1923) and the horned, satyr-like beings in "The Nameless City" (1921). And significantly, Lovecraft in the latter story suggests an analogy between the relation of these satyr-like beings to their dead city and the role played by his beloved she-wolf in the founding of ancient Rome. Clearly,

Lovecraft is still feeling his way in "The Nameless City" toward integrating his fund of classical lore within his weird fiction, a problematic integration that eventually culminates in his more successful investiture of human characteristics within his Old Ones, the founders of the city in *At the Mountains of Madness*, and his attribution of decadent, bestial traits in their barbaric usurpers, the shoggoths.

In his early poem "To Pan" (written in 1902, published in 1919), however, we still find the young Lovecraft describing the "hybrid"[124] Pan in fondly sylvan terms, using language that would not have been out of place in a poem by Oscar Wilde or one of the Vagabond poets of the 1890s. As late as Lovecraft's pro-pastoral story "The Tree" (1920), the "fauns and dryads"[125] are still being depicted as helpful and benevolent creatures, despite what he also refers to as the weirdness of "dreaded Pan"[126] in the same story. The creatures of Kalos' sylvan grove (much like Pickman's ghouls later on) inspire the beautiful visions of the rustic artist, and later aid in his posthumous revenge against the decadent and urban Musides. (Lovecraft was perhaps inspired in his plot for "The Tree" by Virgil's tale of the tree that grew "up out of the unquiet grave of Polydorus"[127] and says "with a piteous groan ... 'I am Polydorus.'")

Intimations of Lovecraft's later inversion of classical myths, however, appear in his early essay "Metrical Regularity" (1915), in which he challenges the modernist idea "that the truly inspired bard must chant forth his feelings independently of form or language, ... blindly resigning his reason to the 'fine frenzy' of his mood."[128] He goes on to describe this "frenzy" using the analogy of the Greek hero Perseus riding the winged steed Pegasus, and makes a poet's attempt to capture the ongoing stream of consciousness within the mind of Perseus himself. As Lovecraft observes, "Most amusing of all the claims of the radical is the assertion that true poetic fervour can never be confined to regular metre; that the wild-eyed, long-haired rider of Pegasus must inflict upon a suffering public in unaltered form the vague conceptions which flit in noble chaos through his exalted soul." He contrasts this image with the later "succeeding hour of calmer contemplation," which is, he argues, better suited to refining such poetic images. As with Lovecraft's later inversion of Arcadian imagery, a simple change of perspective — in this case, from within Perseus to without — is enough to alter the polemical basis of classical imagery.

Whether Lovecraft is correct or not in the context of this poetical debate is beside the point. What interests us in this essay is the relationship between Lovecraft's anti-modernist critique and the classical images with which he characterizes it, as well as their marked similarity to the forms assumed in Lovecraft's later apocalypses, in which such "chaos" as Lovecraft here decries is a hallmark of Cthulhu and his followers. In his later version, Lovecraft will omit the "long-haired rider of Perseus" completely (a description that echoes his contemptuous description, elsewhere, of radical "long-haired anarchists"),[129] and along with him the romantic narrative of Perseus saving a damsel from the sea monster, Cetus, and retain only the monster Cetus himself, in the form of Cthulhu. The only damsel that requires saving from Cthulhu is Western Civilization itself. (Nor can it be any coincidence that Lovecraft describes modern poets in this same essay in derisive terms nearly identical with those later applied to Cthulhu and his followers: as "a race of ... cacophonous hybrids"[130] and "monstrosities," spouting "amorphous outcries.")

Significantly, too, it may be that Lovecraft's choice of imagery in this instance was dictated by the markedly erotic aspects of the Perseus-Cetus myth, either before or after Andromeda's rescue from the sea monster. Art scholar Jaś Elsner, for example, describes what he calls "the intense sexuality of the maiden laid out, tied up and powerless before the viewer's (and the sea monster's) gaze"[131] in classical depictions of this myth, as well as "the erotic gaze" shared between Andromeda and Perseus immediately after her rescue. As Elsner observes, it is ultimately "uncertain whether the panting of the hero's chest is due to his exertions or his anticipation at getting the girl!" Lovecraft, in 1915, associates this panting and exertion with modernistic decadence and radicalism; although here, as usual, the Puritan Lovecraft carefully elides over any overt sexual reference.

H. P. Lovecraft's "The Tomb" (1917) also straddles the fine line between rapturous revelry in the natural world and that danger Lovecraft later and more explicitly finds in natural fertility and vegetative fecundity; his youthful Hellenism and his youthful Poe-infatuation still co-exist side by side, although the macabre is rapidly gaining the upper hand. Here, just as in "The Dunwich Horror" later on — which begins, as Peter Cannon points out, with "a naturalistic description"[132] of the landscape — an Arcadian preamble begins the tale. In lines that parallel Lovecraft's own autobiography, for instance, his narrator Jervas Dudley speaks of a childhood spent "roaming the fields and groves of the region near my ancestral home," coming "to know the presiding dryads of those trees," and watching "their wild dances in the struggling beams of the waning moon — but of these things I must not now speak. I will tell only of the lone tomb in the darkest of the hillside thickets; the deserted tomb of the Hydes."[133] Note how Dudley cannot speak of his ecstatic, sensual, and Dionysian visions, but he can speak of the tomb that later draws him inside. Pagan sensuality is far less open to discussion, it would seem, than morbid necrophilia, which is pretty much a working definition of Puritanism. Indeed, for the Puritan mind, the latter is often a cloak for the former. Lovecraft, however, does provide a hint toward the basically autoerotic underpinnings of Dudley's sylvan fantasies, when he describes Dudley's "strange dreams,"[134] and visions of "the wild dances"[135] of the dryads in the woods. The language bears comparison with Lovecraft's own definition of erotic love in a letter to future-wife Sonia Greene: "'Youth brings with it certain erogenous and imaginative stimuli" involving "visual imagery of classical aesthetic contours symbolizing a kind of freshness and Springtime immaturity which is very beautiful.'"[136]

Tellingly, too, Dudley's discovery of the Hydes' "half-hidden house of death" takes place during the

> mid-summer, when the alchemy of nature transmutes the sylvan landscape to one vivid and almost homogenous mass of green; when the senses are well-nigh intoxicated with the surging seas of moist verdure and the subtly indefinable odors of the soil and the vegetation. In such surroundings the mind loses its perspective; time and space become trivial and unreal, and echoes of a forgotten prehistoric past beat insistently upon the enthralled consciousness.[137]

Dudley's intoxication with the sights and smells of summer, here, prefigures his own later Dionysian and necrophilic ecstasies within the coffins of the tomb, while in his otherwise incongruous reference to a "forgotten prehistoric past," we can perhaps catch a hint of Lovecraft's later insistence, in "The Dunwich Horror," that the legs of the otherwise goat-like Wilbur Wheatley "terminated in ridgy-veined pads that were *neither hooves nor claws*" (italics mine) but rather "resembled the hind-legs of prehistoric earth's giant saurians."[138] Lovecraft here replaces, or identifies, the sylvan with the prehistoric in much the same way that he later on posits the existence of a primal fund of Cthulhu-centered myths, pre-existing (and, indeed, informing) the classical.

Lovecraft further confirms our reading of the Dionysian Eros at the heart of this tale (as well as in the young Lovecraft's own earlier Arcadian interests) when he describes Jervas Dudley's long autoerotic vigils outside the entrance to this tomb, the vegetation combining with the doorway to create "a sylvan bower"[139] that became "my temple, the fastened door of my shrine," during which he dreamed "strange dreams" and swore "to the hundred gods of the grove that *at any cost* I would some day force an entrance to the black, chilly depths that seemed calling out to me."[140] Sexual consummation here is imagined as a necrophilic rape, which is "spurred on by a voice which must have come from the hideous soul of the forest."[141] The voice is that of Pan, no doubt, and what Lovecraft here terms the allied and alluring "call of the dead"[142] is both the prefigurement and the equivalent of his later call of Cthulhu, calling out from his tomb beneath the sea. Lovecraft is gradually feeling his way, here, toward some connection between Arcadian paganism and Poesque horror, the connection is never really fully established, however, in the tale, save perhaps via the depraved Hydes and their "weird rites and godless revels of bygone years,"[143] which were clearly bacchanalian in nature. As yet, however, classicism and Poe still stand side by side, and — like oil and water — do not truly mix. (This idea of forcing an entrance to the tomb is later recapitulated by Lovecraft's weird entities themselves, who likewise yearn to "'break through'"[144] to our world, their periodic appearances being regarded as violent and "sporadic irruptions."[145] Sexual emancipation, in Lovecraft's infantile imagination, inevitably is transfigured into sadistic rape.)

In Lovecraft's World War I poem "On a Battlefield in Picardy" (1918), too, his earlier Arcadian vision is presented side by side with its sinister obverse in a single work, a contrast Lovecraft cleverly uses to dramatize a before-and-after picture of a French battlefield. As Lovecraft writes, invoking a linked Feminine and lunar vision of destruction that will later become characteristic of his weird fiction: "Here all is dead,"[146] "trenches yawn, and craters pit the ground," while "in the night the horn'd Astarte gleams, / And sheds her evil beams." Before this "dread desolation" ruled the scene, however, Lovecraft tells us, "Satyrs sang by Naiad-peopled rills," the "fragrant grove" "bloomed," and the twilight breeze that "stirs at dusk" still sang of the "never-dying Pan and meadows green!" Alternating between pro–Arcadian and anti–Arcadian imagery, here, is as easy as flipping a switch. The switch will later be flipped, with equal facility, in the form of the fruitful Gardner farm and the blasted heath in "The Colour Out of Space." And, reinforcing this connection, scenes of destruction in both this poem and his later "Colour" will be similarly characterized as a form of divine retribution: as a "Scourge of God"[147] in the 1918 poem and as "a judgment of some sort"[148] in the story.

In Lovecraft's collaborative "The Green Meadow" (1918/1919), written with his "A Merchant from Arcady" poetess Winifred Jackson, we can again see him groping (however clumsily) toward a further integration of Arcadian/sylvan themes with both the cosmic and the macabre. Although the marriage, in this case, is not a happy one, the story does contain, as if in embryo, many seeds (the falling meteor, the revelation of the narrator's true identity at the end of the story, as well as the narrator's desire for the supposed "boon of death and oblivion"[149]) that will all later come to full flower in the form of Lovecraft's later apocalypses. The narrative itself is ostensibly translated from a stone notebook discovered in a meteor that has crashed to earth, etched in "*Greek of the purest quality*"[150] (italics Lovecraft's and Jackson's); Lovecraft's early attempt at depicting "very antique things and forms of life in the days when our earth was exceeding young"[151] still is stuck firmly in the context of the classical.

The typically Arcadian landscape of sea, forest, and meadow, too — now charged with a sentient, Algernon Blackwood-like malevolence — forms the backdrop of the story. As the narrator writes, fearfully: "I knew the green scaly forest hated me."[152] Lovecraft hints at some "horrible colloquy" going on between the "swaying green branches" of the grotesquely overgrown forest, and certain unnamed, but still "ghastly and unthinkable things which the scaly green bodies of the trees half hid," doubtlessly to be identified with the sylvan Pan. (Lovecraft was perhaps influenced in his description of the scaly, reptilian vegetation in the meadow by A. Merritt's "The People of the Pit" [All-Story, 1917–1918], in which Merritt writes of "unpleasant, reptilian trees.")[153] Pan and the dryads have begun the process of transforming into "unnamable" cosmic entities. But although Lovecraft is now characterizing these sylvan gods as malignant and daemonic presences, he has yet to hit upon the correct formula to fully cosmicize and polemicize the Arcadian. The "voice" Lovecraft fears here is yet not the "call of Cthulhu" but still "the voice of the swaying branches."

Indeed, just as in "The Tomb," Lovecraft's earlier sense of mystical communion with sylvan nature is here inverted into something macabre, and Lovecraft's own youthful prayers to the gods are transmuted into a prayer "never to comprehend or encounter"[154] the objects of his previous Arcadian quest. The story finally ends, meanwhile, much like "The Shadow Over Innsmouth," with the suddenly self-aware narrator confronting the prospect of an endless life of immortality. The vision of hope at the end of Lovecraft's poem "On a Battlefield in Picardy," which envisioned the return of *never-dying Pan* and *meadows green!* (italics mine), is transformed here instead into a fear of involuntary immortality in a "Green Meadow."[155] An interesting concept, surely, but not the stuff of true horror.[156]

Even as late as his pastoral poem "The Voice" (1920), we can still find Lovecraft presenting a positive vision of the Greek Arcadian ideal: the groves, the fountains, and the Mediterranean sea all singing a bubbling, aquatic song "learn'd in Arcady."[157] Here, too, the "Majestic trees unspoken calls avow, / And subtle juices fill each tingling bough,"[158] prefiguring those sinister but equally unspoken voices of the trees in "The Colour Out of Space," as well as those "unnamable juices"[159] sucked up by the trees in "The Lurking Fear" (1922). The great god Pan, however, is the real hero of the poem, and, much like Cthulhu later on, who lives on even after the death of death itself, Pan "shall never pass away," and, indeed, threatens to reawaken; not, however, when the stars are right, but rather when spring returns to bloom. Indeed, despite Lovecraft's stereotypical use of naiads, fauns, and satyrs in this poem, one can already see hints of the later Lovecraft Mythos in what he calls Pan's "saltant, shadowy choir,"[160] which suggests something of the demonic "cachin-nating chorus of the distorted, hilarious elder gods"[161] mentioned in "The Call of Cthulhu."

All of this, however, is but the prelude to what Lovecraft calls "a wilder hymn"[162] of both Pan and the classical world itself, a "call of antique beauty" that shall cause "Fair forms thro' immemorial years" to "rise." This call is associated alike with the sylvan pipes of Pan and the oceanic "old Nereus and his green-hair'd train," i.e. the well-known "old man of the sea."[163] Lovecraft's juxtaposition of oceanic with sylvan imagery in this instance is just as incon-gruous (and just as striking) as his later association of the bacchanalian swamp-dwellers in "The Call of Cthulhu" with the terrifying rise of the oceanic Cthulhu. Both the depths of the sea and the wilds of Pan's Mount Maenalus are equally Arcadian. Did the later "call" of Cthulhu have its origin here, in this earlier, equally powerful "call" of the Arcadian Pan?

According to scholar William Smith, the god Pan was indeed "said to have had a terrible voice, and by it to have frightened the Titans in their fight with the gods."[164] Lovecraft perhaps reflects this idea at the climax to "The Dunwich Horror," in which the voice of the paternal deity Yog-Sothoth is associated with "deep, cracked, raucous vocal sounds which will never leave the memory of the stricken group who heard them. Not from any human throat were they born, for the organs of man can yield no such acoustic per-versions. Rather one would have said they came from the pit itself."[165] Nor is it any coincidence that such low rumblings in "Dunwich" are accompanied by the furious and bacchanalian piping of the whippoorwills, as further stand-ins for Pan, as well as forming an inversion of Lovecraft's earlier pastoral imagery of the returning birds of spring.

Even more significant in the light of Lovecraft's later apocalypses, how-ever, is a short prose poem by him and Anna Helen Crofts entitled "Poetry and the Gods" (1920), which seems to form a blueprint, of sorts, for most of his later weird mythos. Indeed, much like his seminal prose poem "The Street," whose picture of a devolved and subversive community constitutes a blueprint for both "The Horror at Red Hook" and "The Shadow Over Inns-mouth," "Poetry and the Gods" seems to be a central document in prefiguring the basic form assumed by Lovecraft's later cosmology.

Unfortunately, very little is known about this work, nor has the situation been helped by the fact that "Poetry and the Gods" is generally held in very low esteem among Lovecraft critics. S. T. Joshi, for example, rightly dismisses the work as "peculiar,"[166] "anomalous" within the Lovecraft canon, and "mawkish" in its execution, calling it "a curiosity" that "will become of interest only if more information on its writing and its collaborator emerges"; while early biographer L. Sprague de Camp, for his part, calls it simply "a limp little fantasy wherein Marcia ... reads a piece of free verse and is at once visited by Hermes, winged sandals and all."[167] These criticisms, however, while fair in terms of the quality of the story itself, fail to recognize the central place this story, despite its obscurity, holds in the canon — representing as it does an unalloyed vision of the Greek Arcadian world reborn, in language that was shortly to be subsumed by the risen Cthulhu. And whereas here we find Lovecraft and Croft lamenting the day when "Pan lay down to doze in Arcady, and the great Gods withdrew to sleep in lotos-gardens beyond the lands of the Hesperides,"[168] in Lovecraft's weird canon this lament will gradually be inverted and transformed into a conservative warning about the dangers of the awakening bacchanalia, both to civilization itself and to the those decadent artists sensitive enough, or sensuous enough, to fall under its lascivious and chaotic spell.

"Poetry and the Gods" begins in the present day, with a cultured female protagonist (indeed, a "nymph"),[169] who — seemingly sharing Lovecraft's own disharmony with the modern era and a longing for Arcadian things — suddenly finds herself falling under the influence of some free verse she is reading, whose "wild harmony"[170] seems to predict "a new age of song, a rebirth of Pan."[171] And although Lovecraft disliked free verse, certainly the heroine's reaction to the verse is Lovecraftian enough: the woman quickly falls under the hypnotic influence of archaic and "strange thoughts and wishes," after which her mind is transported "eastward to olive groves in distant Arcady which," much like Henry Wilcox's nightmare-visions of Cthulhu later on, "she had seen only in her dreams."[172]

The female dreamer is then confronted by Hermes, who begins a long disquisition on things Arcadian: he speaks of Pan's home on Mount Maenalus, and refers in Cthulhu-like language to how "Pan *sighs and stretches in his sleep, wishful to awake* and behold about him the little rose-crowned Fauns and Satyrs"[173] (italics mine). The language is suggestive not only of "dead Cthulhu,"[174] who "in his house at R'lyeh ... waits dreaming," but also of those mysterious and eruptive entities later on in Lovecraft's "The Shadow Out of Time," which according to Aboriginal legends threaten "'to awake and eat up the world.'"[175] Indeed, Hermes then goes on to relate what will be familiar to most Lovecraft-readers from the standard emblematic formulae from both "The Call of Cthulhu" and "The Nameless City," that "that is not dead which can eternal lie, / And with strange aeons even death may die."[176] He observes how "in thy yearning thou hast divined what no mortal, saving only a few whom the world rejects, remembered: *that the Gods were never dead, but only sleeping the sleep and dreaming* the dreams of Gods in lotos-filled Hesperian gardens beyond the golden sunset. And now draweth nigh the time of their awakening, when coldness and ugliness all perish, and Zeus sit once more on Olympus"[177] (italics mine). Lovecraft and Croft's description of the incipient gods' process of awakening, too, telling of how "already the sea about Paphos trembleth into a foam which only ancient skies have looked on before,"[178] closely prefigures Lovecraft's own later picture, in "The Call of Cthulhu," of the apocalyptic rising of Cthulhu, whose resurrection is accompanied by "a mighty eddying and foaming in the noisome brine"[179]; just as Cthulhu's followers — called by Lovecraft "his ministers on earth," who, like the satyrs and nymphs, "still bellow and prance and slay around idol-capped monoliths in lonely places"[180] — are prefigured in "Poetry and the Gods" by those "white saltant forms"[181] that dance in the "woods and fields" at twilight in honor of Pan.

By the time we reach Lovecraft's "The Temple" (1920), we see that he has finally succeeded in subsuming the classical as merely one element within the overall plot, although he has not yet inverted his pro–Arcadian stance. And while described as "demoniac,"[182] "hideous,'"[183] and "mocking,"[184] the Grecian/pagan elements in the story are also, just as in "The Tree," still aligned on the relative side of good, exacting vengeance upon a murderous German submarine commander during World War I. And, as in his later story "The Crawling Chaos" (1920/1921), his depiction of the bacchanalia here is still "radiant"[185] and joyous. Lovecraft describes the bacchanale at the end of the tale as a "rhythmic, melodic sound as of some wild yet beautiful chant or choral hymn"[186]; the discordant and animalistic bleating of Cthulhu's orgiastic followers is still nowhere in evidence.

Indeed, Lovecraft's basic story in "The Temple" — of a possibly divine youth being captured by sea pirates (in this case, German terrorists/saboteurs) and then afterward exacting revenge against them — is actually a retelling of a legend of the god Dionysus as related by Homer, in which Dionysus, in the form of a youth, is captured by Tyrrhenian pirates who do not believe he is a god. Eventually, Dionysus unmasks himself, changes into a lion, transforms the oars and the mast of the ship into serpents, causes ivy to grow around the vessel and "the sound of flutes"[187] to be "heard on every side." This so terrifies the sailors that they all jump into the sea, where they are transformed into dolphins; all save for the pilot of the vessel, who alone recognized Dionysus' divinity. The "sound of flutes," so familiar to readers of Lovecraft's fiction, is already being used here as a symbol of terror, although, just as in "The Temple," here it is still a righteous terror, used as a means of divine retribution. The numerous dolphins that appear in Lovecraft's story, too, and which persist in pursuing the drifting German submarine, also reflect the pro–Grecian stance of Lovecraft's tale: dolphins are regarded in classical myth as the pets of Poseidon, the patron god of Atlantis, and also figure in the worship of the gods Apollo, whose shrine at Delphi was named after the dolphins, in the worship of Artemis in her form of the nymph Arethusa, and in the worship of the god Palaemon, whose drowned body was rescued by dolphins.

Despite his successful integration of the classical into the heart of the tale, however, Lovecraft is still not entirely successful in his attempt at the creation of an ancient tradition of primal myth that in some way antedates the classical period. Lovecraft's ineradicable classicism perhaps impedes his attempt, here, at suggesting a truly prehistoric tradition of pre-human lore. And although the sunken ruins that Ehrenstein discovers in a dark undersea valley will be described as representing a "magnificent though unclassified architecture,"[188] this architecture is still "largely Hellenic in idea," imparting "an impression of terrible antiquity, as though it were the remotest rather than the immediate ancestor of Greek art."[189] Still, we are not very far here from such later Atlantis-analogues as Lovecraft's Y'ha-nthlei and R'lyeh, the latter of which is described in similar terms as having existed "behind ... Atlantis; behind fabled Mu, and myth-whispered Lemuria. It was the ultimate fountain-head of all horror on this earth."[190] And while Cthulhu himself clearly cannot be described as "a radiant god"[191] like that worshipped in this story, Cthulhu certainly does have his origin here, in a reversal of such positive imagery.

In "The Crawling Chaos," pagan trees and vegetative fecundity again assume a sinister and semi-articulate aspect, as well as a hypnotic one. At the same time, too, Lovecraft attempts a tentative integration of his socio-political ideas with classical or Arcadian imagery, in this case, his xenophobic and nativist attitudes toward foreign influences; the "omnipresent trees"[192] are "plainly foreign" in their origin, while the nearby architecture likewise displays "a quaint fusion of Western and Eastern forms," "Corinthian columns" being juxtaposed with a "red tile roof ... like that of a Chinese pagoda." (As we shall see later on, a similar juxtaposition of Asian forms and Western modernism will likewise figure in the decadent, proto–Modernist architecture of Ralph Adams Cram, who will himself likewise figure, as we shall see, in interesting ways within Lovecraft's weird fiction.)

Lovecraft and Jackson's larger picture in "The Crawling Chaos," however, still savors of that polemical uncertainty characteristic of Lovecraft's early weird fiction, resulting in a story that, as Joshi points out, lacks "focus or direction."[193] True, the plot in "The Crawling Chaos" is already just as plainly apocalyptic as his later Mythos fiction; Lovecraft even has a choir of gods and goddesses, much like his Cthulhuian entities later on, who filter down to the earth from space, "down through the gloaming from the stars,"[194] in order to preside over the destruction of the earth. Lovecraft describes these entities, too — much like Cthulhu's followers later on — in markedly Dionysian terms; although here, as with those "beauteous faun-folk"[195] he praises in "Poetry and the Gods," the bacchanalian has not yet been subsumed beneath Lovecraft's apocalyptic rhetoric. Lovecraft describes these Dionysian visitors in positive and even in joyous terms as a "throng of half-luminous, vine-crowned youths and maidens with windblown hair and joyful countenance," and even takes pains to contrast the "mellifluous choriambics" and "ravishing strains" chanted by the Dionysian youths with what he calls the "mocking, daemonic discord, [which] throbbed from the gulfs below the damnable, the detestable pounding of that hideous ocean." Of course, these two separate elements — the bacchanalian and the oceanic — will later be merged in Lovecraft's fiction, via the jointly bacchanalian and oceanic rites practiced in "The Call of Cthulhu" and "The Shadow Over Innsmouth." As yet, however, not only are the Dionysian gods or entities in this story apparently *not* the source of the "ruin and decadence"[196] that overtakes the earth, but these same gods also offer to provide salvation to Lovecraft's narrator from the earth's impending doom (a salvation or escape, however, which he apparently throws away by turning back to look as the earth is destroyed, much like Danforth in *At the Mountains of Madness*).

In this story, we can see Lovecraft's halting attempt at integrating his classical themes with his larger apocalyptic impulse, the same apocalyptic Puritan impulse which, in the 17th century, had seen the collapse of the Massachusetts Puritan oligarchy as the end of the universe. But although we can already see here, in Lovecraft's description of the "tottering towers of deserted cities,"[197] a prefiguration of the same decay that later "spreads over the tottering cities of men"[198] at the hands of the subterranean/aquatic Cthulhu, Lovecraft has not yet hit upon the proper idiom with which to convey his message of evil. And although Lovecraft had already, in such prose poems as "Nyarlathotep" and the post-apocalyptic "Memory" (1919), begun using a parable form to clothe his apocalyptic visions (perhaps derived from Edgar Allan Poe's parables "Shadow: A Fable" and "The Colloquy of Monos and Una," and additionally bolstered by his reading of the numerous apocalyptic and post-apocalyptic scenarios of the early pulps, including George Allan England's *Darkness and Dawn* trilogy [*The Cavalier*, 1912–1913] and Dr. Garrett P. Serviss' *The Second Deluge* [*The Cavalier*, 1911] and *The Moon Metal* [book pub. 1900, *All-Story* 1905]), he has not yet worked out the specific mechanisms of that parable.

In Lovecraft's "The Outsider" (1921), an autobiographical Arcadian setting again forms the prelude to a later story of Poesque horror: the titular Outsider spends its childhood in what he calls "awed watches in twilight groves of grotesque, gigantic, and vine-encumbered trees that silently wave twisted branches far aloft. Such a lot the gods gave to me."[199] "The gods," here, as we shall see in chapter 3, perhaps reflect Lovecraft's characteristic projection of his parents onto a gigantic and, indeed, god-like scale. As in "The Lurking Fear" later on, Arcadian vegetative fecundity is here being harnessed to depict interior psychological states. And what Lovecraft calls, in his own autobiography, a watch for "dryads and satyrs in the woods and fields at dusk,"[200] here becomes transformed into a groping search for personal identity, culminating in an ultimate revelation of the narrator's own decay: Lovecraft, just as in his story "Hypnos" later on, seemingly recasts his own youthful Hellenism into a realization of the decadence, madness and corruption inherent in such an Arcadian aesthetic.

Perhaps one of the most significant stories from the point of view of our study is Lovecraft's "The Moon-Bog" (1921); although basically written to order for an amateur St. Patrick's Day celebration in Boston, it is here, as perhaps nowhere else, that we can see Lovecraft's transition from Arcadian classicist to infuriated Puritan, from pastoral poet to Roman caricaturist, in progress. Unfortunately, this tale is, like "Poetry and the Gods," often ignored by Lovecraft's readers: Joshi rightly calls it "elementary," "conventional," and "unusually trite and commonplace"[201]; while de Camp dismisses it as "a mediocre story of supernatural horror."[202] But it is here that we can watch as what Lovecraft calls "all that I recalled of a classic youth"[203] is finally utilized in the service of his chosen medium of the macabre. And although the story is by no means successful, the unavoidably artificial nature of the narrative may ultimately have aided Lovecraft's powers of construction, by requiring him to organize and codify his sizeable fund of classical knowledge in the service of a macabre story structure.

Indeed, although ostensibly an Irish tale, the classical element (what Lovecraft calls the "glory that was Greece")[204] is here strangely predominant, due to Lovecraft telling of the malevolent influence of a buried priestess of Artemis located in a submerged temple beneath an Irish bog. (Lovecraft was perhaps influenced in this association of Ireland with the classical by the fact that Sicily — the "favorite abode of the goddess"[205] Demeter, who is also mentioned in "The Moon-Bog"[206] — was believed to have been first settled by a Celtic people from the Iberian peninsula, called the Siculu or Sicani.) Lovecraft, however, who at this period in his life had no time for the non–Anglo-Irish, even goes so far as to trace such traditionally Irish spectres as "wraiths in white hovering over the waters"[207] and "dancing lights in the dark of the moon" to classical invaders in Ireland's ancient past — much in the same way that later on, in "The Whisperer in Darkness," he attributes "Celtic" and "Scotch-Irish" legends of "malign fairies and 'little people' of the bogs and raths"[208] to his own, entirely fictional Outer Ones.

The greatest advance Lovecraft makes in "The Moon-Bog," in terms of his later cosmology, is his attribution of the main evil in the tale to a classical source: in this case, the Arcadian goddess Artemis, described by scholar William Smith as "a goddess of the nymphs, [who] was worshipped as such in Arcadia in very early times,"[209] and who was possessed, even during the classical period, of both benevolent and malevolent aspects. Regarded as "the personification of the fructifying and all-nourishing powers of nature," Artemis was also associated with the crescent moon in her identity of Selene, as well as being associated, in her Taurian and Brauronian forms, with sadistic rites of bloodletting and human sacrifice. Known to the Romans as Diana, Artemis figured prominently in the Dianic fertility cults of the Middle Ages, which also played so large a role in Lovecraft's weird fiction. Artemis' fellow nymphs also appear in Lovecraft's tale, too — likewise in a sinister context — leading the peasant laborers to their deaths by drowning in the bog (after which some of them are seemingly transformed into frogs). Lovecraft finally invokes the orgiastic spirit of the bacchanalia, no longer solely a force for retribution or righteous vengeance, as a *negative* force, with the dancing, the ceremonial processions, and the hypnotic, feminine rhythms of the followers of Bacchus here leading to unavoidable death and destruction.

Lovecraft also tentatively associates Arcadia with madness here, too, as his narrator crosses the line into temporary insanity, and begins praying, as Lovecraft did during his youth, to the classical goddesses, "as the horrors of the situation roused my deepest superstitions."[210] Later, of course, in *At the Mountains of Madness*, it is Danforth's course of reading in the *Necronomicon* and kindred occult texts that unhinges his mind. The pipes of Pan make their appearance here, too: referred to as the "sound of wild pipes in the night"[211] and described in specifically Arcadian terms as "wild, weird airs that made me think of some dance of fauns on distant Maenalus"[212] — certainly an improvement upon Lovecraft's ambiguous and tentative references to Pan's Mount Maenalus at the beginning of "The Tree."

The wildness that Lovecraft repeatedly associates with the pipes of Pan, above, is also significant. And while Lovecraft critic Joel Pace suggests that Lovecraft's use of the word "wild"[213] to describe Asenath Waite's decadent college set in "The Thing on the Doorstep" is basically a pun "on the surname of the most notorious decadent of his day,"[214] if Lovecraft *is* using "wild" there as a pun on "Oscar Wilde," then such a usage also looks backward to Lovecraft's earlier, and consistent, use of the word "wild" in an exclusively sylvan and Arcadian sense in works including "The Voice" and "The Whisperer in Darkness."[215] Nor are the two usages in any sense mutually exclusive. Indeed, as discussed below in III. Wine, Women, and Song: Vagabonds and Decadence in Arcadia, Arcadia was very much linked with decadence, both in Lovecraft's mind and in the writings of the 1890s decadents against whom Lovecraft was reacting.

Despite the evils wrought by the Feminine or Arcadian forces in this story, however, Lovecraft still remains slightly equivocal in his inversion of Grecian mythology. And, much as in "The Street"[216] and *At the Mountains of Madness*,[217] in which Lovecraft's characters are able to discern vanished mirages of past glory shimmering above now decadent ruins, his narrator here sees a vision of Artemis' original city hanging above the ruins in the bog, rising "majestic and undecayed, splendid and column-cinctured."[218] At the same time, however, he also "watched in awe and terror" as he saw "dark saltant forms silhouetted grotesquely against the vision of marble and effulgence"; here Lovecraft evinces a sort of fractured co-existence between classical grandeur on the one hand, and bacchanalian decay on the other. That insanity which Lovecraft, following Cicero,[219] had once associated with dancing is here contrasted with the beautiful but incarnadined architecture, in much the same way that Lovecraft, later on, differentiates between the civilization of the Old Ones at its height and its period of shoggoth-induced decay. Slowly but surely, we can see Lovecraft gradually assembling all of the ingredients seen in his later apocalypses. Only the larger polemical context is missing — as well as an appropriately Cthulhuian disguise for his nymphs and goddesses.

Lovecraft's "The Lurking Fear" (1922) continues this evolution, particularly with regard to the sylvan or Arcadian landscape and related fertility imagery. As Lovecraft candidly observes in part 4 of the tale: "It was *a peaceful Arcadian scene*, but knowing what it hid I hated it"[220] (italics mine). The Arcadian landscape here, much like the animistic sea, land and sky in "The Crawling Chaos" and "The Green Meadow," represents for Lovecraft "a noxious alliance with distorted hidden powers"; an evil rooted in the basic fructifying powers of nature, and which, in *At the Mountains of Madness*, is extended to a corruption inherent in the structure of space and time itself.[221] And although Lovecraft here attempts to stress the ostensibly sinister, eldritch, and morbid qualities of this landscape, that these fields and hills are ultimately the same ones visited with such pleasure by Lovecraft in his earlier pastoral verse is fairly obvious. Lovecraft simply projects it through a different lens, in order to make it an outward, animistic embodiment of the story's cannibalistic, incestuous, and sadistic events. Indeed, throughout the story, Lovecraft uses elements of the Arcadian landscape in an almost expressionistic way to reflect the feverish mental terrain of the tale, describing the foliage as "maniacally thick"[222] and denouncing the larger landscape itself as "the mocking moon, the hypocritical plain, the festering mountain, and those sinister mounds."[223]

As in "The Outsider" and "The Green Meadow," Lovecraft again emphasizes the unnatural size and luxuriance of the vegetation in this tale, particularly the trees: the "giant oaks"[224] are so thick upon the landscape that even the omnipresent thunder itself is said to be "tree muffled."[225] The other vegetation, too, is described as being "unnaturally thick and feverish."[226] Lovecraft, just as in "The Tomb," suggests a necrophilic inversion of the fertility imagery of pagan worship via his implication that this luxuriousness and giganticism are due to some sort of vampiric relationship with the sadistic, cannibalistic acts taking place beneath the ground. In "The Colour Out of Space," of course, Lovecraft turns this luxuriousness and giganticism of the vegetation toward a supposedly cosmic purpose, but here Lovecraft is still stuck firmly in Roman mode: writing of the trees as leering "above me like the pillars of some hellish Druidic temple,"[227] Lovecraft's early Arcadian mysticism is filtered through the Roman conflict with the druidical tribes on the European frontier. Lovecraft writes, too, of running half-mad "through diseased, precipitous abysses of haunted hillside forest."[228] But by what was this forest originally "haunted," if not by the ghost of Pan? Pan is here recast, however, in the form of a larger, seething, incestuous and cannibalistic assemblage of horrors, in which the devolved hordes of the bestial Martense family form a more sinister version of the dancing, animalistic companions of Pan.

By the time he writes "The Horror at Red Hook" (1925), Lovecraft's fauns, nymphs, and Aegipans are all finally explicitly turned toward an obviously macabre purpose. Even so, Lovecraft's satirical vision in that story is still far from complete, his frenzied denunciations of "cosmic sin"[229] ultimately defeating his own purpose by deflecting attention from the pagan horrors at hand to the Puritan and unbalanced perceptions of his protagonist. (This is perhaps why Lovecraft, later on in "The Shadow Over Innsmouth," decided to attribute such frenzied anti-pagan vituperations to the crazed, pathetic Zadok Allen, in whom they could be reasonably excused.) Only the caricatural aspects of Lovecraft's later mythos, in which the Arcadian and sylvan aspects of his cosmology are appropriately disguised, finally provided him with sufficient distance to properly focus the readers' attention on the fictional horrors at hand.

In "The Colour Out of Space" (1927), Lovecraft's inversion of Arcadian imagery into characteristic Lovecraftian form is complete. As Peter Cannon observes, "a naturalistic account of the landscape"[230] again acts as a preamble to the ensuing tale, the story being firmly set in the "West of Arkham"[231] where "the hills rise wild" (not to say Wildean), and as usual, the malevolence of these "hills and vales"[232] is symbolized primarily by their fecundity and fertility — as if, as critic Maurice Levy observes, "nature were unhinged."[233] As Lovecraft's narrator nervously observes, "The trees grew too thickly, and their trunks were too big for any healthy New England wood."[234] And although critic Peter Cannon suggests that the Gardners' farm in this story "becomes a kind of travesty of the Garden of Eden,"[235] that Lovecraft's earlier and pervasive Arcadian imagery forms a more logical and immediate model than the Eden of the Old Testament.

On the other hand, however, Lovecraft's famous blasted heath, which forms ground zero for the cosmic color's invasion of our world and which becomes the crowning horror of the tale, is a place without any fertility whatsoever, described by Lovecraft as "five acres of grey desolation"[236] with "no vegetation of any kind on that broad expanse," even the trees on its outermost edge are "sickly and stunted, and many dead trunks stood or lay rotting at the rim." Indeed, so horrible does Lovecraft's narrator find the blasted heath that for his narrator, "even the long, dark woodland climb beyond seemed welcome in contrast." Lovecraft's horrors, as in *At the Mountains of Madness*, evidently occupy a sliding scale. Lovecraft's description of the blasted heath as resembling "the outcome *of a fire*" (italics mine) is reminiscent of a childhood anecdote recorded by Lovecraft's friend W. Paul Cook, of Lovecraft attempting to start a fire while a young boy: "He said very positively, 'I wasn't setting a big fire. I wanted to make a fire one foot by one foot.'"[237] In both cases, we have an area of fire denoted by definite lines of demarcation from the untouched lands surrounding it. Save that here, the bonfire from the bacchanale of Lovecraft's Cthulhu-followers has expanded into an entire landscape of desolation and destruction. The green meadow has now become the blasted heath; Lovecraft has finally learned how to control or incorporate the verdant Arcadian fields within his weird fiction. Indeed, it becomes increasingly clear that the "phenomenal size and unwonted gloss"[238] of the fruits in "The Colour Out of Space" are but a symptom of decay, their ripeness and growth acting as a prelude to "a lasting disgust." Nor is it difficult to see a similarity between the "diseased ... tone"[239] characterizing the various botanical and insectoid perversions in this story, and the earlier Arcadian decadence of writers like Whitman and Wilde, whose pederastic and sensuous Arcadian utopia was equally corrupt and perverted.[240]

Lovecraft also revisits many of the other motifs familiar from his earlier Arcadian verse in "Colour," suitably inverted, of course. Just as in "The Haunter of the Dark" (1935), later on, in which it is "in the spring,"[241] "when the delicate leaves came out on the garden boughs" and "the world filled with a new beauty"[242] that "a deep restlessness"[243] grips Lovecraft's protagonist Robert Blake, springtime is here associated with the onset of decadence and decay: Lovecraft writes here of how "April brought a kind of madness to the country folk."[244] The additional detail, too, that "the trees budded prematurely around Nahum's,"[245] prefigures that premature puberty of Wilbur Whately (before the age of five) later on in "The Dunwich Horror." Nor can it be any coincidence that Lovecraft should trace the unnatural motion of the trees and vegetation in this tale to "the sap"[246] within the tree. The same juices are sucked up by the "over nourished oaks"[247] in "The Lurking Fear," and the same phallic sap earlier animated the pro–Arcadian verse of the 1890s decadents,[248] not to mention the early poetry of Lovecraft himself, in which Lovecraft fondly refers to those "subtle juices"[249] that "fill each tingling bough" and which form, in springtime, the "joyous call to new activity."[250]

In "Colour," however, this sap is doing the Devil's work. The trees themselves, at the end of the tale, all are "straining skyward" while "twitching morbidly and spasmodically ... as if jerked"[251] to some epileptic orgasm. Ironically, Lovecraft's ostensible divorce from his previous naturalistic and sadistic themes simultaneously allows him to be more transparent with regard to the latent sexuality underlying his inverted Arcadian imagery. The overt themes of incest and sadism in "The Lurking Fear," for example, are now merely latent or implicit; the same symptoms, in other words — living trees and animated vegetation — are here attributed to an ostensibly different cause, although the symptoms are still rooted in the fundamentally autoerotic aspects underlying Lovecraft's solitary and youthful vigils in the sylvan woods.

In "The Dunwich Horror" (1928), H. P. Lovecraft again revisits the inverted Arcadian landscapes from both his poetry and his youth, with his playful dryads and fauns — here called "strange forest presences"[252] — now cast purely in the role of villains. Indeed, given their lasciviousness, their laziness, their drunkenness, and their bestial, hybrid natures, it is curious that it took Lovecraft, with all of his Puritan crochets, so long to cast Pan's sylvan companions in such a role, unless, again, it was his classical traditionalism that temporarily obscured the true significance of such pastoral imagery within his mind. Lovecraft even speaks in this story of his ostensibly cosmic Old Ones as treading "the fields,"[253] much like the hoofed and horned monstrosity in "The Unnamable"; while Wilbur Whately's unseen father, Yog-Sothoth, is described, despite his ostensible cosmicism, as having "walked on the mountains that May-night"[254] on which he was conceived. Wilbur, too, although described by Lovecraft as being "like the spawn of another planet or dimension,"[255] possesses obviously satyr-like features. And, just like the odorous fauns mentioned in Lovecraft's letter to Edkins, these "cosmic" Old Ones are likewise identifiable by "their smell."[256] Lovecraft has finally found his idiom: a medium that will enable him to harness Greek mythology to his larger personal concerns, in this case, societal and familial decay. The whip is Roman satire, and with it, Lovecraft is able to beat Greek mythology into submission and guide it as he chooses.

Of course, the home of the decayed and incestuous Whately family in "The Dunwich Horror" is, just like the tomb of the Hydes in "The Tomb," and like Henry Akeley's colonial home in "The Whisperer in Darkness," depicted as being "set against a hillside,"[257] the very hills of Pan, no doubt. And here too we find the familiar Arcadian landscape of mountains, deep woods, gorges and ravines, all marked by the usual giganticism and "a luxuriance not often found in settled regions"[258]; the same luxuriance so celebrated by the worshippers of multi-breasted Artemis. Nor are the rites of the bacchanalia absent, either, in the form of "wild orgiastic prayers"[259] made by prehistoric Indian tribes in ancient times in the Dunwich region — orgies that are mirrored by what Lovecraft calls the sinister "dance" and "creepily insistent rhythms"[260] of nature itself, in the form of the whippoorwills, fireflies, and bull frogs. Indeed, even the birds of springtime are here twisted toward Lovecraft's usual necrophilic ends, with the normally lascivious whippoorwills (associated with nocturnal passion in the writings of the earlier Arcadian vagabond poets)[261] transformed into piping psychopomps conveying the souls of the dead.

Of course, and just as in "The Colour Out of Space," this natural luxuriousness becomes but a prelude to dissolution and decay at the end of the tale, when the "green grass and foliage wilted to a curious, sickly yellow-grey"[262] while "over field and forest were scattered the bodies of dead whippoorwills." As with the mounds of skeletons sacrificed to the Magna Mater in "The Rats in the Walls," the ultimate end result of all fertility is death. The Arcadia of the nymphs has something rotten about it, the same rot that, for Lovecraft, infected decadents such as Oscar Wilde and Walt Whitman.

In "The Whisperer in Darkness" (1930), Lovecraft is even more explicit in associating his ostensibly cosmic Outer Ones (here called "unholy woodland presences")[263] with "those universal legends of natural personification which filled the ancient world with fauns and dryads."[264] Lovecraft, in a stunning example of literary cheek, even attributes the origin of Pan's "queer companions,"[265] by whom he himself was once so inspired, to a misidentification of a "queer elder earth-race, driven to hiding after the advent and dominance of mankind."[266] Indeed, Lovecraft will even have his protagonist Wilmarth find "the source of some of the most repulsive primordial customs in the cryptic elder religions of mankind"[267] — i.e., the sadistic and sexual bacchanalia — in cosmic rites inculcated by his Outer Ones themselves. (In "The Dreams in the Witch House," too, Lovecraft will further reverse or invert the purely psychological and mundane origins of bacchanalian Eros by attributing the earthly bacchanalia to a supposedly cosmic "Walpurgis-rhythm,"[268] which "sometimes break[s] forth in measured reverberations that penetrate faintly to every layer of entity.") For Lovecraft, apparently, our faults lie not in ourselves, but in the stars. At any rate, all of this suggests Lovecraft's increasing facility in his use of classical and Arcadian themes in his weird fiction, as well as the increasing autonomy of his own mythos from its embryonic background of myth, although he was never able to completely erase — only obscure — this cosmic versus mundane contradiction at the base of his mythology.

Of course, Lovecraft's Outer Ones in "Whisperer" make their home amid Pan's desolate traditional haunts: in the caves of the nymphs, and "among the remoter hills — in the deep woods of the highest peaks, and the dark valleys where streams trickle from unknown sources."[269] This is all language recognizable from Lovecraft's earlier Arcadian poetry, but here it is linked by Lovecraft with "traces of hidden and unwholesome tenancy."[270] Even so, Lovecraft's attempt to link this Arcadian symbolism with his alien and immigrant Outer Ones naturally leads to some odd contradictions. Lovecraft's description of the ancient, long-standing nature of the aliens' infiltration of the Vermont woods in "Whisperer," for example, is diametrically opposed to Lovecraft's pro–Arcadian language in his 1927 travelogue, in which he contrasts the "Swart foreign forms" to be found in Vermont's "squalid immigrant nests and grimy mill villages"[271] with the traditional and magical forms of the eldritch surrounding natural landscape. In "Whisperer," however — into which Lovecraft has interpolated whole passages from his earlier Vermont travelogue — this contrast is forgotten. The aliens are the original inhabitants of the Arcadian landscape, and the only true transient or immigrant in the Vermont woods, ironically, is Lovecraft's doomed hero, Henry Akeley.

The ultimate flowering of Lovecraft's Roman and neo–Puritan satirical vision, however, is to be found in the apocalypses of his later mythos: in the form of Cthulhu, who is basically an inverted version of the paternal sea gods Poseidon, Neptune, Glaucus, or Nodens; in the aquatic Deep Ones of "The Shadow Over Innsmouth," who represent basically an inverted form of the Greek sea nymphs and naiads; and in the landscape of Lovecraft's *At the Mountains of Madness*, whose desolate caves and mountains represent the ultimate evolution of the desolate fastnesses of Pan, transported whole into polar, and ultimately into cosmic, regions. Here, in Lovecraft's later apocalypses, form and function have been inextricably (and, for some readers, imperceptively) welded together, so much so that Cthulhu is considered, by some, to be an actual deity. Cthulhu has a reality, however, only within the context of a peculiarly specific socio-political worldview. Like the prophet Isaiah in the Old Testament, pronouncing destruction on the corrupt kingdom of Edom: "And wild beasts shall meet with hyenas, the satyrs shall call to one another; There shall Lilith alight, and find for herself a resting place,"[272] the Western world has, for Lovecraft, become populated, if not with the satyrs and Lilith, then by their distant, cosmic kin.

III. Wine, Women, and Song: Vagabonds and Decadence in Arcadia

> Shall not mine incantations bring around me the wonderful
> company of the wood-gods, their bodies glistening with
> the ointment of moonlight and honey and myrrh?
> —Aleister Crowley, *Liber Liberi vel Lapidis Lazuli* (1907)[273]

Lovecraft's stance vis-à-vis the Greeks, Arcadia, its sylvan gods, and the bacchanalia is thrown into greater relief once one considers the stance of his opponents in this polemical battle; and indeed it was a battle, as the strenuous intellectual debates surrounding the issue of literary decadence, the evils of Oscar Wilde, and the danger of Fitzgerald's *Rubaiyat* around the end of the 19th century all demonstrate. And given Lovecraft's own tempestuous relationship with the decadent movement, it is surely no coincidence that it is among the literary decadents of his youth that we find those who were most assiduous in recapitulating and promoting the same pagan and Arcadian imagery that Lovecraft later inverts. Indeed, Lovecraft's rhetoric, both in his stories and in his conservative socio-political essays, presupposes a direct engagement with, and reaction against, various literary movements of his day. He had clearly chosen his side in the argument, and he defended it on many fronts and with all the available weapons in his arsenal. And just as in Lovecraft's "Poetry and the Gods," in which Zeus predicts that a new poet shall soon arise "who shall proclaim our return and sing of the days to come when Fauns and Dryads shall haunt their accustomed groves in beauty,"[274] in "The Call of Cthulhu," Lovecraft will similarly make decadent artist Henry Wilcox one of the prophets of the rise of the sinister Cthulhu, predicting, not a reign of beauty, but rather the end of Western civilization.

As historian Douglass Shand-Tucci observes in his biography of architect and former decadent Ralph Adams Cram, "the art of Bohemia" at the turn of the 20th century "celebrated Arcadia significantly."[275] For gay artists in particular, apparently, Arcadia offered a means of escape from the norms of socio-religious probity. Shand-Tucci wrote of what some scholars call "the propensity of homosexual writers from Whitman to Forster to see in that imagery of Arcadia 'a place where ... gay men could physically effect a pastoral escape route' (as Mark Lilly puts it...)." This calls to mind wealthy decadent photographer Fred Holland Day's rustic retreat in rural Maine, where he used his immense wealth to create a pagan temple, and where he took ostensibly "classical" photographs of naked young boys in the roles of satyrs, fauns, and Pan. There also was Walt Whitman's socialist follower Edward Carpenter, who equated the Arcadian call of Pan with unleashed homosexual desire, and this in turn with the ideal of democracy. As Carpenter writes in *Towards Democracy* (in imagery later utilized, in inverted form, in Lovecraft's "The Unnamable" and "The Dunwich Horror"): "I follow you [Democracy] far afield and into the untrodden woods, and there remote from man you disclose yourself to me, goat-footed and sitting on a rock."[276] Lovecraft, of course, whose earlier aristocratic views later merged imperceptively with his adoption of a form of fascist collectivism, rejected democracy, and for precisely the same reasons for which the pro-primitive Carpenter praises it: calling it "closer to the primal animal or savage state from which civilized man is supposed to have partly evolved,"[277] and writing scathingly of "the dreams of ethics and democracy which clouded the nineteenth century."[278]

And then there were the Vagabond poets of the decadent period: Bliss Carman and Richard Hovey, whose poems of wine, women and song were filled with such familiar Arcadian symbols as Pan (addressed in Baudelairean tones as "Brother, lost brother! / Thou of mine ancient kin!,"[279]) piping flutes,[280] springtime,[281] and the birds of springtime, along with such recurring natural features as mountains, hills, ravines, caves, deep woods, lakes and rivers.[282] There is a rampant eroticism and phallicism throughout the Vagabondia poems, as well as the pervasive appearance of pagan nymphs[283] and goddesses: the Oreads,[284] Astarte,[285] Tanis,[286] Ashtoreth,[287] and Lilith,[288] as well as Lovecraft's Magna Mater herself, referred to in her various guises as the "Allmother,"[289] "Mother Earth"[290] and the "Ancient Mother."[291]

The animated trees and orchards of the Gardner's farm are here too. Vagabonds Hovey and Carman claim membership in "one brotherhood / With leaf and bud / And everything that wakes or wends."[292] As biographer Roger Austin reports, "Carman was truly a vagabond only in the sense that he wished to escape the restraints of society,"[293] while for his part Richard Hovey declared: "Off with the fetters / That chafe and restrain! / Off with the chain!"[294] In this, Carman and Hovey were merely following in the bacchanalian footsteps of their rustic predecessor Walt Whitman, whom the Puritan Lovecraft detested,[295] and who likewise sang of "the mystic deliria, the madness amorous, the [song of] utter abandonment."[296] And it is not surprising to learn that, although Whitman's poems themselves were glaringly (and intentionally) devoid of literary or classical references, Whitman's bedroom walls, on the other hand, were decorated with pictures of Bacchus and a satyr.[297]

But although the Vagabond poets found their preferred home in a rustic, naturalistic Arcadia, this Arcadia was not so much an actual place as a state of mind — a place where one suddenly "wakes and finds himself."[298] As Richard Hovey observes in his poem "The Faun, a Fragment," in which Hovey declares himself to be "half Faun," and observes, "I am weary of clothes":

> For I am woodland-natured and have made
> Dryads my bedfellows,
> And I have played
> With the sleek Naiads in the splash of pools
> And made a mock of gowned and trousered fools.[299]

(Lovecraft's narrator in the coda to "The Shadow Over Innsmouth" also wishes to play naked with the Naiads, even if they are his own grandmother *and* great-great-grandmother.) On the other hand, Hovey goes on, the "trousered fools" (i.e., those respectable gentlemen who seek temporal wealth or power) "shall not find the way to Arcady, / The old home of the awful heart-dear Mother" (Lovecraft's sinister Magna Mater, again, here associated with what Hovey calls "the sense of freedom and nearness of Earth"[300]). Already, as early as these 19th century vagabonds, we find ourselves immersed in the same countercultural rhetoric later mastered by the hippies of the late 1960s. And one thinks that Lovecraft — much like the conservative King Pentheus, whom the decadent Aleister Crowley described as the "representative of respectability,"[301] who also opposed the introduction of bacchanalian rites into his kingdom in Greek myth — himself awoke in Arcady, but simply did not like what he saw. As Bliss Carman concludes in his poem "Romany Signs" (dedicated to the poetess Louise Imogen Guiney, who was also not unknown to Lovecraft)[302]: "I'll warrant here's a road to Arcady / With goodly cheer and merry company."[303] But for H. P. Lovecraft, the road to Arcadia was also the route to apocalypse.

In the Vagabondian cycle of wine, women, and song, too, we cannot forget (and nor could the teetotaler Lovecraft) that it is "wine" that conspicuously heads the list, and it is not hard to see a parallel between the Vagabonds' numerous poems dedicated to the "Clinking of glasses / And laughter of lasses,"[304] and that similarly "liquorish" "effusion" of "Bacchanalian mirth"[305] recited by Jervas Dudley in Lovecraft's "The Tomb." Indeed, the fact that this same nexus of wine, women, and song, which forms such a perfect storm of Lovecraft's Puritan crochets, likewise underlay the bacchanalia (along with such other Lovecraftian crochets as nudity, dancing, and an Eastern or Grecian origin), probably explains why the bacchanalia figured as such a central feature in his weird fiction: the bacchanalia was one of the few aspects of the sylvan Greek world that would pass whole, and without inversion, directly into the Lovecraftian weird canon. (Lovecraft was also doubtlessly influenced in this, too, by the science fantasy stories of the early pulps, including works by writers George Allan England and Edgar Rice Burroughs, in which primitive bacchanalian and orgiastic practices are common.) Nor is it probably any coincidence to note how the surprisingly satanic-sounding Temperance imagery found in Lovecraft's anti-alcohol poem "The Power of Wine" (1915) — which speaks of "hosts of darkness," "black wings," "cloven feet," and dancing or writhing with "ghoulish mirth"[306] — will later find direct analogues in things such as the "faint beating of giant wings"[307] associated with the orgiastic bacchanale in "The Call of Cthulhu," as well as in the devilish hoofed creature in Lovecraft's "The Unnamable," tellingly described as the offspring of a "screaming drunken wretch."[308]

One finds an additional, and ironic, point of agreement between Lovecraft and the Vagabond poets, too, in their mutual insistence that Pan is not dead. In his poem "Pan in the Catskills," for example, Bliss Carman, much like Lovecraft in his raptures over the Vermont scenery later on, identifies the magical scenery of the Catskills with the golden "enchantment"[309] of the "Thracian wild" — a place where once was heard "a slow mysterious piping wild and keen." But whereas Bliss Carman remains content to merely dispute the common assertion that "he [Pan] is dead," and to protest the idea that "now no more / The reedy syrinx sounds among the hills,"[310] H. P. Lovecraft instead warns us of the revival of Pan (and the forces of disorder he represents), which he sees as a prelude to disaster.

Significantly, there were numerous connections and overlaps between these Arcadian Vagabonds of the 1890s and the contemporary decadent movement on both sides of the Atlantic, since both Bliss Carman and Richard Hovey were closely associated with Boston decadents such as Ralph Adams Cram and Fred Holland Day,[311] collaborating with them on artistic and literary projects and also engaging in more dubious, but still closely related, private nocturnal occupations, whose precise nature is now hidden from us by the veil of the unnamable, but which are probably accurately described under the all-encompassing rubric of "wine, women, and song." As Douglass Shand-Tucci observes, "Does vagabondia seem somewhat at odds with *Salome* and *The Yellow Book*? In fact, Bohemian aesthetes of the period were characteristically one thing in winter, another in summer; Wildean in town, as it were, Whitmanic in the country."[312] Both of these would have been equally anti-pathic to Lovecraft. And although both Hovey and Carman would outwardly disavow any direct connection with the decadent Wilde or his aesthetic move-ment,[313] it seems clear that the open and naturalistic sexual freedom espoused by the Arcadian Vagabonds, as well as the more dubious and perverse forms of love espoused by the decadents, shared a similar source, and were both equally well symbolized by the Arcadian Pan, that embodiment of the pleasures of the flesh. Indeed, throughout the late 1800s, one sees a close relationship between Hellenism, decadence, and the lack of restraint advocated by Whit-man.

Thus do we find Oscar Wilde encoding the sexually perverse aspects of his poems in classical terms,[314] while in his poem "Pan," we see Wilde calling for the return of the "goat-footed God of Arcady" to modern England: "Ah, leave the hills of Arcady! / This modern world hath need of thee!"[315] For the decadents, the modern world had need of Pan's return; and if Pan no longer existed, then Wilde, or one of his bacchanalian, homosexual devotees, would assume his place, no matter what the cost (whether in terms of health, rep-utation, or jail time). Indeed, some misguided decadents would take such injunctions literally: pathetic magicians like Aleister Crowley and his followers, for instance, conducting mystical ceremonies in which they attempted to channel and embody the classical gods.[316] Crowley's sadistic poem "Hymn to Pan" (1913), which calls for Pan to "come over the sea / From Sicily and Arcady!,"[317] became a keynote text in Crowley's Thelemite religion. Even in the modern era, we find this same pagan language of "'dryad stillness,'"[318] of "'pagan shrines'"[319] and the lonely woods of "'wild nature'"[320] figuring in the rites and manifestos of Western occult manifestations such as Wicca and neo–Paganism.

Strangely, the similarity of such classical allusions in the works of Crowley to those made by H. P. Lovecraft in his weird fiction would later lead some Lovecraft critics, such as Philip A. Shreffler, to suggest a connection between Crowley's chant of "Io Pan! Io Pan!" and Lovecraft's recurring cry of "'Ia, Shub-Niggurath.'"[321] If there was a connection between Lovecraft and Crow-ley, however, it was only in their mutual use of the same classical sources: their shared use of the term "Ia!" or "Io!" for example, deriving from the prefix of the god Iacchus (often confounded with Bacchus), who was regarded as "the personification of the shouting and the enthusiasm of the initiates"[322] during their ritual processions. At the same time, however, the polemical differences between the conservative Lovecraft and decadents such as Crowley could not be more pronounced: those modern occultists who adopt Lovecraft's cosmology for use in their rituals actually do so in direct opposition to his own use of his cosmology as an anti–Dionysian caricature of Greek cosmology.

There may be a hint of the processes and methodology underlying Lovecraft's later inversion of decadent Arcadian themes in Lovecraft's 1918 critique of a decadent amateur publication entitled *Les Mouches Fantastiques*, published by followers of Oscar Wilde, in which Lovecraft contrasts what he calls the unwholesome "Dionaean Eros" of the decadents with what he calls higher worlds of "pure Uranian beauty" not attainable by the "lower regions of the senses."[323] Lovecraft cleverly turned the tables on his opponents by utilizing, in its original, Platonic, and idealistic sense, a term ("Uranian") later adopted by these same decadents as synonym for pederastic desire.

Something of the same methodology, I would argue, likewise underlies Lovecraft's parallel usage of decadent forms to facilitate the anti-decadent polemic in his own weird fiction. Lovecraft cleverly appropriated the territory of the enemy by reasserting ownership of previously uncontested terms and imagery. It is interesting, for instance, that in his 1918 essay he does not use the words *agape* (Gk. "Brotherly love") or *caritas* (Lat. "altruistic love"), which were also sometimes used to contrast eros, or carnal/sensual love, with idealistic love, but instead uses a word later adapted to a purely homosexual context. (The name of Lovecraft's character "**Kuran**es," too — the dispossessed king in his medievalist fantasy "Celephais"— also appears to derive from this word, "Uranian," as does the name of the sinister "Van **Kauran**" family in his collaborative story "The Man of Stone," although it is also possible, given Lovecraft's lifelong interest in astronomy, that he was inspired in these instances by the name of Urania, the muse of astronomy.[324]) At any rate, Lovecraft's pointed usage of the term "Uranian" adequately demonstrates both the nature of, and the methods behind, his polemical opposition to the decadents, as well as the extent of the difference between Lovecraft's classicism, and that of men like Samuel Loveman and Oscar Wilde.

As Peter Cannon observes, H. P. Lovecraft accepted the decadents, "but only up to a point."[325] And, as with his decadent artist Henry Wilcox in "The Call of Cthulhu"—whom Lovecraft's narrator declares is "of a type, ... which I could never like," although his narrator is "willing enough to admit both his genius and his honesty"[326]—Lovecraft's admiration for the decadents was intermixed with repulsion. Lovecraft spoke in similar terms in his collaborative story "Medusa's Coil" of the Baudelairean painter Frank Marsh, who, despite having "taken his pose of decadence pretty seriously and set[ting] out to be as much of a Rimbaud, Baudelaire, or Lautreamont as he could," was also "as sincere and profound an artist as I ever saw in my life," and "a delight to have around."[327] A similar dichotomy likewise characterized Lovecraft's relationships with his own decadent friends, such as the poet Hart Crane, whose genius Lovecraft respected despite his pitiable alcoholism, as well the horror writer and poet Clark Ashton Smith, whom Lovecraft says he could "'like'"[328] and "'tolerate'" and admit "'to be a social equal,'" despite what Lovecraft saw as his Neanderthalic sexual libertinism.

A similar dichotomy likewise characterized H. P. Lovecraft's troubled relationship with his friend, the decadent poet and bookseller Samuel Loveman, whose poetry, despite Loveman's personally abstemious lifestyle, is often wildly, if somberly, homoerotic. Indeed, although Lovecraft was effusive in his praise of Samuel Loveman's works—calling him "'the last of the Hellenes—a golden god of the elder world fallen upon pygmies,'"[329] and even aiding him in various ways: preserving his poems, defending his work in the amateur press, and preparing his proofs for publication—his praise was by no means unqualified. And although we see Lovecraft declaring Loveman's long poem *The Hermaphrodite* (1926) to be "perhaps the most authentically Greek in spirit of any sustained utterance of recent years,"[330] this is an encomium that, given Lovecraft's own views on the Greeks as effeminate and non-virile, is surely a qualified compliment, and which mirrors Lovecraft's ambivalent stance toward both the Grecian and the decadent throughout his writings. As Estelle Jussim observes in her biography of Fred Holland Day, whose works were often described by critics as purveying "a purely Greek point of view,"[331] "To say that something was Greek in conception was not necessarily a compliment, however much the Victorians admired the ancient sculptures."[332] As Lovecraft himself confirms: "The Hellenes, with their strange beauty-worship and defective moral ideas, are to be admired and pitied at once, as luminous but remote phantoms; the Romans, with their greater practical sense, ancient virtue, and love of law and order, seem like our own people."[333] A feeling of pity perhaps also tempered Lovecraft's admiration for Loveman.

Samuel Loveman, later in life, denounced what he rightly saw as the hypocrisy of H. P. Lovecraft, and although Loveman makes it clear that his bitterness derives from his friend's concealed anti–Semitism, it is possible that Lovecraft's equivocal attitude toward Greek decadence in some way influenced Loveman's charge of hypocrisy. As Lovecraft observed in a 1927 letter, Loveman's work "must be read wholly for imagery and not for ideas, as must every other work of art. Great Scott—if Loveman and I judged each other by our ideas, we'd have long ago suffered the fate of the Kilkenny cats."[334] Although Lovecraft is referring to political differences here, Loveman's Greek point of view may have also figured in his opposition. Samuel Loveman, for his part, apparently cast H. P. Lovecraft in the role of the respectable King Pentheus in his sadistic and erotic poem "Bacchanale," which was dedicated to Lovecraft, and in which Pentheus is stabbed to death by his mother, Agave, the same knife-wielding and castrative Terrible Mother that figures so prominently throughout Lovecraft's writings. Loveman perhaps is making a commentary here upon Lovecraft's seething maternal concerns, as well as upon Lovecraft's Puritanism.

What Lovecraft calls "the underlying sensitiveness"[335] of Samuel Loveman also figures in his characterization of the various decadents throughout his weird fiction: the self-described "'psychically hypersensitive'"[336] sculptor Wilcox, or the decadent painter Marsh, who is described as being, "like all decadents,"[337] "exquisitely sensitive to the colour and atmosphere and names of things." Lovecraft perhaps satirizes this idea elsewhere, too, via that "sensitiveness to beauty"[338] exhibited by his pathetic hybrid ape-man, Arthur Jermyn, who is, like Loveman, "a poet and a dreamer," and whose sensitiveness in this regard is sneeringly attributed by Jermyn's neighbors to his "Latin blood ... shewing itself." Lovecraft, interestingly, was preceded in this simian caricature of the decadents by 19th century American critics of Oscar Wilde, who saw Wilde and his fellow aesthetes as (much like Lovecraft's decadent artist Richard Pickman later on, who is "bound down the toboggan of reverse evolution"[339]) "'tending down the hill'"[340] toward the apes. Publications such as the *Washington Post* and *Harper's Weekly* depicted Wilde as an ape and described him as "a regressive link in the Darwinian chain."[341]

S. T. Joshi's comment, meanwhile, that "the neoclassicism of [Samuel] Loveman's poetry and his general air of languid sophistication could only appeal to Lovecraft"[342] also requires some further qualification: the term "neoclassicism," for instance, is more suggestive of the baroque, ornate, and artificial French and English styles of the 1700s, which Lovecraft would indeed have admired, than of the bacchanalian, decadent, and Hellenic verse that Samuel Loveman produced — although certainly both men respected each other's mutual archaisms. The term "languid," too, has distinctly decadent, and negative, echoes in Lovecraft's weird fiction, being applied to both the decadent Henry Wilcox, who "turned languidly at my knock"[343] in "The Call of Cthulhu," and also to the sadistic emperor Elagabalus, whose perversity Lovecraft associates with necrophilia in "Herbert West: Reanimator."[344] In this conspicuous usage of the word "languid," of course, Lovecraft follows earlier decadent usages, from Park Barnitz to Oscar Wilde, who himself derived it, according to Richard Ellmann, from "Schlegel's *Lucinde*, where it said, with a touch of Wilde's self-mockery, 'Laziness is the one divine fragment of a godlike existence left to man from Paradise.'"[345] It is doubtful that "languid," for Lovecraft, would have been a recommendation. Lovecraft's slyly described, in 1926, Samuel Loveman's poem *The Hermaphrodite* as "The Herm book"[346]; this partly, no doubt, served as merely a convenient abbreviation; but also, possibly, was a reference to the word herm, a phallic figure of the ancient world and a symbol of the fertility god Priapus, which was often depicted in the decadent art of Aubrey Beardsley and Fred Holland Day. As Lovecraft wryly observed elsewhere regarding Samuel Loveman's penchant for detecting "phallic symbolism"[347] in artwork: Loveman had "done enough delving in that line to see phalli in most things from church steeples to mushrooms."

Samuel Loveman was also, according to biographer S. T. Joshi, possessed of an "impressive collection of *objets d'art*,"[348] which Lovecraft "first saw ... in September 1922 and was much impressed by." Joshi even suggests that the morbid collection of necrophilic objects collected by the decadent aesthetes in Lovecraft's story "The Hound" was perhaps inspired by this collection. If so, however, then "The Hound" was surely a curious tribute: the entire story is a wild, over-the-top parody of the standard tropes of decadence, in which Lovecraft transforms the homoerotic male brotherhoods espoused by decadents such as Ralph Adams Cram, Baron Corvo, and Edward Perry Warren into something ghoulish and necrophilic. "The Hound" is also the story in which Lovecraft's famous volume, the forbidden *Necronomicon*, first appears. If the entire story can be interpreted as a caustic satire on the perversities of homosexual decadence, then the *Necronomicon* itself also appears to be a satirical version, in turn, of the various forbidden literary works of the decadent period: whether Whitman's oft-banned *Leaves of Grass*, Beardsley's oft-censored drawings, or Wilde's *Collected Works*, which disappeared from bookstore and library shelves for many years following his scandal.

Lovecraft's partial dedication of his story "Hypnos" (1922) to Samuel Loveman, too, is surely an ambivalent tribute to Loveman's Hellenism, given Lovecraft's immoral characterization of the narrator's supposedly "impious"[349] delvings into the unknown with his imaginary friend, as well as the tragic fate of its narrator, who ends his days "bald, grey-bearded, shriveled, palsied, drug-crazed, and broken,"[350] and who only belatedly learns that "insanity had filled all my tragic life." Indeed, just as with his inversion of the sylvan motifs of Arcadia, in "Hypnos" we can again see Lovecraft turning the tables on his polemical opponents. Hypnos, the Greek god of sleep, had long been a favorite topic for depiction by such decadents as Fred Holland Day and the homosexual Jewish painter Simeon Solomon. Ralph Adams Cram, too, seems to have made use of Hypnos in the title of his volume of occult-themed horror stories, *Black Spirits and White* (1895) (with which Lovecraft was familiar). Hypnos was considered the brother of Death, and the two of them often were represented by Greek artists under the aspect of slumbering youths, one black, one white.[351]

Written in the year following "The Moon-Bog," Lovecraft's "Hypnos" still straddles the line between Poe and classicism, and between being a proclassical story and an anti-decadent portrait. Indeed, as if expressing Lovecraft's despair, or at least his acknowledgment, at having reached the limits of inspiration in his own mechanical, pastoral verse, the story seems to portray his own grudging admiration for the visions of the decadents even as he delineates the sleaziness and tawdriness of their methods and lifestyles. The eyes of the narrator's friend in the story, according to Lovecraft, had looked upon "realms which I had cherished in fancy, but vainly sought."[352] And despite its ambivalence, "Hypnos" clearly reflects the increasing assimilation of decadent ideas within Lovecraft's weird fiction, even if the only way he could assimilate decadence was to absorb it and reflect it within the form of an anti-decadent polemic. Indeed, there may be a parody of Samuel Loveman's contemporary worship of Hellenistic beauty (not to mention of Lovecraft's own youthful classicism) in his description of the narrator in this story sitting alone "for hours, adoring and praying to"[353] the marble bust of "Hypnos" that he himself has carved. The slow devolution from the benevolent and inspired pagan sculptor in "The Tree" to the decadent sculptor Henry Wilcox in "The Call of Cthulhu" has finally begun, eventually culminating in the "decadent sculptures"[354] that Danforth and Dyer discover in *At the Mountains of Madness*.

Although Lovecraft succeeded in "Hypnos" in combining his classical interests with that aerial nightmare imagery that had both tormented and fascinated him since he was a child, the final step toward the Cthulhu apocalypses, with their caricatural

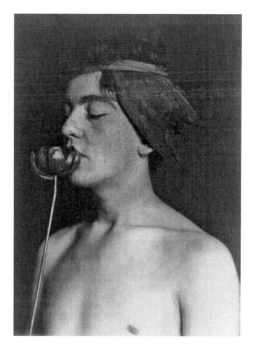

The decadent version of "Hypnos" (circa 1896, photograph by Frederick Holland Day, from Louise Imogen Guiney Collection, Library of Congress, Prints and Photographs Division, used with permission of RPS / Science & Society Picture Library).

inversion of the ancient Greek myths, had not yet begun. However cosmic his guise, the Hypnos in this story is still Hypnos, and not an inverted Mythos double. True, Lovecraft's Hellenic gods are now being filtered through the 19th century lens of the romantics and the decadents, rather than through the more hackneyed and archaic filter of the earlier Georgian, pastoral, and Roman poets. It merely remained for Lovecraft to more accurately define his Puritan stance vis-à-vis the decadents and to integrate this stance into the actual plots of his weird fiction. He would later do this in "The Whisperer in the Dark," in which he saw fit to recapitulate the plot of "Hypnos" in the second half of the story (Albert Wilmarth, much like the narrator in "Hypnos," is tempted with the attainment of ultimate cosmic knowledge by the sylvan, alien inhabitants of the Vermont woods).

It may be, too, that we also catch a further glimpse in "The Whisperer in Darkness" of Boston architect Ralph Adams Cram, author of *The Decadent* (1893) and later a prominent Anglo-Catholic medievalist and conservative. Cram's life seems to have exerted a sort of fascination upon Lovecraft, who mentions Cram at least twice elsewhere in his weird fiction. (In "The Thing on the Doorstep," for example, portions of Cram's biography, such as his "Boston architect's office,"[355] are intermixed with that of Cram's close friend Henry S. Whitehead in Lovecraft's description of Edward Derby's best friend, Dan; while in "The Call of Cthulhu" Lovecraft archly refers to what he calls "a widely known architect with leanings toward theosophy and occultism,"[356] who "went violently insane..., and expired several months later after incessant screamings to be saved from some escaped denizen of hell." As biographer Douglass Shand-Tucci confirms, Cram also maintained a lifelong interest in "Spiritualism and the occult."[357])

Lovecraft's "Whisperer," meanwhile, perhaps has further echoes of Cram in the form of what Lovecraft calls "A Cultivated Male Human Voice,"[358] overheard partaking in a bacchanalian fertility ritual in the Vermont woods, and further described as "a mellow, educated voice which seemed vaguely Bostonian in accent, and which was certainly not any of native of the Vermont hills."[359] Later, one of the Outer Ones describes this cultivated Bostonian, named Mr. Noyes, as having "been one of us for years...."[360] Wilmarth afterward expresses his "particular shock" to "discover that my guide Noyes was the human celebrant in that monstrous bygone Sabbat-ritual"[361]; this shock is vaguely similar, perhaps, to that which one might feel upon discovering the conservative Cram's youthful decadent associations.

The suave Mr. Noyes, however, is merely one of a number of such "human allies"[362] of the Outer Ones in "Whisperer." Wilmarth also refers to "the crude speech of an unknown and evidently rustic man"[363] also overheard during the ceremony, later revealed to be that of Walter Brown, "who lived alone on a run-down hillside place near the deep woods" (yet another friend of Pan, it would seem). And although Lovecraft describes Brown as a "surly farmer"[364] (perhaps a distant kin of Lovecraft's decayed "Gardner" family?), he also represents the Whitmanesque side of the Wilde-Whitman dichotomy that Lovecraft so deplored. Even more insidiously, however, the other human allies of the Outer Ones, according to Lovecraft, include "a few of mankind's philosophic and scientific leaders"[365] (a relationship perhaps akin to that of men such as John Addington Symonds and Walter Pater with decadence, or Harvard's John Reed with Bolshevism?) who are either under the hypnotic influence of the aliens, or else have, as Lovecraft puts it, made a "pact with the Outside Things."[366] Lovecraft's language here, just as with Captain Obed Marsh's rumored "bargains"[367] with the Devil in "The Shadow Over Innsmouth," strangely parallels that earlier, anti–Satanic language propounded by such Puritan polemicists as Cotton Mather, for whom secular dissenters, no less than the confessed witches themselves, had made a covenant with the Devil. Needless to say, the fact that the terms of H. P. Lovecraft's sociopolitical polemic should merge so seamlessly with those of the 17th century Massachusetts divines should give even Lovecraft's most ardent admirers (and apologists) pause. (Perhaps significantly, too, the Rev. Nicholas Noyes, as Lovecraft doubtlessly knew, was also prominent in the 1692 witchcraft trials in Salem. Noyes was known for his fierce and "unforgiving temper"[368] and for having "no mercy" whatsoever "for the sinner who denied his guilt." Mr. Noyes' alliance with the aliens in Lovecraft's story thus perhaps represents the ultimate turnabout of the former Massachusetts hierarchy, and further reinforces the extent of the aliens' infiltration of New England culture.)

This sinister alliance between Lovecraft's Outer Ones and cultured men such as Mr. Noyes also mirrors the cross-cultural and syncretic aspects of the decadents in the 1890s. Indeed, much like Bostonian Fred Holland Day, who evinced a lifelong interest in immigrants,[369] blacks,[370] and foreigners,[371] or Ralph Adams Cram, who combined Eastern with Western forms in his architecture,[372] or Bliss Carman, who declared himself to be "Western in bearing, / And Eastern in breed,"[373] we find Lovecraft's Mr. Noyes actively facilitating the entré of the Outer Ones into human civilization and Western customs. The aliens even adopt the grammar and accent of Mr. Noyes' cultivated, Bostonian voice,[374] although for Lovecraft's narrator, the aliens' buzzing voice is still merely "a morbid echo"[375] of the Bostonian's own voice, "winging its way across unimaginable abysses from unimaginable outer hells."[376] Lovecraft's youthful polemic against sedition was still going strong, save that now it had been expanded from its previous association with the supposed sedition of the American colonies against the Mother Country across the sea to include the Dionysian and cross-cultural interests of New England's intellectual elite. And much like the Lebanese mystical artist Kahlil Gibran — who, beginning as a street waif in Boston, eventually went on to eclipse his generous patron Fred Holland Day, and, indeed, all of the other artists and writers of the Boston decadent milieu[377] — these imitative Outer Ones in "Whisperer" definitely hold a superior position over their human allies. An alien voice, overheard by Wilmarth from another room, exercises what Lovecraft calls "an unmistakable note of authority"[378] over the others in the room, while Henry Akeley's mechanical voice seems "to be in a position of subordination and pleading," and Mr. Noyes' tones exude "a kind of conciliatory atmosphere."

Ralph Adams Cram's interest in Theosophy, too, represents yet another symptom of these cross-cultural impulses in New England during this period — one that also did not go unnoticed in Lovecraft's weird fiction. Lovecrafts, curiously, includes "a theosophical colony"[379] amid the various troublesome anti-imperialist and anti-colonialist rebellions in "The Call of Cthulhu," which are associated with the incipient rumblings of an awakening Cthulhu — what Lovecraft calls, in an echo of his earlier militaristic critiques of ideas about "universal brotherhood,"[380] "some 'glorious fulfillment' which never arrives."[381] As Sylvia Cranston observes in her 1993 biography of Theosophical Society founder H. P. Blavatsky, "the [theosophical] movement's first object" was "universal brotherhood,"[382] in the form of a religious pollination between East and West; a syncretic, multicultural, and revolutionary program that could only have aroused Lovecraft's instant ire, suspicion, or derision. Indeed, as Cranston goes on, Blavatsky's Theosophical movement quickly came to have a huge impact on both Indian nationalism and the development of the Indian National Congress in particular, "which under Mohandas Gandhi's guidance became the dominant power leading to the historic hour when India gained her freedom."[383] This fact may be reflected in Lovecraft's association of the theosophical cult with "serious native unrest"[384] in India and elsewhere. According to Cranston, too, Theosophy was directly instrumental in transforming Gandhi himself from a completely secularized and Westernized Indian into both an activist and a devotee of the Hindu religion. And although Lovecraft himself later drew derision from his friend (and amateur occultist) E. Hoffmann Price for having included Theosophists among the degenerate cultists mentioned in his weird fiction (according to Price, "Clearly he'd been totally ignorant of Theosophy yet had sounded off"[385]), Price himself seems not to have truly understood the exact nature of Lovecraft's own opposition to the religion, or to have realized that the "bland optimism"[386] of the Theosophists, for Lovecraft, also masked still more frightening socio-political implications, reflecting as it did an alliance or attempt at unification between East and West. (Critic Robert M. Price, on the other hand, seems to recognize some hidden meaning in Lovecraft's depiction of Theosophy, observing how the "occasional references to Theosophy per se imply that he used the cult itself as an image of some kind,"[387] although Price stops short of making any political or polemical connections.)

Boston itself, significantly, was initially at this center of the Theosophical movement. H. P. Lovecraft's picture of the alien interests of the Bostonian Mr. Noyes perhaps satirizing this period during the late 1800s, when, as Kahlil Gibran's biographers write, "it was fashionable for Boston Brahmins to enter 'the mystic atmosphere of the Orient circle' by flocking to private lectures given by Siddi Mohammed Tabier on 'The Book of the Dead' or by Swami Vivakananda on 'the Karma Yogi.'"[388] Indeed, as Douglass Shand-Tucci emphasizes in his biography of Ralph Adams Cram, H. P. Blavatsky's "*Isis Unveiled* has distinct New England roots."[389] Blavatsky lived and worked in Boston in the 1870s, published articles in Boston spiritualist journals, and founded one of the oldest Theosophical churches there. Cram and his fellow Visionists, too (the Visionists were an American offshoot of the British Hermetic Order of the Golden Dawn) likewise made their headquarters in Boston, in a room decorated with "symbolic devices of various sorts, mostly Oriental and exotic."[390] The whole place had, as Cram admits in his memoirs, "'a mildly profligate connotation [amongst Bostonians], which misrepresented it utterly.'" Even the vast wooded spaces in Vermont, too, in which Lovecraft's Outer Ones make their home, formed a starting point for the development of Blavatsky's theosophical movement in America; as Douglas Shand-Tucci observes: "rural Vermont ... played a vital part in the history of Theosophy, it having been in the wake of psychic 'disturbances' in Vermont that Madame Blavatsky, the theosophical leader Cram was a follower of in the mid–1880s, journeyed to New England to undertake the study that led to her cofounding of the Theosophical Society."[391]

The more obvious reasons for such cross-cultural pollinations amongst the decadents during this period are sexual reasons, which would have only made such interrelations all the more suspect to the Puritan Lovecraft. From the pederastic intrigues of Fred Holland Day and his friend Herbert Copeland among the immigrant children of Boston's slums, to Oscar Wilde's pederastic exploits in North Africa, or the sexual tourism of aesthetes such as Charles Warren Stoddard's in the South Seas in the 1880s, dark foreigners have long functioned as repositories for Western sexual desire, often cloaked beneath classical and sylvan allusions. As Wilde wrote in a letter to friend Robbie Ross, the "'Kabyle boys'"[392] of North Africa are "'lovely,'" Wilde referring to them in Arcadian terms as "'fauns. Several shepherds fluted on reeds for us. We are followed by lovely brown things from forest to forest.'" Indeed, Lovecraft may have intended a satire of things such as Fred Holland Day's quest for fauns and satyrs among Italian and Mediterranean boys in Boston's slums, in Richard Upton Pickman's secret Boston studio in "Pickman's Model," where he engages in cannibalistic and sadistic pursuits. Lovecraft pointedly calls these, in his story "He," the acts of "uncommunicative artists, whose practices do not invite publicity or the light of day."[393] Indeed, for both the decadents and Lovecraft, the sensuous and ecstatic aspects of Arcadian and bacchanalian revelry were foremost in their vision, albeit clouded in Lovecraft's works by an overlay of cosmic outsideness. And although the immigrant hordes found their unabashed enemy in Lovecraft, he ultimately did far less damage to these immigrants — particularly their young — than their ostensible friends in the decadent movement, whose cloak of friendship concealed a sexual motive.

It is significant, too, with regard to Lovecraft's opposition to decadence, that "The Whisperer in Darkness" is told from Wilmarth's point of view — that is, from the point of view of an outsider and academic — and not, say, from the point of view of Mr. Noyes himself, whose interaction with the alien Outer Ones is, after all, more direct, and whose interest in the cosmic is, presumably, either equal to or even greater than that of Wilmarth. True, Wilmarth is described as possessing what Lovecraft calls a "love of strangeness"[394] and a marked interest in cosmic abysses (a fact that strangely contradicts, however, Lovecraft's portrait of Wilmarth earlier in the story as a conservative who engages in epistolary and academic battles against Fortean believers in unexplained phenomena). Ultimately, however, the distance that Lovecraft presents between the cultivated Mr. Noyes and the narrator Albert Wilmarth is basically the same as that polemical distance that he maintained between himself and the decadents. This distance is further reflected in Wilmarth's conscious recoil from all of Mr. Noyes' alien associations — or, as Lovecraft puts it, Wilmarth's desire "To keep as far as possible from such influences and such emissaries"[395] in the future. Or, as Cotton Mather similarly observes in his *Wonders of the Invisible World* (1692), in words H. P. Lovecraft would doubtlessly have agreed with: "If any among ourselves be"[396] allured into a covenant with the Devil, "my councel is, that you hunt the Devil from you, with such words as the Psalmist had, *Be gone, depart from me, ye evil doers.*"

IV. Conclusions

Lovecraft's use of Roman satirical methods in his weird fiction enabled him to divorce his former, and now regretted, Arcadian mysticism from his conservative and aristocratic Roman classicism, and yet still utilize his considerable knowledge of both. Poe vs. Greece, Arcadia vs. Rome, Roman order vs. the Greek bacchanalia; these are the tensions that give H. P. Lovecraft's later mythos its characteristic parameters and form. It is here, I think, where we must locate Lovecraft's uniqueness as a horror writer, and not in his supposed cosmicism, which, as others have already observed, was certainly not an invention of Lovecraft's, and which in any case is actually very sparse in Lovecraft's mainly mundane weird canon. On the other hand, Lovecraft's most characteristically "Lovecraftian" stories are those stories that most clearly involve an integration of his social and personal crochets with classical and macabre themes, i.e., his later apocalypses. Cosmicism merely forms the backdrop for a basically Roman satire, whose atmospheric genius also hides its uniquely Roman prosaicism.

So hermetic and consistent was H. P. Lovecraft's satirical worldview, however, that it eventually developed a transmutative power of its own, transforming what was originally basically a satire into a cosmology, and from a cosmology into a popular cultural mythos. Many of Lovecraft's younger readers are seemingly unaware of his original satirical intent, and the elaborate biases that underlay its creation. This blindness on the part of some of Lovecraft's readers is also facilitated by the dearth of classical education in the United States, which has rendered many of his classical references incomprehensible to the modern reader.

I do not mean to suggest in any way, however, that Lovecraft's creation of his anti–Arcadian polemic was somehow rigidly or rationally planned. Everything — its slow growth, its tentative nature, its many contradictions — suggests that such a caricatural polemic, if it exists at all in his weird fiction, was largely an organic growth, and one that was characterized (as we have seen) by many exceptions (such as Lovecraft's Dunsanian fantasies and his Vermont travelogue). If my essay has any value, it is in its attempt at a definition of the true nature and boundaries of Lovecraft's classicism. It means nothing to say, for example, that both Howard Phillips Lovecraft and Samuel Loveman were "classicists," given the polemical distances between them. Certainly Lovecraft and Loveman's mutually-held classicism was a point of interest that joined them together; but it also symbolized their inherent differences, including their larger socio-political differences, as well.

Lovecraft's conservative anti–Arcadian polemic was useful, and prescient, in predicting many of those bacchanalian and sensuous social factors that influenced and shaped the latter half of the 20th century in the West, and particularly in the U.S. The wide and seminal influence of black culture on popular music, dance, and sports; the ineluctable growth and influence of feminism and gay liberation; along with the growing power of postcolonial nations in Africa, the Far East, and the Middle East; all have their analogues in Lovecraft's earlier anti–Dionysian critique. And although, as scholar M. I. Rostovtzeff observes, "Cicero would not have recognized his compatriots if by chance he had come to life again in the Rome of the early popes and the late emperors, though some of them still wrote Ciceronian Latin,"[397] Lovecraft probably would recognize something of himself in his current descendants, although for him, it would only be in the sense of recognizing fragments from a nightmare. The lascivious rites of Cthulhu's animalistic followers are now broadcast every night on TV. Glib Satanists and lycanthropic Crowleyites promulgate their absurd mystical doctrines on the Internet. And that bacchanalia from which Lovecraft so recoiled, has, in the form of the sexual revolution, spawned an epidemic that is just as unspeakable, and just as unnamable, as anything he, in his paranoia, could have created.

Two

The Birds and the Bees
(According to H. P. Lovecraft)

As a matter of fact, women are sisters of the flowers, and
are in close relationship with the animals.
— Otto Weininger, *Sex and Character*[1] (1903)

This chapter forms a brief addendum to the previous one, in which I deal with one specific aspect of Lovecraft's Arcadian vision that figured prominently in his later inverted anti–Arcadian satire: Lovecraft's use of bees.

Bees, in the classical world as now, were central to agricultural life, and were thus regarded by the ancients, along with their various analogues (honey, flowers, beehives, etc.) as symbols of fertility and as representatives of the female deity. As anthropologist J. J. Bachofen observes: "'The bee was rightly looked upon as a symbol of the feminine potency of nature. It was associated above all with Demeter, Artemis, and Persephone.'"[2] The goddess Demeter was regarded as the "'pure mother bee,'"[3] and her priestesses also were regarded as bees.[4] (As Lovecraft would have known from his reading of Dr. Margaret S. Murray's *The Witch-Cult in Western Europe* [1921], this curious idea was perpetuated well into the medieval period, when it was subsumed into the rituals of the Witches' Sabbath, during which women were said to have been transformed into "'the likenesse of bees.'"[5]) Bees were also central to the wild and orgiastic rites of Dionysus,[6] and while Bacchus was associated with the grape, Dionysus was known for his mead, produced from fermented honey.

Bees, of course, are vital to the sex life of flowering plants, and are thus, by extension, closely associated with sexuality in general; the phrase the "birds and the bees" is synonymous with sex itself. (So closely associated are bees with the sexual act that amongst the Masai, according to anthropologist H. R. Hays, couples brewing honey wine "must be continent for two days before and during the six days of the brewing or the wine will be undrinkable and the bees will fly away."[7]) More specifically, bees are associated with the male process of fertilization, and women take, as Otto Weininger's quote at the beginning of this essay suggests, the part of the flower.

This constellation of feminine, Dionysian, and sexual meanings is typical of the bee imagery in neoclassical, pastoral, and Arcadian verse. A characteristic example can be found in H. C. Bunner's light-hearted *Airs from Arcady and Elsewhere* (1884), where — amid florid poems dedicated to "spring rustling in the tree"[8] and to the pastoral deities Daphnis and Chloe — we find a roundel entitled "O Honey of Hymettus Hill," which asks:

> Thy musky scent what virginal chaste
> Blossom was ravished to distill,
> O honey of Hymettus Hill,
> Gold brown, and cloying sweet to taste?...[9]

Such bee imagery was also typical of the Arcadian Vagabonds of the 1890s. Bliss Carman, for example, in his poem "A More Ancient Mariner," included the bee among his own band of vagabond poets, calling it "a vagrant bold," who "pilfers from every port of the wind, / From April to golden autumn."[10] In another poem in his collection of erotic verse, *Songs of the Sea Children*, Carman described his love as a "sultry languorous flower," observing: "I was the rover bee, and you — / With the hot red mouth where a soul might drown, / ... / You were the blossom that drew me down."[11]

In Ralph Adams Cram's ghost story "The White Villa," too, included in *Spirits Black and White* (1895), bees form a part of the homoerotic and decadent Arcadia envisioned by Cram's protagonists. His two male protagonists lie together lethargically in the grass beside the ruins of a temple of Poseidon and Ceres, the idyllic scene consisting of "a vague and pulsating murmur"[12] of the sea "that blended with the humming of bees all about us," while "a small shepherd boy, with a woolly dog, made shy advances of friendship" and gathered "flowers for us," including "asphodels and bee-orchids." Photographer Fred Holland Day later referenced much the same imagery in his decadent picture "The Honey Gatherer" (1898), in which a shirtless young man is shown carrying a large vessel, poised beside a smaller male classical statue. A further link between bees and 1890s aestheticism was also provided by Maurice Maeterlinck's book *Life of the Bee* (1900), a collectivist hymn to gynocracy that attempted to provide a scientific basis for the resurgence of paganism and woman-worship of the decadent period. Maeterlinck's vision, according to scholar Mary Warner Blanchard, later influenced Henry Adams' neo–Catholic study *Mont-Saint-Michel and Chartres* (1904), in which he drew inspiration for his own peculiar mystical Mariolatry from the structures of bee society.[13] In Lovecraft's work, of course, we can also see a similar and, indeed, omnipresent concern with the Magna Mater, albeit in her more overtly murderous and terrible aspects. His Great Mother is more closely akin to the restless goddess of the Meso-American myths, who cries out in the night for sacrificial hearts and human blood, than to any saving celestial virgin.

In his early poetry, however, H. P. Lovecraft would likewise revel in such unabashed Arcadian bee-imagery. In his springtime poem "March" (1915), he writes of how "in June we revel in the bees' soft hum, / But March exalts us with the bliss to come."[14] Nor does Lovecraft's later poem, "A June Afternoon" (1918), disappoint: Lovecraft speaks of how "a drowsy hum, as of contented bees / In distant hives, pervades the balmy air."[15] In his 1921 birthday poem to his young friend Alfred Galpin, meanwhile, Lovecraft writes (one hopes satirically) of the Muses descending to Galpin, where

> Thy ruddy lips with wine they stain,
>   And honey from Hymettus' hives;
> And breathe in thee a pure refrain
>   To tell the glory of their lives.[16]

The alliance pictured here, between bacchanalian wine and Dionysian honey, does much to explain Lovecraft's later, and far more sinister, use of bee imagery in his writings, given the pro–Temperance aspect of Lovecraft's larger anti-bacchanalian critique.

In Lovecraft's early short story "The Tree" (1920), in which the Arcadian is still being given a positive spin, bees once again present a benevolent aspect. The story is related to the narrator by "an old bee-keeper who lives in a neighboring cottage,"[17] who alone knows the truth of what occurred — a fact which suggests some more intimate alliance between the beekeeper and those sylvan forces of nature that aid the sculptor Kalos to carry out his revenge. (Later on, of course, in "The Call of Cthulhu," only such decadents as the languid Wilcox — in addition to various other "artists and poets"[18] — are sensitive enough to perceive the "ceaseless, half-mental calling from underground"[19] sent from the sleeping Cthulhu; and significantly, the dead Kalos, too, much like Cthulhu, is likewise described as a sleeper.[20])

At the same time, however, Lovecraft found the bee a useful metaphor for his virginal Puritan polemics: his poem "The Nymph's Reply to the Modern Business Man" (1917), begins (rather explicitly for Lovecraft):

> If all the world and love were young,
> *And I had ne'er before been "stung,"*
> I might enough a dullard prove
> To live with thee and be thy love[21] [italics mine]

"Stung" here forms a sarcastic euphemism for previous sexual experience. (In his caustic response to fellow amateur Edna von der Hyde in 1914, the virginal Lovecraft heaped derision upon the sexually experienced woman, observing dryly of von der Hyde: "The Modern Lothario is fortunate in having so competent and experienced a champion."[22])

Lovecraft later reflected the feminine side of this sexual equation in his collaborative story "Deaf, Dumb, and Blind." Lovecraft and Eddy combined the honey-imagery so familiar from Arcadian and pastoral poetry with the idea of Satanic and sexual corruption, as blind and deaf protagonist Richard Blake hears a "demoniacal"[23] and "pagan pandemonium" of supernatural origin, which he likens to the "lecherous buzzing of bestial blowflies" and the "Satanic humming of libidinous bees"—right before he is pulled by what he calls "devil-fingers" (autoerotic?) into a final "cesspool of eternal iniquity," described in apocalyptically Puritan language as a "sin-steeped night" of "Purgatory" and a "vile vortex of vice." Lovecraft and Eddy are slightly more explicit here than Lovecraft himself usually is when describing the cosmic bacchanalias of Azazoth or Yog-Sothoth in his canonical weird fiction, but the sources of both images—whether the ostensibly cosmic orgies of Lovecraft's stories, or the "Cabirian orgies"[24] here described in this collaboration, are both to be found in Lovecraft's inversion of Arcadian imagery.

In "The Colour Out of Space," too, bees take their place along with all the other examples of overripe pagan fecundity in the Gardner's realm of Arcadian decay. As Lovecraft writes, "In May the insects came, and Nahum's place became a nightmare of buzzing and crawling. Most of the creatures seemed not quite usual in their aspects and motions, and their nocturnal habits contradicted all former experience."[25] These same insects, too, including the bees, also partake of the later decay that quickly follows upon this fecundity, all of them dying out along with the cattle and vegetation. The final manifestation of the cosmic color from space, too, is characterized by an insect simile: Lovecraft describes it as an "unhallowed radiance, ... like a glutted swarm of corpse-fed fireflies dancing hellish sarabands over an accursed marsh."[26] Lovecraft, as usual, transfigures Arcadian imagery via his patented necrophilic processes. For Lovecraft, Life not only leads to Death, Life is a kind of Death. And tellingly, this strange cosmic color is accompanied by a glow from the "bee-hives near the stone wall on the west."[27] (And is it a coincidence, I wonder, that the heroes in Lovecraft's "The Dunwich Horror" utilize "a metal sprayer of the sort used in combating insects"[28] in order to combat the sylvan Wilber Whately's gigantic, unseen brother?)

This same nightmare buzzing of the insects in "Colour" likewise forms a large part of Lovecraft's "The Whisperer in Darkness," in which the immigrant aliens infiltrating the Vermont woods speak in what Wilmarth calls "a buzzing imitation of human speech."[29] Indeed, Lovecraft speaks of this buzzing, at the beginning to his tale, as being "voices like a bee's that tried to be like voices of men."[30] He then goes on to spend two full paragraphs in "Whisperer" attempting to describe these "blasphemous"[31] and ostensibly alien buzzings, which are further likened to "the drone of some loathsome, gigantic insect ponderously shaped into the articulate speech of an alien species"[32] — but the more Lovecraft goes on, adding more adjectives and similes of cosmic alienage, the more it seems like a diversionary overlay over the original Arcadian imagery that first inspired the image. The fact that these buzzing voices are overheard by Wilmarth and Akeley while taking part in a fertility ceremony in the Vermont woods, too, merely reinforces "lecherous" and "libidinous" sexual associations that underlie Lovecraft's bee symbolism.

Lovecraft also incidentally, either consciously or unconsciously, invokes bee imagery in a more subtle, and more thematic way, throughout the weird canon. In "The Shadow Over Innsmouth," for instance, the rising of the Deep One hordes is associated with "a curious sort of buzz or roar"[33] as they pursue Lovecraft's protagonist. The Innsmouth hybrids themselves, meanwhile, are described as "'swarms'"[34] throughout the tale; the language is perhaps retained from "Innsmouth"'s direct precursor, "The Horror at Red Hook," in which Lovecraft speaks of "the squinting Orientals that swarmed from every door"[35] during a police-raid on Suydam and Lilith's Devil-worshipping cult. All of this reflects what critic Maurice Levy rightly calls the "swarming nature"[36] of Lovecraft's entities — language that, as Levy also points out, has numerous echoes in Lovecraft's various racist writings.[37] That Lovecraft, in these tracts, also connects this swarming with a secretive process of sexual "spawning"[38] by these same immigrants further reflects the pagan sexual symbolism of bees and underlines why, for the Puritan Lovecraft, they formed such a perfect symbol. Nor did it hurt that Lovecraft was fond of invoking "insect" language with regard to his various personal squabbles. He compared his opponents, for instance, during his 1915 controversy with Charles Isaacson in the amateur press, to "critical canines and insulting insects."[39] Lovecraft, tellingly, equated insects with his despised sensual and plebian dogs in terms of his polemical antagonisms. His ultimate expression of this seething, spawning collective evil, of course, is the shoggoths, from whom all sense of individuality or personal identity has been expunged.

Bees, of course, form a perfect symbol to describe collective entities or mass evil, which is perhaps why they repeatedly figure as such in the early science-fantasy pulps that Lovecraft devoured as a youth, in which collective evil is frequently depicted in gynocratic or insectoid form. In George Allan

England's post-apocalyptic *Darkness and Dawn* (*The Cavalier*, 1912–1913) trilogy, for example, which Lovecraft highly praised as a youth,[40] the villains take the form of a race of bestial, subhuman ape men collectively referred to simply as "the Horde,"[41] who prove to be the degenerate descendants of African Americans who have been reduced to savagery due to what England speciously regarded as the lack of firm white authority to guide them, and who are compared to "a swarming mass of bees."[42] Even more significant, however, is the swarm of amphibious oceanic monsters in Victor Rousseau's *The Sea Demons* (*All-Story*, 1916), a story that, as early Lovecraft biographer L. Sprague de Camp correctly suggests, had a huge influence on Lovecraft's later depiction of his Deep Ones and Cthulhu spawn[43] and whose gynocratic organizational structure is explicitly referred to throughout the tale as being akin to both the ants and the bees, even to the extent of being "governed by a queen,"[44] while their undersea homes resemble "the cells of the bee."[45]

The collective environments of Lovecraft's various weird entities, too, are described in typically bee-like terms: the Deep Ones live in nests[46] all over the world; while the Old Ones' dead-city in *At the Mountains of Madness* is described as being a "honeycomb,"[47] much like the tunnels of the ghouls in "Pickman's Model,"[48] and the subterranean underground in "The Lurking Fear"[49]—tunnels further described in that story like bee-language as a "hell-hive."[50] In "Pickman's Model," too, Lovecraft further refers to Pickman's ghouls as "ant-like armies of the mephitic monsters."[51] Lovecraft doubtlessly invokes ants in this instance rather than bees due to the subterranean nature of the insect simile involved, although the term "armies" applies equally as well to bees as it does to ants.

It may be, too, that Lovecraft was influenced in his choosing of the original, Arabic name for the *Necronomicon*—*Al Azif*—by this inversion of Arcadian bee-imagery. "*Al Azif*" refers to the sinister hum of nocturnal insects, a sound that in Lovecraft's pastoral poetry had earlier symbolized the fecundity of life, here being used to symbolize the most blasphemous, forbidden, and unmentionable book in the Lovecraftian canon. Lovecraft, of course, had been influenced in his usage of Arabian terms by his childhood reading of the *Arabian Nights*, and also by his appreciative later reading, in July 1921, of William Beckford's *Vathek* (1786), in which Beckford associates "the sullen hum of those nocturnal insects which presage evil"[52] with the demonic songs sung by Vathek's necrophilic mother Carathis, accompanied by her honor-guard of mute black women. Surely this image would have recommended itself to Lovecraft's notice, given his strong association (as discussed in chapter 6, below) of blacks and women throughout his writings as symbols of evil. That both blacks and women were closely associated in Lovecraft's mind with sexuality (hence his aversion) only further reinforces the connections between bees and sexuality that we have been tracing here.

Indeed, one could easily argue that Lovecraft's recurring bee imagery represents merely yet another facet of Lovecraft's lifelong, and ambivalent, engagement with the feminine archetype of the Great Mother, in all her various facets, throughout his weird fiction. As anthropologist Erich Neumann observes in his study *The Great Mother* (1974), bees were closely associated with symbols of motherhood, honey being regarded, like milk, as a worthy sacrifice to the "earth goddesses."[53] Bees were even believed to have nursed both Zeus[54] and Dionysus[55] in their infancy, and honey was regarded (however inaccurately) as "the purest food for mothers."[56] These were all notions of which the classicist Lovecraft, with his own recurring maternal (and nursing)[57] obsessions, was surely well aware. This classical maternal analogy with the bees was doubtlessly suggested by the gynocratic organization of bee society. Lovecraft may have intended to indicate a matriarchal or maternal organization underlying his nests of sub-oceanic creatures in "The Shadow Over Innsmouth," which are represented in the story primarily by female authority figures, in the form of the narrator's grandmother and great-great-grandmother. Neumann directly links the often murderous matriarchy of the bees, in which males are routinely killed after mating, with the recurring cultural symbol of the murderous and bloodthirsty Terrible Mother,[58] which is likewise prominent throughout the entire Lovecraftian weird canon. A similar idea also seems to underlie the gynocratic race of monsters in Edgar Rice Burroughs' *Pellucidar* (*All-Story*, 1914–1915) novels — which critic William Fulwiler has shown to have exerted a huge influence on Lovecraft[59] — in which an intelligent species of evolved dinosaurs called the Mahar have done away with men entirely and are now "fertilized by chemical means."[60]

Lovecraft, interestingly, seems to have firmly believed in the superior evolutionary prospects of insects as compared to man, an idea that had some currency around the early 1900s, as evidenced again by such works as Maeterlinck's *Life of the Bee* as well as Lafcadio Hearn's essay "Beyond Man," in which Hearn writes in idealized terms of the supposed moral and social superiority of the collective social structure of insects, in this case, of the ants (ideas that later came to such dubious fruition in such collectivist societies as Nazi Germany, Stalinist Russia, and Red Cambodia). As Lovecraft wrote in his *Commonplace Book*, "As dinosaurs were once surpassed by mammals, so will man-mammal be surpassed by insect or bird."[61] This idea found subtle expression in his fiction via the "mighty beetle civilization"[62] that Lovecraft predicts will supplant mankind in the future in "The Shadow Out of Time." Lovecraft also seems to have promulgated this theory among other writers in his circle, such as Robert H. Barlow[63] and Frank Belknap Long, who wrote several stories based upon this theme: "The Last Men" (1934), "The Great Cold" (1935), and "Green Glory" (1935), all published in *Astounding Science Fiction*.

Tellingly, Long's stories in this vein are animated by a palpable feminine anxiety: the matriarchal insect-societies of the future are characterized by a marked feminine giganticism (giant female barnacles, giant female ants, and giant female bees) and a male physical miniaturization, in which human sexual intercourse is characterized as a tragic *liebestod* that inevitably leads to death. As Long observes, the "pitiful smallness"[64] of the males in this world fills his hero with a humiliating anxiety, which sends "a cold chill to the core of his being,"[65] due to the enormous matriarchal barnacles in "The Great Cold" that intend to make "the women of the human race as relatively enormous as themselves, and reduc[e] the male to physical and mental insignificance."[66] And it is tempting to read Long's symbolism in this regard as stemming, much like Lovecraft's own (as further discussed in chapter 6, below), from a persistent maternal obsession; what H. P. Lovecraft himself, in a revealing letter to friend Helen V. Sully written around this same period (1934), called Long's "maternal fixation & kindred neuroses," fostered by Mrs. Long's lifelong "oversolicitude"[67] of her son. Lovecraft knew whereof he spoke.

Given my hypothesis that Lovecraft's later weird fiction embodies an inverted satire of Greek Arcadian myth, one would naturally expect many of the elements of Lovecraft's earlier pastoral vision to have undergone inversion in his stories. As we have seen, this is certainly the case with the fruits, the fields, the fauns, and the bees of Greek legend. A similar study of birds in Lovecraft's fiction, too, would doubtless reveal a similar inversion of pagan symbolism; and although I have not yet undertaken such a study, Lovecraft's recasting of mating whippoorwills, as we have seen, as sinister psychopomps in "The Dunwich Horror," and his picture of the nightmarish hippocephalic shantak-birds in his *The Dream-Quest of Unknown Kadath*, seem to at least tentatively bear out this hypothesis.

THREE

Secrets Behind the Locked Door
Lovecraft and the Theseus Myth

I. The Myth of Theseus

Lovecraft's lifelong engagement with the myth of Theseus illuminates his fictional concerns in striking ways, intertwining with the recurring parental, paternal, and prohibitive or forbidden themes throughout his weird writings. The son of King Aegeus of Athens, Theseus was hidden away after his birth: his father concealed "a sword and a pair of sandals"[1] beneath "a great rock at Troezen" and gave "instructions that when Theseus was strong enough to lift the rock, he should be allowed to travel to Athens in search of his father." Later, according to scholar William Smith, Theseus was recognized by his father "by means of the sword which he carried, acknowledged as his son, and declared his successor."[2] The deeper psychological and symbolic meaning of the story is just as clear today as it doubtless was to the ancient Greeks who invented it. (This issue of a resemblance to the father likewise animates the narratives of H. P. Lovecraft, such as "The Dunwich Horror," in which the resemblance of Wilbur Whately's twin brother to his invisible father forms the climax to the narrative,[3] *The Case of Charles Dexter Ward*, in which Ward sees "his own living features in the countenance of his horrible great-great-great-grandfather,"[4] and "The Lurking Fear"[5] and "The Shadow Over Innsmouth,"[6] in which the issue of inherited ocular characteristics [what Lovecraft calls "The Horror in the Eyes"] forms the clue to a shared paternal ancestry.)

A classic example of the Greek hero, Theseus went on to destroy many of the "robbers and monsters that infested the country"[7] and nearby areas, including the Minotaur, the centaurs, and the ghastly, sadistic robber

Bas relief of Theseus with his mother, Aethra, lifting the trapdoor beneath which is hidden his paternal inheritance, his father's magical weapons. "When he reached maturity, he [Theseus] took, by his mother's directions, the sword and sandals, the tokens which had been left by [his father] Aegeus, and proceeded to Athens" (William Smith, *A Classical Dictionary of Biography, Mythology, and Geography* [Albemarle Street: John Murray, 1881], 766). An analogy for Lovecraft and his mother, and his own father's absence? Terracotta "Campagna" plaque showing Theseus, Roman (from *Greek Myths* by Lucilla Burn, © 1990. Courtesy the University of Texas Press. © The Trustees of the British Museum).

Damastes Procrustes, in addition to figuring "in almost all the great heroic expeditions" of classical mythology, including the story of the Argonauts, wherein he fought alongside such well-known heroes as Hercules, Jason, and Orpheus. We also find Theseus leading the heroic fight against the sinister Feminine/Matriarchal principle, whether he was defeating the femme fatale Medea, who usurped his mother's place and attempted to poison him at a banquet, or engaging in what William Smith calls his "celebrated" "adventures" during "his expedition against the Amazons," kidnapping their queen and routing their invasion of Athens. H. P. Lovecraft himself later resumed this standard, during his anti-sex battles in the pages of *The Argosy*, in which he attempted to stem what he calls the "reckless fury"[8] of the Amazons' "charge.")

It is interesting, therefore — given Theseus' status as a classic hero, and Lovecraft's repeated engagement with Thesean themes — that Lovecraft's weird fiction (aside from a few notable examples)[9] should be so basically devoid of obviously heroic narratives and clearly heroic themes. Indeed: given the nightmare aspect of most of Lovecraft's weird fiction, why did he even bother to invoke the myth of Theseus at all? If critic Victoria Nelson is correct, however, in her supposition that "the origin of Lovecraft's pustulating horrors"[10] is to be found in an awareness of the horrific aspects of his father Winfield's fatal illness, the progress of which is so vividly described in S. T. Joshi's biography of Lovecraft,[11] then it is there — in the marked patriarchal and paternal aspects of the Theseus myth,[12] and not in Theseus' heroic deeds — where his engagement with Theseus legend must be located. The Theseus myth perhaps enabled him to come to grips with, as well as to somehow channel, his paternal longings for the sometimes terrifying father whom he barely knew.[13]

Nor, as I discuss elsewhere,[14] is the Theseus myth the only childhood reading that Lovecraft later twisted toward paternal uses in his fiction: his readings of Sir Arthur Conan Doyle's Sherlock Holmes mysteries, for example, as well as the weird fiction published in the early Munsey magazines, and even the passion narrative of the New Testament (as noted by Maurice Levy),[15] fastened on the latent paternal meanings inherent in the texts. Lovecraft's use of the classical myth of Palaemon and Leucothea in his revealing poem "On a Grecian Colonnade in a Park" (1920) perhaps also reflects this paternal obsession: the mother Leucothea threw herself and her son Palaemon into the sea to escape the madness of her husband, Athamas,[16] and Lovecraft may have seen a parallel here with the madness of his own father. And although, as Maurice Levy observes, Lovecraft "spoke little of his father"[17] in his writings, at the same time, as we shall see below, it could be said that he spoke volumes.

Admittedly, some of Theseus' adventures were already suggestive of the macabre long before H. P. Lovecraft ever got to them. Indeed, Lovecraft seems to have been strongly inspired by the legend of Damastes Procrustes in his ultra-mundane story of New England grotesquerie, "In the Vault" (1925), which is notable in the Lovecraftian canon for its regionalist and non-cosmic setting. According to Lucilla Burn in her book *Greek Myths*, Theseus, during his heroic journeys, once fell into the clutches of an "infamous"[18] robber called Polypemon or Damastes Procrustes, who urged Theseus "to spend the night on his wonderful bed, a couch guaranteed to provide the perfect fit for all comers. Procrustes would invite travelers down and then set to work to make them fit the bed: if they were too short, he pounded them with a mallet in order to stretch them out, and if they were too long, he lopped off their feet and heads." Indeed, the surname "Procrustes" literally means "the stretcher," and the phrase the "bed of Procrustes"[19] later became proverbial throughout all of Greece. Theseus, of course, finally gives Procrustes his just deserts. In Lovecraft's version of the story, however, he puts a typically Poesque twist on the tale, adding the framing device of a revenge scenario, in which the corpse of a miser takes revenge against a drunken undertaker named Birch for the cutting off of his feet at the ankles, in order to make his body fit into a noticeably cheaper, smaller coffin. Poe and classicism were indeed the twin antipodes of Lovecraft's mind; but they were not, as this admixture proves, mutually exclusive.

In Lovecraft's rather prosaic collaboration with Clifford M. Eddy, "The Ghost Eater," along with "The Shadow Over Innsmouth" and "The Whisperer in Darkness," we can perhaps detect further echoes of the story of Theseus and Procrustes. Lovecraft's narrators worry that they might somehow be molested in their sleep, and instead sit up watching in their chairs,[20] or else attempt (however successfully) to forego sleep.[21] Indeed, in "Innsmouth," Lovecraft seems to make a direct reference to the myth, Lovecraft's narrator debating "whether I had better try to sleep at all.... Was this one of those inns where travellers were slain for their money?"[22] Another echo occurs in the cannibalistic old patriarch's loving description in "The Picture in the House" of how "the butcher cut off [the] feet"[23] in one of the *Regnum Congo* illustrations, upon which the depraved old man dwells with such sadistic relish. Clearly, the more sadistic aspects of the Theseus myth also made a huge impact upon the young Lovecraft.

With its motifs of mysterious paternity, magical gifts, battles with monsters, and heroic quests, the legend of Theseus follows a familiar archetypal pattern common to most heroic fairy tales, a pattern that is directly rooted in the attempts of children to emancipate themselves from the paternal and maternal yoke. As Freudian psychologist Ernest Jones observes in his classic study *On the Nightmare* (1951), the typical hero of the fairy tale eventually wins a wife and treasure, with his attainment of one or both being "usually aided by either some magical instrument, sword, etc., or some living agency, often an animal,"[24] with the ultimate (and unconscious) goal of "overcoming the father and winning the forbidden mother."[25] (One instance of this can be seen in Obi-Wan Kenobi giving Luke Skywalker his father's lightsaber in the original *Star Wars*, immediately followed by the deaths of Luke's adoptive aunt and uncle, and his later confrontation with [and defeat of] the Satanic black father, who is himself merely a cybernetic version of Lovecraft's equally sinister father, Yog-Sothoth.) This "idea of obtaining the magic weapon," Jones goes on, "is often associated with places symbolizing the womb," such as a "cavern or valley," or a "hole in a mountain," an idea that refers back to what Jones calls the "primordial penis-womb phantasies of infancy"[26] (and what Randolph Carter's Uncle Chris, in "The Silver Key," refers to as "an old unopened box with a key in it,"[27] much to the discomfiture of Carter's aunt). It is symbolized, in the Theseus myth, by that giant rock beneath which the magical weapons are secreted.

All of these "places symbolizing the womb," of course, have their clear analogues in the numerous subterranean tunnels, caves, basements, trapdoors, mounds, attics, and holes in H. P. Lovecraft's weird fiction. In his stories, however, these places, normally symbolizing emancipation, sexual or otherwise, from the parents, are subtly altered to reflect Lovecraft's troubled relations with parents Winfield and Susan Lovecraft, as well as his own lack of any overt emancipation. As Lovecraft himself admitted, "Always a recluse, with no varied events of life to mark the transition from boyhood to manhood, I have retained more of the old juvenile point of view and sympathy than I would care to acknowledge publicly. I have grown up without knowing it."[28] But "acknowledge it publicly" Lovecraft did, in the form of his weird fiction. By the time of the writing of "The Silver Key," Lovecraft's version of the Thesean heroic quest has become a mere feedback loop; the adult cannot go forward, he can only slip back into a realm of helpless familial and childhood nostalgia. Randolph Carter's search for "his old ancestral country around Arkham"[29] leads him to the hill "where *his mother and her fathers* before her were born"[30] (italics mine), where he magically returns to the state of a child. For Lovecraft, positive change is only possible by maintaining a proximity to one's maternal parents or ancestors, who form the only stable oasis in an ultimately indifferent universe of darkness and paternal abandonment. And significantly — given the symbolism discussed by Jones — this renewed infantilism of Carter is facilitated by what Lovecraft calls a "strange cave in the forest slope, the dreaded 'snake-den' which country folk shunned."[31] The vaginal orifice is here combined, as with the simultaneously male-female Asenath Waite later on, with the phallic masculine in one giant amalgamated, parental mass, in which mother and father are joined into a single form. As Lovecraft explains, in typically necrophilic language, this cave of Carter's fathers is a "sepulchral" place: the curious "eagerness"[32] with which Carter enters its precincts is directly akin to that "hot eagerness"[33] with which the necrophilic Jervas Dudley earlier attempted to enter his own ancestral tomb. Thus, the sexual "emancipation" that Randolph Carter experiences at the end of his heroic quest is far more akin to a return to the womb, in the form of necrophilic, maternal incest, than to actual sexual liberation. Carter's voluntary reabsorption into the cave of his ancestors merely forms a more benign analogue to the more malevolent and vampiric usurpation of identity — whether by one's undead ancestors, or by invisible, ostensibly "cosmic" entities — found elsewhere throughout Lovecraft's weird fiction.

In his fantasy story "The Quest of Iranon" (1921), too — whose plot recapitulates the basic outlines of the Theseus myth, with a supposed prince named Iranon searching for the lost land of his father, where he supposedly rules as king — Lovecraft again inverts the heroic contours of the story to reflect his desire, not for the attainment of adulthood, but rather for a return to the world of his childhood. As Iranon explains, his goal is not to supplant the aging father or to win himself a bride, but rather to return to the native soil of his parents, which is invested with "memories and dreams"[34] and "things remembered of childhood." Unfortunately, even in this meager wish Iranon finds himself thwarted: like a Theseus in reverse we learn that his supposedly royal father was merely a beggar. After this Lovecraft's poet commits suicide, and does so using a method which, as we shall see, is quite typical of his writings: by drowning himself in a swamp. (Lovecraft's identification of Iranon's home-city with his father in this story is also suggestive of his later maternal identification of Providence, Rhode Island, with the Mother Earth that bore him.)

Of course, it would be foolish to criticize Lovecraft's horror stories for their morbidity and their lack of heroism, or even for their consciously anti-heroic stance, all of which are endemic to the horror genre. But that is precisely the point: many authors create horror fiction, but few of them are classicists who consciously incorporate an inverted satire of the Theseus legend into their narratives. Lovecraft did; and his reasons for doing so are very revealing. As Peter Cannon observes, although Lovecraft's *The Case of Charles Dexter Ward* exhibits certain aspects of the traditional bildungsroman, its hero yet "experiences none of the customary coming-of-age trials"[35] of such stories — a statement that could characterize much of Lovecraft's weird oeuvre, in which this theme of youthful emancipation is turned on its head. Lovecraft's characters come of age: but to do so means death.

The narrator of "The Shadow Over Innsmouth," for example, first discovers the decayed, seaside town of his ancestors upon his "coming of age,"[36] while in "The Tomb," Jervas Dudley's necrophilic adventures will be likened to the losing of his virginity: Dudley tells us that after his first night spent alone in the tomb, "I was no longer a young man, though but twenty-one winters had chilled my bodily frame."[37] In "The Shunned House," too, as the narrator tells us, the story takes place after the character's attainment of adulthood, when his uncle finally "set before me the notes and data which he had collected concerning the shunned house"[38]—notes that have numerous analogues to the various Thesean gifts bestowed by other father-surrogates throughout Lovecraft's weird fiction: from the mysterious "hereditary envelope"[39] in "The Rats in the Walls," to the notes and artifacts on the Cthulhu Cult bequeathed by Prof. Angell to the narrator in "The Call of Cthulhu." As Peter Cannon observes, too, oftentimes in Lovecraft's weird fiction, such communications "never reach their intended recipients."[40] Randolph Carter's father, for instance, never has any idea that his secret ancestral key even existed,[41] while in "The Rats in the Walls," the all-important hereditary envelope is destroyed by fire during the Civil War. This idea is perhaps inspired, as I argue in "More on H. P. Lovecraft and Sherlock Holmes," by Lovecraft's reading of Conan Doyle's "The Four Orange Pips," but it ultimately derives from the cataclysmic void that Winfield Lovecraft's death left in HPL's psychology. Indeed, Lovecraft's influences are deeper than bildungsroman and deeper, ultimately, than literature itself, reflecting instead psychological commonalities with the darker aspects of both infantile and primitive psychology. And if, as critic Maurice Levy suggests, his weird fiction represents "a mythical quest"[42] in the form of "a series of ordeals that strangely recall the initiation stages of yore," it is also an anti-heroic quest, commensurate with Lovecraft's pessimistic, nihilistic philosophy, what critic Robert M. Price cleverly calls Lovecraft's "'cosmic futilitarianism.'"[43]

For Lovecraft, indeed, the Thesean inheritance is not one of heroism, but rather one of horror, often accompanied by loathsome sounds and disquieting odors emanating from behind the locked Thesean door (whoever said the womb smelled *good*?), with all his narrator's attempts at emancipation being fractured or tortured. Robert Suydam's "June wedding"[44] in "The Horror at Red Hook," for example, ends in "murder-strangulation"[45] during the honeymoon voyage, followed by the sacrifice of Suydam to the naked nymph Lilith during an apocalyptic bacchanalia. After his honeymoon in "The Thing on the Doorstep," meanwhile, Edwin Derby looks "slightly changed,"[46] wearing what Lovecraft calls "a look of almost genuine sadness," presumably due to the revelation of Asenath's true identity as wife, father, and mother all in one; no emancipation from the parents is to be found in *this* marriage. And then there is Denis de Russy's murder-lynching of his wife in "Medusa's Coil," followed by Denis' own suicide in front of his father after the revelation of his wife's true identity. As Maurice Levy observes of Lovecraft, with a certain degree of understatement, "The author decidedly has a bad opinion of conjugal habits."[47] Marriage for Lovecraft is an occasion, not of emancipation or joy, but rather — as with the castrative rites of Atys and Cybele in "The Rats in the Walls" — an invitation to male sacrifice. The only true emancipation lies within the tomb, in which death either returns to life, as in "The Outsider," or lies dreaming, as in "The Unnamable" and "The Call of Cthulhu." Indeed, instead of emancipation from the parents, in Lovecraft's weird fiction we often see the ancestor return by clawing his way out of the ground, and drag his lone descendant back down along with him. In Lovecraft's weird fiction, the Theseus door is not unlocked by the hero from without; instead, it is broken down, or threatened to be broken down, from within. Lovecraft's father was dead, but the curse of his sexuality could not remain buried; thus, the two — sexuality and death — became confused in his mind. True, Lovecraft could have derived this idea from Poe; but Poe also extolled Romantic love, a theme strangely absent from Lovecraft's fiction. No: Lovecraft took from Poe only what he wished to take from Poe; and he took it for paternal reasons.

Perhaps the extent of Lovecraft's deviation from this heroic template can be gauged via his tortured reading of Sherwood Anderson's *Winesburg, Ohio,* a book that ends on a markedly heroic note with the beginning of a heroic quest, as Anderson's young hero George Willard finally embarks into the world after the death of his mother — his experiences in Winesburg, Anderson writes, having "become but a background on which to paint the dreams of his manhood."[48] As Lovecraft wrote to *Weird Tales* editor Edwin Baird, he had intended his short story "Arthur Jermyn" to be a riposte to what he called "the tame backstairs gossip of Anderson's *Winesburg, Ohio.*"[49] "Jermyn" also was, as S. T. Joshi suggests, a fractured retelling of the circumstances of Lovecraft's father's own mental and physical degeneration as a result of tertiary syphilis.[50] One thinks that these two ideas, the heroic and the paternal, were intimately connected in Lovecraft's mind. And whereas the departure of Anderson's Willard is presumably merely the first step of lifelong journey, Lovecraft's Arthur Jermyn — like Lovecraft himself, the last of his family line — cuts his own journey short by choosing suicide (in the form of self-immolation). Lovecraft's own choice to become what he called a non-entity was merely another form of suicide.

As Jervas Dudley revealingly explains, after his discovery of the locked door of the ancestral mausoleum of the Hydes in "The Tomb":

> Reading the life of Theseus, I was much impressed by that passage telling of the great stone beneath which the boyish hero was to find his tokens of destiny whenever he should become old enough to lift its enormous weight. The legend had the effect of dispelling my keenest impatience to enter the fault, for it made me feel that the time was not yet ripe. Later, I told myself, I should grow to a strength and ingenuity which might enable me to unfasten the heavily chained door with ease; but until then I would do better by conforming to what seemed the will of Fate.[51]

Ironically, Lovecraft's narrator takes the story of Theseus not as a spur or impetus to heroism or greater action, as one might expect, but rather as an excuse for staying put, Dudley afterward spends his time waiting before the door of the tomb "for hours at a time each day"[52] and even "listening very intently at the slightly open portal,"[53] presumably for the sound of familial echoes, reverberating from the undead life stirring furtively within. (By contrast, in Charles Kingsley's 1900 retelling of the Theseus myth for children, Theseus utilizes the period of waiting before he is able to lift the stone in order to train himself physically, spending "all his days in wrestling, and boxing, and hurling"[54] in order to grow strong enough to lift the rock.) As we shall see, this act of listening at the Thesean door will occur throughout the Lovecraftian canon and seems to reflect Lovecraft's own youthful curiosity regarding his father's condition.

That this tomb of the sinister and bacchanalian Hydes is representative of Winfield Lovecraft's death seems quite likely, since Robert Louis Stevenson's Mr. Hyde is a notably male figure of depravity, animalistic degeneration, and sexual and sadistic horror, whose name, for Victorians, evoked crimes unnamable either by probity or decency: all very much like the disease which so cruelly afflicted Lovecraft's father. Significantly, too, Jervas Dudley conflates his Hyde lineage with his Dudley patrimony, observing, "Last of my paternal race, I was likewise the last of this older and more mysterious line."[55] His eventual claiming of the tomb thus is equivalent to the claiming of a lost paternal inheritance.

As with Randolph Carter later on, the liberation that Jervas Dudley seeks within the portal is not a spur toward heroism but rather a withdrawal, not only into the past, but toward death: what Lovecraft convolutedly, but significantly, refers to in this tale as "things that are not, or are no longer, living."[56] Death, in Lovecraft's weird fiction, if not in his mechanical-materialist philosophy, always preserves some transient trace of life. And although a frantic Dudley vows to "some day *force an entrance* to the black, chilly depths that seemed calling out to me"[57] (italics mine) (language that sounds suspiciously like rape, representing, perhaps, an infantile and sadistic rationalization of the sexual process), he is patently unsuccessful in his tentative endeavors to open the door. So inept is Dudley in his endeavors, indeed, that entire "months following my discovery were spent in futile attempts to force the complicated lock of the slightly open vault."[58]

And ultimately, although Dudley eventually loses his virginity by finding his way inside and sleeping inside an empty coffin,[59] Dudley's supposed emancipation turns out to be nothing more than an illusion — for as Dudley (and his father along with him) both learn, he had never in fact entered the tomb at all, but rather "*had spent the night in the bower outside the tomb*; my sleep-filmed eyes fixed upon the crevice where the padlocked portal stood ajar!"[60] (italics Lovecraft's). Dudley's heroic attainment of the womb has merely been illusory, visual, and masturbatory. He has penetrated the crevice solely with his eyes and with his mind; indeed, he has had his sight "fixed upon the crevice"[61] for hours — and even, as he tells us (in a childish simulation of intercourse), "once ... thrust a candle nearly within the closed entrance"[62] — but was capable of nothing more. Even more embarrassingly, not only was the entire village aware of this failure (like a heroic Theseus in reverse), but his father, whom he was supposed to overthrow or supplant, is now the one who visits, counsels, and retains authority over him; even visiting Dudley "frequently"[63] in the madhouse, in a grim and ironic reversal of the actual situation, not only of the Theseus myth but also with regard to Lovecraft's parents, both of whom were hospitalized due to nervous disorders.

Dudley's failure is compounded on the night on which he is captured, during which it is his father, and not he himself, who discovers the "treasure-trove"[64] that was concealed in the sub-cellar of the ruined Hyde mansion: a lightning bolt revealing a Thesean box containing a miniature portrait that (as with the portrait of Curwen found later on in *The Case of Charles Dexter Ward*), confirms the maternal ancestry of the hero. Whereas in the legends of yore we see Theseus uncovering his father's "treasure-trove" while his mother stands by, Lovecraft inverts this, and instead shows us Jervas Dudley standing by while his father, Mr. Dudley, discovers a lost link in his son's maternal ancestry, essentially transferring his son's patrimony from himself to his mother, much as occurred in Lovecraft's actual life.

This Theseus-door from "The Tomb" recurs throughout Lovecraft's fiction (usually, however, without any direct attribution to the Theseus legend) and often, as we have seen, in the form of trapdoors, attic doors, basement doors, brass doors, or stone doors located in a subterranean vault. And, just as with the hapless young Dudley, the opening of these doors is no easy matter for Lovecraft's protagonists. The door in *The Dream-Quest of Unknown Kadath*, for example, forms an obstacle due to its sheer size; Lovecraft here (as in "The Call of Cthulhu," written around the same time) associates the Theseus door with an ultimately parental giganticism. As Lovecraft writes,

> To open so vast a thing was completely not to be thought of, but the ghouls hoped to get it up just enough to slip the gravestone under as a prop, and permit Carter to escape through the crack.... Mighty was the straining of those three ghouls at the stone of the door above them, and Carter helped push with as much strength as he had.[65]

Here, just as in "The Tomb," the emancipation symbolized by the Theseus legend is transfigured via necrophilic processes: a tombstone is used as a lever, and cannibalistic, necrophilic ghouls aid an impotent narrator to do what Lovecraft's ghoulish Outsider had accomplished unaided. (Lovecraft's ghouls even have to carry his hero Carter part of the way up the steps of the tower![66])

In "Pickman's Model," the Theseus door appears again — in both a literal sense, in the form of the "great well in the earthen floor"[67] of Pickman's secret studio, which has "a heavy disk of wood" as its cover, which allows entry to Pickman's ghouls — as well as in a figurative sense, in the form of what Lovecraft calls that "forbidden gate" that Pickman himself had "found a way to unlock." The Theseus-inheritance, in this case, is represented by Pickman's regression into the cannibalistic, sadistic practices of his ghoul-witch heritage; what Lovecraft (perhaps with some sense of autobiographical tragedy) calls the "strange shadow"[68] under which Pickman was born. Pickman's emancipation, like that of Jervas Dudley before him, thus entails a violation of societal probity and societal norms, due to a descent into bacchanalian sensuality.

In "The Rats in the Walls," meanwhile, in what we shall come to see as a typical act of paternal inversion in his works, Lovecraft inverts the heroic archetype of emancipation from the father even further, and instead presents us with a *father* coming to terms with a *son's* death or degeneration. Even so, however, and just as in "The Tomb," the paternal Delapore is initially stymied in his attempts to open the primal Theseus door in the Exham Priory's deepest sub-cellar. "What secret would open the gate," he observes lamely, "wiser men than me would have to find."[69] This "wiser" man finally turns out to be one of Lovecraft's recurring patriarchal academics and father surrogates: classical archeologist Sir William Brinton, who "within an hour"[70] of examining the portal manages to figure out how to cause the altar door "to tilt backward"; the portal, like Cthulhu's trapdoor later on, being "balanced by some unknown species of counterweight."[71] As we shall see below, this division of paternal figures into benevolent (Sir William Brinton) figures and malevolent (the cannibalistic Delapore) figures is a recurring feature of H. P. Lovecraft's weird fiction.

In Lovecraft's collaborative "The Mound," he likewise invokes this idea of a cryptic, and in this case hidden, portal; but while the shrubbery-covered stone doorway in this tale displays signs of having once possessed a "hinged door or gate,"[72] the door itself is now gone, so that his narrator finds his entry a bit easier. Tellingly, too, this tunnel will be associated by Lovecraft with what he calls "a sort of hereditary secret"[73]: the family of Zamacona's wife T'la-yub are the only ones in the subterranean city of T'sath who know about this secret passage leading to the surface world. Here, however, Jervas Dudley's marked eagerness to penetrate the portal is matched by the eagerness of Lovecraft's narrator "to get away from that black aperture which still yawned open"[74] once he sees what lurks within: an underworld of dead-alive beings, feminine entrapment, and corrupt interracial sexuality.

In the fantasy "The Strange High House in the Mist" (1926), the Theseus door will take the form of an "ancient door of nail-studded oak beyond which lay only the abyss of white cloud."[75] Lovecraft here dispenses with the attic of his youthful classical discoveries (or the basement of Pickman's degeneration) entirely, and instead has the portal open directly onto the celestial realm of the classical gods themselves. Even here, however, there is also a patriarchal relation, in the form of the old-fashioned gentleman with "a great black bearded face whose eyes were phosphorescent with the imprint of unheard-of sights,"[76] and who (like Lovecraft's own grandfather) regales Olney, the hero, with "tales of marvelous ancient things."[77] As we shall see below, such beards are a typical signifier of patriarchal or paternal figures in Lovecraft's fiction, whether benevolent or malevolent.

The Theseus-type door also appears in Lovecraft's collaborative parody "The Horror in the Museum," described as a padlocked "door which was never opened, and above which was crudely smeared that hideous cryptic symbol from the fragmentary records of forbidden *elder magic*"[78] (italics mine). Lovecraft here pointedly (if playfully) connects his Thesean symbolism with his "elder" (i.e., parental) themes. This idea that the door "was never opened," too, likewise suggests the by-now familiar impenetrability of such a door, as well as the related theme of the forbidden as related to adult or parental sexuality. In his collaborative "Out of the Aeons," too, the curator Pickman observes that he is glad that the risen volcanic island in the story "had sunk before that massive suggestion of a trap-door could be opened"[79]—so that here, just as in "The Tomb," true penetration or emancipation is indefinitely deferred, lest the sleeping, ravening sexuality dwelling within be released.

Lovecraft also revisits the Theseus door, and further inverts it, in *The Case of Charles Dexter Ward*, by having both the Charles Dexter Ward's father and Dr. Marinus B. Willett (yet another academic father-surrogate) investigate a "trim concrete surface with an iron manhole"[80] located at sinister father-surrogate Joseph Curwen's Pawtuxet farm, a door "to which Mr. Ward at once rushed with excited zeal" (in a further reflection, and inversion, of young Jervas Dudley's "hot eagerness" to enter the tomb.) As Lovecraft goes on (in a clear recapitulation of his various paternal inversions in "The Tomb"): "The cover was not hard to lift, *and the father had quite removed* it when Willett noticed the queerness of his aspect. He was swaying and nodding dizzily, and in the gust of noxious air which swept up from the black pit beneath the doctor soon recognized ample cause" (italics mine). Ward's father here, despite his atypical success in opening the Theseus portal, is quite literally overwhelmed by the claims (and corruption) of Curwen's far more ancient (and far more malevolent) patrimony. (It is notable too that the younger Ward, for his part, seems quite unaffected by such charnel odors: claiming, for instance, that the stench accompanying Curwen's resurrection was "absolutely harmless and unfortunately necessary."[81] Young Ward, like necrophilic Jervas Dudley before him — not to mention the narrator of Lovecraft and Eddy's "The Loved Dead"— has perhaps having become "bewitched"[82] by the charnel odors of the grave, and possessing a homeopathic immunity to, or even a necrophilic desire for, the processes and manifestations of morbid decay.) Lovecraft completes his numerous inversions in *Charles Dexter Ward*, by having Dr. Willett's disposal of young Ward's body take place "behind the bolted door"[83] of Ward's room: the locked portal of the youthful hero's emancipation in the Theseus legend instead becomes the son's *grave*.

Lovecraft also makes use of the Theseus door, albeit without direct attribution, in one of his earliest surviving weird story efforts, "The Alchemist" (1908), written while he was still a teenager, in which the young narrator Antoine, in what Lovecraft calls "the culminating event of my whole life"[84] (i.e., the coming-of-age theme again), lifts "a small trapdoor with a ring," beneath which he discovers the immortal alchemist responsible for his generations-long familial curse. And although his narrator here actually succeeds "with difficulty in raising it," this door proves to lead merely to yet another, this time a "massive oaken" door located in a subterranean passage, which is pictured of course as "stoutly resisting all my attempts to open it."[85] Indeed, not only does the narrator does *not* succeed in opening it, it finally creaks open only from within, under the volition of the evil, immortal alchemist who resides inside. Fittingly too, given the marked inversion of Thesean and heroic themes in Lovecraft's weird fiction, although young Antoine notices a horde of treasure behind the locked door at the climax to the story, he takes no interest in it whatsoever, observing simply, "In one corner was an immense pile of shining yellow metal that sparkled gorgeously in the light of the torch. It may have been gold, but I did not pause to examine it, for I was strangely affected by that which I had undergone."[86] Although he has completed the Thesean quest and won the treasure (if not the love of a woman), Antoine is not interested in it. Lovecraft's pseudo-aristocratic disdain for the capitalistic-industrial creation of wealth, as well as his appalling powerlessness to profit from his own imaginative efforts, both come to mind. And although Lovecraft's economic views, outwardly at least, were an ostensible manifestation of his philosophical adherence to what Oswald Spengler calls "the classical ideal"[87] of "indifference ($\alpha\pi\alpha\theta\epsilon\iota\alpha$) to the course of the world"—what Lovecraft himself refers to in a juvenile poem as "the Vanity of Human Ambition"[88]—such ideas were basically psychological in their origin, having their basis in Lovecraft's despairing rejection of the possibility of heroic human attainments, and his painful failure to secure complete parental emancipation.

II. The Door Opens Both Ways

The Thesean door in Lovecraft's weird fiction is not solely a limiting or prohibitive barrier, however; indeed, it often permits of egress from beyond the grave, as well as offering awful hints as to the appearance, shape, and size of the horrors beyond them, even as they prevent a total revelation of the full picture of these horrors. From behind the Theseus door, one often hears what Lovecraft calls a "padding or shuffling,"[89] or "unaccustomed stirrings and bumpings and scrapings,"[90] as well as "a curious jumble of soft, furtive sounds,"[91] language equally as suggestive of infantile curiosity regarding nocturnal parental coupling as it is of any indescribable cosmic entity. (As we shall see, a similar infantile curiosity seems to underlie Lovecraft's notion of the "cyclopean" as well.) In his parodic collaboration "The Horror in the Museum," too, Lovecraft (clearly having fun with the story) keeps adding more and more (and increasingly incongruous) sonic and odorous modifiers to his description of the unknown creature on the other side of the Thesean door. Even here, in a collaborative story, written purely for remuneration, Lovecraft has seen fit to include aspects of what was clearly an obsessive and insistent theme in his mind: the Theseus myth, and the troubling problem of opening the ancestral portal.

He may have heard rumors, as a child or young adult, regarding the nature and origin of his father's illness, distorted echoes or hints that may have reached him through the locked doors, or thin walls, of his family home—awful hints of deviancy, madness, perversion, or what Lovecraft later called "obscure vice"[92] and "sins." As Joshi observes in *H. P. Lovecraft: A Life,* "The trauma experienced by Susie Lovecraft over this excruciating period of five years"[93] of her husband's illness "can only be imagined." Joshi surmises that while Lovecraft was "intentionally kept in the dark about its specific nature," he also probably "wondered a great deal." Thus, in *The Case of Charles Dexter Ward* we find the young Ward desperately chasing down what Lovecraft calls "vague reports"[94] and "scattered allusions relating to" his mysterious male ancestor, also called an "apparently 'hushed-up' character,"[95] the careful erasure of whose past leads Ward to suspect that "a conspiracy had existed to blot him from memory." As Lovecraft observes, too — emphasizing as he does so the husbandly aspect of Joseph Curwen's disgrace — his wife Eliza later changed her name "on the ground 'that her Husband's name was become a publick Reproach by reason of what was known after his Decease,'"[96] in what Lovecraft suggestively calls "a whispered series of highly peculiar and disquieting stories." This theme of whispers and rumors, already endemic to the weird fiction genre, is especially heightened in Lovecraft's stories.

A similar change-of-name, interestingly (from "Wilde" to "Holland"), likewise figured in the paternal disgrace of Oscar Wilde's family during the late Victorian era, his family being compelled not only to change their name but also to flee their country. (Oscar Wilde, too, was unable to publish any works under his own name, resorting instead to his prisoner number, "C.33": the man who had stood as the public symbol of perverse and unnatural practices himself became the very embodiment of "the unnamable.") And, given the many parallels between Lovecraft's *The Case of Charles Dexter Ward* and Wilde's *The Picture of Dorian Gray,* as well as between the scandal that overtook Oscar Wilde himself and the near-contemporaneous tragedy that overtook Lovecraft's father, it is not hard to see in Lovecraft's story a commentary upon both tragedies, whether conscious or unconscious. Lovecraft himself explicitly associates the aura of scandal surrounding the vampiric Curwen with that surrounding Wilde, observing that it "can be compared in spirit only to the hush that lay on Oscar Wilde's name for a decade after his disgrace."[97]

This conspiracy to hide the "paternity"[98] of Ann Curwen eventually leads to the mutilation of Curwen's tombstone. The effacement of a father's grave echoes the similar "blank slate slab"[99] of the alcoholic father in "The Unnamable" who sires the eponymous monster in the tale; not to mention the defaced statue of what Lovecraft describes as "long-bearded"[100] man in Lovecraft's poem "The City," the sight of which causes the poet to flee in panic "from the knowledge of terrors forgotten and dead." All of these suggest some basic, if unnamable, paternal anxiety on the part of Lovecraft. Lovecraft further reinforces the basically sexual nature underlying such paternal effacements in "The Haunter of the Dark," in which the Pharaoh Nephren-Ka is said to have built a temple "with a windowless crypt"[101] around a mysterious egg-shaped stone — a feminine, intra-uterine and womb-like space, within which, as Lovecraft tells us, the Pharaoh "did that which caused his name to be stricken from all monuments and records." The language is suggestive of some sexual or sadistic transgression, here committed by a king (which is, along with the godhead, the ultimate symbol of the father). Compare the language here, for instance, with that in Kingsley's 1900 children's book of Greek myths, telling of how the inventor Daedalus "did a shameful deed, at which the sun hid his face on high"[102] (which is writer Charles Kingsley's delicate way of explaining, to children, Daedalus' construction of a device allowing the wife of King Minos of Crete to have intercourse with a sexually-aroused bull). Lovecraft's complicated language of unspeakable and unnamable deeds pre-serves a similarly infantile vernacular, rooted in circumlocutions of adult acts for children.

One perhaps catches an glimpse of this somber, secretive atmosphere that surrounded the young Lovecraft — what Lovecraft in his *Commonplace Book* of plot ideas calls an "atmosphere of considerable mystery"[103] — in "The Alchemist," in which the young narrator Antoine notes "the manifest reluc-tance of my old preceptor to discuss with me my paternal ancestry,"[104] a refusal which "gave rise to the terror which I ever felt at the mention of my great house." A similar reluctance is experienced by the youthful Jervas Dudley, who spends the months following his discovery of the Hydes' tomb making "careful guarded inquiries regarding the nature and history of the structure."[105] In "The Rats in the Walls," too, father Delapore (Lovecraft again inverting his father-and-son obsession) speaks of the "ignorance"[106] in which he was deliberately kept about his family, due to "the policy of reticence always main-tained by the Delapores." Such "frightened reticence and cloudy evasions," of course, has the unfortunate but also completely understandable effect of rendering the legends about Delapore's ancestors "all the ghastlier."[107] As we have already seen, too, in "The Silver Key," young Carter's aunt tries to prevent his uncle from telling him about his ancestral box, "saying it was no kind of thing to tell a child whose head was already too full of queer fancies"[108] — although Carter later consults this very box, despite her objections.

In his memoir, *Son of Oscar Wilde,* the adult Vyvyan Holland writes sim-ilarly, and equally poignantly, of how he was kept in the dark regarding the nature of his father's crime for many years, and how his inquiries about his father to his mother's stuffy Christian and Victorian family "were always side-tracked."[109] His inability to obtain any clear answer to the question gave him "vague misgivings,"[110] which only increased over time. As Holland observes, "The reticence of my mother's family through the years had led me to conjure up all kinds of pictures of what my father might have done."[111] Holland erroneously supposed his father had been guilty of such crimes as embezzlement, thievery, and even bigamy. In the same way, too, in Lovecraft's twisting of the Theseus myth to reflect some sloshing, unmentionable horror, the elongated shadow of similarly vague crimes and unconfirmed fears can be seen — fears that eventually grew too large even to be mentioned in human language, and which were replaced instead by incomprehensibles (or unmentionables and unnamables) such as "Cthulhu" and "*Phtagn*"; fears that were enlarged, twisted, and distorted by their tortured passage through a locked and forbidden door.

Something of this same youthful atmosphere of "furtiveness and secretiveness"[112] can also be discerned in Zadok Allen's pathetic narrative in "The Shadow Over Innsmouth," in which the events leading up to both the Deep Ones' insurrection in Innsmouth and the murder of young Zadok Allen's father, are presented from the point of view of Allen as a child. As Allen observes (revealingly suggesting a conflation of his own identity with that of Lovecraft's narrator as he does so): "'Mebbe *ye'd like to a ben me in them days*, when I seed things at night aout to sea from the cupalo top o' my haouse. Oh, I kin tell yew' *little pitchers hev big ears*, an' I wa'n't missin' nothing' o' what was gossiped about Cap'n Obed an' the folks aout to the reef!'"[113] (italics mine). This "gossip" about the narrator's ancestor, Captain Marsh, perhaps parallels similar whispers, gossip, or rumors about Winfield Lovecraft. And if, as often observed, Lovecraft's narrator Olmstead in this story is a stand-in for Lovecraft himself, then so, in some ways, is the aged derelict Zadok Allen, whose "big ears" perhaps reflect Lovecraft's own childhood curiosity: what Lovecraft, in "The Tomb," similarly calls "the traditionally receptive ears of the small boy,"[114] when referring to the innate inquisitiveness of young Jervas Dudley. (Not only his ears, however, but Lovecraft's mouth appear to have gotten him into trouble: Lovecraft wrote in 1924 of how "when I was six or seven I was of course curious about the allusions which I did not understand in adult books, and about the prohibitions imposed by *elders* upon my conversation"[115] [italics mine]. The language which again suggests something of the etiology underlying Lovecraft's later and obsessive references to things such as "unnamable things" and "Elder Gods.")

Despite such cryptic familial evasions, however, Antoine (perhaps like Lovecraft himself) is slowly "able to piece together disconnected fragments of discourse, let slip from an unwilling tongue."[116] And although Lovecraft later alleged in his letters that his father's hospitalization was the result of exhaustion, he may have been deliberately fudging the truth in the interest of gentlemanly propriety, rather than being unaware of the true facts — much in the same way that he would, at other times, fudge the facts about his high school career, his divorce, his mother's illness, or the suicide of Robert Nelson. Lovecraft had nothing but contempt for those writers who acted like the modernist novelist Theodore Dreiser, who made what he calls "unsavory revelations ... in the public press about his own family."[117] The fact that one of Lovecraft's uncles, Dr. Franklin Chase Clark, was a physician further suggests he would have been made aware of the true facts underlying his father's medical condition. Lovecraft was particularly close to Clark, describing himself as hanging "'upon his conversation as Boswell hung upon Dr. Johnson's,'"[118] which, coming from Lovecraft, was certainly high praise indeed. The obvious syphilitic imagery throughout the Lovecraftian canon, too — the venereal disease that afflicts the proboscis of Sir Wilful Wildrake (more Oscar Wildean language, once again); the "'spotted snake'"[119] mentioned by the deranged father in "The Rats in the Walls"; as well as the "sin-pitted"[120] and "pockmarked" faces seen in "The Horror at Red Hook," suggest that Lovecraft was well aware of the nature of his father's affliction, though he was too reticent to express his anguish directly. (True, Lovecraft apparently derived this spotted snake from Conan Doyle's "The Speckled Band"; but I would suggest that he only did so because of the paternal connotations aroused by the tale, which also involves a murderous father.)

As Peter Cannon has observed (and much like the perhaps overly-protective Phillips family), Lovecraft himself engaged in some odd evasions and transferals in this regard; Cannon sees in father Delapore's caring for his maimed son in "The Rats in the Walls," for instance, a "role reversal of Lovecraft's feelings over the loss of his father."[121] Indeed, Lovecraft pointedly draws our attention to this transferal by having father Delapore, in the context of discussing the death of his own father in 1904, refer to his son Alfred as the "*boy who reversed the order of family information*"[122] (italics mine). The boy perhaps represents none other than Lovecraft himself, who via his chosen literary medium bequeaths to us, the readers, the truth about his father, rather than having his father confidentially bequeath it to himself. (There is a similar act of obvious transposition in Lovecraft's inversion of the dates of his father's death in "The Rats in the Walls" and "The Shadow Over Innsmouth," from July 19 to July 16, as pointed out by S. T. Joshi and David E. Schultz.[123]) In *The Case of Charles Dexter Ward*, too, Lovecraft presents us with a father "grieving"[124] for his apparently disturbed son, whose mental aberrations first began, significantly, when he began a "strangely persistent search for his forefather's grave"[125]; i.e., yet another Thesean search of the son for his father. All of his peculiar inversions in this regard perhaps reflect something of that common process of obfuscation among artists that was earlier noted by Sigmund Freud, and which Philip Rieff refers to as "a certain amount of 'resistance' against the detective work of the interpretive authority, even (and especially) when this authority was oneself"[126]; the ultimate "work of the imagination" consists of "self-concealment."[127] That Lovecraft himself understood the psychological sources of such imagery is further suggested by the fact that young Ward's own perceived eccentricities in the story are, revealingly, being laid by his doctors to "some profound subconsciousness"[128] that overwhelms his life; as if Joseph Curwen were somehow a revived and reanimated aspect of Ward's own subconscious. The only subconscious at work in this story, however, was none other than Lovecraft's own; and it is Lovecraft, and not Ward, who created the undead Joseph Curwen, with his revealingly paternal and maternal characteristics.

Lovecraft frequently attributed his father's insanity to the sons in his stories, just as he attributed his own spasmodic childhood chorea (tic) symptoms to the mothers in "The Shunned House" and "The Colour Out of Space." In lieu of any outward emancipation from the familial bond, fiction, and fiction alone, allowed Lovecraft to exercise some measure of control over his life, especially given the fact that more traditional outlets of control (a job, the fathering an actual family of his own, etc.) were denied to him (self-denied, as may be). Very often, too, sons predecease their fathers in Lovecraft's weird fiction: Welcome Harris dies two years before his father, in battle,[129] for example, while Richard Pickman's painting "Ghoul Feeding" is left in the possession of Pickman's father,[130] after Pickman himself suddenly goes missing. Lovecraft here cleverly inverts his association of patriarchal cannibalism with a picture, seen earlier in his short story "The Picture in the House," by having a depraved son leave a cannibalistic picture with an older man.

In "Beyond the Wall of Sleep" (1919), too, Lovecraft's protagonist, a young staff intern, is warned in a "*paternal way*"[131] (italics mine) by "*the head* of the institution" (italics mine), called "old Doctor Fenton," that "I was overworking; that my mind needed a rest." Here Lovecraft again inverts the dynamics of his father's illness, by imputing Winfield's supposed nervous exhaustion to a younger man, and making a specifically paternal figure (in this case, one of his recurring academic father-surrogates) the voice of reason in the tale. (Old Dr. Fenton finds his paternal opposite, meanwhile, in the depraved mental patient in the tale, Joe Slater, significantly described as the "head"[132] of his family, whose periodic need for forced restraint by the hospital staff mirrors the facts of Lovecraft's father's own confinement.) As discussed in my essay "A Reprehensible Habit: H. P. Lovecraft and the Munsey Magazines" (forthcoming),

Lovecraft was apparently influenced in the setting and characters of this story by the beginning chapters of the *All-Story Weekly* science fiction serials *Palos of the Dog Star Pack* (1918) by J. U. Giesy and *Draft of Eternity* (1918) by Victor Rousseau — although with the former story, just as with his alterations of the Theseus myth, Lovecraft is assiduous in his subversion of Giesy's heroic themes in the service of his paternal obsessions, transforming the comatose patient Jason Croft and the slow-witted alien Jasor into slavering beasts.[133] A similar paternal inversion occurs in "The Tomb," in which the young Jervas Dudley speaks of "the physician with the iron-grey beard"[134] who, along with Dudley's father, "comes each day to my room." Lovecraft's benevolent paternal figure, as in *The Case of Charles Dexter Ward* later on, here is divided into two separate characters: the actual father on the one hand, and a learned academic surrogate on the other, almost as if Lovecraft was unable, given his knowledge of his father's illness, as well as his father's capitalistic, commercial career, to openly impute such scholarly attributes to an actual paternal figure.

In "The Shadow Out of Time," Lovecraft cloaks this issue of paternal inheritance in an even more elaborate and ironic fashion. As usual in a Lovecraftian story, the hero of the story is the father, Nathaniel Peaslee, not the heroic, Thesean son. But unlike in "The Rats in the Walls," paternal information is successfully conveyed from one to the other. The father Nathaniel decides "that my son at least must be informed"[135] about his hallucinatory encounters with the Great Race. Indeed, father Peaslee is anxious to "test the horror" he experienced by bringing back an artifact of his experiences "and shewing it to my son."[136] The father even leaves it up to his son to decide "whether to diffuse the matter more widely,"[137] a decision that — given that the story eventually *was* published (under Lovecraft's hand) — Peaslee's son surely made in the affirmative. Lovecraft was masquerading, for the purposes of fiction, as both the son and as his own father, thereby giving himself permission to use his own father's madness for fictional purposes, and informing both himself and us, the readers, of the secret facts of his pathology that his own father was unfortunately unable to provide to him. In his fiction, if not in his life, Lovecraft was able to assume the mask, and the role, of the father, and with none of the messy aftereffects of STDs, wives, or possession by an all-consuming and all-destroying sexuality. (Lovecraft further confuses the identities of father and son in this story by dating the night of father Nathaniel's descent into the ruins roughly to the date of his own father's death,[138] as S. T. Joshi and David E. Schultz point out in their annotated edition of "The Shadow Out of Time," while at the same time dating Nathaniel's amnesia to the period of Lovecraft's own withdrawal "into hermitry."[139])

Tellingly too, Lovecraft also skillfully evades or displaces the circumstances of his own childhood listening to or overhearing of parental whispers and rumors. In *The Case of Charles Dexter Ward*, for instance, it is young Ward's mother and father who are depicted as morbidly "listening ... in the night"[140] "in the hall outside the locked door"[141] of the attic, while their son engages in ghoulish, necrophilic rites within. Later on, too — and much like young Antoine at the hands of Pierre in "The Alchemist" — Ward's mother is "kept in as complete ignorance" about young Ward's doings as possible, and is "not told of the change"[142] in his behavior. These changes suggest the similar alterations of behavior earlier undergone by Winfield Lovecraft, and the entire scenario suggests that the young Lovecraft was far more informed of what was going on around him than his nervous elders perhaps intended. Indeed, Lovecraft further reverses his paternal dynamic by having the doctors diagnose young Ward with a case of "dementia praecox,"[143] thus mirroring his father's own diagnosis of paresis — a diagnosis that is doubly ironic, as it is actually the ancestral father-figure Curwen, and not young Ward, who is being so diagnosed.

A similar psychological sleight-of-hand may also underlie Lovecraft's odd depiction of himself, in private correspondence, as "grandpa," and his slightly-younger male correspondents as his "grandsons." Lovecraft here merges his father's and grandfather's identities with himself, much in the same way that Joseph Curwen subverts and replaces Ward's identity. A similarly odd, but equally characteristic, conflation of father and son roles occurred when Lovecraft, as a toddler, would playfully refer to his father Winfield as a looking like a "*young* man"[144] (italics mine), an idea that the adult Lovecraft strangely revisits at the climax of "The Green Meadow," in which he refers to the horrific "land of Stethelos, where young men are infinitely old."[145] In "The Strange High House in the Mist," too, he incongruously observes how "the bearded host"[146] in the story "*seemed young*, yet looked out of eyes steeped in the *elder mysteries*" (italics mine). "Elder" here is defined by Lovecraft as "the first age of chaos before the gods or even the Elder Ones were born." Even Lovecraft's ordinary *Elders* are mere infants compared to this idea of an all-encompassing, and all-birthing, cosmic primordial age. In "The Quest of Iranon," something of "youth"[147] itself will be said to depart this "elder world" when Iranon, who has heretofore remained youthful-appearing throughout his entire life, finally learns the true facts of his beggarly paternity and suddenly becomes a "very old man" in appearance. Iranon's extended period of youth perhaps corresponds to Lovecraft's own extended infantilism, while his later death and old age symbolizes Lovecraft's own adopted persona as both a non-entity and an old man, respectively. Strikingly, too, Lovecraft's prematurely tall Wilbur Whately is represented as a man in a child's body; indeed, Whately is said to have a bearded face at the age of ten! If nothing else, such odd inversions suggest that the ideas of age and youth were very much on Lovecraft's mind.[148]

One of Lovecraft's earliest surviving horror stories, "The Alchemist," is already replete with all of the strange phenomena we have been tracing, above: inversions and reversals; a doubling of the father-figure into opposing benevolent and malevolent figures; and strongly paternal themes, in the form of the fatherly longings of the young protagonist, Antoine, the last descendant of a once prosperous line of noble aristocrats, much as Lovecraft envisioned himself to be. (Significantly, Lovecraft later reuses this same name, "Antoine," in his racist, collaborative story "Medusa's Coil." However, there he will invert it, and apply it not to the son but to the father, described as "Antoine de Russy, of an ancient, powerful, and cultivated line of Louisiana planters,"[149] and who, like the father in "The Rats in the Walls," is mourning the loss of his son. And here too — in yet another act of inversion — father Antoine tells us that his own father died when he was so young that he "can just barely remember him,"[150] so that he had to be raised, like Lovecraft, by his mother and aged grandfather.)

As in "The Shunned House" later on, not only does young Antoine's father in "The Alchemist" predecease him, but none of the previous holders of Antoine's family title have ever lived beyond the age of thirty-two years as Antoine lamely observes, "I had hitherto considered this but a natural attribute of a family of short-lived men,"[151] Lovecraft may be projecting the circumstances of his father's demise onto a grand scale. The benevolent vs. malevolent paternal doubling in this tale is likewise very pronounced, with the two contrasting lineages of the Comtes de — — on the one hand, and the evil father-and-son alchemists Michel and Charles le Sorcier on the other, being mirror images of each other. The unconscious or repressed aspects of Antoine's lineage seemingly are overtly manifested within the evil, sadistic lineage of the le Sorciers, who are associated with the rumored sacrifice of "many *small* peasant children" (italics mine) (a theme of infanticide which likewise runs throughout the Lovecraftian canon). And just as the mother of young Antoine dies at his birth, so too are the evil alchemists rumored to have burned Michel's "wife alive as a sacrifice to the Devil" — a punishment that Lovecraft will later, in "Arthur Jermyn," reserve for the unfortunate offspring of a corrupt maternal ancestor.

Significantly, however, even these murderous father-and-son alchemists have what Lovecraft calls "one redeeming ray of humanity; the evil old man loved his offspring with fierce intensity, whilst the youth had for his parent a more than filial affection,"[152] a fact that strongly underlines the overwhelming paternal anxieties underlying the tale (as well as prefiguring the later devotion shown by the cannibalistic Delapore for his maimed son). Admittedly, this love between father and son is partially the result of plot mechanics: Lovecraft needs to inordinately stress this love between father and son in order to explain precisely why the evil Charles le Sorcier will later go to such lengths to carry out his elaborate and murderous curse against Antoine's family throughout the coming centuries: as revenge for the murder of his own father by Antoine's ancestor. But Lovecraft could just as easily have created a narrative in which the accidental death of Charles le Sorcier's fiancée spurs him on to a course of lifelong revenge, and not his father. The fact that Lovecraft chooses the latter and not the former course merely underlines the paternal themes discernable throughout the whole work, as well as the puritanical aspect of Lovecraft's work as a whole (with these two aspects doubtlessly being related). Indeed, when Antoine tells us, "I should never wed, for, since no other branch of my family was in existence, I might thus end the curse with myself,"[153] it says as much about Antoine's familial "curse" (syphilis?) as it does about Lovecraft himself, and the extent to which his father's fall from grace, and his mother's reaction thereto, perhaps affected his own attitudes, including Lovecraft's related renunciation of Thesean heroism in his work. As critic Maurice Levy observes, Lovecraft seems to have had a "more or less clear consciousness"[154] of the "corrupted blood" in his paternal heritage, as evidenced, Levy argues, by Lovecraft's frequent and "anguished reveries on the ever possible perturbation of hereditary patrimony."

Also noteworthy is the immortality of the Satanic alchemists in this story: the father and son create an "elixir which should grant to him who partook of it eternal life and youth."[155] And just like the undead Cthulhu later on, the evil Charles le Sorcier sustains his life deep underground, where the life-giving, fertility properties of the subterranean womb are transmuted by the tomb into a darker, corruptive version of life; an immortality that is a caricature of sexuality and of that rampant, paternal lust that also spelled Lovecraft's father's, and consequently his own family's, doom. In "The Shadow Over Innsmouth," too, the Deep Ones partake of a similar paternal immortality. Zadok Allen observes how it is not unusual to see a man "'a-talkin' to his own five-times-great-grandfather who'd left dry land a couple o' hundred years or so afore.'"[156] Immortality is presented here as part of a paternal tradition.[157] One thinks here, too, of Lovecraft's pervasive idea of a possession of the child by the (immortal) parent, in lieu of true emancipation, such as Ephriam Waite taking over the identity and body of his daughter Asenath in "The Thing on the Doorstep," or Joseph Curwen supplanting the identity, if not the body, of his young descendant Charles Dexter Ward. Indeed, perhaps part of the problem with the Theseus myth, for Lovecraft, with its idea of emancipation via processes of inheritance, is the fact that truly inheriting the gifts of the father would likewise entail possession by the negative (most likely sexual) aspects of the parent as well; the same aspects that led to the death of Lovecraft's father in a madhouse.

Throughout *The Case of Charles Dexter Ward*, for example, there is a confusion between *ancestor* and *descendant*, particularly in the second half. Curwen masquerades as Ward for the much of the narrative, all as part of what Curwen's friend Jedediah Orne describes, in blatantly paternal language, as the "plan by which I came back as my Son."[158] Nor is it any coincidence that Lovecraft's own father, who was remembered by some of his acquaintances, as biographer L. Sprague de Camp writes, "as a 'pompous Englishman,'"[159] is mirrored in this by Joseph Curwen, who although American, had left home at age fifteen and returned at age twenty-four "with the speech, dress, and manners of a native Englishman."[160]

This idea of the possession of a son by the father likewise brings to mind the common Victorian idea of the inheritance of sin and vice by one's progeny — the pre-genetic belief that a profligate father would, in turn, spawn a profligate child. This idea of the father's sins revisiting themselves upon the sons — either in the form of divine punishments or in the form of inherited vices — seems to have been especially active, for example, in the morbid aura of strangeness that surrounded Oscar Wilde's two boys while in the care of their straight-laced maternal family. Wilde's son Vyvyan described one particularly dreadful episode in his memoirs, in which an off-color limerick that he recited to a playmate was blown into a major incident. As Holland relates, "I came in for a terrifying lecture into which my father's name entered; the general idea being that unless I was very careful I would come to a bad end."[161] Nor can it be any coincidence that the same vices for which the young Holland was carefully watched by his mother's relatives during his childhood — drunkenness, sexual profligacy, blasphemy, and even *studies of Greek* — are directly mirrored in the very things that later came to symbolize degeneracy throughout Lovecraft's weird fiction.

Lovecraft's "The Outsider" (1921) revisits many of these same paternal and Thesean themes, with Lovecraft this time taking us deep within the Thesean threshold itself and showing us the mechanics by which it opens from within: with the undead paternal inheritance itself clawing its way out of the grave to revisit its descendants. And whereas in "The Tomb" it is "the mansion"[162] of the evil, decadent Hydes, that, "gone for a century, once more reared its stately height to the raptured vision," in "The Outsider" Lovecraft directly reverses this and instead presents us with a resurrected ghoul, alone, who returns to the mansion of his former revels. Of course, the fact that the ghoul, in this instance, is Lovecraft's protagonist, necessarily means that the traditional trajectory of a Lovecraft story (proceeding from above ground downward into forbidden, primal, subterranean spaces) is entirely reversed, with the ghoul instead proceeding upwards from "the stone crypts deep down among the foundations."[163] And whereas the young Jervas Dudley is impelled downward by a morbid, necrophilic desire for what he perversely calls "that charnel conviviality"[164] of the tomb, the ghoul of "The Outsider" is conversely impelled upward from his charnel world by a "frantic craving for light"[165] and for the company of the "gay crowds in the sunny world beyond the endless forest."[166] In both cases, however, the essentially ancestral or paternal nature of this restless death remains the same.

Not surprisingly, either, given the Theseus themes we have been discussing, the immortal ghoul's emancipation from his underworld realm is facilitated by a heavy, stone "slab or door,"[167] which he lifts by using his head and both hands — the ghoul's only failure in this endeavor being his inability to prevent the trapdoor from "falling back into place" after he passes through it. Further reversing the order of events in "The Tomb," Lovecraft's ghoul then passes from a cemetery out into the world, visiting a modern revel, some of whose celebrants, given the fact that their "expressions ... brought up incredibly remote recollections,"[168] are presumably the ghoul's own relatives or descendants. (Later on, in *The Dream-Quest of Unknown Kadath*, Lovecraft again associates "a great trap door of stone with an iron ring"[169] in the forest floor with a similar such interface between the underworld and the surface world; and, significantly, he likewise connects this trap door with what he calls "the Great Ones' curse,"[170] which causes the door to be avoided by the gigantic Gugs. As Lovecraft writes, the Gugs "realize that all which is forgotten need not necessarily be dead, and they would not like to see the slab rise slowly and deliberately."[171] Lovecraft, just as in "The Outsider," associates a trapdoor with the restless dead, and the term "Great Ones," here, suggests a parental force, both ancient and gigantic, that will not remain in its grave, while the "curse" again suggests Lovecraft's obsession with corrupted paternity.)

Unfortunately in "The Outsider," this particular Great One does not stay buried, but instead returns to haunt his descendants, who, like the family of Joseph Curwen, are horrified by this personage from the past. Save that here, it is not merely the lettering upon a paternal tombstone that has been effaced, but rather the memory of Lovecraft's ghoul himself that has been obliterated: the ghoul only realizes at the end "all that I had been."[172] Nor is it surprising that, after this climactic revelation of his identity in the mirror, the Ghoul immediately returns to the cemetery, to find "the stone trap-door immovable"[173] and his return to the tomb now impossible. The Theseus door provides revelations for the parents as well as the children, it seems; but here, just as for Jervas Dudley in the asylum, there is no going back. As Robert Waugh observes, in Lovecraft's weird fiction "the way up is not the same as the way down."[174] (Admittedly, this is not true for Lovecraft's later fiction: witness father Peaslee's descent into the depths of the earth, and compare this with father Delapore's earlier descent into the same abyss: the lessening of Lovecraft's sense of the macabre in "The Shadow Out of Time" perhaps represents a more general lessening of his paternal anxieties in later years.)

In "The Outsider," notably, Lovecraft forgoes the figure of the son completely; the Thesean inheritance itself is the protagonist. It lifts the trapdoor itself and goes in search of its offspring. But instead it only finds a mirror — a mirror such as young Jervas Dudley and Charles Dexter Ward form for their ancestors. Even so, Lovecraft's outsider-ghoul does win wife and treasure, of a sort: even if the wife is the ghoul-queen Nitokris, and their liaison is — as with so many such pairings in Lovecraft's weird fiction — a cannibalistic, necrophilic revel. Indeed, with its themes of escape and self-realization, "The Outsider" is, aside from a few exceptions, one of the closest things to a heroic narrative in Lovecraft's weird fiction.

But what is the hidden revelation experienced by the Outsider? What is it that Lovecraft's risen ghoul suddenly realizes about himself? Clearly, his main realization is that he is dead, but that merely skims the surface of a deeper, more substantial revelation, which involves some hidden truth about his very identity. The answer, I think, is at least partially to be found in Lovecraft's pointed description of the Outsider's body as "unclean,"[175] "abnormal, and detestable," "the putrid dripping eidolon of unwholesome revelation; the awful baring of that which the merciful earth should always hide." This is precisely how one would describe the disease-pustules of syphilis, the baring of which, in Lovecraft's father's case, "the merciful earth" not only "should" hide, but did hide. Indeed, the suggestion of syphilis in the description of the ghoul is unmistakable, and it is perhaps telling that in the same year in which "The Outsider" was written Lovecraft also composed a bawdy satire, "The Pathetick History of Sir Wilful Wildrake," which also invokes, albeit from a darkly comedic perspective, much the same pathological imagery. As Lovecraft writes, although "Pain'd, pox'd, and putrid with his Woes,"[176] Wildrake laments that he still

> ...must crave
> And ogle vainly to my Grave,
> Whilst even then (if Crones err not)
> My itching Ghost will haunt the Spot!

This same "itching Ghost," of course, likewise haunts the place of his burial in "The Outsider," and the "Crones" mentioned in the poem perhaps mirror the aged nurse of Lovecraft's story.

The fact that Lovecraft prefaces "The Outsider" with a quote from the Keats, too, referring to a "be-nightmared"[177] baron and his guests, who "dreamt of many a wo," is, I think, another clue: Lovecraft's story represents a fairly standard revenant dream of the child for a deceased parent. As Ernest Jones observes in his classic study *On the Nightmare*, "Dreams of people who are dead occur most frequently, and are most heavily charged with emotion when the dead person represents the father or mother."[178] Jones goes on to directly associate such parental dreams not only with the various common myths about undead revenants (vampires, werewolves, and ghouls, creatures with the power "of returning from the grave and visiting the living, especially by night"[179]) but also with the pervasive ancient practice of ancestor worship throughout the world; and this, in turn, with the development of the basic idea of a god-like or all-powerful deity.

One could adduce numerous instances of such revenant dreams in literature and life: in Denton Welch's bizarre coming-of-age novel *In Youth Is Pleasure* (1945), for example, the youthful narrator has recurring necrophilic dreams about his dead mother, whose name, much like the similarly effaced graves in Lovecraft's stories, "was quite banned"[180] within the family, and even considered so "unmentionable that it was necessary to use elaborate circumlocutions in speaking about the past"; circumlocutions with which the equally reticent Lovecraft would also have been quite familiar, and which, in the form of his weird fiction, became very elaborate indeed. (Lovecraft himself would have been aware of this link between the parental and the unnamable from his reading of Sir J. G. Frazer's *The Golden Bough* [1922],[181] which, in its discussion on primitive tabooed words in chapter 22, treats in depth this origin of forbidden words in the names of family relations, the dead, and the names of kings [i.e., the tribal father-surrogate.]) Movie director Stuart Gordon, too, refers to a similar such paternal revenant dream on the commentary track to his film version of H. P. Lovecraft's *Re-Animator* (1985), observing "My father passed away when I was a teenager, and I often had dreams about him. And as a matter of fact, one of the dreams that I remember having, was one in which my father came back from the dead, and looked *horrible*. And ... I didn't care, I was just glad to see him."[182] Lovecraft's "The Colour Out of Space" similarly ends with such a paternal-revenant dream: his narrator has repeated dreams about what he calls the "good old man"[183] Ammi Pierce (language with decidedly paternal overtones: "old man" is common slang for father, not to mention its parallel with Lovecraft's equally parental Old Ones), in which Pierce repeatedly assumes the form of "a grey, twisted, brittle monstrosity which persists more and more in troubling my sleep" — language that applies just as well to the corpse-like monstrosity in "The Outsider." In "The Silver Key," too, Randolph Carter's grandfather appears to Carter in his dreams, described as a "grey old scholar"[184] who "spoke long and earnestly of their ancient line" and who reminds Carter of the familial key hidden in the "antique box ... handed down from his ancestors."[185] But whereas Carter's benevolent grandfather sends him dreams of English ancestral glory, in "The Call of Cthulhu" the restless, undead, and phallic father sends nightmares, rooted in a ravening and sadistic sexuality.

Further hints of this familial basis of Lovecraft's restless dead can be discerned in the second half of his poem "The Poe-et's Nightmare" (1916), which is set in a macabre and sadistic nightmare-world, populated by "werewolves, *and the souls / Of those that knew me well in other days*"[186] [italics mine], language that surely, given Lovecraft's lack of emancipatory and sexual relationships, refers to some familial, and perhaps paternal, connection. And while critic James Goho suggests that the presence of the revenant dead in "The Unnamable" "illustrates a longing for the past, perhaps a longing for death, perhaps for a dead lover,"[187] it seems much more likely — given the strong anti-sexual impetus of Lovecraft's works — that a parental bond, and not a "dead lover," forms the primary animating force in this and other tales of the revenant dead in Lovecraft's canon. (Notable here, too, is the odd fact that the only male god mentioned in the mad ramblings[188] of Lovecraft's narrator in "The Moon-Bog" is Plouton, more familiarly Pluto, god of the underworld and lord of the dead. This unconsciously reflects, perhaps, Lovecraft's own all-pervading concern with the death of his father or other male relatives. The gigantic Unknown God of the Dead that appears at the end of "Under the Pyramids" shares a similar fatherly [and necrophilic] association, with the word *unknown* here reflecting Lovecraft's hazy memories of his father.)

As psychologist Ernest Jones explains, this "attitude of awe and fear in respect of dream visitors from the dead"[189] gave rise to the apotheosis of one's ancestors, and, ultimately, to the creation of such familiar figures as the "Heavenly Father"[190] (still potent for a vast majority of people even today) and the Mother Goddess, personages who ultimately derive from the infantile perception of the parent as an all-powerful figure. Lafcadio Hearn, for example, discusses the role of ancestor worship in Japan, by which "'All the dead became gods,'"[191] a practice directly rooted in the Japanese feeling of filial devotion toward living parents and grandparents. And as critic Maurice Levy similarly observes in his study of Lovecraft's works, discussing the close connection between dreams and Lovecraft's weird fiction: "The dream process is always inseparable from mythical patterns."[192] And it is here too (especially given the markedly infantile aspects of Lovecraft's weird fiction) where we must also look for the origins of Lovecraft's all-pervasive Old Ones and Elder Ones, which also combine aspects of dream, the ancestral, and the cosmic.

This dream-inspired ancestor worship even permeated Lovecraft's beloved classical Rome: historian Edward Gibbon, for example, wrote of how "the ardour of the Roman youth was kindled into active emulation, as often as they beheld the domestic images of their ancestors."[193] Roman tombstones, too, were usually, historian Keith Hopkins writes, "dedicated to the Manes, the revered spirits of the dead.... Originally, these Manes were ghostly shadows, without personal or individual shape. They were transient beings which *inhabited the underworld for the period between leaving one body and entering another*"[194] [italics mine]. And it may be that in "The Outsider" we see a reflection of this same restless tendency in its most primitive and prototypical form. And although Maurice Levy dubiously locates what he calls "the phenomenal originality of Lovecraft"[195] in "this intimate fusion of oneiric vision and mythic elaboration," in reality this fusion of myth and dream is only as original as the superstitious dogmas of a tribal shaman. Indeed, Lovecraft's stories are replete with this archaic belief in the persistence of life after death, the animistic idea, as expressed in "The Thing on the Doorstep," that a paternal soul can somehow be "half detached"[196] from its body, and yet keep "right on after death as long as the body lasts." Jervas Dudley speaks in "The Tomb" of "my rather original ideas regarding life and death,"[197] which "had caused me to associate the cold clay with the breathing body in a vague fashion." The grave in Lovecraft's works becomes, as Maurice Levy observes, "a *functional place*"[198] of "*animated*" life. This is the origin of the Puritans' Invisible World, which had such a huge impact on Lovecraft's imagination. Children too, with their limited store of experience, have an equally difficult time conceiving of the permanence of death; instead believing, as child psychologist Leontine Young observes, that the sudden disappearance of the beloved adult is a purely voluntary desertion, perhaps even an intentional punishment of the child for some unknown infraction. And for said child there is always the additional and eerie possibility—which is just as real to the child as it is to any mystic or Christian theologian (and which actually occurs in some of H. P. Lovecraft's weird fiction)—that the loved one will eventually and unexpectedly return.[199]

In "The Colour Out of Space," both Mrs. Gardner and the animals of her farm persist in living on even after being almost totally consumed by the vampiric entity from space, as will some of the corpses discovered by Randolph Carter in *The Dream-Quest of Unknown Kadath*. Here Lovecraft's undead and undying Cthulhu perhaps represents the paternal apex of this infantile fear. Lovecraft's trademark observations that "life and death are all one to those in the clutch of what came out of R'lyeh,"[200] and that "that is not dead which can eternal lie, / And with strange aeons even death may die,"[201] are just as applicable to the ghoul of "The Outsider" and to the vampire of traditional myth as they are to Lovecraft's ostensibly cosmic entities. And just as Jervas Dudley in "The Tomb" speaks of "the call of the dead"[202] that impels him in his necrophilic quest, so too does Lovecraft speak of a "Call of Cthulhu," which speaks in dreams to men.[203] Ultimately, the two "calls" are one and the same.

In "The Silver Key," tellingly, this same "call" language reappears yet again, likewise in relation to the ancestral and paternal dead: Lovecraft observes how "they [Randolph Carter's ancestors] were *calling* him back along the years, and with the *mingled wills of all his fathers* were pulling him toward some *hidden and ancestral* source"[204] (emphases mine). Cthulhu's "call" merely represents the malevolent, obverse form of this ultimately familial, psychological phenomenon. Indeed, Lovecraft's repeated description of how the "entombed"[205] "dead bodies" of the Old Ones "told their secrets in *dreams* to the first man, who formed a *cult which had never died*"[206] [italics mine] constitutes as accurate a description as those provided by Ernest Jones for the origins of ancestor worship in the mists of prehistory. As critic Peter Cannon elsewhere admits, although he does not elaborate further on the topic, Lovecraft's description of the undead Cthulhu "clearly lends itself to religious and hence psychological interpretation"[207] — an interpretation Lovecraft cleverly forestalls, however, by substituting the mechanisms of his own imaginary cosmology for inner psychological processes. Ultimately however, Cthulhu seems to represent merely yet another form of a vampiric revenant, occupying the top rung in a gradual process of development beginning with the restless ghoul in "The Outsider," and continuing with the vampiric entity in Lovecraft's "The Hound," all representing the mixed feelings that the living project upon their restless and supposedly undead kin.

The strongest of all feelings, of course, is love, a force which, as Ernest Jones observes, "reaches its greatest intensity between lovers, married partners or children and parents."[208] And it is here, I would suggest, in a persistence of infantile fears of being abandoned by a beloved parent, where Lovecraft's recurring image of the restless revenant has its origin. This idea is especially brought home by the poignant scene in Lovecraft's "The Silver Key," a story that, as Maurice Levy observes, is shot through with a desire to return to one's "first childhood,"[209] and in which Randolph Carter "would often awake calling for his mother and grandfather, both in their graves a quarter of a century."[210] Unfortunately, however, love is rarely unmixed, often being combined with feelings of hate, fear, and desire; hence the restlessness of the dead in our dreams, whose nocturnal visits are animated by a strength of emotion commensurate with their horror. As Ernest Jones explains elsewhere, "The motives which are supposed to activate a dead person to return to the living"[211] are often "so firmly bound up with the point of view of the corpse that it sometimes needs an effort to remember that they can only represent ideas projected onto him from the minds of the living." Hence such things as the oral sadistic desires of the reanimated vampire, or the cannibalistic desires of the ghoul, which actually represent the suppressed and incestuous desires of the relatives of the deceased (and it is notable that revenants are most often said to visit members of their own family). In "The Unnamable," too, we find Lovecraft engaging in a similar process of projection or inversion: Randolph Carter suggests that the "monstrous apparitions"[212] sometimes sighted in cemeteries have their origin in projections from the minds of the dead themselves (here called "psychic emanations" that were "moulded by the dead brain of a hybrid nightmare"). Lovecraft's inversions as usual serve mainly to hide the unconscious sources of his own fictional ideas. Nor does it take much imagination to see in these "apparitions of gigantic bestial forms" a mundane prefiguration of Lovecraft's later and ostensibly cosmic weird entities.

Lovecraft will further underline the obviously paternal nature of Cthulhu's dreams in *The Dream-Quest of Unknown Kadath*, via what he calls the "*archaic father* of all the *rumoured* shantak-birds"[213] (italics mine), a creature that is said to reside within the aptly named "Temple of the *Elder Ones*" (italics mine) at Inquanok, and who, just like Cthulhu, is said to send "out queer dreams to the curious." Tellingly, too, and much as in "The Alchemist" and *Charles Dexter Ward, et al.*, Lovecraft goes on to invoke his recurring language of whispers and rumors with regard to this blatantly paternal creature, writing breathlessly: "It is *whispered*, that the *rumored* shantak-birds are no wholesome things; it being indeed for the best that no man has ever truly seen one (for *that fabled father* of shantaks in the king's dome is fed in the dark)" (italics mine). Of course, this idea that "no man has ever truly seen one," as applied to a clearly paternal animal, has obvious resonances with Lovecraft's own largely unseen father and his admittedly vague memories of him,[214] an idea that also extends to such invisible paternal entities as Yog-Sothoth. Typically, too, Lovecraft also provides a more benevolent version of this malevolent sleeping father in the same story, in the form of the "patriarch Atal,"[215] who likewise resides within the Temple of the Elder Ones in the land of dreams, and who becomes so drowsy during his talk with Randolph Carter that Carter "laid him gently on a couch of inlaid ebony and gathered his long beard decorously on his chest."[216] One hopes that his sleep, at least, is less restless and troubled than that of Cthulhu. Sleeping, of course, is how the infantile mind often interprets death; and children are often told, or often assume, that dead loved ones are merely "sleeping." (In *At the Mountains of Madness*, significantly, Lovecraft himself blurs the distinction between the two, writing of the "dead or sleeping polar waste."[217])

Given the parallels we have been discussing concerning the connection between the undead Cthulhu and the restless dead at the heart of primitive ancestor worship, it should perhaps come as no surprise to find that Cthulhu, in yet another recapitulation of the trapdoor in Thesean myth, himself sleeps behind an "immense carved door"[218] "like a great barn door," the door of Theseus' magical inheritance finally having swelled to gigantic and ostensibly cosmic proportions. And whereas Jervas Dudley was initially frustrated in his (essentially coital) attempts at entry due to his own infantile passivity, here the men's comprehension of Cthulhu's portal is frustrated by the otherworldly nature of the barrier itself, which baffles any attempt at human understanding. The parental has become the divine. The all-powerful has become the god-like.

III. Lovecraft's Great Old Ones

Just as with the dreaming Cthulhu, Lovecraft's trademark terms for his various cosmic entities; whether they are called "Old Ones," "Elder Ones," or the "Great Old Ones," are less reflective of the cosmic context in which they are usually taken or of Lovecraft's intimations of an "unwholesome"[219] "antiquity" than of this more basic familial and psychological context, suggestive of an ambivalent parental obsession on Lovecraft's part, and indicating perhaps a certain restiveness under domineering maternal control on the one hand, and a retreat from overt and threatening paternal sexuality on the other.

As critic John Salonia observes, "Lovecraft uses the titles 'Old Ones' and 'Great Old Ones' *to characterize different races of alien beings in various tales*"[220] (italics mine); in other words, the aliens themselves are interchangeable, but the conception of old or aged entities remains the same. The fact that this "Old Ones" usage persists throughout the Lovecraftian weird canon, even in different contexts (whether in application to the malevolent entities of "The Dunwich Horror" or "The Call of Cthulhu," or the ostensibly benevolent entities of *At the Mountains of Madness*), testifies to the extent to which Lovecraft's horror fiction is permeated by unconscious and underlying parental concerns, for which his ostensible concern with the cosmically "ancient" is a convenient vehicle. (And even within the same story, such as *At the Mountains of Madness*, a single race can be variously referred to as Elder Things, Elder Ones and Old Ones; the words change, but the signification of [ultimately familial] age remains the same.) And while other Lovecraftian scholars, like Robert Waugh, are quick to describe things like the primordial or pre-human rites in "The Horror at Red Hook" as deriving "from extraterrestrials,"[221] although technically correct, this unfortunate tendency to take Lovecraft at his word also obscures the obvious elements of domesticity preserved via his patented older or primordial language, elements that are further reinforced by the suggestive elements of gender that Lovecraft consistently applies to his ostensibly cosmic Great Old Ones (Cthulhu is described as a *he*, for instance, and Yog-Sothoth is both the *husband* of Shub-Niggurath and the *father* of Wilbur Whately, etc.). Writer Will Murray comes rather closer to the truth when he points out that Lovecraft's "Old Ones" is "an actual Native American term"[222] but he too stops short of aligning his fictional inspirations with the propensity of various peoples for ancestor worship. Lovecraft himself, however, will go so far in his 1929–1930 collaborative story "The Mound" as to directly identify his Old Ones both with the ghosts of Native American myths and also as "the ancestors of all men."[223]

The primary function of parental, ancestral gods, of course — in both mythology and in the family unit itself— is the creation of life: whether the creation of all mankind or the universe itself, or the making and birthing of children; these are mysterious processes which are therefore invested with solemn rites of ritual and mystery. Thus do we find the forces of fate that control the ghoul's life in "The Outsider" being described in undisguised divine terms, with the Outsider glumly observing, "Such a lot the gods gave to me."[224] Nor is it a surprise to find Lovecraft, in *At the Mountains of Madness*, attributing the creation of life on earth itself to his fictional Old Ones, referred to as "*Elder Things* supposed to have *created all earth-life as jest or mistake*"[225] (italics mine); Lovecraft's parental portrait here, much as in "The Outsider," is invested with his typical pessimism and cynicism with regard to life and fate. Lovecraft pointedly describes Arthur Jermyn's great-great-great-great grandparents as a "white ape-goddess"[226] on the one hand and as "a great white god who had come out of the West" on the other. The "strange progenitors"[227] of Arthur Jermyn here are described explicitly by the African natives as gods, in a possible caricature of both Lovecraft's own parents and what Lovecraft saw as a primitive processes of tribal apotheosis. Divested of its cosmic context, Lovecraft's language reveals its firmly parental basis. (Lovecraft's association of the Old Ones with the swastika in "The Shadow Over Innsmouth"[228] also suggests the degree to which Lovecraft's racism was likewise a search for the ultimate father, the ultimate ancestor — a father in the form of a collective racial soul.)

Lovecraft himself underlies this essentially domestic conception of his Great/Elder/Old Ones terminology. In "The Tomb," for instance, Jervas Dudley uses such terms purely in reference to family, without any obfuscatory cosmic element, when he refers to the ancestral Hydes as an "*older* and more mysterious line"[229] than his own; and we have already noted Lovecraft's description of the paternal double in "Beyond the Wall of Sleep" as "*old* Doctor Fenton"[230] (italics mine). The necrophilic Herbert West, too — who, significantly, will remain unnaturally youthful in his appearance throughout his life,[231] and thus forms an example of the eternally defiant and disobedient son (as well as of Lovecraft's recurring old-young inversions) — grudgingly admits the medical abilities of such "tradition-bound *elders*"[232] (italics mine) as "the learned and benevolent"[233] Dr. Allan Halsey, who himself represents yet another one of Lovecraft's conservative, academic father-surrogates. In "The Silver Key," too, it is "An *old* servant"[234] (italics mine), and not Randolph Carter himself, who finally "forced the carven lid" of the ancestral box with its magical weapon hidden within. Lovecraft's recurring Old Ones forever usurp or preempt all attempts at adult or Thesean emancipation.

Lovecraft's recurring theme of cyclopean giganticism, too, whether of beings or things, likewise reflects an underlying parental basis. As Ernest Jones observes in *On the Nightmare*, "legends ... told of *giants*"[235] merely reflect that "mythological transformation of the child's conception of its parents." Lovecraft's fiction definitely provides more than enough examples of such legends, from the (again, paternal) shantak-birds, which are "larger than elephants,"[236] to the "titan *elbow*"[237] uncovered in "The Shunned House," which proves to represent merely one portion of a surviving and vampiric patriarch, lying buried and sleeping, like Cthulhu, for centuries. Peter Cannon's *Twayne* study of Lovecraft provides an excellent list of such instances of giganticism in Lovecraft's early weird fiction,[238] and although Cannon elsewhere criticizes Lovecraft's combination of gigantic, ghostlike, vampiric, and lycanthropic characteristics within a single entity in "The Shunned House," saying that "he overloads the horror to the point of absurdity,"[239] this combination of ultimately parental and ancestral characteristics also serves to reveal the psychological sources of his imaginary creatures, in an overt concern with corrupted parental or paternal heredity.

In her book *Life Among the Giants* (1966), child psychologist Leontine Young discusses this issue of children's perceptions of their parents from the child's perspective, portraying a world of parental legs, and shins, and towering paternal heads, the parents' greater size and height giving them a longer reach, a greater stride, and the arsenal with which to wield almost total power and control over their child's movements — or at least the ability to suggest they are capable of doing so. "This matter of size is one way all children are alike and one way they all differ from grown up people," Young writes; "It is a very important matter, as all children know."[240] And although, in her chapter entitled "The Giant Killers," Young sees in the fairy tale of Jack and the Beanstalk the embodiment of a dream "every child born must have" of "demolishing his own particular giant and demonstrating to one and all that he is not to be trifled with," in Lovecraft's weird fiction we often (but not always) see the triumph of the giant, and the reification of infantile helplessness. (In "The Shunned House" and "The Dunwich Horror," it is true, we do see the vanquishing of the giant; the uncle in the former story partakes of the giant's general dissolution, while in the latter story we see a father figure, Dr. Armitage, vanquishing the gigantic son, in another one of Lovecraft's patented inversions.) At the same time, however, as Young points out, this common giant-killer fantasy of the child is tempered by the love and dependence that the child also feels for the giant, so that "the good giant and the bad giant have a disconcerting propensity for amalgamating into one. This creates a long succession of complications." Hence, too, the strange ambivalence discernable in the Lovecraft weird canon, in which the gigantic Cthulhu, despite his horror, is still able to exert a paralyzing power of hypnotic fascination, and in which Lovecraft's cannibalistic paternal devils are often countered by an equal and opposing force of paternal rationality and good.

Certainly, it does not take a great stretch of the imagination to discern in Lovecraft's basic formulation, the "Great Old Ones,"[241] an obvious combination of two of the most prominent aspects of the parent-child relation: size and age, with the epithet "great" itself likewise containing elements of age as well as size. As Alex Houstoun observes in his 2011 essay on H. P. Lovecraft and the Burkean/Kantian sublime, Lovecraft frequently "amplifies sublime characteristics such as size, obscurity, and depth"[242] throughout his works, inventing "horrors the size of mountains." But although Houstoun emphasizes Lovecraft's ostensible concern with supposedly cosmic horror, these very tangible attributes actually suggest a more visceral origin in direct parental issues, a fact that more than explains, too, the recurring fear which Lovecraft's characters express regarding their ancestry and maternity or paternity throughout his weird fiction; concerns that any objective assessment must agree are very far removed from the "cosmic." There is a curious domesticity in the giganticism of the Great Race in Lovecraft's "The Shadow Out of Time," in which the huge scale of the aliens is associated as much with such mundane and familial objects as tables ("whose height could not be under ten feet"),[243]

Jack the Giant Killer: the infantile fantasy of the child revenging itself against the gigantic, ogreish parent. In Lovecraft's weird fiction, the giant is sometimes defeated, but usually, as in the case of Cthulhu, only to rise up once again. From *Jack the Giant Killer and Other Stories* by Anonymous, frontispiece, Mother Goose series (Philadelphia, PA: Henry Altemus, 1903).

doorways ("15 ft high"), and houses ("1000 ft tall"),[244] as it is with alien or cyclopean ruins. The telepathic mental omniscience that Lovecraft associates with this Great Race, too, is ultimately to be identified with the apparent omniscience of the parent, as felt by the child in his or her power.

Tellingly, Lovecraft further combines these *old* and *gigantic* themes (along with related themes of *dreams* and *sleeping underground*) in "The Shadow Out of Time," where (in a passage he copied nearly word for word from the *Encyclopædia Britannica*) he speaks of certain legends among the Australian aborigines about "'Buddai, the gigantic old man who lies asleep for ages underground with his head on his arm, and who will some day awake and eat up the world.'"[245] Lovecraft's patented "old" language again is paired with gigantic stature in the form of a tribal and clearly ancestral spirit, which Lovecraft clearly takes as an analogue (or a precursor) to his own cosmicized version of the same conception. Lovecraft, as always, is adept at evading and concealing, even as he reveals, the basic psychological sources of his cosmic conceptions. Indeed, this strange image of the *giant-headed father* seems to have been much on Lovecraft's mind. He referred to it at least twice as early as 1922, associating the horrors that stem from "the paternal roof"[246] of Jan Martense's cannibalistic family in "The Lurking Fear" with "dead men's skulls swelled to gigantic proportions,"[247] imagery suggestive of some corrupt masculine influence proceeding upward from below. In his prose poem "What the Moon Brings," too, Lovecraft combines this same paternal head with images of kingship and giganticism via a "black basalt crown of a shocking eikon"[248] seen by his protagonist submerged in a swamp, crowning a buried mile-high horror whose head alone is visible above the waters, the sight of which prompts Lovecraft's narrator to commit suicide. (This idea of the giant paternal head is surely a very ancient one; anthropologist Erich Neumann, for example, refers to the "Chinese ideogram for the god of heaven,"[249] which literally means "'man with big head,'" language that also suggests our more familiar idea of the "head of the family.") We have already noted, above, Lovecraft's pointed use of the word "head" to describe both Dr. Fenton and Joe Slater's respective paternal roles in "Beyond the Wall of Sleep." In his "The Nameless City," too, we find Lovecraft referring to the totemic ancestral spirits of the buried city as having a huge head, which Lovecraft goes on, tellingly, to link to both the archetypal father-god, Jove ("Not Jove himself had so colossal and protuberant a forehead"),[250] as well as the lascivious and horned Satyr, which further suggests the darker, sexually active aspects of the father.

Lovecraft's language is also revealingly paternal in his pro–Allied World War I poetry, in which England is referred to in patently familial terms as the "Isle of my Fathers!,"[251] with the paternal again being given a larger ancestral and racial complexion. Lovecraft's recurring exclamation in his correspondence, too, "God Save the King!" also testifies to the strength of this paternal obsession within his imagination. The all-powerful father is symbolized by both "God" and the "King" in this statement; Lovecraft's injunction for God to "save" this king represents the benevolent obverse to Lovecraft's undead Cthulhu, who also survives semi-alive through endless aeons. The latter manifestation perhaps is indicative of the more troubling and perhaps sexual anxieties that underlie Lovecraft's overt devotion to the family, and his failure to achieve complete divestment from his parents' identities. (Lovecraft himself repeatedly emphasizes this identification of the king with the father in "The Quest of Iranon," in which Aira, the imaginary lost city of Iranon's quest, is repeatedly referred to as the place "where my father once ruled as king,"[252] while the townspeople among whom Iranon grew up once belittled him for thinking "himself a King's son."[253])

Lovecraft's weird fiction perpetuates this same dichotomy between an emulation of the father on the one hand (in the form of his academic, benevolent paternal heroes) and defiance on the other (in the form of his revenant, malevolent paternal entities). Lovecraft's weird fiction, just as much as his childhood tic symptoms from which he suffered as a child, constitute a symptom of what child psychologist Margaret S. Mahler calls an "ambivalent conflict"[254] toward one's parents. But whereas psychoanalyst Ernest Jones writes of the jealous son who envies the sexual potency of the father, in Lovecraft's case one thinks he was less envious than livid. Indeed, Walter Delapore's deliberate "slaughter"[255] of his entire family, including his father, in "The Rats in the Walls," after the revelation of the deviant cannibalistic practices of his family line, followed immediately by his fleeing to Lovecraft's beloved "Virginia," ultimately seem to reflect the violence of Lovecraft's revulsion against his father's perceived sins, and a Puritan fleeing toward a virgin (Virginia) paradise. Lovecraft's love for the state of Virginia throughout his lifetime[256] may have had just such a simple psychological explanation, aside from the numerous racial and social reasons that he cites for his attachment. (In "Arthur Jermyn," too, we see a father, called an "old man," carry out a similar "madly murderous scheme"[257] against what he perceives to be his corrupt family. Lovecraft perhaps inverted his feelings in this regard by having Sir Robert Jermyn "put an end to all three of his children.")

Lovecraft's division of the father figure into two opposing halves — commonsense academics on the one hand, and bestial monstrosities on the other — symbolizes what Leontine Young saw as the ambivalent nature of this parental giant to the child. Sometimes these two opposing characteristics are even combined in one person, as with Lovecraft's ambivalent Terrible Old Man, who

Table 2. Benevolent vs. Malevolent Old Father Figures in HPL's Weird Fiction.

Benevolent Paternal Figures	*Malevolent Paternal Figures*
"Beyond the Wall of Sleep"	"Beyond the Wall of Sleep"
"Old Dr. Fenton," who speaks to the narrator in a "paternal way" (*D* 31).*	Rural degenerate and sadistic killer Joe Slater, called the "head" (*D* 29) of his family. He reduces his victim's body to ribbons, and it takes "the combined efforts of four men" in order "to bind him in the straightjacket" (*D* 28).
"The Call of Cthulhu"	"The Call of Cthulhu"
Prof. George Gamwell Angell, the "grand-uncle" (*D* 126) of the narrator; with the "queer bas-relief" which he bequeaths to his grand-nephew being an analogue to the cannibalistic pictures earlier shown by the old man to Lovecraft's genealogist narrator in "The Picture in the House."	Cthulhu, priest of the "Great Old Ones" (*DH* 139), who spoke "in dreams to the first men" (139).
"The Alchemist"	"The Alchemist"
Antoine's "aged guardian" (*D* 329) Pierre, called "an old and trusted man of considerable intelligence" (*D* 329).	The evil sorcerer Michel Mauvais, who has a "sinister reputation" (*D* 330) (the theme of whisper/rumors, again).
"The Silver Key"	*At the Mountains of Madness*
Randolph Carter's "grandfather and his great uncle Christopher" (*MM* 412), the only close relatives that "understood his [Carter's] mental life" (412), and who are both "long dead" (412), as well as his uncle's hired man, Old Benjiah Corey (yet another "Old One").	Note here too, Lovecraft's likening of the Old Ones' dissection of the explorers' bodies to the work of "a careful butcher" (*MM* 37), which recalls that subterranean "butcher shop and kitchen" (*DH* 43) that awakens Delapore's cannibalistic desires, as well as the image in "The Picture in the House," showing "'whar the butcher cut off his feet'" (*DH* 122).
"The Dunwich Horror"	"The Dunwich Horror"
The conservative academic Dr. Armitage.	The unseen father/husband Yog-Sothoth.
Charles Dexter Ward	*Charles Dexter Ward*
The physician Dr. Willet and the elder Mr. Ward, described as a "practical man of power and affairs" (*MM* 155).	The old and evil Joseph Curwen, as well as "the evil old man called Josef Nadeh" (*MM* 223), one of the vampiric Joseph Curwen's closest companions.

Benevolent Paternal Figures	Malevolent Paternal Figures
"The Shadow Over Innsmouth" The ancient tippler Zadok Allen.	"The Shadow Over Innsmouth" Captain Obed Marsh.
Unknown Kadath The helpful tavern keeper, described as "a very old man" (*MM* 327), who takes Randolph Carter "to an upper room" to show him "a crude picture" (327) of the Elder Gods of dreamland, and imparts to him legends that "the old tavern-keeper's great-grandfather had heard from his great-grandfather" (327) (paternal transmission of tradition again, and doubtlessly an elaboration on the classical picture book given to the young Lovecraft [Joshi, *Lovecraft: A Life*, 23.])	"The Picture in the House" The old man with the "patriarchal" beard (Joshi, notes to "The Picture in the House," Lovecraft, *Call of Cthulhu*, 372), who likewise shows the protagonist a picture. (In "The Shadow Out of Time," Lovecraft speaks cryptically of one of his Antarctic Old Ones, as chiseling "certain pictures" [*SOT* 77] on the walls of the tower room where he is imprisoned: Lovecraft here combines the imprisonment of his father with the picture imagery of "The Picture in the House.")
"The Shunned House" The narrator's uncle Dr. Whipple, "a sane, conservative physician of the old school" (*MM* 239).	"The Shunned House" The "swarthy" (*MM* 248) vampiric/lycanthropic patriarch, Etienne Roulet.
"The Rats in the Walls" Sir William Brinton, who actually solves the riddle of the portal in Delapore's basement.	"The Rats in the Walls" The cannibalistic father Delapore.
"The Tomb" The "physician with the iron-grey beard" (*D* 6) and Mr. Dudley.	"The Tomb" Dudley's decadent ancestor, Jervas Hyde.
Unknown Kadath The "older men" near Mount Ngranek, who give Randolph Carter "blessings and warnings" (*MM* 329) regarding his quest.	*Unknown Kadath* The patriarchal father of all the gigantic, horse-headed shantak-birds, whose existence is surrounded by rumors and whispers, and who is hidden from sight in the darkness.
"The Colour Out of Space" The good old man Ammi Pierce, with his "white beard" (*DH* 56), who haunts the dreams of the narrator.	"The Dreams in the Witch House" The Black Man of Arkham, consort of witch Keziah Mason.
"Herbert West: Reanimator" Dr. Halsey, one of the "tradition-bound elders" (*D* 139–140) who opposes West.	"Herbert West: Reanimator" Dr. Halsey after his reanimation by West, described as a mad simian monster (*D* 143).

Benevolent Paternal Figures	Malevolent Paternal Figures
"The Shadow Out of Time"	"The Shadow Out of Time"
Father Nathaniel Peaslee, who despite his madness returns to sanity alongside his son.	Peaslee's case is associated with Joe Slater from "Beyond the Wall of Sleep" (*SOT* 41).
"The Thing on the Doorstep"	"The Thing on the Doorstep"
Edward's father, "old Mr. Derby" (*DH* 285).	Asenath's "wolfish" (*DH* 280) and evil father, Ephraim.
"Polaris"	
The "grave bearded men" (*D* 21) of Lomar, who are known for their "scruples of honour" (*D* 22).	
*See endnotes for a list of abbreviations.	

is at times sinister and at other times benevolent. Indeed, even Lovecraft's benevolent father figures, whom Peter Cannon perceptively traces to Lovecraft's "uncles and grandfather"[258] (what Herbert West in "Reanimator" somewhat impatiently calls examples of "'the professor-doctor type'"),[259] are fraught with caveats: West's best friend observes that "age has more charity for these ... tradition bound elders"[260] than he. These are the men who, as Randolph Carter similarly complains, in markedly paternal terms, still persist in believing in the "gentle churchly faith"[261] associated with the "naïve *trust of his fathers*" (italics mine); men such as Dr. Willett in *The Case of Charles Dexter Ward*, who in his distress speaks seriously of things such as the "'Blessed Saviour'"[262] (a notion that Lovecraft will slyly invert in the same story by giving Ward's resurrected ancestor Jesus Christ's own initials; this echoes, as well, the name of Carter's uncle Chris in "The Silver Key").

In "The Strange High House in the Mist," too, it is the supposedly wise "patriarchs"[263] of Kingsport who "dread" the house perched high on the cliffs above, while it is the "young men" and "venturesome youths" of the town who "long to extract some hint of the wonders that yawn at the cliff-yawning door." Lovecraft's attitude here toward these conservative elders perhaps provides a revealing window on Lovecraft's own ambivalent and perhaps restive response to his male relatives. The benevolent and respected Dr. Halsey in "Reanimator" is ultimately reduced by the youthful Herbert West from a heroic figure to the very epitome of bestiality and cannibalistic degradation; and whereas even West could not help but admire Halsey's previous fortitude and strength as he helped to fight a typhoid epidemic in town, after his reanimation poor Halsey is described as being like "a malformed ape or anthropomorphic fiend,"[264] and later (in a grotesque caricature of Lovecraft's own father) as being locked into an asylum cell "where it beat its head upon the walls of a padded cell for sixteen years."[265] Thus the difference between Lovecraft's benevolent and malevolent father figures is sometimes razor thin, and his later cosmic and elder entities also reflect such inherent ambiguities.

Interestingly, psychoanalyst Ernest Jones traces the dichotomy discernable between God the Father and The Devil to much the same paternal ambivalence. And whereas the idea of God has its origin in the infantile experience of the all-powerful, all-knowing, and all-punishing father, the Devil symbolizes the father in his more capricious, violent, or sexually active aspects. Jones directly traces the origin of the medieval Devil, or Black Man, to what he calls the "darker, 'evil' side of the father's nature and activities,"[266] which the son wishes to both emulate and defy. The Devil, revealingly, often plays "the part of the friendly father"[267] in medieval legends. (Nathaniel Hawthorne alludes to this same paternal–Devil connection in *The Scarlet Letter*, in which the pagan elf-child Pearl innocently asks if her tortured Puritan father is the "Black Man."[268]) Later, too, H. P. Lovecraft will (and entirely without the irony of Hawthorne) present this same Black Man as the consort of the witch Keziah Mason in "The Dreams in the Witch House," where he will likewise be characterized by Lovecraft's trademark giganticism, described as both "tall"[269] and "huge."[270] (In "The Thing on the Doorstep," too, Lovecraft will specifically call the bizarre father figure Ephraim Waite "that devil."[271] In "The Call of Cthulhu" he revealingly refers to as "a supreme elder devil or *tornasuk*,"[272] who is made the subject of "certain queer hereditary rituals" of the Cthulhu Cult. The language strangely recalls that sacrifice of the wife and mother of the father-and-son alchemists' to the Devil in "The Alchemist," and is symbolic, perhaps, of an unconscious belief in the betrayal of his own mother at the hands of his father. And perhaps Lovecraft feared that he would, like Charles le Sorcier, follow his father in perpetuating such paternal rites.)

The Devil also has numerous other, less obvious, corollaries in the Lovecraftian weird canon. The Devil, as we have seen, is often being depicted as a "giant,"[273] again reflecting that giganticism that characterizes the infantile perception of the parents. The Devil, too, much like the classical giants before him, was also known for his cyclopean architecture. As Ernest Jones observes, in medieval legends the Devil often demonstrates an interest

> in building, one that we would trace ontogenetically to one of the infantile conceptions of parental child-making; according to this babies — and therefore other interesting objects — are constructed out of intestinal contents, an interest which later becomes transferred to the idea of formations out of sand, mortar, etc. Wunsche writes: "On closer examination all the sagas in which the Devil erects

mighty dams that run straight across lakes, cyclopean walls, and bridges that range high into the sky and lead over abysses, ravines and valleys prove to be Christianized giant sagas of various localities."[274]

Although Lovecraft's recurring uses of the term "cyclopean" are far too numerous to ever be listed here, it is in an infantile conception of the life-giving abilities of parents that we must similarly locate the equally grand scale of Lovecraft's recurring cyclopean constructions, including masonry that "soared up beyond the sight"[275] in *The Dream-Quest of Unknown Kadath*, the "dizzy giganticism"[276] and "titan terraces" in "The Mound," and the "hideously ancient wall or causeway"[277] discovered in "Celephais," described by Lovecraft as being "too gigantic ever to have risen by human hands, and of such a length that neither end of it could be seen." Occasionally, such constructions even reveal their parental origins, such as "those brooding ruins that swelled beneath the sand like an ogre under a coverlet"[278] in "The Nameless City" (but do *ogres* hide under coverlets, or do *parents*?)[279] As Ernest Jones points out, "The sadistic view of sexual functions which so many children hold explains why the parent so often appears in the dream in the symbolic guise of an aggressive animal or monster"[280] (an idea that is perhaps reflected in Lovecraft's transformation of the primal scene [i.e., parental intercourse] into the cosmic chaos witnessed by Danforth at the end of *At the Mountains of Madness* [further discussed in chapter 6]).

Lovecraft likewise replicates the most primitive aspects of father-worship in his repeated association of his gigantic entities with wind and thunder. The god Zeus, for example, was called both "'the Thunderer'"[281] (an appellation later used in "Poetry and the Gods"),[282] and "'the Great Father,'"[283] with "All-Father"[284] being an additional paternal epithet. The one reinforces the other: thunder and the masculine, eruptive phenomena of lightning are typically regarded as manifestations of the masculine principle, and, by extension, as a divine (paternal) punishment for the violations of some fatherly infraction. (Zeus punished Semele by consuming her with lightning.) Tellingly, anthropologist H. R. Hays describes Zeus' character in Hesiod's myths as that of an "irascible parent who will not tolerate the desire of his children for the privileges of an adult,"[285] an attitude that likewise characterizes the equally retributive, and likewise archetypal paternal, Yahweh of the Old Testament. Such paternal authority is likewise, by extension, often invested in the figure of the tribal king; the kings among the Polynesians, for instance, were believed to possess a *mana* that they "transferred to the land and the people from the sky — a power dramatized by such phenomena as thunderstorms and heavy surf."[286]

Lovecraft himself reflects something of this paternal thunder symbolism at the climax to "The Dunwich Horror," in which the thunder and lightning attendant upon the abortive appearance of the unseen father, Yog-Sothoth, are described in obviously archetypal and ancestral terms: "from what unplumbed gulfs of extra-cosmic consciousness or *obscure, long-latent heredity*, were those half-*articulate thunder-croakings* drawn?"[287] (italics mine) — language that strangely recalls Charles le Sorcier's "rumbling voice"[288] in "The Alchemist." Indeed, in "The Strange High House in the Mist," Lovecraft practically underlines this paternal aspect of thunder: he describes "The Terrible Old Man" as a fount of lore imparted to him by his father and his grandfather. Significantly, part of this patriarchal lore involves "lightning that shot one night up from the peaked cottage to the clouds of higher heaven"[289]; while the ancient gods that Olney encounters there will be said to vanish amid "echoes of thunder."[290]

There are numerous instances in which Lovecraft, improving upon the climax to Poe's "House of Usher," has a helpful (and divine?) thunderbolt come to the aid of his protagonists at a climactic moment, such as in "The Picture in the House," when "the titanic thunderbolt of thunderbolts"[291] blasts the patriarchal, cannibalistic house in which the narrator is trapped, or in "The Tomb," in which "the older inhabitants of the region sometimes speak in hushed and uneasy voices; alluding to what they call 'divine wrath,'"[292] with reference to "a peal of thunder, resonant even above the din of the swinish revelry,"[293] which long ago destroyed the bacchanalian mansion of the decadent Hydes. In both cases, the divine and benevolent aspect of the masculine principle swoops down to destroy the bestial and degenerative aspects of this same masculinity. In "The Lurking Fear," however, we see the characteristic obverse of this divine association; here Lovecraft incongruously combines the idea of divine retribution with the cannibalistic and orally sadistic, writing of how "on a summer night a bolt had come out of the heavens and left a dead village whose corpses were horribly mangled, chewed, and clawed."[294]

Indeed, "The Lurking Fear" in particular showcases Lovecraft's fascination with the symbolism of thunder. The paternal, hereditary horrors of the story are obsessively linked with the omnipresent "thunder in the air,"[295] since the murders that so oddly stir the narrator's macabre interest are most frequent after particularly violent thunderstorms. "Some said the thunder called the lurking fear out of its habitation,"[296] as Lovecraft explains, "while others said the thunder was its voice." The incestuous and cannibalistic Martense family is even called "thunder-crazed,"[297] while the monster that stalks the countryside is described simultaneously as "a giant"[298] and "a thunder-devil." None of this makes any sense whatsoever, unless, of course, one accepts the connections that we have been tracing regarding these related themes of paternalism, giganticism, and the Devil. Lovecraft's narrator even observes how "the increasing thunder must have affected my dreams,"[299] a statement that reads as nothing less than an earlier version of the connection between paternalism and dreams as seen with Lovecraft's later Cthulhu.

This horrific aspect of paternal or familial thunderstorm imagery continues throughout the Lovecraftian canon. The narrator of "The Tomb," for example, after his necrophilic loss of virginity within the tomb, "conceived my present fear of fire and thunderstorms,"[300] of which "I had now an unspeakable horror." This anxiety is later paralleled by an equal dread of thunderstorms exhibited by Robert Blake in "The Haunter of the Dark"[301]; while Asenath Waite in "The Thing on the Doorstep" (who, again, actually is her own father) claims "to be able to raise thunderstorms."[302] In *The Case of Charles Dexter Ward*, too, young Ward exhibits "a curious interest in the weather"[303] while resurrecting his vampiric, father-figure ancestor, Joseph Curwen; and indeed, Curwen's resurrection itself is accompanied by what Lovecraft suggestively calls "a sharp thunderstorm, anomalous for the season, which brought with it such a crash that Mr. and Mrs. Ward believed the house had been struck."[304] In Lovecraft's "The Other Gods" (1921), meanwhile, the hero Atal is repulsed by the gods when he attempts to witness their bacchanalian dancing upon a high mountain peak; his repulsion is accompanied, characteristically, by a "terrible peal of thunder."[305] Afterward, an enormous (and indeed, cyclopean) symbol is found chiseled on the enormous summit; Atal's quest to see the gods' forbidden bacchanale thus mirrors both the earlier bacchanalian revels of the Hydes (admittedly writ large) attended by a curious Jervas Dudley, as well as the child's curiosity about parental fornication, here accompanied by infantile perceptions of parental giganticism and punishment, presented in an almost biblical story about transgression and guilt.

The well known odor that invested the Devil's person, too — called by Ernest Jones a "hellish stink"[306] — was likewise, according to Jones, "largely associated with his capacity of making thunder." Jones goes on to speak of what he calls the "well known" "flatus symbolism of thunder," an association that has its origin, he writes, and like so much else, in "infantile sexual symbolism."[307] (Indeed, this thunder-flatus connection is so prevalent that numerous examples could be adduced: from Aristophanes' *Clouds* to the recent movie trailer for the film *Ted* [2012]. Note too the obvious paternal imagery in the familiar nursery rhyme, "It's raining, it's pouring / The *old man* [the father?] is snoring." The familiar dare of the atheist, too, i.e., for God to strike him or her dead where they stand [presumably via lightning], in punishment for their disbelief, reflects a similarly patriarchal connection between the father and thunder.) Lovecraft's "The Dunwich Horror" shows that he himself was well aware of this thunder-odor connection: one of his rustic locals, in describing the path of destruction left behind by Wilbur Whately's gigantic, invisible brother, observes: "'They's suthin' ben thar! *It smells like thunder*'"[308] (italics mine). Lovecraft's overt concern with things such as "Mephitic vapors"[309] and "strange, evil odors" throughout his weird fiction, of course, is too well known to require further commentary here, save to say that its connection with the malevolent aspects of the paternal in his writings, however unexpected or unlikely, has possibly been overlooked.

This association of Satanic thunder with flatus has its obviously corollary in the idea of the divine and masculine properties of the wind. Ernest Jones, for example, cites several illustrative beliefs in this regard, reflecting a belief in the fertility of wind in ancient Greece, such as the fertilization of Ocyrhoe-Hippe by the West Wind,[310] while anthropologist Erich Neumann discusses the Ancient Egyptian belief that female vultures were impregnated by the wind[311]— an idea essentially rooted, Jones suggests, in the neurotic-infantile idea that "the act of procreation may consist in the passage of Flatus from one body to another."[312] And although the intense early interest in farts (remembered by anyone who has been to kindergarten) is intensely repressed throughout adult life, it still persists, as Jones argues, in such seemingly loftier forms as the spiritual idea of divine "action at a distance"[313] "or of peculiar powers of searching and penetrating." These ideas directly relate to something "penetrating in the manner of a gas," and are all ideas that Lovecraft recapitulates, in a cannibalistic and incestuous sense, via the seemingly omnipresent and far-reaching danger in "The Lurking Fear," in which the wholesale slaughter of an entire settlement is associated with the haunted Martense mansion, although the localities were "over three miles apart."[314]

Thus, too, do we find Dutee Harris in "The Shunned House" becoming "*a father* on that memorable night of September 23, 1815, *when a great gale drove the waters of the bay over half the town*"[315] (italics mine). The wind is directly linked, in this instance, with both fatherhood and heredity. The ghostly, undead male-female couple that guard the portal in "The Mound," too, are likened by Lovecraft, in their immaterial spirit form, to "a sudden wind blowing against me,"[316] and are further described as "unseen, formless, opposing hands laid on my wrists" (perhaps reflecting issues of overt parental control). The unseen but still horrifying tentacled Elder Things of the inner earth, which so terrify the Great Race in "The Shadow Out of Time" (and which are linked by Lovecraft with the paternal legend of the giant Buddai), are notorious for "their control and military use of *great winds*"[317] (italics Lovecraft's). This language recalls Lovecraft's military symbolism with regard to the patriarchal cats in *Unknown Kadath*, as well as his virile and manly view of the Roman republican army. (Lovecraft may have been influenced in this wind-imagery of the Elder Things by Perley Poore Sheehan's lost race story *The Abyss of Wonders* [Argosy, 1915], in which the mysterious, black, apelike slaves of the Golden Race sometimes travel in the form of a menacing hurricane or tornado, which moves with the "noise of a Cyclopean express."[318] This language prefigures Lovecraft's pervasive "cyclopean" language, as well as his famous shoggoth-as-subway imagery in *At the Mountains of Madness*.) Tellingly, any mention of these Elder Things is regarded as a strict taboo in the Great Race's society, much like any mention of the deceased mother in Denton Welch's *In Youth Is Pleasure*, or the ancestral spirits of some religions. Equally tellingly, Lovecraft describes the periodic attacks of these Elder Things as having "permanently coloured the psychology of the Great Race,"[319] perhaps testifying, again, to the extent to which Lovecraft himself recognized his own paternal obsession.

In "The Nameless City," too, Lovecraft directly confounds the "night-wind"[320] that "rattles the windows" with the restless ancient spirits that "stalked among the spectral stones of the city."[321] As the narrator observes — combining the symbolism of the wind with the animistic superstitions of the witch-doctor — he "must always remember and shiver in the night-wind till oblivion."[322] This is the very same night wind upon which the (fatherly?) ancestral ghoul later rides at the conclusion to "The Outsider," along with the other "mocking and friendly ghouls."[323] There is no reason, of course, for such undead creatures as ghouls, which traditionally haunt tombs and cemeteries, to ride the night wind, unless Lovecraft is explicitly identifying the deceased and the ancestral with the wind.

Significantly too, Lovecraft further connects this wind in "The Nameless City" with the familiar symbol of the Thesean door. The wind or reanimated spirits that stalk the city streets prove to emanate from "a small and plainly *artificial* door chiseled in the solid rock,"[324] which in turn (and just as in "The Alchemist") leads to yet another, this time already-opened, door, described as "a massive door of brass, incredibly thick and decorated with fantastic bas-reliefs." As usual, of course, Lovecraft's narrator finds it impossible to budge or close this final, intrauterine obstacle, observing instead that "I touched the open brass door, and could not move it. Then I sank prone to the stone floor." The exhausted narrator, just like Jervas Dudley before him, is content to simply sit and look "at the steps" leading downward into the womb-like realm, but "for the nonce dared not try them."[325] Like a Lovecraftian version of *Waiting for Godot*, that strange lassitude that, in the wake of Lovecraft's adolescence, gripped his entire life and prevented him from trying to build a new existence outside the familial home, is here given symbolic form.

It is significant, too, that this Thesean door of brass is found already open: the ancestral or revenant winds of the ruined city's restless dead apparently make a nightly transit between the desert ruins and the subterranean vault down below. As in "The Outsider," written in the same year, the ancestral spirits have left their grave; but unlike Lovecraft's Outsider, they have retained a means of returning into the earth. Thus, the climactic revelation of the story, when it comes, involves not the opening of the Theseus door by the young hero, but rather the slamming shut of this door in front of the hero, under pressure from the onrushing winds as they pass within. As Lovecraft observes: "The great brazen door clanged shut with a deafening peel of metallic music whose reverberations swelled out"[326]—a metallic version, of course, of thunder. Here, as elsewhere throughout his weird fiction, unseen parental forces, and not the significant hero, control the mechanisms of opening and liberation. (As we shall see in chapter four, a similar transit of windy spirits seems to play a role in Lovecraft's later conception of the moon-ladder in *At the Mountains of Madness*.)

In both "The Nameless City" and *At the Mountains of Madness*, too, Lovecraft speaks of the "rage"[327] of the wind and of its apparently "conscious malignity."[328] This is suggestive, again, of the angry Satanic obverse of divine retribution. Curiously, too, Dyer at first attributes the tampering with the equipment at their base camp to these same winds, which, he argues, "must have harbored singular curiosity and investigativeness."[329] The tampering, of course, has been done by the revived Old Ones, a term which, if we take *Mountains of Madness* as an elaboration upon the earlier plot of "The Nameless City," surely preserves something of the earlier story's ancestral or revenant conception, especially its association of winds with the restless dead. (Just as in "The Tomb" and elsewhere, in "The Nameless City" we see the usual Lovecraftian confusion between spaces symbolizing the womb and the tomb: the tunnel beneath the city proves to contain numerous cases that Lovecraft can only describe as being "hideously like coffins in shape and size,"[330] and he further refers to the innermost space of the tunnel as "the grave of unnumbered aeon-dead antiquities." As we shall see in chapter 6, this view of the maw of the inner earth as a realm of both fertility and death, is characteristic of the Mother Goddess, in both her beneficent and her malevolent aspects.) And just as with the immortal Cthulhu later on, Lovecraft's obsession with the revenant or restless dead in this story also takes the form of an ostensible immortality[331]; indeed, it is here, in "The Nameless City," that we first come across Lovecraft's famous immortality couplet later reproduced in "The Call of Cthulhu," although its basis here is clearly ancestral and necrophilic, rather than cosmic, in its complexion.

Immaterial parents and ancestors also loom large in Lovecraft's collaborative "The Diary of Alonzo Typer" (based upon a draft written by William Lumley), in which an occult investigator named Typer, exploring the haunted van der Heyl mansion, becomes aware of a number of sinister presences in the house, manifesting themselves at first as "the dissolving outlines of a gigantic black paw."[332] Soon, however, this paw begins to resolve itself into two separate forms; as the narrator tells us, "I have seen the paw again — sometimes alone and sometimes *with its mate*"[333] (italics mine). Lovecraft here specifically identifies the paw not only with the former ancestral denizens of the house, but also with a male-female (i.e., parental) pair. (This idea appears to be Lovecraft's own; for although in his original draft of the story, William Lumley does refer to the presences in the house as being male and female, nowhere does he speak of either mates or a specific male and female pair.) As we shall see, such married couples, doubtlessly representing Lovecraft's parents, later reappear (in both benevolent and malevolent guises) throughout his fiction.

Lovecraft's interesting choice of the word "paw" to describe the clutching, immaterial entities in this story, rather than the words *claw, fang,* or *talon,* found elsewhere throughout his weird fiction, recalls his use of the same term to describe the hand of that enormous (and perhaps paternal) "Unknown God of the Dead"[334] in "Under the Pyramids," whose giganticism and apotheosis both suggest aspects of the ancestral. (Tellingly, too, the narrator's vision of this God of the Dead is later dismissed as being a mere dream — again, much like Wilcox's dreams of the risen Cthulhu.) Lovecraft called his father "'Papa'"[335] while a toddler, "pa" (or "paw"), of course, merely being a common, shortened form of "papa." (In his original draft of the story, again, Lumley simply refers to these paws as "black clutching hands"[336] and "a black claw-like hand,"[337] and not "paws.") In "The Shadow Over Innsmouth," Lovecraft specifically uses the word "pa" in the highly suggestive context of old Zadok's tragic story of the death of his father during the Deep Ones' insurrection in the previous century: "'They rattled our door, but *pa* wouldn't open ... then he clumb out the kitchen winder with his musket to find Selecman Mowry an' see what he cud do ... never heerd o' my *pa* no more'"[338] (italics mine). The depth of emotion as Allen tells his story, with "tears ... coursing down his channeled cheeks into the depths of his beard," perhaps testifies to the extent of the adult Lovecraft's continuing anguish.

IV. The Patriarchal Beard

Yet another recurring aspect of the paternal found throughout Lovecraft's weird fiction is the patriarchal beard, a fact which is both ironic and significant, given his own marked aesthetic dislike for male facial hair. "Lovecraft hated all facial hair,"[339] L. Sprague de Camp writes; "He said: 'I'd as soon think of wearing a nose-ring as of growing a mustache.'" Lovecraft even managed to connect this curious antipathy with his polemical alignment with ancient Rome: Lovecraft wrote disgustedly, if playfully, in his letters about the "tufts and fringes of sickly fur!"[340] commonly found among the ancient Greeks, which he would contrast with the "decent, clean-shaven Roman nobleman of equestrian rank and consular dignity." As William Arrowsmith confirms, the "first trimming of the beard"[341] amongst ancient Romans was traditionally seen as being "symbolic of a boy's having attained to his manhood," immediately "preliminary to his donning of the man's garb, the *toga virilis*." But while ancient Rome certainly provided Lovecraft with a useful justification for his prejudices, there is also a reflection, here, of a reaction against the Victorian era of which his older male relatives formed a part, and during which excessive facial hair was common (Lovecraft's father even sports a mustache in a family photograph). Lovecraft's contemporary, Edmund Wilson (born 1895)—whose own fiction, despite Wilson's later reviling of Lovecraft's works in a review, presents numerous similarities to Lovecraft's own — similarly wrote in his *Memoirs of Hecate County* (1946) of "those unpretentious mustaches, characteristic of my father's era, that shaved off squarely at the ends as they were, with no smart points or rakish flourishes, make one wonder why they should have been thought ornamental."[342]

Lovecraft's arch-paternal figure Joseph Curwen notably adopts a false beard to disguise himself throughout the latter portion of *The Case of Charles Dexter Ward*; indeed, Lovecraft at first simply calls him "the bearded man,"[343] in addition to his Poe-like (and Zadok Allen–like) pseudonym of "Mr. Allen." The cannibalistic old man in "The Picture in the House," too, displays a long white beard that Lovecraft, in an earlier version of the story, explicitly declares to be "patriarchal."[344] As discussed in my essay "A Reprehensible Habit: H. P. Lovecraft and the Munsey Magazines" (forthcoming), Lovecraft seems to have been influenced in this latter image by his reading of George Allan England's *Darkness and Dawn*, although here as elsewhere, Lovecraft inverts the positive, heroic protagonist of England's story, who despite his "patriarchal hair and beard"[345] and ragged appearance is still a noble and resourceful man of action, into a bloodthirsty, sadistic, and subhuman brute.

Lovecraft's old man in "The Picture in the House" (December 1920) is a problematic figure. Unlike his earlier and more ambivalent Terrible Old Man (January 1920), the old man in this story is really and truly terrible, a devouring patriarchal figure whose immortality has bypassed the grave entirely, although like a vampire, he also survives upon human blood. At the same time, however, Lovecraft's use of a Puritan figure as an agent of evil in this story seems to be a sign of its technical immaturity, Lovecraft not yet having succeeded in fully integrating his pro–Puritan polemics within his weird fiction. (His decrying of Puritanism in "The Unnamable," too, as a poisonous straitjacket, also savors of this same polemical and technical immaturity.) Certainly, there is a very wide gap, here, between his picture of one of the Puritan or colonial fathers as a raving and animalistic beast, and his picture, elsewhere, of the "pious bliss"[346] previously enjoyed by the "rugged men" of New England's early period, who obeyed what Lovecraft revealingly calls the "laws and virtues *of our fathers*"[347] (italics mine). The bearded old man's casual allusions to his own acts of serial murder in the past, of course, including his successive killing of a district schoolmaster and a parson, read almost like the Deep Ones' insurrection in "The Shadow Over Innsmouth" in miniature. Their successive destruction of all of Innsmouth's churches, and the subsequent institution of a regime of cannibalism and idolatry are all due to yet another depraved New England patriarch, Captain Obed Marsh. By the time "Innsmouth" was written, however, Lovecraft had finally resolved the potential polemical ambiguity inherent in this idea of having a patriarchal, late-colonial figure acting as the basis for decay and degeneration, by splitting this paternal figure into two characters, having the elderly (and "bushy-bearded")[348] Zadok Allen represent the benevolent, if decayed, remnants of New England's aristocratic tradition, and Captain Obed Marsh act as an agent of idolatrous, perverse, and bacchanalian paternalism.

Significantly, as we have seen, Lovecraft practically dates the destruction of Innsmouth to the very night on which Zadok Allen's father died in 1846. The destruction of New England cultural continuity thus is intertwined together with the destruction of familial and paternal continuity. (As S. T. Joshi and David E. Schultz point out, too, Lovecraft roughly dates his narrator's flight from Innsmouth to the date of his own father's death: although, characteristically, he chooses to invert the date from July 19 to July 16.[349]) And significantly, Lovecraft praises artist Frank Utpatel's illustrations to "Innsmouth," "even if he does represent a long-bearded nonagenarian [Zadok Allen] as smooth-faced in one of them."[350] This *caveat* suggests how important the possession of a beard by his patriarchal figures was to him.

Lovecraft's ambivalent Terrible Old Man is also described as having "long white hair and beard"[351] about which the "small boys" in the neighborhood "love to taunt" him. Note here Lovecraft's suggestive and, ultimately, very odd juxtaposition of the Terrible Old Man's age with the size of the "small" boys, thus representing yet another formulation of Lovecraft's standard parental giganticism, albeit one that is stated in inverted terms, while at the same time still managing to convey the centrality of this issue to Lovecraft's mental (and literary) conceptions. Why *small* boys, for instance? Why not simply young boys, or children, or teenagers? Lovecraft's description of the children in this story as small, however, is quite typical of his weird fiction, in which children are usually described in diminutive terms: the sacrificial victim in "The Dreams in the Witch House," described as "a small white figure"[352]; the "small child"[353] taught by the old witch in "The Horror at Red Hook"; "small Romnod"[354] in "The Quest of Iranon," who is at times simply called the "small one"; the "small child"[355] who is taught to engage in acts of cannibalism and necrophilia by Pickman's ghouls; "the little boy with no father or mother"[356] in "The Cats of Ulthar," also called "small Menes,"[357] as well as his diminutive cognate-figure in the same story, called "little Atal the innkeeper's son," who Lovecraft emphasizes is "so small a boy"[358]; etc. — all are described in language so strikingly opposed to the standard terminology of giganticism and vastness used with regard to Lovecraft's enormous cosmic entities, and so consistent, that it is almost a classic formulation (and dichotomy). We have already noted, too, the numerous "*small* peasant children" murdered by the father and son in "The Alchemist," as well as the receptive ears of the "*small* boy" noted in "The Tomb." Needless to say, Lovecraft's continual opposition of small vs. large, vast, and ultimately cyclopean, preserves, on into adulthood, what is arguably the essential condition of childhood.

V. Conclusions

Lovecraft's engagement with the Theseus myth reveals a lifelong concern with — indeed, an ongoing obsession with — issues of family and paternity. Acutely intelligent, curious, and observant as a child, Lovecraft was doubtless very much aware of how different he was from other children due to his lack of a father. And, as he became aware of the real reasons behind his father's absence (whenever and however this realization occurred), this awareness of difference seems to have evolved into a feeling of profound alienation, closely linked with fears of disease, corruption, and the unclean. As Maurice Levy observes, "Just like the character of the tale of that name, he was an 'outsider.'"[359]

In his obsession with the figure of the Father, Lovecraft's works reveal an interesting commonality with the equally macabre expressionist and proto-expressionist artists and writers during this period (especially Alfred Kubin and Otto Weininger), who likewise evince a similar, albeit patricidal, obsession with the Father. Franz Werfel's novella *Not the Murderer*, Walter Hasenclever's play *The Son*, the overwhelming paternal anxieties of Franz Kafka, and the anti-patriarchal diatribes of bohemian German psychologist Otto Gross, typify the uneasy German relationship with the Father during the early 20th century; save that there, *contra* Lovecraft, these expressionist polemics were colored by the largely socialist, pacifist, and radical orientation of the expressionist movement, which saw the Father as a reflection of the larger patriarchal order of war, oppression, and social hypocrisy. (These same attitudes later merged seamlessly with the feminist progressive politics of the 1960s, which included a fanatical repudiation of patriarchy.) As scholar Mel Gordon observes of Hasenclever's *The Son*, "For the returning wounded and mentally-torn enlisted men, *The Son* fixed a clear blame for the world's problems on the old and powerful, with their rigid, controlling, and cowardly ways."[360] Lovecraft's association of the Father with sex, degeneracy, and sadistic decay is merely a conservative parallel of this European expressionist polemic. But whereas the themes in the expressionistic stories and plays are frankly patricidal, in Lovecraft's weird fiction we are instead confronted with an undead and homicidal father, whose curse and whose crimes are not stilled by the grave but rather stir in the night, like rats in the woodwork. The murder of the Father in Germany is replaced, by Lovecraft, with the unmanning or degeneration of the son, reflective, perhaps, of that tragedy unleashed on Winfield's family by his illness. True, Lovecraft's father only fell victim to a disease, but it was a disease that at the time, much like AIDS is now, was fraught with moral implications.

"Those tragedies of the turn of the century!"[361] as Edmund Wilson exclaims in his story "Ellen Terhune" while describing the death of Terhune's businessman father, whose financial ruin was followed by his suicide "in a cheap little New York hotel" after a life of dissipation and drink. The death of Lovecraft's father was very much the same: succumbing not during the glory of the Civil War, like Delapore's grandfather, or during the glory of World War I, like Delapore's son, his death was instead much more like that of Delapore himself, raving and unheroic, stripped of sanity and dignity in a nightmare cell. Lovecraft's own dreams of heroism died there with him.

As Ernest Jones observes in *On the Nightmare*, the "deepest conflicts"[362] in one's life are those related to one's "earliest relationships to the parents." And in much the same way that, as Jones writes, "the conception of the Heavenly Father is a subjective projection of the child's feelings about the earthly Father,"[363] so too do Lovecraft's gigantic "cosmic" entities reflect a giganticism of paternity: the father is rendered large by the furtive echoes of his presence, rendered frightening by the possessiveness of his sexuality, and rendered cosmically "indifferent" by his absence. This absence, however, is not untroubled by a certain restlessness and guilt, in the form of an undead and unnamable sexuality, signifying either the social curse of sexually transmitted disease or possibly the disquieting advent of puberty. (In his collaborative "The Diary of Alonzo Typer," for instance, Lovecraft writes of Typer's realization of his own ancestral "degeneracy"[364] and that "nameless sin" that he must "expiate" — an idea completely absent, one notes, from Lumley's original draft of the tale, in which there is no intimation whatsoever of a blood relationship between the hero and the sinister family of wizards whose home he is investigating.)

Lovecraft seems to have known all this; and although natural probity or Puritan reticence did not allow him to explicitly mention it, he seems to have consciously sought out and identified with the Theseus myth, in an attempt to wrestle with, and make use of, his hopeless paternal longing. And if this longing underlies the genesis of Lovecraft's best weird stories, then Lovecraft was bequeathed a magical inheritance indeed, even if (his father being, like Charles Dexter Ward's father, a "mere" businessman) Lovecraft was ultimately forced to forge his magical inheritance himself.

FOUR

From the Moon to the Pit
Lovecraft's Moon-Ladder

They laughed at me as "Prof. Moon,"
As a boy in Spoon River, born with the thirst
Of knowing about the stars.
They jeered when I spoke of the lunar mountains,

...

And the littleness of man.
But now my grave is honored, friends...
—"Alfonso Churchill," *Spoon River Anthology*, Edgar Lee Masters[1]

I. Describing the Indescribable

Fictional "evil entities,"[2] as H. P. Lovecraft told his young protégé Robert H. Barlow in the summer of 1934, "must be more fully described than mere formless shadows. It must be handled very carefully, he said ruefully." One can well appreciate Lovecraft's difficulty. On the one hand, it is exceedingly difficult to describe the patently indescribable, and disappointing to the reader to have fictional horrors too clearly etched. On the other hand, too much vagueness will, as S. T. Joshi observes, create "'a suspicion that the author himself did not have a fully conceived understanding of what the central weird phenomenon of the story is actually meant to be.'"[3]

In the latter camp, Joshi includes such Lovecraftian stories as the early, collaborative "The Green Meadow," whose "meandering vagueness,"[4] as Joshi writes elsewhere, robs it "of any cumulative power." But ironically, while "The Green Meadow" is rightly described by Joshi as "quite frankly, a pretty sorry excuse for a story," it is also, like much of Lovecraft's earlier, classically-inspired poetry, quite valuable in a critical sense, since it aids us in identifying key concepts and ideas underpinning the more complex cosmology of his later fiction. And in the various "weird and terrible things"[5] that Lovecraft's Grecian narrator sees in this tale, such as those "dark vaporous forms" that "hovered fantastically" in the sky, we find something that helps to illuminate — however fitfully — some of those things about which the half-mad Danforth so disjointedly and irresponsibly whispers at the end of *At the Mountains of Madness*, including Lovecraft's cryptic and mysterious "'moon-ladder.'"[6]

Interestingly, Lovecraft has Danforth himself, during his more lucid moments, attribute the curious elements in this final vision "to his curious and macabre readings of earlier years"[7] — a statement that, although it refers to Danforth's unwise delving into the pages of the *Necronomicon*, also suggests to us the role played in his own weird fiction by Lovecraft's course of early reading in Edgar Allan Poe, classical writers in 18th century translation, the

Greek vase painting showing the ancient ceremony of women "drawing down the moon." Could this be an earlier version of HPL's mysterious moon-ladder from *At the Mountains of Madness*, which seems to connect Gaia, the primal goddess of the earth, with the sinister and Astartean moon above? From William Hamilton, *Collection of Engravings from ancient vases...* (1791–1795), vol. 3, plate 44 (Art & Architecture Collection, Miriam and Ira D. Wallach Division of Art, Prints and Photographs, The New York Pubic Library, Astor, Lenox and Tilden Foundations).

cramped writings of the Puritan divines, vast amounts of pulp and mystery fiction, and astronomical (but still no less classical),[8] scientific texts. Nor is it any coincidence, perhaps, that Lovecraft's staid academic narrator, Dyer, tries to disguise Danforth's mad visions by using terms that echo those earlier "dark vaporous forms" that hovered in the sky in "The Green Meadow," observing dryly: "The higher sky, as we crossed the range, was surely vaporous and disturbed enough; and although I did not see the zenith, I can well imagine that its swirls of ice dust may have taken strange forms."[9] Ultimately, as we shall see, it seems as if these two seemingly unrelated conceptions: (1) Lovecraft's moon-ladder, and (2) his idea of immaterial, intangible, and upper-atmospheric forms in the mist—what he calls in "The Dunwich Horror" shapes "without sight or substance"[10]—were somehow intimately connected. This connection, however, given the overt interest of many Lovecraft readers in the more famous aspects of the his cosmology, such as Nyarlathotep or Cthulhu, has seldom been addressed.

II. The Moon-Ladder

> Carmina Vel Caelo Possunt Deducere Lunam.
> (Charms can even bring the moon down from heaven.)
> —Virgil, *Eclogues*[11]

The meaning of Lovecraft's "moon-ladder" has remained obscure. As critic Robert Waugh once asked, referring to the more bizarre aspects of Danforth's final vision: "Or what can we say at all of the windowless solids or the moon-ladder? At this point our hermeneutics collapse, and we have to regard Danforth, as does Dyer, as too susceptible to his reading, too deeply read in the Necronomicon, so that his learning obstructs his ability to understand his experience."[12] To say this, however, is to take the strained and desperate hypothesis of Lovecraft's staid narrator at face value, as well as to suggest that Lovecraft himself was somehow insensible as to the meaning and implications of his own fiction, in defiance of Lovecraft's own views about the insufficiency of "mere formless shadows" as the embodiment of the "evil entities" within weird stories.

On the contrary, the moon-ladder itself appears in various guises—as a beam, a path, a road, a bridge, and simply as a rapid rising and falling—throughout Lovecraft's writings. Usually it features four components: (1) the moon at the top of the ladder; (2) the pit or inner earth at the bottom (what the crazed Danforth calls the "'black pit'"[13] during his final vision); (3) grasping and tactile, yet somehow still immaterial and unseen entities lurking in between; and (4) some sort of hypnotic influence that afflicts Lovecraft's characters, very often resulting in their deaths, usually by drowning. Unlike the biblical Jacob's Ladder (Genesis 28:10–19), which formed a bridge between Heaven and Earth, and facilitated the travel of angels ascending and descending the ladder, Lovecraft's moon-ladder seems to facilitate the travel of misty alien entities, who travel an endless circuit of lunar and subterranean corruption. And like the moon itself, which appears throughout Lovecraft's writings in various feminine, lycanthropic, and sentimental or romantic aspects, his moon-ladder also includes feminine, mythological, and sexual echoes, and ultimately seems to represent a cosmicized version of the Astartean or Dianic aspects of the moon and the allied Gaia-aspects of Mother Earth, of which Lovecraft was well aware in his earlier classical poetry.

One recalls, again, Lovecraft's *Poemata Minora or, Minor Poems* (1902), whose "Ode to Selene" sings ecstatically of the "maiden splendour"[14] of Diana, the goddess of the moon. As late as 1921, in his poem "To Mr. Galpin," Lovecraft writes fondly of how "Adown the *moonbeams' misty road* / The nymphs celestial dance their way"[15] (italics mine); here the misty road is already conceived as both a means of transport from the moon to the earth and as a conveyance for the cosmically feminine. In his poem "Revelation" (1919), however, this feminine road is imagined in much more sinister terms. Lovecraft this time uses the goddess Astarte as a synonym for the horned moon. And although the poem begins in a "gorgeous glade,"[16] akin to those in Lovecraft's earliest pastoral poetry, the poet, in a fit of immoral (and seemingly autoerotic) avarice, wishes to ascend to the "celestial poles of light" above him:

> Madly on *a moonbeam ladder*
> > Heav'n's abyss I sought to scale,
> Ever wiser, ever sadder,
> > As the fruitless task would fail.
>
> Then, with futile striving sated,
> > Veer'd my soul to earth again,
> Well content that I was fated
> > For a fair, yet low domain;... [italics mine]

But although the poet returns to earth, he now finds nothing about him but burning desolation and terror, with the sylvan "dell, of shade denuded / By my desecrating hand." The trip up and down the moon-ladder has brought (masturbatory) destruction. Lovecraft's language here is suggestive of the autoerotic aspects of Asenath Waite, who could "make any dog howl by certain motions of her right hand,"[17] or his narrator in "The Shadow Out of Time," for whom, as Lovecraft writes, "In my whirling brain there had begun to beat a certain rhythm which set my right hand twitching in unison. I wanted to unlock something,'"[18] shortly before he begins his own dizzying journey up and down the moon-ladder. There is, too, the "huge grey quill"[19] that the old witch Keziah Mason thrusts "into Gilman's right hand" during his nightmarish and sexual initiation into the witch-cult in Arkham; and then, of course, there is the "satyr-like"[20] Erich Zann's "long, cold, bony right hand,"[21] which plays such an important part during his solitary orgies alone in his room. For Lovecraft's poet, too, the (sexual) pleasures of heaven were unscalable, being undermined by their brutish, erotic origin; the poet ultimately is unable to escape his "low domain."

In his Poesque poem "Unda; or The Bride of the Sea" (1916), too, Lovecraft describes what he calls "*a bright bridge* made of wavelets and beams"[22] (italics mine), which grows "*Straight from the moon to the shore* where I'm sighing," "Wand'ring *from earth to the orb* of sweet dreams." At the same time, the face of the maid whom the poet loves appears in the moonlight, hypnotically beckoning the poet out along what Lovecraft calls this "beam bridge" toward her. Her urging, however, cloaks deception and leads to the poet's death by drowning:

> Currents surround me, and drowsily swaying,
> Far on the *moon-path* I seek the sweet face.
> Eagerly, hasting, half panting, half praying,
> Forward I reach for the vision of grace [italics mine].

The waters then close over the head of the poet, but he does not care, enveloped in the primordial liquid medium of the eternal Feminine. (As we shall see, this image of drowning recurs throughout Lovecraft's life and writings, where it seems to represent a return to the eternal womb of nature.) In "Nyarlathotep" (1920), too, Lovecraft speaks of "something coming down from the greenish moon"[23] at the beginning of Nyarlathotep's apocalyptic reign, eventually resulting in a form of mass hypnosis that causes people to begin to form "curiously involuntary marching formations," although there is no hint of drowning here: the narrator's dissolution occurs in darkened chambers beyond time, in which the universe itself disintegrates into cosmic chaos (an image perhaps inspired by Garrett P. Serviss' *The Moon Metal*, in which the evil Dr. Syx hypnotizes an audience with an apocalyptic magic lantern show depicting the destruction of the earth by the moon).

This same curious marching formation later reappears in a specifically feminine context in "The Moon-Bog," in which a fatal hypnosis is instilled in a line of peasant laborers, either by the naiads, the priestess of the moon, or by the goddess Artemis herself; Lovecraft's story never makes it quite clear which (although such confusions between priestess, nymph, and goddess are characteristic of the archetype of the eternal Feminine). Reduced to a state of "doglike"[24] submission by the feminine forces emanating from within the buried temple of Artemis, the workers follow a line of naiads "with blind, brainless, floundering steps as if dragged by a clumsy but resistless demon-will," until they are finally drowned or transformed into animals. And, just as in *At the Mountains of Madness* later on, the story climaxes with a sighting of the moon-ladder — described here by the narrator, like Danforth's later maddening vision, as one of the "fantastic incidents"[25] that "unhinged me utterly" — that takes the form of "a beam of faint quivering radiance having no reflection in the waters of the bog."[26] And it is "upward along that *pallid path*" (italics mine) that Lovecraft's narrator thinks he sees the wraithlike shadow of his friend Denys Barry "slowly writhing, a vague contorted shadow struggling as if drawn by unseen demons." The lascivious naiads of Lovecraft's 1921 "Galpin" poem are here reduced to demons akin to those in Cotton Mather's Puritan theology, in the context of what is essentially a sexualized night flight, characteristic of nightmare and dream imagery (as discussed further below).

For example, in Cotton Mather's *The Wonders of the Invisible World* (1692) (which we know that Lovecraft read), Mather refers to what he calls "those *Wicked* Spirits, whose temptations trouble us,"[27] and which make their home in what Mather calls "the *High Places* of Our Air," the same zone of the upper atmosphere in which Dyer and Danforth see the strange mist-effects in *At the Mountains of Madness* and that are suggestively described in "The Shadow Over Innsmouth" as "the unknown arcana of upper air and cryptical sky."[28] (Nathaniel Hawthorne reflects some of these curious Puritan beliefs in *The Scarlet Letter*, in which witch Mistress Hibbins offers to take the elf-child Pearl for a flight with her "some fine night"[29] to meet the "Prince of the Air," i.e., the Devil.) Indeed, although critic Maurice Levy traces Lovecraft's "major theme"[30] — what Levy calls his interest in "the diffuse and enveloping presence of the invisible"[31] — to the influence of Hawthorne, a more direct antecedent of both authors is Mather himself and the larger Puritan elite of which he was a part, whose archaic views (including a defense of slavery, a belief in the importance of a strictly hierarchical rule, and an apocalyptic belief in imminent societal decay) are so close to Lovecraft's own.[32] Like children peopling the dark with imaginary and frightening monsters, so too was the Puritan's world perpetually alive with unknown and invisible menace.

Significant, too, is Mather's odd and allied belief that once the Messiah returns, and what he calls the "the *Spiritual Wickedness in High Places*"[33] is done away with, the Devil will afterward "be clap't up, as a Prisoner in or near the Bowels of the Earth."[34] This idea prefigures, as we shall see, Lovecraft's repeated association of the upper air with the inner earth or the pit — what he himself calls "that inner world of subterrene horror of which dim legends tell, and which is litten only by the pale death-fire"[35] — not to mention prefiguring Lovecraft's repeated depiction of his weird entities as dwelling in some sort of a subterranean bondage, like the sleeping Cthulhu, forever awaiting the time when he can rise again. (Lovecraft perhaps makes a direct acknowledgement of this Puritan connection in "The Dunwich Horror," in which he admits that the odd acoustic phenomena in the tale inevitably suggest to the imagination "a conjectural source in the world of non-visible beings,"[36] an idea that immediately suggests the title of Cotton Mather's notorious 1692 book.) Mather's idea of the Devil's possession of "the Utmost parts of the Earth"[37] also figures equally strongly into Lovecraft's later mythos, with its almost Fortean implication of a non-human dominion and ownership of our planet. Typically, however, one notes that Lovecraft inverts the order of Mather's theology, so that whereas Mather believes God will confine the Devil in the inner-earth at end of time, for Lovecraft the apocalypse comes when Cthulhu is finally released from such bondage. Still, the close similarities between Lovecraft and Mather in this regard, as well as in other, socio-political issues, could easily account for what the oft-criticized August Derleth saw as Christian underpinnings of Lovecraft's fictional cosmology.

Lovecraft revisits, in more sophisticated form, the same interrelation between the moon, drowning, and the hypnotic in his collaborative "The Horror at Martin's Beach" (1922), written with his wife-to-be, Sonia, in which the deaths by drowning of dozens of sailors are caused by what Lovecraft and Greene call "'Hypnotic Powers,'"[38] here emanating from the eye of a seemingly feminine and maternal sea monster. And although often regarded as a minor effort (at best), and grouped, in Arkham House's volume of Lovecraft's revisions, among Lovecraft's secondary revisions (since, as Joshi observes, Lovecraft never regarded it as a true collaboration),[39] "Martin's Beach" is actually a very revealing work, at least insofar as it relates to his recurring weird symbolism and the complex cosmology later proffered in *At the Mountains of Madness*.

The story involves the revenge of a gigantic sea monster against the sailors who killed its apparent offspring, an enormous larval or infant creature nearly fifty feet long. Weeks later, a strange phenomenon begins offshore: an "unearthly ululation"[40] that the sea-captain and the scientists studying the infant monster believe to represent a party in distress and requiring help. Significantly, this ululation first begins "in the twilight, when ... *a rising moon* began to make *a glittering path* across the waters" (italics mine), a prototypical version of Lovecraft's later moon-ladder. Lovecraft suggests some additional sort of connection between the moon, the monster, and the waters:

> There is no exact record of the time the thing began, although a majority say that the fairly round moon was "about a foot" above the low-flying vapors of the horizon. *They mention the moon because what they saw seemed subtly connected with it*—a sort of stealthy, deliberate, menacing ripple which rolled in from the far skyline *along the shimmering lane of reflected moonbeams*, yet which seemed to subside before it reached the shore[41] [italics mine].

The "vapors of the horizon"—also called "the demons of the black waves and the night-wind"[42]—recall both the oceanic vapors in "Unda" as well as those mysterious "dark vaporous forms" seen in the sky in "The Green Meadow"; the vapors perhaps signify those immaterial alien entities that traverse the distance between the inner earth and the moon along the moon-ladder.

Tossing a life preserver toward the source of the cry from the waters, soon dozens of would-be rescuers are pulling without effect on the lifeline in a futile attempt to draw it back to shore. Lovecraft and Greene tell us in strangely masturbatory language of how, "hard as they tugged, the strange force at the other end tugged harder; and since neither side relaxed for an instant, the rope became rigid as steel with the enormous strain."[43] Indeed, the narrator goes on to describe the rope as growing "harder and harder"[44] in the water, its "strands" swelling "with the undisturbed soaking of the rising waves." This image has so much in common with the climactic first date of James Joyce and Nora Barnacle at Ringsend (as well as the ribald Latin poetry of Juvenal),[45] that one wonders whether Lovecraft and Greene's story was based upon an actual holiday that Lovecraft and Sonia Greene spent together at a seaside resort "in Gloucester and Magnolia"[46] in 1922, and whether Lovecraft and Sonia are, in this image, having rather a ribald joke at our expense. And just as in "The Moon-Bog," in which the hypnotized "line of followers, never checking their speed,"[47] tread unstoppably down beneath the waters and disappear, the line of rescuers here find themselves stuck in some "mysterious bondage to the hempen line which was slowly, hideously, and relentlessly pulling them out to sea,"[48] walking forward single-file in a "monotonously" "swaying" line to their doom.

Of course, assuming that Lovecraft is the primary author of the tale, it is more than likely he was influenced in this imagery by the various earlier hypnotic sea monsters in science fiction, such as the hypnotic-eyed (and, as we have seen, feminine) reptilian Mahars in Edgar Rice Burroughs' *Pellucidar* novels, or the saurian Cay monster in Frank Savile's *Beyond the Great South Wall: The Secret of the Antarctic* (*The Argosy*, 1899). In Burroughs' *At the Earth's Core* (*All-Story*, 1914), for example, human slaves, especially fattened for the kill, are hypnotized into walking one by one into a tank filled with staring-eyed, autocratic reptiles, who slowly proceed to eat them piece by piece, keeping them alive even after the most horrific mutilations,[49] an image that also influences Lovecraft's similar picture of the dead being "mechanically reanimated"[50] and then "mutilated" for the amusement of the decadent Tsathians in "The Mound." Lovecraft may also have been influenced by a similar hypnosis-sequence in *Beyond the Great South Wall*, in which Savile describes the "baleful glare"[51] of his giant saurian monster, whose "fascination"[52] drags its victims toward him "'like a puppy on a string,'" prefiguring both the later doglike simile for the victims in "The Moon-Bog" and the weirdly erectile aspects in his and Greene's later story. As Savile observes, the monster's long neck becomes "stiffened"[53] as it stares at its hapless victim, becoming as "stiff as a rope that warps a ship from the harbor" as it sways back and forth, accompanied by a corresponding rigidity and swaying in the body of the hypnotized sailor. (The title of Savile's novel may have influenced the title of Lovecraft's "Beyond the Wall of Sleep"; indeed, there are a number of close parallels between the titles of early *Munsey* science-fantasy tales and his later weird fiction, not the least of which is the similarity between Burroughs' *At the Earth's Core* and the title of *At the Mountains of Madness*.) Lovecraft's association of hypnotism with drowning, too, although doubtlessly rooted in his own thoughts of suicide, is also anticipated by Burroughs' saurian Mahar, who like the later Deep Ones are said to "habitually indulge their amphibian proclivities"[54] and who enjoy enacting their anthrophagous rites in special temple-pools constructed for the purpose.

"Martin's Beach" finally ends with the moon-path beginning to fade out as an apocalyptic blast of thunder crashes from the sky, described in incongruously cosmic terms as a "planet-rending peal of Cyclopean din,"[55] followed by a final "faint and sinister echoes of a laugh" heard "from some abysmal sunken waste" (an intimation of the sub-oceanic Cthulhu?). Danforth's final backward glance in *At the Mountains of Madness* is foreshadowed here by the "livid face of a backward-glancing victim gleaming pale in the darkness"[56] as the final cataclysm falls. As S. T. Joshi observes, apocalyptic passages such as these in this story come "off sounding forced and bathetic,"[57] mainly because "there has been an insufficient build-up." But even so, Lovecraft and Greene's curious attempt to somehow link an "infuriate *sky*"[58] and a "voice of *heaven*" with a "laugh" emanating from "some *sunken* waste" (italics mine) already prefigures the parameters of Lovecraft's later moon-ladder, in which above is somehow connected with below, and the cosmic is connected with the subterranean.

Lovecraft and Greene's curious notion that this satanic alliance between

Above and Below has the ability to rend a planet, too, further foreshadows the cosmological idea in *At the Mountains of Madness* (perhaps derived from England's *Darkness and Dawn*, in which a similar cataclysm is presented)[59] with regard to the origins of the moon in an ancient cataclysm, in which the future lunar matter was somehow ripped from the bowels of the earth. This cataclysm is simultaneously linked by Lovecraft with the sudden rising of a sinister land mass from the bottom of the ocean in the nearby Antarctic, a place "which had come to be shunned as vaguely and namelessly evil"[60] by the Old Ones. Lovecraft seems to be suggesting some sinister and perhaps alien agency at work here, one that makes its home in the corrupt spaces of the inner earth, and that somehow threw off the moon and pushed these mountains (called by Dyer the "focus of earth's evil")[61] up from below, and whose corruption now spans both bodies, earth and moon, as well as the linked tether between them. (Lovecraft locates the moon's origin in the South Pacific,[62] which suggests a connection with Lovecraft's allied picture of the South Seas as a hotbed of activity for both the Deep Ones and the Cthulhu Spawn. This idea perhaps partially owes its origin to stories such as A. Merritt's "The Moon Pool" [*All-Story*, 1918] or Francis Stevens' "The Nightmare" [*All-Story*, April 1917], which were likewise set in the Pacific. In his sequel to *Polaris—of the Snows* [*All-Story*, 1916], too, entitled *Minos of Sardanes* [*All-Story*, 1916], *Munsey* author Charles Stilson also associates the South Seas with the Antarctic in this fashion, observing: "As islands appear suddenly from the depths of the South Pacific, so had volcanic forces upheaved the Antarctic sea bottom."[63] If nothing else, such passages suggest the incubation of Lovecraft's later cosmology in the recurring motifs of early pulp fiction.)

This new and evil mountain range, which arises in the neighboring Antarctic after the moon is torn away from the earth, meanwhile, is perpetually concealed from view by what Lovecraft calls a "vague opalescent haze"[64] in the distance; a churning western mist that again recalls to mind those vaporous forms in both "The Green Meadow" and "Unda," and which Lovecraft significantly connects with "primal mists of the pits at earth's core"[65] in this same story, suggesting some means of transit between the inner earth and the mountains high above. (This misty/vaporous polar imagery was also quite common in the early science-fantasy stories that Lovecraft read as a youth, such as Stilson's *Polaris of the Snows* and possibly Lee Robinet's *Thyra, a Romance of the Polar Pit* [book pub., 1901], in which hidden colonies of lost races surviving at the poles are often hidden from view by smoking volcanic mountains or craters,[66] which provide a temperate environment amidst the ice and snow. Lovecraft likewise hints at some process of volcanism[67] to account for this rising mist.) Lovecraft may also have been influenced in his association of the subterranean pit with the celestial zenith by A. Merritt's masterful "The People of the Pit" (*All-Story*, 1918), in which a sinister range of mountains in the northern wilderness looks over an enormous, abyssal canyon on the other side, whose bottom is clouded with vapors; Merritt likens the experience of looking out over the canyon to "'peeping over the edge of a cleft world down into the infinity where the planets roll.'"[68]

Lovecraft, too, as if to accentuate this sinister alliance between the moon and the inner earth, describes this forbidden mountain range to the west as being "like the serrated edge of a monstrous alien planet about to rise into unaccustomed heavens"[69] — something, again, which in fact happened earlier, when the moon was either expelled or torn away from the early earth. Evil above is equated with evil below, with perhaps a meeting place between them, located in the westward mountains, a meeting place perhaps identical with that private, forbidden bacchanalia of the gods that Atal, in "The Other Gods," so desired to surreptitiously observe upon the mountain top. That bacchanale is ultimately identical to that commerce with the gods (cosmic copulation) that was once enacted upon the tops of the Babylonian ziggurats, whose summit was seen as the house of the God. Indeed, Lovecraft's forbidden mountains, forever hidden in that subterranean haze that is piped up from below, are even provided with a rampart (whether naturally occurring or not, Lovecraft does not specify)[70], perhaps for that purpose.

Of course, if Lovecraft's inner earth is the home to some unknown and intangible force of absolute evil, and the moon was wrenched out of this same inner earth, it makes sense that the moon should continue to provide a residence for these same forces, and that the feminine forces of the satanic or corrupt underworld should somehow be related to or aligned with the hypnotic and feminine forces of the Dianic moon. And if the same evil forces dwell in both locations, there should remain a line of connection or communication between them via a link, or a tether, or ... a ladder. Indeed, Lovecraft hints at just such an idea in "The Shadow Out of Time," when his narrator speaks of having once made contact with "a mind from a large asteroid on which had survived much of the archaic life and lore of the primal planet whereof it formed a fragment."[71] In much the same way, one thinks, the sinister lore and corruption of the inner earth could have gone on to survive upon or infest the moon. Hence, too, Lovecraft's explicit linking of what he calls the supposed lifelessness of the "sterile disc of the moon"[72] to the landscape of the Antarctic wasteland explored by Dyer and Danforth: the two locales mirror each other, share a common origin, and, ultimately, form a habitat for the same immaterial, unnatural, and perhaps eternal forms of life.

III. A Rising and a Falling

> "I remember the square of moonlight on the floor, that wasn't
> like any other light, and the visions that danced in the
> moonbeams when my mother sang to me."
> — H. P. Lovecraft, "The Quest of Iranon" (1921)[73]

Lovecraft refers to this connection between the upper air and the inner earth throughout his weird fiction. In "The Dunwich Horror," Dr. Armitage's battle with Wilbur Whately's cosmic brother gives rise to "a rumbling sound brewing beneath the hills, mixed strangely with a concordant rumbling which clearly came from the sky."[74] Listeners later hopelessly confuse the two, speaking of a "deafening, cataclysmic peal whose source, be it inner earth or sky, no hearer was ever able to place."[75] Indeed, many other critics have noted this apparent confusion in Lovecraft's works between upper and lower: critic Robert Waugh calls it the apparent connection between "the journey up and the journey down,"[76] and critic Maurice Levy similarly calls it a "coming-and-going between two gulfs."[77] As Levy observes, to rise in Lovecraft's stories is also often "to descend or to fall"[78]; and with Lovecraft, the "deep is *also* above." But although both Waugh and Levy both note Lovecraft's curious obsession with the abyss, and Levy perceptively links Lovecraft's conception of "hidden abysms of the Cosmos"[79] with the "secret depths of the earth," neither make the obvious connection between the Feminine and this obsession with dark abysms, despite the clearly sexual basis of Lovecraft's recurring night flight imagery.

Consider the characteristic form taken by Lovecraft's cryptic moon-ladder near the end of "The Call of Cthulhu," when Johansen's ship is caught up in a (possibly cosmic) storm during his escape from a risen R'lyeh. Lovecraft writing of "a sense of spectral whirling through liquid gulfs of infinity, of dizzying rides through reeling universes on a comet's tail, and of *hysterical plunges from the pit to the moon and from the moon back again to the pit*"[80] (italics mine). As he later makes clear, this vision is but a "dream,"[81] but it is a dream replete with psychological meaning, especially given what psychologist Ernest Jones has written on significance of such travel or night flight experiences in his classic study *On the Nightmare*. Folkloric beliefs in witches on broomsticks, or in shamanic astral travel, are also ultimately derived from what Jones calls "the familiar 'flying dream' experiences,"[82] which are themselves, in turn, rooted in a feeling of sexual arousal in the sleeper. One thinks of John Webster's *The Duchess of Malfi* (1623), where Webster writes of "this rage, which carries you, / As men conveyed by witches through the air, / On violent whirlwinds!"[83] This imagery already betrays an essentially sexual origin, in this case the basic masculine fantasy of men riding upon women. The idea parallels the "carrying" imagery so common to Lovecraft's writings, such as the riding of the cultists upon the hybrid winged creatures in "The Festival," the carrying away of Kuranes by his nurse in Lovecraft's "Celephais"[84] (an idea later cosmicized via Keziah Mason's carrying away of a sleeping Walter Gilman in "The Dreams in the Witch House"),[85] or the carrying away of the five-year-old Lovecraft himself by the ambivalently sinister night gaunts of his nightmares, which tickled him even as they terrified him. (That the "hybrid winged things"[86] upon which the cultists ride in "The Festival" stand in some relation to "'the wings'"[87] likewise sighted by Danforth at the end of *At the Mountains of Madness* seems likely.) According to Jones, too, the common belief in "the idea of the psychopompic bearing away of souls"[88] can likewise be traced "to the 'angstvolle Traumfahrt' (the dreadful dream travel or flight)," an idea that likewise has numerous affiliations in Lovecraft's dream-inspired weird fiction, from the psychopompic whippoorwills in "The Dunwich Horror" to the psychopompic vampire in "The Hound," with its "accursed web-wings."[89]

The etiology of all this night flight imagery in his early nightmares about the night gaunts is significant, as it conforms to Jones' locating of these dreams in a specifically "infantile"[90] mindset, with their "ultimate source"[91] in "the sexual excitation of various movements (dandling, chasing, etc.) in early childhood; the phenomenon of erection is in both sexes the kernel of the whole conception of flying." Indeed, children, because of their relatively small size as compared to adults, are far more susceptible to such treatment than most grownups; as psychologist Leontine Young observes, the child is often "patted, pinched, even kissed and picked up by perfect strangers."[92] Lovecraft, of course, illustrates this idea perfectly, with the tickling forced upon him by the night gaunts surely representing an analogue to those forms of infantile excitation noted by Jones; this sadistic infantilism in Lovecraft's fiction is later perpetuated even on into adulthood, via the night gaunts' tickling of the grown-up Randolph Carter in *The Dream-Quest of Unknown Kadath*, the tickling which the old man associates with sadistic sexual desire in "The Picture in the House,"[93] as well as via Lovecraft's own recurring dreams of flying or floating. Indeed, Lovecraft himself does much to confirm this nightmare-origin of his night flight imagery, describing the vaporous fall through space of his narrator Peaslee, for instance, as "the essence of pure nightmare."[94] (Lovecraft had an odd nostalgia for how the poet's mother used to rock him to sleep when he was a child in "The Quest of Iranon." Iranon's persistence in dwelling upon this rocking while a young man testifies to the degree to which infantile sensations persisted in gripping Lovecraft's adult imagination.)

Very often, too, as with Randolph Carter's adventures in Dreamland, Lovecraft's night flights are characterized by a repeated movement up and down; as Maurice Levy confirms, Carter "moves more often vertically, in height or in depths, than horizontally,"[95] with "flights and falls" following "one upon the other," although Levy, again, stops short of noting the basically sexualized origin of such imagery. In William Beckford's *Vathek,* for instance — which Lovecraft appreciatively read in July 1921[96]— we can also discern a hint of this same highly sexualized night flight imagery, when Baba-balouk (Prince Vathek's Black eunuch servant) is trapped upon a swing in Vathek's harem by the sexy Nouronihar and the other harem women, and jerked up and down. Later, a terrified (but obviously very stimulated) Baba-balouk dreams "that the phantom of Nouronihar, having mounted him once more on her swing, had just given him such a jerk, that he *one moment soared above the mountains, and the next sunk into the abyss.*"[97] Beckford here, like Lovecraft later on in *At the Mountains of Madness*, combines typically sexualized dandling imagery from infancy with mountainous and abyssal imagery. Beckford, indeed, was as interested as Lovecraft in the imagery of the feminine subterranean chasm, later, fearfully, associating the sound of Vathek's mother's approach with "a group of spectres, ascended from the abyss."[98] These are doubtless the same unseen, Satanic presences, with which the abyss is also populated in Lovecraft's weird fiction.

In "Hypnos," the sacrilegious cosmic explorations of the narrator and his mysterious friend are similarly described as *"plungings or soarings,"*[99] during which they repeatedly encounter a curious series of immaterial obstructions that continually impede their flight and are "describable only as viscous, *uncouth clouds of vapors*" (italics mine). This idea again recalls those bodiless vapors and invisible aerial presences prevalent throughout Lovecraft's weird fiction, here associated with a process of astral travel, such as was often found in the early science-fantasy published in the *Munsey* magazines. In "Under the Pyramids," too, Houdini's descent into a seemingly bottomless pit will be tellingly described as a "rising"[100] and a "diving," again in alliance with such related concepts as "bat wings" and "gulfs of hell" — archetypally feminine gulfs and abysses that Lovecraft here links to "the core of the planet itself"[101] and later on, in *At the Mountains of Madness*, similarly calls those "unfathomed regions of earth's core."[102] Indeed, Lovecraft practically underlines the joint feminine and orgasmic aspects of this night flight, as Houdini is captured, bound, and then lowered into a well of "prodigious, almost incredible depth"[103] (the archetypal Feminine pit), after which he undergoes a "mental cataclysm," described as the ecstasy of nightmare and the summation of the fiendish. The suddenness of it was apocalyptic and daemonic — one moment I was *plunging agonizingly down* that narrow well of million-toothed torture, yet *the next moment I was soaring* on bat-wings in the gulfs of hell; swinging free and swoopingly through illimitable miles of boundless, musty space; ... Thank God for the mercy that shut out in oblivion those clawing Furies of consciousness which half-unhinged my faculties, and tore Harpy-like at my spirit! [italics mine].

Just as with the tickling of the night gaunts, which the young Lovecraft felt to be a sort of torture, here the orgasmic suddenness of this aerial cataclysm is, despite the ecstasy which it also entails, simultaneously linked with the horrible. (Indeed, as Ernest Jones observes, this alternation between the voluptuous and the frightening is one of the essential traits of the nightmare, one which betrays the nightmare's origin as an essentially sexualized anxiety reaction.) The mention of furies and harpies, too, further underlines the feminine nature of this ultimately sexual rising and falling, an idea Lovecraft subtly revisits in *Mountains of Madness*, in which Dyer links the piping Antarctic winds with the call of the Sirens.[104] (It may be that Lovecraft was also influenced in this imagery by the second volume in England's *Darkness and Dawn* trilogy, *Beyond the Great Oblivion* [1913], in which hero Allan Stern's plummeting descent into the great abyss from which arose the earth's new moon is described in strikingly demonic [and, indeed, proto–Lovecraftian] terms as being like a "nightmare — a horrible dream of darkness and a mighty booming wind — a dream of stifling vapors and an endless void that sucked them down, down, down, eternally,"[105] Stern feeling as if he were being flailed by "some sinister and ghoul-like demon." In England's description of Stern's seeming battle against "the intangible" during his series of "mad downward rushes," during which his own screams are "mingled with wild, demonic laughter," one can again see an intimation of Lovecraft's later semi-demonic and intangible entities; although Lovecraft alone adds the specifically feminine aspects of Houdini's descent into the abyss, aspects that are merely latent in England's own abyssal imagery.)

Lovecraft also evinces a more localized and domestic fascination with such rising and falling imagery throughout his works, such as the "'black cellars an' attics'"[106] of Innsmouth, in which unknown monstrosities lurk, or the cellars and attics of the sinister Joseph Curwen.[107] Even in his ostensibly cosmic *At the Mountains of Madness*, Lovecraft is unable to resist referring to the subterranean tunnels of the Old Ones' city as existing in "the basement,"[108] language that suggests something of his own barely containable fascination in real life, when some buildings in his home town of Providence were razed and pits were found in some of the basements. As an excited Lovecraft intently asked mystified acquaintance Dorothy C. Walter and her chaperone, "Could we imagine for what purpose they might have been constructed?"[109] The structure of Lovecraft's moon-ladder is merely a cosmicized version of this same, more domestic fascination, one that mirrors his larger fascination with the omnipresent and all-powerful Feminine archetype, which also (as we shall see in chapter 6) encompasses both underworld and celestial aspects. The goddess Hecate, for example, was regarded as a three-fold goddess: identified with "Selene or Luna in heaven, Artemis or Diana in earth, and Persephone or Proserpina in the lower world,"[110] her body formed a microcosmic model for the moon-ladder itself. Like the vapors of the great abyss in *At the Mountains of Madness*, Hecate got around.

Such archetypal imagery is potent even today, with modern Wicca and neo–Pagan enthusiasts still promulgating a ceremony involving "drawing down the moon," whose imagery suggests something of Lovecraft's moon-ladder. As Margot Adler observes in her book *Drawing Down the Moon* (1979), many covens "have rituals in which the goddess, symbolized by the moon, is 'drawn down' into a priestess of the coven who, at times, goes into trance and is 'possessed by' or 'incarnates' the Goddess force."[111] The goddess often is "symbolized by the phases of the moon" and is "known by a thousand names,"[112] language which, not uncoincidentally, recalls Lovecraft's use of the cribbed chant "'Gorgo, Mormo, thousand-faced moon'"[113] in "The Horror at Red Hook." Indeed, although critics are often quick to note Lovecraft's usage of a passage from the *Encyclopædia Britannica* in this portion of "Red Hook," few have addressed the polemical reasons underlying his choice of this particular passage, which specifically invokes imagery of the Feminine and the lunar, and its relation to his larger concern with feminine evil in his writings. The moon-ladder also encompasses these same sexual and Feminine aspects.

Lovecraft's own poetry, as we have seen, was already filled with this joined imagery of the Feminine and the lunar, in the form of the goddesses Astarte, Selene, and Diana. And although critic T. R. Livesey suggests that interpreting Lovecraft's use of the moon as "a female symbol"[114] in his fiction is more problematic than it seems, given "the many different ways Lovecraft uses it," such a criticism ignores, as we have seen, the central role played by the moon in Lovecraft's cataclysmic cosmology in *At the Mountains of Madness*, and also his larger conception of the moon-ladder itself, which runs throughout Lovecraft's writings, eventually culminating in Danforth's final, startling revelation. Nor should the moon's different phases throughout Lovecraft's writings, or the "fact that the moon's appearance — and the mood it sets — changes radically during the course of lunation,"[115] act as any bar to such a feminine interpretation. True, Lovecraft associates the *full* moon with feminine sentimentality and romance in "Medusa's Coil," comparing it to "a spotlight at the varieties!"[116] But he also associates the horned *crescent* moon with Astarte in a 1933 letter to Clark Ashton Smith.[117] The moon's phase is different; the connection with the Feminine remains the same.

IV. The Origins of the Moon-Ladder

> [Art] makes and unmakes many worlds, and can draw
> the moon from heaven with a scarlet thread.
> — Oscar Wilde, "The Decay of Lying"[118]

Lovecraft's readings in the early pulps, even more than his classical studies, provided numerous suggestions of his later moon-ladder. In Dr. Garrett Putnam Serviss' novella *The Moon Metal*, for example, the mysterious mad scientist Dr. Syx uses a machine to draw down a new metal called artemisium (named after the moon goddess Artemis) along "'a shaft of flying atoms extending in a direct line between'" his laboratory "'and the moon.'"[119] (Lovecraft once admitted to having read every single published work by Serviss,[120] and also wrote a 1903 essay about the same streaks that radiate from the crater Tycho from which Syx derives his artemisium.[121]) Dr. Syx himself seems to have some mysterious link with the moon that Serviss never explicitly explains; the story ends with the defeated scientist suddenly rising toward the moon from a mountain top, at the very point at which the full moon seems to touch the distant mountains: "As I continued to gaze, as if entranced, the face and figure of the doctor seemed slowly to frame themselves within the lunar disk, until at last he appeared to have quitted the air and the earth and to be frowning at me from the circle of the moon."[122] In Victor Rousseau's *The Sea Demons*, too, Lovecraft would have noted the means by which the sinister amphibious fish-men ascend to conquer the world of men: via a continental shelf located in the North Sea, which rises from a deep oceanic abyss to being within just a few feet from the ocean surface (an idea later used in "The Shadow Over Innsmouth"), thus providing what Rousseau perhaps significantly calls "an actual ladder"[123] up to humanity. Did Lovecraft similarly view the high mountains of the Antarctic as facilitating a similar invasion of the earth from the moon?

The moon-ladder first emerges into something like its final form, however, in A. Merritt's masterful pulp horror story "The Moon Pool," which Lovecraft regarded as one of his top ten favorite weird stories),[124] and whose plot, style, setting, and technique had an incalculable impact on the form of the Lovecraft Mythos. And here, much as in Lovecraft's early poetry, we read of how "*a lane* of moonlight"[125] appears at "the rim of the sea" as a frightened Dr. Throckmartin tells the story of his capture by a mysterious and alien moon-entity, further described in proto–Cthulhuian terms as "a gleaming gigantic sea serpent racing over the rim of the world straight and surely toward the ship." (And, just as in Lovecraft and Greene's "The Horror at Martin's Beach," written approximately four years later, there is a marked stiffening in response to this phenomenon, Throckmartin gazing "as though turned to stone. He stiffened to it as a pointer does to a hidden covey.") But although Lovecraft's works usually tend to accentuate the horror of such phenomenon, Throckmartin's hypnotism instead induces both horror and ecstasy.

Merritt goes on to directly refer to this moon path throughout this chapter, describing it as a sort of cosmic passage or portal between two worlds. As Merritt observes, this path

> stretched to the horizon and was bordered by darkness. It was as though the clouds above had been parted to *form a lane*— drawn aside like curtains or as the waters of the Red Sea were held back to let the hosts of Israel through. On each side of the stream was the black shadow cast by the folds of the high canopies. And *straight as a road* between the opaque walls gleamed, shimmered and danced the shining, racing, rapids of moonlight[126] [italics mine].

Did Lovecraft also look upon his own moon-ladder as being somehow akin to a cosmic parting of space, allowing something alien to pass through between dimensions or worlds? It seems so: hence the horror evinced by Danforth at the climax to *At the Mountains of Madness*; Lovecraft's obsessive fear of foreign infiltration is projected onto a cosmic and, indeed, apocalyptically religious level. Merritt will go on to speak of a "moon door"[127] and "moon pool" throughout the remainder of the story, and it is but a small step from such a moon door and a moon pool to Lovecraft's later "Moon-Bog" or "moon-ladder." Abraham Merritt also reflects something of the archetypal feminine aspect of the moon in his story, in the form of a superstitious Swedish woman named Thora, who accompanies Throckmartin's doomed expedition and who is also strangely affected by the alien rhythms projected by the mysterious alien entity beyond the pool. As Merritt writes, she raised her arms and made "a curious gesture to the moon. It was — an archaic-movement; she seemed to drag it from remote antiquity —!'"[128] Thora resembles "some ancient priestess of Odin" as she does so.[129] The language here sounds very much like the pagan ceremony of drawing down the moon, discussed above, and it seems possible that the feminine association here influenced the form taken by Lovecraft's own later conceptions.

Merritt speaks, too, of a mysterious mist arising from the sea, here called an "opalescent mistiness"[130] and described in strangely animistic terms as "those strange little swirls of mist that steam up from the Southern Ocean like the breath of sea monsters, whirl for a moment and disappear,"[131] thus prefiguring Lovecraft's own mist-like entities, which likewise had their origin in or near the South Pacific. (One wonders if Lovecraft also thought of his own mysterious ocean mists as the breath of Cthulhu.) Intriguingly, too, Merritt's oceanic mists increasingly begin to take on what he calls "the suggestion of some winged creature in darting flight."[132] Merritt goes on to associate the winged creature with that "winged messenger of Buddha — the Akla bird whose feathers are woven of the moon rays," but the alert Lovecraft-reader will perhaps associate it with "'the wings'"[133] of Danforth's final vision, as well as with those nightmarish sensations of flight experienced by Lovecraft's hapless narrators, as they are conveyed up and down by the equally immaterial wings of the moon-ladder. Indeed, just as Lovecraft's later narrators are hurled about by what he calls a "viscous, sentient darkness,"[134] Merritt's narrator intimates some conscious organization behind this mist, suggesting that the vapors that make up the "white path"[135] of his "moon stream" are no regular "mist born of sea and air," but rather "spirals of *living vapor*" (italics mine).

This idea of sentient vapors or living powers of immaterial darkness are likewise common in early science-fantasy. In J. U. Giesy's *Palos of the Dog Star Pack*, for example, which ran just one month after "The Moon Pool," (and whose plot, as we have seen, seems to have strongly influenced "Beyond the Wall of Sleep"), we watch as occult investigator Jason Croft is assaulted by intangible and likewise sentient "shapes and forms, whose warp and woof was darkness,"[136] which "floated and writhed about him" while traveling in astral form through the depths of outer space. As Giesy writes, in strikingly Lovecraftian terms:

> They thrust against him; they gibbered soundlessly at him. They taunted him as he passed.... He recognized these shapes of terror as those elementals of which occult teaching spoke, things which roamed in the darkness, which had as yet never been able to reach out and gain a soul for themselves.

These "unthinkable hurricanes" toss Croft's astral form along as he drifts through the void, described as an "almost palpable darkness." Giesy even suggests some sort of a connection between these entities and a punishment of Croft for his forbidden delving into cosmic secrets, much like the supposedly impious risings and fallings seen in Lovecraft's "Hypnos," later on. (Giesy describes such entities as *elementals*, which is reminiscent of publisher August Derleth's oft-criticized [and seemingly inexplicable] identification of Lovecraft's fictional pantheon with *elemental* entities. Perhaps it had its basis here, in the more recondite and pulp-based facets of Lovecraft's cosmology.)

Lovecraft later alludes to similar such immaterial deep-space entities in

"The Haunter of the Dark," where they are called "solid and semi-solid forms"[137] seen in a black cosmic gulf, which "are known only by their windy stirrings" — "cloudy patterns of force" that "seemed to superimpose order on chaos and hold forth a key to all the paradoxes and arcana of the worlds we know." How such winds can actually be seen in the black gulf of space itself, Lovecraft does not explain, although perhaps their ethereal substance is somehow visible against the black void of space itself. In "The Horror at Red Hook," too, a similar wind from "the bottomless pit"[138] coils "sentiently about the paralyzed detective" — a wind that Lovecraft says has no linkage with either *earth or heaven*" (italics mine), language already suggestive of that cosmic alienage later associated with the forbidden mountain range in *At the Mountains of Madness*. The cosmic wind from the abyss, it seems, is equally at home in the subterranean abyss and among the high mountain tops. In *The Dream-Quest of Unknown Kadath*, meanwhile, these ethereal beings are described in collective terms, as invisible "shoals of shapeless lurkers and caperers in darkness, and vacuous herds of drifting entities that pawed and groped and groped and pawed."[139] And although critic John Salonia suggests that such creatures reflect an interest in "germlike or protozoalike imagery"[140] on Lovecraft's part, I would suggest an origin for such images, not in Lovecraft's scientific pursuits — which in any case were continually at war with his weird-fiction impulse — but rather in the primeval viewpoint which permeates Lovecraft's weird fiction as a whole, which portrayed the world through a pantheistic and childish lens, and continually projected inward psychological conflicts into sinister outward forms; what critic Maurice Levy perceptively calls the "subtle and progressive intrusion of the Invisible"[141] in Lovecraft's works, resulting in an atmosphere swarming with "satanic presences."[142]

Consider Lovecraft's description of his 1928 trip to the Endless Caverns in Virginia, whose "unknown chasms"[143] inevitably suggested to him the presence of invisible disembodied intelligences populating the subterranean realm; what he calls unseen creatures that inhabit the "frightful and obscure frontiers of the material world, ... suspicions of vague and unhallowed dimensions whose formless beings lurk ever close to the visible world of man's five senses ... unsuspected orders of beings and influences that haunt the sightless depths." Cotton Mather could not have said it better. (Lovecraft, interestingly, goes on in this same passage to associate these visions with John Uri Lloyd's occult-novel *Etidorhpa, or The End of Earth* [1895], which Lovecraft read in 1918, and which later played a highly influential role in the semi–Lovecraftian underworld stories of writers Ray Palmer and Richard S. Shaver in *Amazing Stories*. Aside from a few synesthesian "fleeting creatures"[144] briefly encountered in the novel, however, the intangible entities that Lovecraft here describes nowhere appear in *Etidorhpa*, although Lovecraft's picture of Nyarlathotep in "The Rats in the Walls" as a "mad faceless god"[145] dwelling in the "grinning caverns of earth's centre" definitely seems to derive from *Etidorhpa's* similarly faceless [although completely benevolent] man-creature, which leads protagonist Llewelyn Drury deep into a cave leading into the inner earth in the story.)

And although a more complete discussion of the bottom rung of this moon ladder — what Lovecraft calls, in "The Call of Cthulhu," the pit, and what he calls in "The Mound" "the gulfs of nether horror"[146] — must await my larger discussion of the archetypal feminine abyss or underworld in chapter 6, we can simply note here Lovecraft's direct association of his immaterial sentient entities with this same pit, from which they seem to emanate, as if from some central, corrupted source. In *At the Mountains of Madness*, as we have seen, the "queer Antarctic haze"[147] that haunts the alien mountains to the west of the city proves to be the result of what Dyer calls a "torturous-channeled rising of some such vapor" from the center of the earth; indeed, Lovecraft repeatedly emphasizes the subterranean aspects of this mountainous mist, later calling it a "kindred mist"[148] to that which Dyer and Danforth encountered in the "blasphemous, horror-fostering abyss." As in Cotton Mather's Puritan mythology, however, these "gaseous wraiths"[149] also people the "tenuous atmospheric strata" of the upper air, having been sighted from time to time, Lovecraft says, by "rash flyers" who "have barely lived to whisper" of them "after unexplainable falls" — falls very much like those undergone by Johansen during his dream in "The Call of Cthulhu," or the "hideous fall"[150] experienced by Peaslee in "The Shadow Out of Time." (Lovecraft, as we have seen, was just such a "rash flyer" himself during the night, whether he was being tickled by the night gaunts or simply floating over a cyclopean alien city.) Lovecraft may also have been influenced in this idea of rash flyers, however, by Sir Arthur Conan Doyle's masterful weird story "The Horror of the Heights" (1913), in which a wealthy and intellectual gentleman-pilot, described (like many of Lovecraft's heroes) as a "poet and a dreamer,"[151] comes to believe in the Fortean notion of "jungles of the upper air," which he blames for the inexplicable falls of high-altitude pilots. (Among the various "ghost-like creatures" that Doyle's hero discovers are "serpents of the outer air," composed of "long, thin, fantastic coils of vapour-like material," as well as larger and more dangerous tentacled monsters that anticipate Lovecraft's Elder Things, described as "a purplish patch of vapour" and composed of "some transparent, jelly-like substance"; all imbedded within a fine, greasy substance resembling "organic matter," which floats high above the earth like a sea of plankton, before "fringing off into the void" of space. Lovecraft's immaterial creatures interact with outer space in much the same way.) (See Appendix.)

These ghost-like creatures from Conan Doyle's weird fiction merged easily with Lovecraft's wide fund of classical knowledge, in which the visible world was already peopled by innumerable faery presences and nature spirits — what he calls in his sylvan poem "The Voice" "formless beings"[152] that "rov'd the spangled blue" in the light of the "sinking moon." In "The Dunwich Horror," too, these mysterious sylvan (and now malevolent) vaporous forms again appear, in both an aerial and a subterranean context. Lovecraft observes how "the wind gibbers with Their voices, the earth mutters with Their consciousness,"[153] and describes them as "rushing airy presences to be heard faintly at certain hours from stated points at the bottom of the great ravines."[154] Intriguingly, Lovecraft also goes further in depth regarding their exact nature and origin, suggesting that their immaterial structures seem to preserve some facet of a different, or earlier, state of physical being; what he tantalizingly calls "another plane of phase of entity from which it [the planet earth] had once fallen, vingtillions of aeons ago."[155]

What this previous "phase of entity" was, Lovecraft does not say, although it obviously refers to some immaterial or ethereal form of matter that predates our own: either the plasmatic primal *materia* of the archetypal feminine abyss, which so shatters Danforth's mind in *At the Mountains of Madness*, or else what mystics and occultists commonly identify, as John Uri Lloyd does in *Etidorhpa*, as "invisible worlds"[156] and "unreachable centers of ethereal structure about us that stand in a higher place of development than earthly matter." This is a fairly common idea in Platonic lore, but Lovecraft characteristically inverts it into a more sinister conception. And although for the Platonist as for Lovecraft the earth itself has long since become mired in the evils of physical matter, deep in the inner earth, however, such a primordial (or alien) state of being may conceivably still linger: hence Lovecraft's repeated references to the evil or corruption of the inner earth. (Indeed, in *Etidorhpa* Lloyd suggests that the interior of the hollow earth is comprised solely of "a shell of energy,"[157] a highly energized gravity sphere around which the crust of the earth first coalesced long ago, like dust around a soap bubble. Are Lovecraft's ghostly entities the original inhabitants of this hypothetical energy sphere, which later gave form to the earth?)

Intriguingly, the bodies of some of Lovecraft's more famous cosmic entities will also partake of this same Platonic etherealness: Cthulhu, for example, is called a "cousin"[158] of those "serene and primal, undimensioned and to us unseen" things that walk between the "spaces we know." Indeed, Lovecraft is at pains, in *At the Mountains of Madness*, to contrast the completely organic and material Old Ones with the only partly tangible Cthulhu-spawn.[159] This strongly suggests that the arrival of Cthulhu and his kin, which as we have seen is coincident with the cataclysmic wrenching of his sinister continent of R'lyeh up and out of the Pacific, was either facilitated by or connected in some way with some allied force deep within our planet itself, with whom he is somehow intimately related or allied. (Critic Will Murray, in his 1990 essay "Buddai," convincingly argues that these immaterial Cthulhu-spawn are identical with the equally immaterial Elder Things in "The Shadow Out of Time," although his suggestion that these things be called "Buddai" is much less convincing, especially since Lovecraft already called them Elder Things himself.)

And it is in "The Shadow Out of Time," written just two years before his death, that Lovecraft finally supplies a history — as fragmentary as it is — for these immaterial entities of earth's prehistory. He tells us of their mighty cities of stone (now ruins) and of their wars with the Great Race, after which they were driven down into "those caverns of inner earth which they had already joined to their abodes and begun to inhabit."[160] Even so, Lovecraft still reveals very little about them, not even their name (the very embodiment, indeed, of his unnamable), simply calling them either Elder Things or else simply very dangerous and "utterly alien entities,"[161] who so threaten the Great Race that the very mention of them becomes taboo; although perhaps they are also to be identified with that "Magnum Innominandum"[162] or the great "Not-to-Be-Named One"[163] mentioned throughout his writings (although, admittedly, these latter creatures are described purely in the singular, not the collective). That this apparently cosmic taboo had some more direct or visceral origin in Lovecraft's own familial (and paternal) situation, however, seems very likely, especially given the masculine gender of this Not-to-Be-Named-One, as well as the resemblance between the periodic "irruptions"[164] of these Elder Things onto the surface of the earth and those periodic irruptions of madness on the part of Lovecraft's father. (Lovecraft would have been familiar with such a connotation of the word "irruption" from *Munsey* author Victor Rousseau's *Draft of Eternity*, in which the psychologist-narrator refers to a patient's attack of hysteria as an "irruption"[165] of madness.) And interestingly, it is while unsuccessfully attempting to leap across a cleft situated above a (feminine?) subterranean gulf that father Peaslee is snatched up by these disembodied entities, in the form of a blasting and seemingly conscious wind from below: a "materially tangible blackness"[166] that takes him upon a "bat-like flight through half-solid air"[167] (Danforth's "'wings,'"[168] once again), while plucking and tickling him just like Lovecraft's night gaunts. And of course Lovecraft again links this frenzy of maternal power and resurgent infantilism with what he calls the "secrets of the primeval planet and its immemorial aeons"[169]: i.e., the aged (and feminine) core of Mother Earth.

Fascinatingly, even Lovecraft's curious recurring image of mist surrounding a mountain peak (presumably on its way to the moon), reflects aspects of the archetypal Feminine. Anthropologist Erich Neumann, in *The Great Mother*, writes of what he calls the archetypal symbolism of the moon as "the great lamp, the vessel of light, of the female godhead, who is also seen as a container of souls in which the *souls rising up from the earth like vapor* are gathered and conveyed onward in their scent to the great round"[170] — yet another psychopompic conveyance of souls, via a night flight into the great feminine abyss. This transit made by the mist from the subterrene abyss to the Mountains of Madness seems to constitute an outward physical embodiment of Lovecraft's more immaterial and trans-dimensional moon-ladder. And just as at the end of "The Horror of Martin's Beach," Lovecraft spends a great deal of time in *At the Mountains of Madness* describing the simultaneously cosmic and meteorological aspects of this upper atmospheric mist. Dyer observes how "At a very high level there must have been great disturbance, since the ice-dust clouds *of the zenith* were doing all sorts of fantastic things"[171] (italics mine). This is suggestive, perhaps, of some otherworldly or alien disturbance at the edge of space, which Dyer here associates with the formation of supposed mirages, but which could just as easily represent images from some cosmic intrusion into our universe. (Somewhat amusingly, too, we again find Lovecraft echoing his earlier vagueness with regard to the vaporous forms in "The Green Meadow": Dyer describes how the outlines of these "restless ice-vapours"[172] sometimes "seemed on the point of settling into some bizarre pattern which they feared to make quite definite or conclusive." Lovecraft must have believed, at least in this latter instance, that he had finally presented his readers with enough clues to understand, at least partially, the meaning underlying his cryptic imagery.) And significantly, Lovecraft directly connects these mirages, which manifest themselves at the zenith of the sky, with the inner earth: Dyer describes how "the entrance to the great abyss"[173] located beneath the Old Ones' city is "impressively though decadently carved to a likeness of the primordial celestial dome" — an interesting juxtaposition, again, of upper with lower, of zenith with "nadirs."[174] It seems likely that the Old Ones, who produced this carving (perhaps under the influence of the shoggoths), saw some sort of connection, and perhaps worshipped via sacred rites, some otherworldly transit between this upper zenith and the lower abyss. And, not uncoincidentally, it is in this chamber carved with the celestial dome where Dyer perceives a stream of warm air proceeding upward from the aperture leading to "the limitless void below."[175] For Lovecraft, just as with the Starry Wisdom cult in "The Haunter of the Dark," which proves to represent but a cloak for a creature of some dark and cosmic abyss, the archetypal feminine power of celestial and heavenly ascents never forsakes its intimate connection or, ultimately, its identity with the vaginal and the abyssal, the all-devouring feminine underworld of the aged and forever-copulating womb.

IV. Conclusions

The moon, with its archetypal or symbolically feminine powers, was apparently much on Lovecraft's mind, as his conversations with friend George Kirk clearly show. Kirk's journals tell of "an all-night conversation"[176] that Lovecraft had with his friend on the eve of his separation from his wife, in which the points of discussion ranged from Sonia herself to "the curious aspect of the moon, boy's books, friendship, certain aspects of the sex, etc." Kirk's latter reference (as his next sentence confirms) clearly refers to an in-depth discussion of sexuality and, perhaps, sexual experiences. This easy progression of subjects, from Lovecraft's disintegrating marriage, to astronomy, to aspects of the moon, to sex, does much to suggest a relation between these topics in his mind, even if we did not have the additional confirmation of the moon symbolism in Lovecraft's writings.

So what was the moon-ladder? I theorize, again, that it was a sexualized version of Jacob's Ladder in the Old Testament, in which the transit of angels from the earth into the presence of god has been replaced with a darker trans-action. Throughout *At the Mountains of Madness*, Lovecraft hints that the origins of humanity and even of all life on earth were brought about by the actions of his Old Ones. But these Old Ones also feared something else, something dark and forbidden, and it is possible that our ultimate origins, and the origins of life itself, lie there, in some dark and unknown facet of space and time, which was, to Lovecraft at least, unwisely utilized by these Old Ones sometime in our dim prehistory. Elsewhere in the story, making the unlikely transition from geologist to art critic, Dyer decries what he calls an "alien element"[177] that he detects among the sculptures of the latter-day and decadent Old Ones, perhaps referring to the influence of the shoggoths, now liberated from slavery. And it seems likely that the shoggoths, whom Lovecraft tells us eventually "conquered the abyss"[178] beneath the Old Ones' city, and who were in any case probably not restrained by the cultural fear that had hitherto characterized the Old Ones' worship of these dark forces, perhaps either awakened something or allied themselves with some cryptic dark force (a force that perhaps likewise figured into the shoggoths' own origin); an alliance of convenience, or perhaps an alliance of twin malevolence, with those unknown misty entities who traverse without fear the same murky depths as they. Much like the worshippers of Cthulhu in the Louisiana swamps, perhaps the shoggoths were willing to go farther, and lower, in their propitiation of this alien force than the Old Ones had been.

Ultimately, Lovecraft's cosmicized origin of life (and all cosmologies are ultimately a search for human origins) is nothing more than a projected version of the primal sexual act, refracted through the infantile lens of his imagination. Indeed, Lovecraft's vaunted cosmic beyond was nothing more than a *mental* beyond, with "mental" here being equal to the subterranean strata of the repressed and seething unconscious. And in this way, Lovecraft's vaunted "cosmic" realm did indeed represent a true confusion of upper with lower, of subterranean forces with lunar malevolence, of bestial desires with alien intrusion — a true moon-ladder, if you will, negotiating a path upward from the pit (i.e., from the depths of the mind) out into the gulfs of space, and then back into the pit once again.

FIVE

Lovecraft's *In Memoriam*
Phillips Gamwell and the Innsmouth Coda

...the pen that would his praise bestow / Pauses for words,
and halts from recent woe!
— H. P. Lovecraft, "An Elegy on Phillips Gamwell, Esq." (1917)[1]

I. The *"Innsmouth"* Coda

As biographer S. T. Joshi has observed, it is Olmstead's "spectacular con-version at the end"[2] of "The Shadow Over Innsmouth"—in which Lovecraft's protagonist comes to gradually accept his sinister maternal ancestry, and is preparing to join his immortal grandmother in her kingdom beneath the sea—that is "the most controversial point of the tale." Many of Lovecraft's correspondents, such as August Derleth and Clark Ashton Smith, although they appreciated the decadent atmosphere of the tale itself, balked at this end-ing, feeling it had not been sufficiently foreshadowed earlier in the text,[3] and Lovecraft was very discouraged by these criticisms.[4] Later Lovecraftian criti-cism has been equally divided about the Innsmouth *coda*: Joshi, for example, suggests that the narrator's transformation actually acts "as an augmentation of the horror"[5] in the tale, while, conversely, other readers, such as Bruce Lord, have interpreted the narrator's decision to join the Deep Ones in their nest beneath the sea as a "switching of sides,"[6] alleging that it represents "a radical departure from Lovecraft's style" of racism and xenophobia. Scott Connors, too, emphasizes Lovecraft's apparent identification of himself with his hybrid narrator, and calls Lovecraft's unexpected ending "one of the most beautiful and spellbinding pieces of 'adventurous expectancy' in the entire Lovecraftian oeuvre."[7]

The transformation of Lovecraft's narrator in this story, however, is nei-ther as unexpected, nor without precedent, or even as decisive as it at first

---

Table 3. Parallels Between HPL's poem "On a Grecian Colonnade in the Park" and his controversial *coda* to "The Shadow Over Innsmouth"

"On a Grecian Colonnade in a Park"	*Coda to "The Shadow Over Innsmouth"*
The poet desires to descend into the "templed deeps" (*AT* 139) of the ocean.	The narrator desires to descend to "many-columned Y-ha-nthlei" (*DH* 367).
Lovecraft evokes the memory of the classical in relation to the ocean depths, speaking of the "haunting memory" (*AT* 138) of the "deserted gods of years remote and blest" (*AT* 139).	The narrator evokes the classical-sounding "wonder and glory" (*DH* 367) of his grandmother's undersea realm (cf. Edgar Allan Poe's "To Helen" [1831]), with its "sunken porticos and labyrinths of weedy Cyclopean walls" (*DH* 366).
The poem ends with the poet planning to "tread again those ancient ways, / And in the templed deeps sink down to rest" (*AT* 139).	The narrator plans to "dwell amidst wonder and glory forever" (*DH* 367).

*See endnotes for a list of abbreviations.

---

might seem. One notes, for example, that the story ends with the narrator still on land, as yet only planning to descend into the depths. It is by no means clear that he will definitely do so. And although he claims that his desire for suicide—his other option—has been steadily lessening as his need to delve into the ocean depths increasingly takes hold, it may be that he will still, in one final fit of rationality, choose this grim alternative. And in this, Innsmouth's *coda* closely resembles Lovecraft's earlier poem "On a Grecian Colonnade in a Park" (1920), which likewise deals with the poet's desire to descend into templed deeps on the ocean floor, and which likewise ends with the poet standing "on the shore / In the cold present, alien and alone."[8] Nor do the parallels between these two works end there. As we shall see, delving into the meaning of this earlier poem also enables us to delve deeper in Lovecraft's later, and seemingly incongruous, *coda*.

In both works, for example, we find the ocean depths being linked for some reason with an older female and a younger male figure: the sea nymph Leucothea and her son, Palaemon, in "Colonnade," and the great-grandmother Orne in "Innsmouth," who torments the narrator in his dreams, as well as his poor cousin Lawrence, whom he plans to liberate from the madhouse and bring with him into the sea. And tellingly, much like the mythical sea nymph Leucothea, who could be described as the prototypical mermaid, Lovecraft will directly connect mermaids with the aquatic Deep Ones in "Innsmouth": the crazed Zadok Allen suggests that the Deep Ones were "'Mebbe ... the kind o' critters as got all the mermaid stories an' sech started.'"[9]

Just as with those numerous instances, too, discussed in the previous chapter, of a suicidal drowning in the sea in Lovecraft's writings, usually in relation to hypnotic feminine power, in both "Colonnade" and the "Innsmouth" *coda* Lovecraft evinces an ambivalence about descending into the depths, which are equated with both immortality and death. Indeed, one can hardly doubt that "the marble gate"[10] through which Lovecraft's poet wishes to pass in this poem is the same as that "irrepassable gate"[11] of life and death through which Lovecraft had sought oblivion in "Ex Oblivione" (written around this same time period); a doorway referred to throughout "Colonnade" as the "dark gate,"[12] "the portal," and the "wat'ry door," which promises a "rest"[13] that is basically synonymous with death. And ultimately, both alternatives considered by Lovecraft's narrator in "Innsmouth"—either shooting himself or leaping into the sea—also represent a form of suicide, physical in the former instance, spiritual and mental in the latter, since Olmstead's identity would be overwhelmed and erased by the darkness of the sea's greater and maternal power.

II. Palaemon Reborn

As critic Maurice Levy observes, H. P. Lovecraft "seriously and frequently considered putting himself to death"[14] throughout his lifetime, a fascination perhaps reflected throughout the canon in his recurring references to poisoning and drowning.[15] Before his marriage to Sonia Greene, Lovecraft, by his own admission, had "'no goal but a phial of cyanide when my money should give out,'"[16] a statement later bolstered by Samuel Loveman, who claimed that he "'carried a phial of poison with him'"[17] while he lived in New York City (although Joshi, inexplicably, disputes this account). The young Lovecraft experienced tentative fantasies during the summer of 1904 of drowning himself in the local river. Lovecraft, in his own words, was "tempted"[18] by "the warm, shallow, weed-grown Barrington River down the east shore of the bay," where he contemplated wading "out among the rushes" and lying "face down in the warm water till oblivion came." As Lovecraft observed:

> There would be a certain gurgling or choking unpleasantness at first—but it would soon be over. Then the long peaceful night of non-existence ... what I had enjoyed from the start of eternity till the 20th of August, 1890.... I liked to think of the beauty *of sun & blue river & green shore & distant white steeple as*

enfolding me at last— it would be as if the element of mystical cosmic beauty were dissolving me[19] (italics mine).

In his prose poem "What the Moon Brings," Lovecraft is even more explicit in this association of submersion with death, and about his own fascination thereof. The piece ends with the poet plunging "gladly and unhesitatingly into the stinking shallows,"[20] in which "fat sea-worms feast upon the world's dead," Lovecraft's almost lifelong philosophical pessimism and nihilism, his studied indifference to the greatness of humanity, and his feeling of being a plaything of fate, whether cosmic or parental, all culminating in this basic, self-destructive act. In the surviving notes to his unwritten (or lost) prose poem "Life and Death," in which he gives voice to his philosophical antipathy to life, we again find death being described in partly aquatic or submarine terms: "'Death — its desolation and horror — bleak spaces — sea-bottom — dead cities.'"[21]

After the death of Lovecraft's mother in May 1921, Lovecraft again contemplated suicide, this time in obliquely incestuous terms, as a mirroring or paralleling of his mother's own desire for death. And although oblivion ostensibly forms the ultimate goal of such an endeavor, it would also mean (just as with the narrator's joining with his grandmother and cousin beneath the sea in the Innsmouth *coda*), a re-merging with the maternal life force, within which he had so wished to dissolve in 1904. As Lovecraft wrote:

> For two years she [Susan Lovecraft] had wished for little else [than death]—just as I myself wish for oblivion. Like me, she was an agnostic with no belief in immortality.... For my part, I do not think I shall wait for a natural death; since there is no longer any particular reason why I should exist. During my mother's life-time I was aware that voluntary euthanasia on my part would cause her distress, but now it is possible for me to regulate the term of my existence with the assurance that my end would cause no one more than a passing annoyance.[22]

In "The Shadow Over Innsmouth," typically, Lovecraft inverts this desire for death on his part by having the mother of Olmstead's uncle Douglas apparently kill herself after Douglas' own suicide — Douglas killing himself in response to her (symbolically incestuous) overtures to join her beneath the sea. Indeed, as if to underline this maternal inversion, Lovecraft additionally describes the poor health of the narrator's beloved cousin Lawrence as being a "major cause of his mother's death"[23] in the same story. One can only speculate as to the reasons behind Lovecraft's inversions in this regard, but, just as with the numerous inversions of his father's illness in his weird fiction (as discussed in chapter 3), Lovecraft's fiction seems to have enabled him to control and manipulate the ineradicable parental demons that beset him even from beyond the grave.

That the sub-aquatic "bliss"[24] sought by Lovecraft's poet in "Colonnade" is identical (just as in "The Tomb") with this basic death wish on Lovecraft's part is confirmed by the numerous additional references to death throughout the poem: the woods beside the colonnade are a place where "forgotten shadows come to dream and brood,"[25] for example (more of Lovecraft's windy, immaterial spirits), while in the deep waters of the sea "old thoughts rose spectral from the grave." Just as in "The Shadow Over Innsmouth" and "Ex Oblivione," however, this grave could also be interpreted as a form of new and immortal life, via a merging with or dissolving into that "element of mystical cosmic beauty"[26] about which Lovecraft so fantasized during his suicidal reveries as a youth, referred to in "Ex Oblivione" as a "new realm"[27] in which there is "only the white void of unpeopled and illimitable space," allowing his narrator to dissolve "again into that native infinity of crystal oblivion from which the daemon Life had called me." The language is curiously similar to that intrauterine twilight existence previously enjoyed by the Outsider in his subterranean womb.

Indeed, as we have seen, Lovecraft's works also evince a curious and recurring interest in this idea of immortality, as well as death; whether the elixir of eternal life concocted by the father and son in "The Alchemist," the "bodily immortality"[28] enjoyed by the Deep Ones in "Innsmouth," or the more dubious undead immortality demonstrated by such revenants as Lovecraft's Outsider ghoul or Cthulhu himself. (In this, Lovecraft may have been influenced by the recurring motif of the search for the key to eternal life, which, along with the creation of vast amounts of gold, was a theme endemic to the early science fiction pulps.[29]) It is Lovecraft's desire for death, combined with his twin desire for a merging with the forces of nature (the archetypal Great Mother), that gives form to that dubious "immortality" conjured up in the Innsmouth *coda*, in which the immortality offered by the Deep Ones and the suicide chosen by Olmstead's uncle Douglas in that same story represent two sides of the same coin.

This same state of being simultaneously dead and immortal, significantly, directly figures into the myth of Leucothea and young Palaemon invoked in "Colonnade." And, like those Deep Ones in "Innsmouth," who, as Olmstead assures us, "would never die,"[30] both of these figures were made immortal, deified after first drowning in the deep: Ino throws herself and her child, Melicertes, into the sea to escape the madness of her "raving"[31] husband, Athamas, after which they are both transformed into "marine deities."[32] Ino is reborn as Leucothea, and Melicertes as Palaemon, described as a radiant young boy riding a dolphin or large fish. (Such instances of apotheosis after drowning are common in Greek myths of maritime deities, such as Ameirake (Penelope), or Artemis and Arethusa.)

According to scholar William Smith (with whose works Lovecraft was closely familiar), there was some confusion surrounding the Leucothea/Palae-mon myth. Some sources say that Melicertes was in fact reborn as the sea deity Glaucus, who is also mentioned in Lovecraft's poem (where he plays a role closely akin to Cthulhu's, as a hoary old man of the deep); whereas other versions of the myth instead "say that Glaucus is said to have leaped into the sea from his love of Melicertes."[33] A similar such leap into the sea, significantly, also figures into Lovecraft's "Innsmouth" *coda*, but from an incestuous rather than a homoerotic perspective: Olmstead tells us how his grandmother, after her son's suicide, "had gone to a spot her dead son had learned about, *and had leaped to a realm*"[34] (italics mine) of undersea "wonders," after which "she had never died." It is striking, indeed, that Lovecraft should frame the grand-mother's descent into the sea as a leap rather than as a sudden disappearance, for instance, or as an accident while swimming; the language is clearly sug-gestive of suicide, and perhaps of a later divine apotheosis.

A similarly dead-and-alive state of undead immortality also seems to obtain throughout Lovecraft's sub-oceanic R'lyeh, in which, intriguingly, it is not only Cthulhu who is undead: Frank Marsh's painting of R'lyeh in "Medusa's Coil," for example, depicts the submerged denizens of that conti-nent "deep under water — though everybody seems to be breathing freely."[35] (Lovecraft may have been influenced in this imagery by the last story in Charles Stilson's *Polaris*-trilogy, *Polaris and the Goddess Glorian* [*All-Story*, 1917], in which, much as in Lovecraft's "The Temple" later on, sailors rescue a man from the sea, a "*man that breathed when his head was under water!*"[36] [italics Stilson's] and who later proves to be from lost Atlantis.) There is also the narrator's fearful description in "The Call of Cthulhu" of what he reveal-ingly calls the "nightmare *corpse-city* of R'lyeh"[37] (italics mine), as well as his revealing declaration that "When I think of the extent of all that may be brooding down there *I almost wish to kill myself forthwith*" (italics mine). Here, just as in Lovecraft's "Innsmouth" *coda*, suicide forms the immediate response to an apparently immortal life beneath the waves: the "corpse-city" of R'lyeh forms an undead analogue to that *liebestod* that Lovecraft's narrator both shuns and desires alongside his grandmothers and his cousin.

But exactly who is this "poor little cousin Lawrence"[38] mentioned so pointedly in the "Innsmouth" *coda*, whose escape from the insane asylum is so assiduously planned by Lovecraft's narrator, and whose appearance is so strangely described as being "an almost perfect duplicate of his grandmother"? And why is Olmstead so adamant in saying that "*together* we shall go to marvel-shadowed Innsmouth"[39] (italics mine), instead of the narrator descend-ing into the maternal depths alone? To find out, we need to delve deeper into

Lovecraft's own family, which, as we have seen, provided the basic blueprint for his later macabre fantasies.

III. H. P. Lovecraft and Phillips Gamwell

One of the most significant family relationships in H. P. Lovecraft's life was his close friendship and correspondence with his younger cousin, Phillips Gamwell (1898–1916). In a largely female household, Phillips represented, as S. T. Joshi observes, "the only male member of Lovecraft's family of his own generation,"[40] and, as Joshi goes on, "Lovecraft's various references to him make it clear that he was very fond of Phillips." "My cousin was a great kid,"[41] Lovecraft later reminisced in 1923, "a [Frank] Belknap [Long] and Alfredus [Alfred Galpin] rolled into one. They remind me of him — he was my best and earliest grandson! I can still see myself training him when he was three and I was eleven!" Lovecraft ended up giving Phillips Gamwell his own stamp collection as a gift in 1915, and (despite his own admitted weakness in these fields) tutoring his younger cousin in algebra and geometry.[42] Some aspects of the Lovecraft-Gamwell friendship even suggest, intriguingly, that had he lived, Phillips might well have succeeded in altering, or at least in somewhat tempering, Lovecraft's otherwise intractable racism. Lovecraft, for instance, later described his cousin's great enthusiasm for Japanese-American silent film actor Sessue Hayakawa, who was famous for his villainous, sexually magnetic roles, and who was, Lovecraft writes, Phillips' "favourite."[43]

Lovecraft's comparison of Phillips with his later correspondents Frank Belknap Long and Alfred Galpin is significant, since the basic parameters of his earlier friendship with Phillips — an older man writing to and instructing a more naive and inexperienced younger man — seem to have provided the basic template for many of his subsequent relationships with his pen-pals for the rest of his life: younger men such as Robert H. Barlow, Willis Conover, Donald Wandrei, Robert Bloch, and August Derleth, with whom Lovecraft routinely adopted the pose of a more experienced and wiser grandfather, tutoring his grandsons in issues of philosophy, literature, and sociology. As Frank Belknap Long later observed, Lovecraft was "convinced that he was 'the old gentleman from Providence-Plantations'"[44] and rarely deviated from this playful yet eccentric grandfatherly pose.

Unfortunately, Phillips died at the end of 1916, succumbing to tuberculosis at age 18.[45] H. P. Lovecraft's elegy on his death was printed just a few days later, in the January 5, 1917, issue of the *Providence Evening News*. Lovecraft spoke of Phillips' "earnest face, in equal measure bright / With beauty's and with virtue's inward light"[46]; while in Lovecraft's comparison of Phillips with both "tender Hyacinthus, lately slain," and "lost Adonis," too, one can perhaps see an early, albeit still embryonic, suggestion of that immortality later promised in the "Innsmouth" *coda*. Hyacinthus, for example, was reborn as a flower, whose leaves were imprinted with "the exclamation of woe AI, AI"[47]; while the slain Adonis was granted the ability, much like the similarly reborn underworld goddess Persephone (Kore), to live six months of the year in the underworld, and the other six months with Aphrodite upon the earth.[48]

Gamwell Phillips figured prominently in several key areas of Lovecraft's weird fiction. In "The Thing on the Doorstep," for example, narrator Dan described himself and his best friend, protagonist Edward Derby, as having known each other "all my life. Eight years my junior, he was so precocious that we had much in common from the time he was eight and I sixteen. He was the most phenomenal child scholar I have ever known."[49] H. P. Lovecraft, of course, born in 1890, was also eight years older than Phillips; and although some critics have rightly seen aspects of Lovecraft's own life, childhood, and marriage in his description of the life of Edward Derby,[50] it is equally obvious that the larger contours of Dan and Edward's lifelong relationship — which is characterized by secret knocks on the front door, and an almost paternal regard of Dan for Edward — reflect the similar regard that the elder Lovecraft had for the younger Phillips. In "The Quest of Iranon," too, the poetic dreamer Iranon will find his soul mate, temporarily at least, in a much smaller and much younger boy named Romnod, who for several years shares his quest for the lost paternal and maternal city of Aira. And like Gamwell, Romnod predeceases his friend, leaving Iranon to weep over his grave. However, quite unlike Gamwell, Lovecraft traces Romnod's death to a spate of drunken dissipation, using his passing to further his anti-decadent and pro–Temperance polemic.

In "The Colour Out of Space," meanwhile, Lovecraft (as is typical in his weird fiction) inverts the dynamics of his friendship with Gamwell, in the form of the close relationship between Thaddeus Gardner and his younger brother Merwin, describing Merwin's loneliness after older brother Thaddeus suddenly goes mad and leaves him alone and bereft. As Lovecraft observes, "Merwin was getting frightfully imaginative, and his restlessness was worse after the shutting away of the brother who had been his greatest playmate."[51] In "The Shunned House," too, Lovecraft similarly inverts the dynamics of this cousin-relationship, describing how Rhoby Harris' son William (described as having degenerated from "a sturdy infant"[52] to "become a sickly, spindling lad") would "seem to improve" during his visits with his cousin, Peleg Harris. As Lovecraft revealingly observes, "had [his nurse] Mercy been as wise as she was well-meaning, she would have let him [William] live permanently with Peleg."[53] As we have seen, Lovecraft later achieved this permanent residence with his cousin (at least in the world of fiction) at the end of "The Shadow Over Innsmouth," in the "lair of the Deep Ones."[54]

In "The Shunned House," what Lovecraft calls a "sad and curious decay"[55] eventually comes to characterize all of the residents of the sinister Roulet home — a decay characterized, much like the tuberculosis that killed Phillips, by a "hollow voice and disconcerting pallor" as well as by a constant feeling of "weakness," followed quickly by death. As with TB, this "wasting-away or decline"[56] is described by Lovecraft as being highly "contagious," at least among the inhabitants of the former residence of vampiric lycanthrope Etienne Roulet. In the *coda* to "The Shadow Over Innsmouth," the slow transformation of Olmstead and cousin Lawrence into hybrid batrachians is described in similarly pathological terms as being akin to "the slow ravages of disease,"[57] which "are not pleasant to watch." (This same association of tuberculosis with bestial decay also figures in one of Lovecraft's earliest surviving weird stories, "The Beast in the Cave," in which prolonged residence in a cavern for TB patients results in horrifying physical changes in their bodies. Lovecraft strongly hints that the beast in the tale is one of these former patients, who has taken up permanent residence in the cavern.)

This does nothing to explain, of course, the strangely feminine aspects of Lovecraft's "Innsmouth" *coda*, such as the narrator's recurring nightmares involving his great-great-grandmother. And although the larger contours of Lovecraft's incestuous engagement with the archetype of the Great Mother must wait for the final chapter in this book, we will now examine the feminine aspects of Lovecraft's desire for suicide and the meaning of Lovecraft's odd juxtaposition of these themes of suicide, drowning, oblivion, immortality, and classicism in both the "Innsmouth" *coda* and "Colonnade."

IV. Merging with the Great Mother

> There are many different kinds of women in every man's ancestry,
> but one kind always predominates and establishes an individual
> norm preference which corresponds to the ancient tribal preferences
> of his remote ancestors in a general way. She would undoubtedly
> resemble quite a few of my great-great grandmothers.
> — Frank Belknap Long, *It Was the Day of the Robot* (1963)[58]

There is a close resemblance between Lovecraft's oft-expressed desire for oblivion and a merging with sun, water, and shore, and what psychologists have identified as that primal, sadomasochistic desire for death or Thanatos — what psychoanalyst John Munder Ross similarly calls an incestuous desire "to plunge back into the boundless beginning,"[59] in the process making oneself "permeable, open, utterly vulnerable, unbounded, unprotected, unmodulated — like a helpless infant melting into its mother's breast." Eugene O'Neill refers to this common conception in his play *Strange Interlude*, observing "'that death meant reunion with Her,'"[60] "'God, the Mother,'" and "'a passing back into Her substance, the blood of Her blood again, peace of Her peace!'" (A similar idea also seems to underlie the common practice of burying the dead in jars or other vessels, symbolizing the womb of the feminine underworld.)

This desire for a reunion with the mother animates much of Lovecraft's life, and by extension much of the Lovecraftian weird canon: critic Maurice Levy, for instance, rightly describes his obsessive desire to return to New England in 1926 as a "primordial"[61] "return to the maternal breast"; while "The Shadow Over Innsmouth" itself begins, as Levy points out, with the narrator's return to Arkham, the "cradle of his mother's family."[62] As Lovecraft himself observed, in revealingly incestuous language, "Like Antaeus of old, my strength depends on repeated contact with the soil of the Mother Earth that bore me."[63] True, this desire was an ambivalent one on Lovecraft's part, his desire for a return to the maternal womb being strongly coupled with an allied fear of this same gaping and overpowering maternal abyss; but unlike Lovecraft's "The Outsider," whose ghoul-hero desires to escape (at least for a time) from the maternal nepenthe of the subterranean womb, in "The Shadow Over Innsmouth," Lovecraft has come full circle and has chosen (or is at least contemplating) a final return to the maternal nest. Ironically, by dying young, Phillips Gamwell was enabled to obtain that unending and infinite oblivion which the nihilistic and pessimistic Lovecraft so desired himself.

Lovecraft's youthful fantasies of merging with the beauties of nature merely represent a more extreme manifestation of this tribal perspective, which identifies the Great Mother with such natural things as "stone or tree, pool, fruit or animal,"[64] in the common belief, as anthropologist Erich Neumann observes, that the Mother Goddess "lives in them and is identified with them." Lovecraft's "Innsmouth" *coda*, too, with the strange equivalency that it presents between the "smoking pistol"[65] used by the narrator's suicidal uncle on the one hand and the narrator's planned leap into the sea on the other, seems to closely conform to what Neumann and anthropologist J. Bachofen call this "death character of the material-maternal,"[66] which "takes everything that is born of it back into its womb of origination and death." Both Bachofen and

Neumann see this belief as an expression of an "archetypal domination of nature and the unconscious over ... the *undeveloped childlike, or youthfully helpless, ego consciousness*" (italics mine), such as Lovecraft, by his own admission, possessed for much of his early adult life.

This domination of the male consciousness by the overpowering unconsciousness of feminine nature (what Lovecraft, in his poem "Mother Earth," calls that feminine power "Too *old* for man's fugacious sway,"[67] which was "of *sentience old* ere thy *weak* brood / Appear'd in *lesser* magnitude" [italics mine] — his trademarked Old Ones again, this time in transparently maternal guise) manifests itself in "Innsmouth" via the narrator's recurring nightmares of his grandmother and great-great-grandmother (both of whom are, quite literally, old ones), in which loathing is equally intermixed with exaltation and desire. Indeed, Olmstead's description of the staring visage of his grandmother sounds very much like the staring visages of such ancient demonesses as the hypnotic Medusa or the Balinese nightmare witch, Rangda, in whose mythologies nocturnal sexual arousal by the all-devouring feminine principle is equated with paralytic suffocation and vampiric death. Tellingly, too, Olmstead's nightmares coincide with his degeneration into a "secluded ... invalid"[68] near the end of the story, a description that sounds very much like Lovecraft himself, during the period of his greatest domination by his own mother. Such dreams would be perfectly normal, of course, if Olmstead were a lonely sailor, lost far out at sea, who was having recurring dreams about a lascivious and beckoning mermaid. Olmstead's dreams, however, are experienced by a grandson about his older female relatives, who are beckoning him to join them in the deep — and that is where the pathological and incestuous element enters in.

Here, again, are suggestions of an incestuous contact between grandmother Orne and her son Douglas — who, Lovecraft tells us, had "spurned"[69] the "wonders" of his mother's underwater "realm" (her vulva/womb?) "with a smoking pistol" (autoerotic ejaculation); instead of incest with his mother, Douglas chooses physical death rather than the ignominy of psychic death. This incest with the mother, however, is merely symbolic of that larger incest of oblivion and death within the ocean, which represents the primordial, intrauterine world of maternal darkness, water, and death. As Erich Neumann observes in *The Great Mother*, very often in myth, "renewal, rebirth, and immortality"[70] (the same immortality that is promised by Lovecraft's Deep Ones) "is possible only when what is to be transformed enters wholly into the Feminine principle; that is to say, dies in returning to the Mother Vessel,"[71] after which follows rebirth in a new form.

The extent to which Lovecraft's ideas in this regard directly parallel similar archaic tribal psychological conceptions is shown by a Polynesian myth cited by H. R. Hays in his study of misogyny, *The Dangerous Sex* (1964), in which death and immortality are depicted as being conjoined and attainable within the vagina of the ancestress of the trickster-hero, Maui. (There are striking similarities between Olmstead's planned rendezvous with his Polynesian Deep One ancestress Pth'thya-l'yi in "Innsmouth," with her fishy and batrachian characteristics, and the myth of Maui's "mighty ancestress"[72] "'Hine-nui-te-po, Great daughter of Night,'" whose "'hair is like the tangles of seaweed and her mouth is like that of a barracoutu" [barracuda], symbolic of the *vagina dentata*, or toothed vagina.) Attempting to defeat his ancestress by crawling into her vagina while she sleeps and out her mouth, Maui is unfortunately killed when she wakes up in the middle of the process and crushes him to death (symbolic of the common male fear of castration by the phallic or devouring woman). It is thus, the myth explains, that "'death came into the world, for Hine-nui-te-po is the goddess of both night and death. And had Maui entered into her body and passed safely through her, men would have died no more." Here, just as in Lovecraft's "Innsmouth" *coda*, the attainment of immortality is seen as a matter of returning to the maternal/ancestral womb; and, just as in the *coda*, death is ultimately seen as immortality's equivalent. By ending his story with his protagonist apparently planning to acquiesce to the Deep Ones' plans, Lovecraft was enabled to envision a prolonged existence with his deceased mother and his cousin once again, but without having to stake his claim upon one form of death or the other.

V. Conclusions

> We are committed with the lone pagan on the seashore, with he
> who worships in the fastnesses of a mountain range or she who
> sings the old chant in a lost valley far from the metalled road.
> — Tony Kelly, "Pagan Musings" (1970), a neo–Pagan manifesto[73]

Incongruous as it may have once seemed, Lovecraft's ending to "The Shadow Over Innsmouth" is now at least understandable. In the Deep Ones of Lovecraft's "Innsmouth" *coda* is a twisted version of both his beloved classical past and the departed ghosts of his family. Olmstead's apparent "switching of sides" perhaps indicates an ambivalent reification of Lovecraft's own earlier Arcadianism and that love for the Greek (also reflected in his poem "On a Grecian Colonnade in a Park") that always co-existed uneasily with the overriding Romanism and the satirical impulse in his writings. Ultimately, however, Lovecraft's youthful love for the naiads could scarcely compete with the intellectual joy he later obtained from skewering these same naiads on the point of some sharp, asexual witticism. Only within the reassuring vacuum of posthumous oblivion could Lovecraft truly let himself go and slip back unashamed into those sensual Greek waters of pantheism and decadence that he had earlier abandoned for the cold, hard realities of stark Roman realism and anti–Grecian, anti–Dionysian caricature.

And while it may be true that Lovecraft's controversial *coda* to "The Shadow Over Innsmouth" represents, in part, an indictment of his own youthful Greek fancies, with the narrator's gradual nocturnal acceptance of his horrific descent (both literally and figuratively) exposing the decadence and corruption underlying the Grecian aesthetic, it may also parallel the grudging acceptance that Lovecraft himself, as time went on, was willing to give to decadent aesthetics and decadent values, at least in the artistic sphere, if not with regard to socio-political values. Partly, too, his *coda* may also reflect something of that ambivalent atmosphere of nightmares, in which, as we have seen, the voluptuous and desirable often alternates with the nightmarish and the horrific.

Ultimately, however, Lovecraft's family is the key to understanding the forces underlying his works: his ever-present desire for, and fascination with, the idea of suicide, death, and oblivion, are intermixed in "Innsmouth" with a kindred (and semi-incestuous) desire to rejoin his deceased relatives in an immortality that forms but a poetic circumlocution for death. Just as in his poem "On a Grecian Colonnade in a Park," however, Lovecraft's desire for sub-oceanic oblivion is tempered by a rational need to remain, for awhile at least, standing on the shore. The narrator's plan to descend into the ocean depths at the end of "Innsmouth" remains just that: merely a plan, subject to change or last-minute reversals. As with a dreamer in a nightmare, sanity at the last moment may suddenly reassert itself and the dreamer wake up. Incestuous immortality may thus, at the last minute, still be spurned or supplanted by the smoking pistol. The fact that Lovecraft juxtaposes this pistol with the Deep Ones' supposed immortality, however, does not negate the fact that, ultimately, both choices are basically the same: death. The only difference between them is the difference between killing oneself with one's pistol (masturbation) and submerging oneself in the "wonders" of the aquatic maternal womb (incest).

• Six •

H. P. Lovecraft and
the *Magna Mater*

I. *The Daemon Heroine*

A misconception, both great and strange, has arisen with regard to H. P. Lovecraft's weird fiction: namely, the idea that he did not represent women in his horror stories. Pulp writer E. Hoffman Price, for example, in his memoir of Lovecraft, describes his wife's critical reaction to his stories as follows:

> Wanda never met Lovecraft, and had, understandably, downgraded him because, as she expressed it, *"He's ignored women, writing around them."* I had never disputed the validity of the statement nor the fact that his ignoring slightly more than half the human race was indeed a weakness in his writing[1] [italics Price's].

Similarly, in horror-writer Barbara Hambly's introduction to a 1996 *Del Rey* edition of Lovecraft's works, she writes: "At the moment I cannot think of a single Lovecraft story in which a woman was the linchpin of the plot's evil — even Asenath Waite was actually a man."[2] "Mothers and wives hardly exist"[3] in Lovecraft's writings, according to critic Peter Cannon. Even the great horror-film director Stuart Gordon, on the commentary tracks for his film adaptations of *Re-Animator* (1985) and *From Beyond* (1986), respectively, declares: "H. P. Lovecraft does not ever write female characters"[4] and "Lovecraft never writes girls." The cover blurb on the back of Penguin Books' 1999 edition of Lovecraft's selected works describes how "H. P. Lovecraft reinvented the horror genre in the Twentieth Century, *discarding* ghosts and *witches* and envisaging instead mankind as a tiny outpost of dwindling sanity in a chaotic and malevolent universe" (italics mine). This assumption is rather commonplace in Lovecraft criticism, and numerous additional examples could be adduced.[5]

Women are not absent from his weird fiction, however; rather, it is merely the traditional romantic structure of desire, pursuit, and bonding that he eschewed — what the disdainful young Lovecraft once called "the following of imaginary nymphs and swains through the labyrinthine paths of amorous adventure."[6] And when they are present, it is usually as villains, whether in the form of Lady Margaret Trevor in "The Rats in the Walls," who figures as "the daemon heroine of a particularly horrible old ballad not yet extinct near the Welsh border,"[7] and who participates in the castrative and cannibalistic rites of the *Magna Mater*; or in the form of the ghoul-queen Nitokris in "Under the Pyramids" and "The Outsider," beautiful on one side, skeletal on the other. In "Psychopompos," the sinister Dame de Blois takes a lycanthropic and serpentine form, epitomizing the archetypal bestial and phallic demoness (an image later recapitulated via the equally phallic Asenath Waite). There are the numerous witches who populate "witch-cursed, legend-haunted Arkham"[8] and Kingsport: the "bent *old* woman"[9] (italics mine) who sits spinning at her wheel near the "cavernous fireplace" (a symbol of the abyssal Feminine) in "The Festival"; or the ancient crone Keziah Mason in "The Dreams in the Witch House," who, like the tickling night gaunts (perhaps a clever Lovecraftian circumlocution for night "aunts"?), exercises a paralytic and hypnotic control over the hapless Walter Gilman; or those witches in "Pickman's Model," whose faces hold such a "close kinship"[10] with those of Pickman's ghouls, and who join with these ghouls in populating Boston's secret and teeming underground. And as we shall see — and as Lovecraft himself observed in his notes to "Medusa's Coil"[11] and in his collaborative story, "Out of the Aeons"— there was a "strong connexion"[12] between his own invented cosmology of alien and elder lore, and things like "the witchcraft movements in Europe, against which the bulls of the popes were vainly directed." His fictional Cthulhu Cult ultimately was as neo–Puritan as it was quasi–Spenglerian, and as firmly rooted in primal ideas of the "Mother Goddess"[13] as the anti-witch fulminations of Cotton Mather.

We have already noted, in chapters 1 and 4, the equally numerous instances of vengeful goddesses found throughout H. P. Lovecraft's horror stories: the fertility goddesses of "The Moon-Bog"; the cannibalistic Magna Mater and the castrative Cybele in "The Rats in the Walls"; the vampiric succubus Lilith in "The Horror at Red Hook"; and, most significantly, Lovecraft's own fictional Shub-Niggurath, also known as the Goat with a Thousand Young, who functions, much like the ape goddess in "Arthur Jermyn," as a sort of darkly satirical version of the sometimes multi-breasted and often animalistic fertility goddesses worshipped in antiquity, and who is described in "The Mound" as both *the All-Mother and wife* of the Not-to-be-Named One"[14] (italics mine) and as being "a kind of sophisticated Astarte." Indeed,

Lovecraft's satirical edge, here — identifying the great procreative mother with a rutting goat — is particularly savage, and closely parallels, as I will argue later on in this essay, the general process by which feminine, Jewish, and black characteristics are later coalesced by Lovecraft in the form of his abysmal shoggoths. (The relative openness, too, with which Lovecraft identifies Shub-Niggurath with the Mother Goddess in "Out of the Aeons" and "The Mound" — both of which were merely collaborative or revisionary stories, written purely for money — is also highly suggestive, and seems to indicate the degree to which Lovecraft, in his canonical fiction, was perhaps disguising the true nature of his ideas with regard to the Feminine behind a symbolic and figurative veil. Even in his canonical "The Whisperer in Darkness," however, we also find his ostensibly cosmic Outer Ones — who are associated by Lovecraft with "the nighted and abysmal secrets of the infinite and the ultimate"[15] — also for some reason taking the time to engage in nocturnal fertility rites deep in the Vermont woods, in a ritual replete with sexual and procreative innuendos.[16])

Far from being banned from Lovecraft's works, as some critics seem to believe, in truth it is his readers and critics themselves who have, in effect, banned women from the Lovecraftian corpus, through the simple expedient of ignoring his numerous statements throughout his works regarding them. Certainly the biographical image of him which has generally obtained — that of an ascetic, Puritan, and sexually reticent person — may have influenced readers and critics in suggesting this general assumption or interpretation. But an aversion to women, which Lovecraft most definitely possessed (as evidenced by his provocative statement in his essay "Travels in the Provinces of America" [1929], which describes blacks and women as being joint "troubles"),[17] is not the same thing as absence. Women indeed had a presence in Lovecraft's works, and that presence is as disturbing to Lovecraft as it apparently is to some of his readers. Nor, as we shall see, is Lovecraft's pointed combination of feminine with black characteristics, either in his "Travels in the Provinces" essay, quoted above, or in his pointed combination of the black with the Astartean in the form of "Shub-*Niggur*ath" (italics mine), in any way accidental or coincidental: both the dark abyssal Feminine (in the form of the primordial void of the Great Mother) and the symbolic darkness of blacks themselves have a linked archetypal symbolism in the darkness of the seething, repressed unconscious; a darkness that Lovecraft went on to identify with the larger cosmic darkness underlying existence itself.

And it is here, too — in Lovecraft's basic reaction to the Feminine — where we might also locate the psychological sources of his inversion of Greek Arcadian themes, as discussed in chapter 1. Certainly, it is no great stretch to suppose that feminine symbolism may have played such a role, given the fact that Lovecraft's numerous later references to witches, she-devils, and female ghouls in his weird fiction possess an obvious figurative origin in the naiads, dryads and nymphs of his childhood Arcadia. As to precisely what it was about the Feminine that provoked Lovecraft's ire, I of course cannot say; although doubtlessly Lovecraft's ambivalent relationships with his mother, aunts, and maternal grandmother would have played a large role in this regard, as would the sexual aspects of his father's illness. Lovecraft's devotion to such Roman figures as Cato, too — who regarded women as a necessary evil — also certainly did much to shape his general attitude toward the Feminine, although this would still not account for what I see as the caricatural bitterness revealed in his later weird fiction. If the final trigger were to be found in the circumstances of Lovecraft's cryptic relationship with amateur "Arcadian"[18] poetess Winifred Jackson, however, then certainly such nasty images as his Shub-Niggurath, with her thousand young (the epitome of the sexually active woman), as well as his naked and blood-drenched Lilith with her swarthy followers (the very epitome of the scarlet woman), would be readily explained, as would the general cannibalistic and sadistic role played by the Feminine in Lovecraft's weird fiction from the 1920s onwards. This dark view of the Feminine eventually found historical confirmation in the thesis of Dr. Margaret S. Murray's *The Witch-Cult in Western Europe* (1921).

II. The "Monstrous Mother"[19]

As noted in chapter 3, the women in Lovecraft's stories often figure as the female half of a married pair. The married couples in his weird fiction, just like the paternal figures, generally are divided into benevolent married couples on the one hand, and malevolent married couples on the other, perhaps reflecting Lovecraft's own ambivalent and infantile relationship to his parents' memory, in which overt devotion is combined with unconscious anxiety at covert and incestuous attachment.

Very often such marriages reflect a marked exogamic anxiety on the part of Lovecraft, very similar to that which once obtained in ancient Greece and Rome, where marriages outside one's race or culture also were frowned upon. As anthropologist Erich Neumann observes in *The Great Mother*, exogamy ultimately reflects the "cohesion of the female group of grandmother, mother, daughter, and children, vehicles of the matriarchal psychology and of the mysteries characterized by the primordial relation between mother and daughter."[20] Lovecraft refers to such feminine sodalities throughout his weird fiction, in such instances as the dark rumors shared by whispering grandams sitting

Table 4. Benevolent vs. Malevolent Wives and Mothers in HPL's Weird Fiction.

Good Wives in HPL's Weird Fiction	Evil Wives in HPL's Weird Fiction
Mrs. Ward in *The Case of Charles Dexter Ward,* who becomes helplessly paralyzed by nervous exhaustion after Ward is supposedly "possessed" by Joseph Curwen, retiring to "Atlantic City" for a rest (*MM* 185).*	Dame de Blois in "Psychopompos," who "was like a serpent in her gait" (*AT* 31), and who was the source, Lovecraft says, of "all her husband's mystery" (*AT* 31).
The nurses in "The Outsider" (*DH* 47), "The Thing on the Doorstep" (*DH* 277), *The Case of Charles Dexter Ward* (*MM* 113), and "Celephais" (*D* 85), all of whom function mainly as ambivalent, controlling, or maternal figures.	Wife Marceline Bedard/de Russy in "Medusa's Coil" (1930), a "she-daemon" (*HM* 187) who turns out to be the very source of "the myth of the gorgon's glance which turned all beholders to stone" (*HM* 196) in antiquity.
The two mothers in "The Alchemist," one who "died at my birth" (*D* 329), and the other who was "burnt" "alive as a sacrifice to the Devil" (*D* 330).	The "monstrous mother" (*DH* 365) who was married to Captain Obed Marsh in "The Shadow Over Innsmouth."
The overly controlling mother in "The Thing on the Doorstep," who likewise dies.	The hybrid white-ape wife of Sir Wade in "Arthur Jermyn."
The solicitous mother of Jervas Dudley in "The Tomb," never named directly.	Lilith, supplantive consort and devourer of Robert Suydam in "The Horror at Red Hook."
The supportive Mrs. Armitage in "The Dunwich Horror."	Lavinia Whately, consort of Yog-Sothoth in "The Dunwich Horror."
Lovecraft's numerous paeans to "Mother England," the "Mother Country," and to its queen; and also to ancient Rome, called the "Mistress of the World."	The degenerative Mrs. Gardner in "The Colour Out of Space."
The "dryads and satyrs" (*MW* 534) of Lovecraft's youthful classical reveries, who form the equivalent of a married pair.	The witch Keziah Mason, consort of the Black Man in "The Dreams in the Witch House."
Maiden aunt Mercy Dexter in "The Shunned House," who acts as a surrogate mother to sickly nephew William Harris.	The widowed Rhoby Harris in "The Shunned House," who, like Mrs. Gardner, goes mad.
The "strange child" and "radiant pair" (*HM* 14) in "The Crawling Chaos."	The first wives "sent out" (*MW* 336) along with the "first cargo of African blacks" to the North American colonies, which only goes to prove, Lovecraft wrote, that "troubles never come singly."

Good Wives in HPL's Weird Fiction	*Evil Wives in HPL's Weird Fiction*
	The goddess Ashtaroth (*D* 260), mentioned in connection with the god Moloch in "The Horror at Red Hook."
	Queen Nitokris and husband Pharaoh Kephren in "Under the Pyramids."
	The marriage of "Jack Manly" to his "beauteous bride, the fair Bridget Goldstein" (*MW* 44), in Lovecraft's satirical story "Sweet Ermengarde."
	The undead T'la-yub, who seizes and traps her love Zamacona in "The Mound"; as Lovecraft explains, T'la-yub, "conceived for him [Zamacona] a curious individual infatuation based on some hereditary memory of the days of monogamous wedlock in Tsath" (HM 150).
	Later on, this squaw becomes the female half of that male and female (and ultimately parental) pair who guard the entrance to the Mound, in the form of an invisible wind.
	The murderous "old man and his wife" (*D* 56) in "The Cats of Ulthar," also called "the sinister couple" (*D* 57).
	The sinister "Etienne Roulet and wife" (*MM* 248) in "The Shunned House."
	Mother Hydra, consort of Father Dagon in "The Shadow Over Innsmouth."
	Shub-Niggurath, "wife" (*SL* V:303) of Yog-Sothoth (also called the *Magnum Innominandum*, the Not-to-Be-Named-One).

*See endnotes for a list of abbreviations.

by the fire,[21] and the transmission of the witch-tradition itself from grandmothers to their progeny; an image that, for Lovecraft, forms the crowning horror at the end of "The Horror at Red Hook," in which a "swarthy squinting hag"[22] is shown "teaching a small child some whispered patois in the shadow of an archway." (Lovecraft may also have been influenced in this picture by his reading, in late 1923, of Dr. Murray's *Witch-Cult*, which makes it clear that "the profession of the witch religion"[23] was "hereditary," with witches' familiars often being "descended from mother to daughter," and with mothers and grandmothers often bringing their female children to the Sabbaths for initiation.[24]) There is also the close and ultimately exogamic connection that Lovecraft suggests between the Medusean priestess Marceline Bedard and the "very old"[25] Zulu witch, "Old Sophonisba," who worships her; here, Lovecraft's *Old Ones*, yet again, are given a very human and, in this case, feminine, complexion.

On the other hand, such exogamic horrors often form but the prelude to even more troubling, incestuous horrors located within the family home itself. In "The Shadow Over Innsmouth," for instance, Lovecraft manages to combine Captain Obed Marsh's exogamic sin in marrying outside his native race and tradition with the decay later found within the narrator's own family. Lovecraft's Outsider earlier attempts to escape from similar such interfamilial feminine control, which takes the form of both the elderly nurse who cares for him, and the larger underground (and womb-like) space in which they both live; and Edward Derby attempts to do so later on in "The Thing on the Doorstep." The Outsider's final, unalterable expulsion from his feminine underworld perhaps corresponds to what Erich Neumann calls the male "rejection from the uterine paradise,"[26] associated with both birth and later adult sexual emancipation.

Biographer S. T. Joshi, in his discussion of this story, dwells in depth on this issue of the strange twilight existence enjoyed by the Outsider in his subterranean castle, asking, "What exactly is the nature of the 'castle' in which the Outsider dwells? If it is truly underground, how is it that the creature spends time in the 'endless forest surrounding it?"[27] Joshi ultimately concurs with critic William Fulwiler that the entire story represents a dream. But if it is a dream, then it is also a dream that conforms, in its basic themes and structures, to the fundamental archetypal dictates of Lovecraft's feminine-bound unconscious, representing what Neumann calls the "uroboric existence of unconscious perfection"[28] found only within the mother's womb, which he goes on to identify with the "original Psychic Situation"[29] of mankind. (There is also a similarity here between this "endless forest"[30] in "The Outsider" and those deep dark woods that anthropologist H. R. Hays associates with the devouring witch of medieval fairy tales, which often contains the vulvic witch house within which the unwary traveler [such as Hansel and Gretel] becomes entrapped and then devoured.[31] Lovecraft's Walter Gilman, too, finds it difficult to escape from such a house.)

Nor is it any coincidence that the evil ancestors in Lovecraft's weird fiction are most often maternal ancestors, even when the ancestor himself is male, whether in "The Tomb," "Arthur Jermyn," *The Case of Charles Dexter Ward*, "The Man of Stone," or "The Diary of Alonzo Typer." (In his notes to "The Shadow Over Innsmouth," too, Lovecraft specifies that the "record of madness & suicides"[32] in Olmstead's family tree occurs solely in his "maternal line.") As Erich Neumann observes of primeval societies, "Even when the matriarchal stratum is repressed, it can appear in male form; for example, as a mother's brother"[33]; so that very often, as H. R. Hays confirms elsewhere, it is "a maternal 'uncle'"[34] who is tasked with initiating an adolescent male into the masculine rites of the tribe: this so-called "clan uncle" sometimes makes ritualistic cuts in the boy's body; or, as in New Guinea, helps him to "to spear a bound captive.[35] These initiatory rites are perhaps akin to those numerous instances of coming-of-age (all too often accompanied by usurpations of identity) so common in the Lovecraftian canon. Behind such male surrogates, however, whether in tribal rites or Lovecraft's stories, lurks the eternal specter of the Great Feminine, against which such masculine rites are merely phallic, magical imprecations, designed to ward off the frightening totality of the female's primordial power.

As noted above, it seems clear that that Lovecraft's older female relatives loom large in these proceedings, transfigured (via nightmarish, unconscious processes, similar to those transformations of the paternal revenant discussed in chapter 3) into the all-devouring mother goddesses of his weird fiction. And here we again find Lovecraft invoking the standard motifs of size and age that also characterize the Great Race and the Old Ones. It makes no difference whether it is an aged witch, an elderly nurse, or an Elder god; whether it is the "shockingly aged"[36] nurse in "The Outsider," or what Lovecraft calls the "aged moon-priestess Cleis"[37] in "The Moon-Bog" — each reflects the persistence of Lovecraft's infantile view with regard to the maternal. (In his poem "Mother Earth," too, as we have already seen, the primary characteristic of the mother deity in the poem, and the fact about her that causes the "'ephemeral'"[38] poet so much horror, is her great age.)

Lovecraft practically underlines this maternal aspect of his Old Ones in *At the Mountains of Madness*, where, as we have seen, they are endowed with the most fundamental power possessed by the maternal: namely, the power of the creation of life. Lovecraft further describes them as "the makers *and enslavers* of that life"[39] (italics mine) during the prehistoric era, language that perhaps suggests something of that maternal domination and control beneath which he chafed, despite his repeated and fevered protests of motherly devotion. (In his discussion of the mythological symbolism of the primordial mother anthropologist Erich Neumann describes the Babylonian sea monster Tiamat in similar terms as being "not only the genetrix but also the true mother of her creatures"[40]; "all of the star gods and all destiny" are the arbitrary *"products of her caprice"* [italics mine], language equally reflective of Lovecraft's generally pessimistic feelings about fate and life itself.) Tellingly, the Old Ones are further described in *At the Mountains of Madness* as being "*supreme on the planet* except for one shadowy fear about which they did not like to speak"[41] (italics mine) — an idea which, in more domestic terms, directly corresponds to both parental power within the home ("supreme on the planet") and parental reticence (especially in Victorian households) about the subject of sex; but a reticence which also, in Lovecraft's special case, suggests a particular reference to the circumstances of his father's illness.

As H. R. Hays observes in *The Dangerous Sex*, due to the "anxieties of the family situation"[42] (and Lovecraft's family life certainly seems to have been more than fraught with repression and anxiety), "The sexually attractive mother and the competing, potentially dangerous father *loom as all-powerful* and both cause tensions in the helpless infant. In primitive myth, which probably arises from childhood compulsions, *both can become magical entities*" (italics mine). Compare this, again, with the numerous married and parental couples in Lovecraft's fiction (table 4), from the divine "radiant pair"[43] seen in "The Crawling Chaos" to the murderous old couple in "The Cats of Ulthar." This parental obsession reaches its apotheosis, as we shall see, in the form of that confused version of the "primal scene" witnessed by a disturbed Danforth (much like the mystified Atal before him) high above the mountains at the end of *At the Mountains of Madness*. Much of the domestic etiology of Lovecraft's entities, however, tends to be lost on Lovecraft fandom and the vast majority of Lovecraft readers, a small fraction of whom actually persist in worshipping his entities as if they were real gods (which perhaps only serves to substantiate the psychological validity of Lovecraft's own innate, and primitive, unconscious inspirations).

For many psychologists, such infantile views of parental giganticism are paramount in influencing child psychological development, especially as regards the relation of the young son with his mother. As psychologist John Munder Ross observes, (combining age and size in a very Lovecraftian manner as he does so): "the child's parents are *older*, *stronger* and *much bigger* than their sons and daughters"[44] (italics mine). As Ross goes on,

> The little boy is awed by his compelling, alluring and large mother. He imagines that her vagina, like her breasts, which he actually sees, and like the womb that is said to have borne him, is very large. It is, he senses, far too large for his little pink button of a penis — too huge, hairy and wonderful. He wants her but cannot have her. He and his penis are just too small. He could be swallowed up alive. Or he would fail her altogether. He would make a fool of himself.

As H. R. Hays confirms in *The Dangerous Sex*, although possibly excited by the spectacle of the primal scene, the child is "at the same time is afraid that his own small organ will be inadequate in comparison with those of his elders."[45] In "The Dreams in the Witch House," for example, we watch as the simultaneously phallic and castrative sacrificial knife wielded by Keziah Mason is wrenched by Walter Gilman "from the old woman's claws; sending it clattering over the brink of the *narrow triangular gulf*"[46] (italics mine). Note that the phallic knife does not merely penetrate the vulvic gulf: it goes over the edge and vanishes; just like the infantile penis described by Ross and Hays, above. Note here, too, the candle that the young and virginal Jervas Dudley thrusts into the entrance of the tomb that he finds himself unable to enter, but which only reveals still further "stone steps leading downward"[47] into darkness: the phallic male becoming lost within the overarching uterine chambers of the necrophilic feminine underworld. (Such candles likewise figure throughout the accounts of witches' Sabbaths cited in Murray's *Witch-Cult*, where they often figure as phallic symbols.[48])

Nor is Walter Gilman's own candlestick any more effective, it would seem, in preventing the egress of Brown Jenkin from his tiny mouse-hole in the wall: despite being wedged in a hole described by Lovecraft as "about the right size,"[49] the trans-dimensional realms of the (ultimately feminine) cosmic beyond are far too large, it seems, to be stopped up by such a small, thin (and masculine) expedient — at least within Lovecraft's tormented imagination. Edward Derby, it is true, has rather more luck with *his* candlestick, when he uses it to bash in his wife Asenath's skull,[50] in a rather brutal victory of the Masculine over the Feminine principle; even here, however, Edward's victory is only temporary, as he is quickly swallowed up by the all-devouring feminine underworld. This (basically castrative) fear of male inadequacy is also reflected, as we have already seen, in the standard *large-vs.-small* dichotomy with regard to Lovecraft's weird entities as compared to children, who are invariably described as *small*, *tiny*, or *little*, in contrast with his creatures of enormous or cyclopean size.

These same notions of maternal giganticism are fairly common among ancient and aboriginal peoples, as well as in ancient and classical art. Erich Neumann, in *The Great Mother*, cites several examples of feminine giganticism in archaic art with regard to both mother figures and the Great Goddess herself, who are often depicted as being very large compared to the child, or the men, beside them. In some Peruvian and African carvings, indeed, according to Neumann, the mother is depicted as almost a "mountain like mass,"[51] suggestive "of fusion with the earth" (symbolic of the woman as Earth Mother), a conception perhaps later given concrete form via Lovecraft's *Mountains of Madness* (emphasis mine), which are regarded as the "focus of earth's evil,"[52] and whose rootedness deep within the sinister underworld permits of the transit of forces of sexual and shoggothian evil from the inner earth to the moon and perhaps beyond. (Is it merely a coincidence that Lovecraft's _Mou_ntains _of M_adness forms the acronym "MOM"? Given what Donald R. Burleson has noted elsewhere regarding Lovecraft's talent for cryptic acrostics in his verse,[53] one cannot be too sure.) Those enormous and gargoyle-like living mountains in _The Dream-Quest of Unknown Kadath_, although not specifically described as being feminine, are said to have "squatted there atop the world" in "a great half circle,"[54] while from their laps (wombs?) arise hordes of "evil shantaks of elephantine bulk."[55] The latter image definitely suggests a feminine or maternal conception, either the act of birth itself, or the resting place of a child in its mother's lap. Indeed, according to Neumann, all such instances of maternal giganticism in ancient art stem from one central fact of life: the unchangeable physiological and psychological relation of mother to child. "Nowhere perhaps is it so evident that a human being must be experienced as 'great,'"[56] Neumann explains, "as in the case of the mother" in relation to "the infant or child," which is "utterly at" her "mercy." And although Lovecraft famously attempted to utilize a similar "great" language in the service of science fiction and his invented cosmology, it too ultimately stems from this more basic, and unchanging, psycho-physical formulation.

It is significant, too, to note both the increasing specificity and the increasing domesticity of Lovecraft's "aged" language through time: the alien Old Ones of _At the Mountains of Madness_ (written early 1931) immediately give way to the 80,000-year-old great-great-grandmother of "The Shadow Over Innsmouth" (written late 1931), and finally to the ancient witch Keziah Mason of "The Dreams in the Witch House" (written early 1932), who is only a few hundred years old or so. The cyclopean giganticism and great age of the Old Ones gradually align themselves with more personal (i.e., biographical) specifics with regard to gender and size. And so, just as we can see the cannibalistic hunger of Delapore and his invisible army of rats being reduced, in "The Dreams in the Witch House," to a single hybrid human/rat/masculine figure, (Brown Jenkin); and just as the endless piles of humanoid bodies in the Magna Mater's underground grotto in "The Rats in the Walls" are, in "Witch House," reduced to a single pile of children's skeletons concealed within Mason's sealed overhead garret, in the figure of Keziah Mason herself we can perhaps see H. P. Lovecraft adhering somewhat closer to the maternal origins of his ambivalent feminine anxieties. Lovecraft slowly zeroes in on the unconscious sources of his inspiration in the form of that loved and hated figure of his mother; both the endless piles of skeletons, and the castrative rites of both Cybele and Keziah Mason, symbolize what he saw as his own masculine death at the hands of this overpowering mother-figure. Gigantic and alluring; the source of life, love, and sustenance; the giver alike of pleasure, pain, and death; as unavoidable and unarguable as fate itself; it is in Lovecraft's ambivalence toward the all-powerful mother that we can trace his larger ambivalence toward both fate and life, an ambivalence that colored the peculiar contours of his life, informing the nihilism and pessimism of his philosophy, as well as the macabre and nightmarish obsessions of his literary career.

In *The Great Mother*, Erich Neumann quotes from a Cora Indian belief about the eagle hero who destroys the (feminine) night; the Indians liken him to a fire, which begins small but which "'vanquishes the Old Ones as they sleep, for he wakes.'"[57] In Lovecraft's works, however, instead of a heroic dawn, we instead see the beginning of, or at least the desire for, the return of a new dark age (as at the beginning of "The Call of Cthulhu"), a dark age that is basically identical with a return to the primordial unconscious state of the maternal womb; the same state of oblivion sought out by Lovecraft himself via a lifetime of self-abnegation, conservatism, and fantasies of suicide; the state of the Outsider before his eventual escape. Although long dead, Lovecraft's Old Ones still manage to vanquish or at least co-opt his protagonists. The vast cosmic immensities that Lovecraft charted, explored, and hinted at are nothing more than the parental immensities whose psychological gap he was unable to bridge. His intruders from "beyond," whether the *Colour Out of space* or the *Haunter of the dark*, ultimately come from the maternal darkness of a primordial sea in which Lovecraft, quite literally, threatened to drown, whether in real life, or in the *coda* to "The Shadow Over Innsmouth."

III. Myrionymus, the Goddess with 10,000 Names

> Shall I find my task in the vault itself, or must I burrow
> deeper into the nighted heart of our planet?
> — H. P. Lovecraft and William Lumley,
> "The Diary of Alonzo Typer"[58]

According to classical scholar Charles Seltman, the Great Goddess had "one nature, but many different names,"[59] eventually passing "something of herself to almost every goddess and many a nymph."[60] At Thebes, she was called Demeter Cabiria[61]; in Phrygia and Syria she was called Cybele[62] and was regarded "the mother of the gods,"[63] an epithet certain to have draw H. P. Lovecraft's attention, given his overwhelming maternal preoccupations. In Lovecraft's "The Rats in the Walls," indeed, she is called both Cybele and the Magna Mater; while in "Out of the Aeons," in the form of Shub-Niggurath, she is simply called the "Mother Goddess."[64] But no matter what one calls her, this wide-ranging belief in her greatness and all-important stature ultimately derives, according to anthropologist Erich Neumann, from the wide "scope of the basic feminine functions,"[65] which encompass the entirety of life: from birth to death, from earth to heaven, from basic sustenance to ecstatic pleasure — functions extending from the mother of the household to Mother Earth herself. And all these same feminine archetypal functions, from the growing green things of the earth, to the vacuity of the cosmic abyss, can likewise be traced throughout H. P. Lovecraft's weird fiction.

As the personification of growth and fertility, the Great Goddess was naturally associated with things like trees, vegetation, flowers, and fruits, which were believed to have been born from the womb of the earth; all things which, at least at first, show such a clear increase in size and gloss in Lovecraft's "The Colour Out of Space." This belief in the feminine aspects of fecundity and fertility had many troubling aspects, however, as demonstrated by the numerous taboos surrounding menstruating women in ancient societies, which seem to have had a homeopathic basis. Anthropologist H. R. Hays, for example, cites Roman author Pliny on the belief that "contact of menstruous women with new wine or ripe fruit will sour both,"[66] such women also being "forbidden to plant seedlings or work in the garden." This disruptive power of feminine fertility is likewise reflected in those destructive abilities traditionally attributed to witches, most of which appear to be rooted in similarly homeopathic superstitions. And so, whereas mothers and midwives were naturally associated with childbirth and with the raising and nurturing of children, witches were conversely, as Dr. Margaret Murray observes in *The Witch-Cult in Western Europe*, said to "suffocate, extinguish, and cause to perish the births of women,"[67] and also to make "men and women, flocks and herds and other animals" "suffer." (A similarly homeopathic principle also probably underlay the superstitious belief that witches were required to "'kill one child ... at the least euerie [sic] month,'"[68] an idea that again suggests an obvious connection with menstruation.) The widespread belief in such infanticidal demonesses as the Babylonian Lilith, the Greek Empusa or Lamia, and the Balinese Rangda also has its origin here; such practices of ritualistic infanticide likewise are quite frequently depicted throughout the Lovecraftian weird canon,[69] where they arguably represent yet another, and usually unrecognized, manifestation of the Feminine in his writings.

It is hard, of course, not to see a similar homeopathic connection between witches' (and menstruating women's) supposed connection with *drying up* milking cows, souring milk, spoiling wine, etc."[70] (italics mine), and the similarly decay-inducing properties evinced by the Colour that inhabits the Gardners' farm in "The Colour Out of Space," which literally dries up the cows and other farm animals until they disintegrate and shrivel up into mere husks. Indeed, Dr. Murray's observation that witches were known for both "causing [and] or *blasting* fertility"[71] (italics mine), (a statement made *twice* by Murray), immediately recalls Lovecraft's own "*blasted* heath"[72] (italics mine), a place where, as Murray quotes from a 1521 Catholic Epistle written against witchcraft, an evil agency has "'destroyed the Fruits of the Earth.'"[73] (Elsewhere, Murray gives a lengthy definition of this "blasting," quoting from *Witchcraft in Bute* [1920], which explains that "'blasting is a whirlwinde that the fayries raises [sic] about that persone quhich [sic] they intend to wrong.'"[74]) Of course, if the abilities evinced by witches are rooted in a homeopathic connection between women and the domestic and natural spheres, doesn't it naturally follow that Lovecraft's Colour is likewise connected with the natural world in some way? And that Lovecraft's cosmic beyond, from which this Colour originates, is perhaps also a *feminine* beyond? As critic Maurice Levy observes, Lovecraft's "horror out of space"[75] finds itself "buried immediately in the depths of the earth," thereby suggesting some linkage between these two locations; but although Levy aptly recognizes space as being a "reversed abysm" in Lovecraft's weird fiction, he never goes so far as to acknowledge or discuss the feminine etiology underlying both images, in which the abysses of space, and the abysses within the earth, both figure as embodiments of a fundamentally feminine abyss of the womb, and by extension, the human unconscious. (In his later collaborative story "Medusa's Coil," interestingly, Lovecraft inverts this projection of the Feminine onto the cosmic level by depicting an individual woman, Marceline Bedard, as possessing "some marvelous links with the outside"[76]— the same "outside," presumably, where Lovecraft's cosmic Colour also had its origin. As Lovecraft observes, Marceline was "a splendid focus of cosmic forces who has a right to be called divine if anything on earth has!"[77]) The apparently feminine aspects of Lovecraft's meteor in "The Colour Out of Space" are also prefigured by Trobriand tribal beliefs, reported by anthropologist Bronislaw Malinowski, about sinister witches, who supposedly "'can fly through the air *and appear as a falling star*'"[78] (italics mine). This suggests a clear connection between meteors and feminine night flight imagery, a connection likewise perpetuated in such things as the ancient Ephesian belief that the goddess Artemis came to the earth as a falling stone. Her meteor still was being worshipped as late as the time of St. Paul.

Given her intimate connection with the natural world, Woman is often seen as the archetypal seeress, priestess, or muse: the woman who, as Erich Neumann observes, can understand "the murmuring springs and fountains"[79] and the language of "rustling of the trees and all the signs of nature, with whose life she is so closely bound up"; much in the same way, perhaps, that Mrs. Gardner, in "The Colour Out of Space," is depicted as listening to some odd phenomenon that no one explains but which manifests itself in the movements of the strangely animate trees and some unknown fluttering that has nothing to do with the wind. When Mrs. Gardner *listens*, is she actually listening to the inner life of her own cosmically feminine self?—that voice of the Mother Earth, which Lovecraft makes the locus of all the earth's horrors in his 1919 poem? As one feminist witch similarly claims in Margot Adler's 1979 study of modern paganism: "'Trees talk to me. My plants are telling me right now that they could use some more water. I am surrounded by my ancestors and by spirit friends.'"[80] The unseen fluttering things of the Gardner farm here are paralleled by pantheistic animism and blatant ancestor worship. Certainly, too, the strange interconnectedness of all the odd phenomena evident on the Gardner farm—the contamination of the well water being connected with the animals, which are in turn connected with the plants and with the direct sustenance of the family—closely mirrors the basic interconnectedness of all natural and environmental phenomena under the sway of Mother Nature, although it could also symbolize the ineluctable reach of the maternal within Lovecraft's infantile imagination.

Even more troubling for Lovecraft, however, is the fact that the rites celebrating such natural fertility processes very often involve dancing and intoxication, in which the female is the focal figure.[81] Lovecraft refers to these in his essay *Supernatural Horror in Literature* as "revolting fertility rites of immemorial antiquity,"[82] often combining the feminine, the sexual, the alcoholic, the phallic, and the sadistic. And while it may be true, as scholar Dennis Quinn suggests, that Lovecraft's aversion to the bacchanalia (as evinced by the orgiastic rites of the Cthulhu Cult) is rooted in the historical accounts of Livy, this does nothing to explain the more basic etiology of his polemical aversion, which I would argue had its origin, along with his lifelong and Ciceronian opposition to dancing, in his rather complex relationship with the Feminine archetype. (Ultimately, however, Lovecraft's fascination with the bacchanalia probably stems not from Livy, but rather from his voluminous reading of the early *Munsey* magazines, in which all aspects of the Feminine archetype—including the lascivious Feminine bacchanalia—are common and recurring images.)

The most outstanding characteristic of the Feminine archetype, of course, is the power of giving birth, an idea that also finds expression throughout the Lovecraftian canon, often with regard to the most horrible, awful, and loathsome of creatures. One notes again Lovecraft's image of birthing horrors in his poem "Mother Earth," which ends with the declaration: "I AM THE VOICE OF MOTHER EARTH, / FROM WHENCE ALL HORRORS

HAVE THEIR BIRTH."[83] Notable, too, are those deformed moon-calves in "The Horror at Red Hook," embryonic abortions who persist in bleating aloud their devotion to the Magna Mater, despite their half-formed grotes-querie — what Lovecraft in his earlier poem called those "living things that yet survive, / Tho' not to human ken alive."[84] Lovecraft's hateful references to immigrants throughout his writings, too, will derive much of their impetus from his intimations of furtive breeding or other unknown processes of sub-terranean reproduction: Lovecraft calls them creatures that seem to be "vaguely molded from some stinking slime of earth's corruption."[85] This imagery later gives rise to the shoggoths of *At the Mountains of Madness*, which are similarly described in Lovecraft's preparative notes for that story as being the "'*spawn of inner earth*'"[86] (italics mine), and whose unwise breeding upon our planet instills such horror into both Dyer and Abdul Alhazred.[87] (Anthropologist Erich Neumann refers to a similar such archetypal conception in *The Great Mother*, in the form of an eleventh-century medieval drawing [Neumann's plate 29] that depicts the earth as a woman, and her earth-body as "nourishing monsters"[88]; in this case, a slithering Cthulhuian tentacle, covered with octopoid-suction cups.)

Here too belongs Lovecraft's recurring imagery of underground repro-duction in "The Lurking Fear" (there called "isolated spawning, multiplica-tion")[89] and "Pickman's Model" (with its picture of ant-like breeding underground), eventually culminating, again, in Danforth's final vision at the end of *At the Mountains of Madness*, in which, like a child lifting a rock, and recoiling at the sight of the living bugs, worms, and larvae swarming under-neath, Lovecraft finally unveils the secrets concealed beneath the earth when the cosmic rock is lifted from above. It is as if the unending piles of skeletons discovered at the climax to "The Rats in the Walls" — what Lovecraft calls, in his prose-poem "What the Moon Brings," "the perfume-conquering stench of the world's dead"[90] — are symbols not merely of death but of the original sin of life itself, which gave form to those murdered beings in the first place. Lovecraft, in the notes for his abortive literary piece "Life and Death," calls this "life!— the greater horror!"[91] bemoaning the fact that (to him, at least) "life is more horrible than death." In "The Outsider," too, the damp and obviously intrauterine castle passages are pessimistically associated not with life but with death: Lovecraft likens the presiding smell of his castle to "the piled-up corpses of dead generations"[92]; the same unceasing processes of Fem-inine sexual generation, personified by Shub-Niggurath with her Thousand Young. It is but a small step from such a despairing formulation to an overall condemnation of that Feminine engine that is most closely associated with the generation of life.

Table 5. Elements of the Primal Scene in Danforth's Final Vision, *At the Mountains of Madness*	
Danforth's Vision in Mountains of Madness	*Parental Primal Scene (Sexual Intercourse)*
"'primal white jelly'" (*MM* 106)	Seminal fluid?
"'black pit'" (*MM* 106)	Uterus/underworld?: what J. J. Bachofen calls the "'primordial mother of dark matter'" and "'the primordial shadow, the dark womb'" (quoted by Neumann, *Great Mother*, 259).
"'the carven rim'" (*MM* 106)	The vulva?
"'the nameless cylinder'" (*MM* 106)	The phallus? (Which is here presumably gigantic, as compared with the "tiny" [*D* 148] hand of the castrated and child-like "cylindrical object" in "Herbert West: Reanimator").
"'the eyes in the darkness'" (*MM* 106)	The feminine eyes of sexuality or sensuality.
"'the original, the eternal, the undying'" (*MM* 106)	What the Egyptians called Net, the Goddess of Sais, who declared of herself, "'I am all that has been, and is, and shall be'" (Plutarch, quoted in Neumann, *Great Mother*, 220).
"'the elder pharos'" (*MM* 106)	*Elder* = parental? *Pharos* = god-king? Thus, yet another version of the divine apotheosis of the all-powerful elder or parent, here engaged in the primal sexual act.

As anthropologist Erich Neumann observes, in terms that eerily coincide with Lovecraft's own fictional outlook, "Wherever the antival fanaticism of the male spiritual principle predominates, the Feminine is looked upon as negative and evil, precisely in its character of creator, sustainer, and increaser of life."[93] This is because, as Neumann goes on, "this male principle of consciousness, *which desires permanence and not change*, eternity and not transformation, law and not creative spontaneity, 'discriminates' against the Great Goddess and turns her into a demon" (italics mine). This could almost be a description of Lovecraft himself, whose philosophy, in all its aspects, whether social, political, architectural, literary, or aesthetic, was based upon just such an unswerving devotion to permanence, tradition, and lack of change. The horrors of Lovecraft's socio-political essays, as well the more general amorphous and formless horrors of his weird fiction, all are rooted in a basic aversion to (an ultimately feminine) mutability and instability.

And although Lovecraft apparently never completed his prose-poem "Life and Death,"[94] the nihilistic philosophy informing it went on to inform the corrupted images of breeding and fertility found throughout his weird canon (what Lovecraft cryptically calls, in "Medusa's Coil," "furtive midnight cult-practices"),[95] images that have their origins in an infantile view of the primal scene of secretive parental sexuality. As noted above,[96] the revelation of the primal scene to the infantile mind is often a traumatic event, which is often interpreted in a sadomasochistic fashion as a battle or an act of violence between man and woman. H. R. Hays, in his book *The Dangerous Sex*, cites the example of Freudian anthropologist Geza Roheim's analysis of Australian aborigines, who "weave myths about erunchas, demonic copulating monsters, which Roheim felt were projected images dramatizing the anxiety awakened on viewing the primal scene."[97] I would suggest that the moon-ladder and all the other "bizarre conceptions"[98] witnessed by Danforth at the end of *Mountains of Madness* represent just such a projected image: a cosmicized version of what Lovecraft elsewhere calls the "snarling chaos and grinning fear that lurk behind *life*"[99] (italics mine) in "The Lurking Fear." "Life" is the operative word here: not the terror of oblivion, which Lovecraft in any case welcomes, or the pain of death, but rather the terror of existence itself, as brought into being and nourished via the mother, and created during the primal act.

As Maurice Levy tellingly observes while discussing Lovecraft's mythic impulse, his weird fiction evinces an overwhelming concern with what Levy calls "the times signifying the beginnings, the Great Time at the beginning of time,"[100] also called "the first Act." Levy goes on to quote from historian Mircea Eliade on the basic concern of mythology with those "'times of the beginnings,'"[101] which is to explain how we have "'come into existence.'" But although Levy does not say so, such language applies equally well to the more basic and infantile mystery of the sex act, parental beginnings, and sexual origins, as it does to wider mythic cosmologies. And although Levy notes such disparate and recurring Lovecraftian themes as an obsession with the primordial beginning of time, with his familial line, with genealogical quests, and with "the 'ancients'"[102]—even going so far as to point out how Lovecraft's Old Ones are, "par excellence, the actors of a primordial drama played at the beginning"[103]—nowhere does he refer to this more basic, and immediate, connection with the parental and the familial.

One sees intimations of this primal parental scene in the island described in *The Dream-Quest of Unknown Kadath*, which Lovecraft tells us had "never been sought by any vessel *because of the sounds that came from it at night*"[104] (italics mine)—nocturnal parental sounds, possibly, which closely mirror those other, equally nocturnal sounds created by the sinister "old cotter and his wife"[105] in Lovecraft's highly personal "The Cats of Ulthar" (also called "sounds heard in the night" and "sounds heard after dark"). That these sounds are here associated with murder, in this case, the sadistic murder of cats by the old (parental?) couple, merely reinforces Lovecraft's sadistic transmutation of this primal parental act. While the fact that Lovecraft explicitly equates the murdered cats in this story with children (as Lovecraft writes, the villagers, upon hearing such sounds, console themselves by thanking "Fate"[106] that it was not one of their own children "who had, thus vanished") is suggestive of that infanticidal maternity of the witch and the vampiric she-demon, whose sexual act is also equated with child sacrifice. (Lovecraft further reinforces this connection with the primal scene by his inclusion of the same small or little boy Atal, from "The Cats of Ulthar," in his later story "The Other Gods," in which, as we have seen, Atal takes part in an expedition to observe the gods [his parents?] during their secretive and forbidden mountaintop revels [sexual intercourse?]; the same primal scene whose sight later drives Danforth mad.)

And although such things as "'the original, the eternal, the undying'"[107] may seem at first to be the most abstract and least identifiable aspect of Danforth's final vision, it also proves to be an identifiably feminine conception, and closely aligned with what anthropologist Erich Neumann calls the elementary character of the primordial feminine: that Great Mother of the beginning who exists beyond space and time, lurking in the cosmic darkness — what Jung called, in the words of Neumann, "the Archetypal feminine as the world-governing totality in all its aspects."[108] Now *that* is cosmism. And it is also feminine, too: a cosmism in which the unending void beyond existence is identified with the procreatory power of the mother, who births and feeds and then kills, thus creating the life-and-death structure of uroboric infinity.

In the bloody myths of Meso-America, she was called "'Our Ancestress and Heart of the Earth,'"[109] the primal feminine underworld here combined with ancestor worship. She was propitiated by the natives with brutal acts of human sacrifice, and is described in proto–Lovecraftian terms as the "*primordial goddess of matter*, whose terrible character with *its eyes* and voracious gullets bursts forth from all her joints"[110] (italics mine), an image that forms an almost word-for-word prefiguration of Danforth's vision at the end of *At the Mountains of Madness*, with its "primal white jelly" and "eyes in the darkness."[111] As Wallis Budge observed of Egyptian goddess Net, this primal and "'all-pervading'"[112] female principle was seen as "'self-sustaining and self-existent'" in both a cosmic and a parthenogenic sense. This is an archetypal idea that retains its power even now, via the familiar image of Virgin Mary and her child, but which is transformed by Lovecraft, in Danforth's final vision, into an image of the unending and corrupt fecundity of nature: some fundamental, immortal mother-principle, unstoppable and plasmatic, dwelling either beneath the earth or upon the moon, or in some trans-dimensional warp stretching between these two locations, and perhaps giving birth in an unceasing stream to some sub-shoggothian form of life ("'the proto-shoggoths'"),[113] which pass up and down the moon-ladder in endless streams.

Lovecraft even hints at his own form of parthenogenesis in this process, in the form of that "'carven rim'" and "'nameless cylinder'" also mentioned in Danforth's final vision: feminine and masculine images, respectively, that mirror the actual architecture of the Old Ones' ruined city, which also contains what Dyer calls "a monstrous cylindrical tower"[114] that resembles "a prodigious round aperture from above." Similar images are seen in that (masculine) steeple in "The Haunter of the Dark," which also contains within it both a (feminine) egg-like stone and an entity from the (feminine) cosmic abyss; as well as in the sinister parental hermaphroditism of the wife and father Asenath Waite in "The Thing on the Doorstep," all perhaps representing what the ancient pagans saw as the endless parthenogenic fecundity of nature itself. That reabsorption back into the peaceful womb of nature, which the young Lovecraft had wished to accomplish via the expedient of suicide, here isn't achieved; instead, Danforth sees the bosom of nature itself while it is sexually active, and in fact caught in the middle of a sex act. A return into the womb is hardly possible with a phallus in the way.

At the same time, according to Erich Neumann, this messy and sadistic primal scene, as conceived by Lovecraft and the Australian aborigines alike, is often countered in mythology by the idealistic, celestial image of the Good Mother as a celestial or cosmic virgin (the goddess Sophia, or the Virgin Mary), who is conceived of as spiritually conceiving and giving birth to a "luminous son"[115] or "'divine child,'"[116] who often "springs from a rock, a tree, the earth, the mouth."[117] Lovecraft utilizes this idea in "The Crawling Chaos," in which that "radiant pair" of parents, noted above, are accompanied by what he calls a "strange child,"[118] who apparently springs forth from a tree. And tellingly, although "The Crawling Chaos" is an apocalyptic story, the nasty procreative fecundity at the end of *At the Mountains of Madness* is nowhere in evidence; instead, the glowing cosmic realm of the radiant pair is presented as being in complete opposition to the apocalyptic imagery of subterrene decay that transpires beneath it.

Lovecraft's view in "The Tomb" and "The Outsider," of the womb as tomb, also reflects another basic feminine archetype, of the Feminine as a container or vessel; whether a vessel for seed and child, or as a dispenser of milk and nourishment. (Some have even argued that the fabled Holy Grail itself was not a chalice, but actually the womb of Mary Magdalene [i.e., the womb of the fertility goddess] — an idea that Neumann argues also forms the source for the image of the cornucopia.[119]) This vessel-symbolism also seems to underlie the notion of "Pandora's Box," which was originally described by Hesiod as a great "'jar,'"[120] and which later generations would, as writer H. R. Hays observes, directly associate with "'that part'"[121] (i.e., the vagina), "'from which so many troubles and sorrows have flowed out upon mankind.'" The works of H. P. Lovecraft contain numerous closed or windowless spaces: Danforth's cryptic "'windowless solids'"[122] in *At the Mountains of Madness*, which are paralleled in "The Haunter of the Dark" by that "windowless crypt"[123] in which the pharaoh's great and unnamable sin was committed; what Lovecraft, in his fragmentary story "The Book," similarly calls "a great square building of stone in an open space,"[124] which the author says causes an inexplicable and "hideous fear" to begin *clutching at me* (italics mine) (the feminine/grandmotherly night gaunts, tickling him again); these are all dense, unlit, airtight spaces, which critic Robert Waugh elsewhere declares to be impervious to hermeneutic elaboration,[125] but which easily yield to exegetic explanation via the black box of the intrauterine.

This feminine vessel imagery also gave rise to the archetypal imagery of the witch with her cauldron.[126] Dr. Margaret Murray, for instance, cites recipes for the witches' (basically sexual) flying potion, which was supposedly created from boiling "'the fat of young children'"[127] in a "'brazen vessel.'" This reads almost like a parody of the actual feminine processes of gestation and maternity, and is perhaps later reflected in that "large covered vat"[128] in "Herbert West: Reanimator," in which bubbles the proto-shoggothian "cell-matter" that the necrophilic West uses in his experiments in the creation of life. (Lovecraft may also have been influenced in this imagery by the similar chemical vats that figure in Edgar Rice Burroughs' earlier mad-scientist story *A Man Without a Soul* [*All-Story*, 1913], which also deals with the artificial creation of life.) Tellingly, too, witches' familiars were also said to inhabit such familiar domestic (and traditionally feminine) vessels as pots, boxes, and jars,[129] a fact that strengthens the essentially maternal nature of the witches' supposed power.

This vessel archetype of Great Mother also underlies what Erich Neumann calls the recurring image of "the sacrificial blood bowl"[130] throughout history, which often figured in the sadistic sacrificial rites of the Meso-American natives. As Neumann observes, "the kettles of Mexico, the blood bowls, like the cauldrons of the underworld, are vessels of transformation on which depend fertility, light, and transformation."[131] Lovecraft himself refers to a "pale metal bowl"[132] covered with ancient designs in "The Dreams in the Witch House," which has "ominous brown stains"[133] on the bottom, and which is used by witch Keziah Mason to collect the blood from sacrificed children. As Neumann observes, "The terrible symbol of the blood bowl still inhabits the unconscious; it occurs in the fantasies and dreams of the sane as well as the insane." Neumann cites in this connection the case history of English mass-murderer John George Haigh, who also claimed to have been impelled in his murderous acts "by a higher power — a higher thing that was outside him and dominated him,"[134] an image disconcertingly similar to the strange paralysis and hypnotism experienced by Walter Gilman at the hands of Keziah Mason in the same story. Murray also mentions such infanticidal blood-bowls in her *Witch-Cult*.[135] And although it may be that Lovecraft derived these symbols of Keziah's knife, her bowl, her fanged familiar, and the beclawed and aged crone herself from previous writings, either Murray's book or else the science-fantasy stories of the early *Munsey* magazines, which are replete with imagery of primitive rites involving human sacrifice, this in no way explains Lovecraft's choice of this particular set of symbols, especially in a weird *oeuvre*, which is noted by most critics for its authorial independence and originality. Instead, they indicate an authorial obsession on the part of H. P. Lovecraft, and one that, as we shall see below, involves typical and recurring characteristics of the archetypal Terrible Mother.

It is to this vessel symbolism of the feminine body that we must also look for the meaning of what Neumann calls the idea of the underworld as "the 'belly' or 'womb' of the earth."[136] This idea in turn gives rise to such familiar feminine symbols as the "chasm, cave, abyss, valley, depths, which ... play the part of the earth womb that demands to be fructified." Lovecraft in "Arthur Jermyn" calls this "the darkness of abysmal treasure-vaults and inconceivable catacombs,"[137] words used by Sir Wade Jermyn in his ravings about Africa, and the woman he met (and married) there. (Lovecraft, it is true, derives the underground treasure-vault imagery in this story from Edgar Rice Burroughs' *Tarzan and the Jewels of Opar* [*All-Story*, 1915], in which Tarzan visit's the underground treasure vaults of a decadent Atlantean city ruled by a lascivious and terrible priestess named La; but once again his personal choice of this imagery reveals his archetypal preoccupations.) In his poem "Mother Earth," too, the final declaration at the end of the poem is preceded by a welter of such traditional symbols of the female earth-womb as the "gully, ravine, abyss"[138]: Lovecraft's poet passes into what he calls "a deep valley, hush'd and dank,"[139] whose "walls contracted as I went" (and whose vaginal symbolism is unmistakable), after which the poet then "crouch'd within a rocky cleft." (Even there, however, Lovecraft's poet finds no relief;

and although he attempts to trace with his hands the surface of the ancient stone around him, he writes, "The clinging lichens moist and *hoary* / Forbade me read the *antique* story"[140] (italics mine), typically combining vaginal dampness and pubic roughness with an infantile view of maternal age.)

It was into just such rocky clefts and ravines that the dismembered body parts of sacrificed pigs were once thrown during the rituals of the (feminine) Greek Thesmophoria — sacrifices, Neumann writes, that fulfilled what was seen by the unconscious mind as "the need for fecundating and reviving the feminine earth with blood, death, and corpses."[141] The same psychology underlies Lovecraft's subterranean and sacrificial imagery in "The Rats in the Walls" and "Under the Pyramids," and also led to the homicidal regimes of the Meso-American natives. (In *At the Mountains of Madness*, too, the Old Ones' city is pitted with enormous, circular gulfs with stairways leading down below, suggestive of some dark and ancient rite. Were these pits used by the Old Ones in a manner similar to the Aztec or Mayan sacrificial pits, i.e., for sacrifices to propitiate the undying feminine force located beneath them?)

This is the place of the lower goddess, what Neumann calls the well-known "deadly devouring maw of the underworld,"[142] an image common to popular myths and Lovecraft's weird fiction alike. For Lovecraft, this dark force at the heart of the underworld was seen as being even more powerful than his aquatic Cthulhu: Lovecraft, in his collaborative "The Crawling Chaos," refers to those "dark gods of the inner earth that are greater than the evil god of waters."[143] Amongst the native tribes of Tierra del Fuego, according to anthropologist H. R. Hays, this goddess was called Tanowa, and was said to dwell in a cave called "the Mouth of the Underworld,"[144] "from which the terrible feminine spirit was supposed to emerge." This idea, Hays writes, is "clearly symbolic of the female genital organ," here reimagined as a castrative or devouring orifice. Amongst the Polynesians, too, we find a female underworld goddess, whose femininity was also associated with "the west"[145] where the sun sets, and therefore with a land regarded as a place of "darkness and death" (a nocturnal analogue with the unconscious mind). (Coincidentally or not, the west is also, one notes, the location of those forbidden mountains "which the Old Ones had shunned and feared"[146] in *At the Mountains of Madness*.) In John Uri Lloyd's occult-novel *Etidorhpa*, which Lovecraft read appreciatively, the subterranean inner earth is likewise pictured as the abode of a feminine goddess called Etidorhpa ("Aphrodite" spelled backwards), although Lloyd's goddess is far more benevolent and celestial than Lovecraft's later conceptions.

Even now, this feminine, vaginal imagery of the underworld is still associated with doom and destruction. In Brian De Palma's brilliant and darkly

The maw of the underworld: the vulvic entrance to the supposed womb of the inner-earth, Udayagiri Hill, India. A similarly devouring image of the subterranean or inner world likewise obtains throughout Lovecraft's weird canon. From James Fergusson, *The History of Indian and Eastern Architecture*, vol. 2, ed. J. Burgess and R. Phene Spiers (London: J. Murray, 1910).

satiric cult film *Body Double* (1984), the protagonist's fear of subterranean tunnels, graves, and other intravaginal spaces is linked with Hollywood's larger necrophilic aesthetic of Gothic horror, vampirism, and sadism. In the television series *Buffy the Vampire Slayer* (whose creator, Joss Whedon, was heavily influenced by Lovecraftian conceptions), this subterranean doom takes the form of a dimensional portal called the "Hellmouth" that exists below the vampire-infested town of Sunnydale, and which causes doom to rise up from below (what H. P. Lovecraft similarly calls "'The Burrower Beneath.'"[147]) Indeed, in the final season of *Buffy*, the villain Buffy has been fighting throughout the entire series, called the First Evil or simply the First — the first source of all the evil in the universe — conveniently assumes human form. Significantly, the form it assumes is that of a female; indeed, not only a female, but a duplicate of Buffy herself: the feminine savior (symbolized in Buddhism by the goddess Tara, and in Gnosticism by the heroine Norea), here locked in eternal struggle/uroboric embrace with the Terrible Mother/feminine power of darkness, who is none other than herself. Indeed, on the elementary level of the primordial mother, both manifestations of the feminine archetype are essentially the same.

Perhaps the oddest — and most illuminating — example of this feminine underworld that I have yet seen can be found in a 1999 video produced by the publishers of *Weird New Jersey* magazine, in which we are treated to a tour (of the exterior, anyway) of what local inhabitants call "The Gates of Hell," which turns out to be nothing more than a concrete storm drain with a strikingly vulvic layout and angle, obviously the hangout of local teenagers (the walls are covered with graffiti, the ground littered with trash), around which many local rumors have gathered. According to local resident Ralph Sinici, local accounts tell of "many levels"[148] of subterranean rooms located within, including chambers "with large axes on the doors," "rooms filled with skulls, skeletons, and various other objects.... Bones have been found here from animal sacrifices.... Just a very eerie place in general." These ideas bear a direct, albeit more populist, parallel with Lovecraft's own picture of a subterranean grotto filled with skulls and skeletons in "The Rats in the Walls," as well as with the castrative rites of Atys and Cybele in the same story (rites symbolically represented here by the castrative "axes on the doors," an example of the familiar image of the *vagina dentata* of the Terrible Mother, whose "door" cuts off the penis like a guillotine; and represented as well as by the special reference to skulls in both accounts, beheading being a common symbolic representation of castration).[149] A not-unrelated and very large amount of racist, sexual, and Satanic (what Lovecraft would doubtlessly call "blasphemous") graffiti also adorns the walls outside this fabled New Jersey storm drain. Much of it is painted or scrawled precisely where the awaiting thighs of an outstretched, reclining woman would be: phrases such as "All Niggers Will Die," "K.K.K.," "White Power," a Nazi swastika, "Fuck You All," "I Hate All Jews," "666 Is Motherfucker," "Gates of Hell," etc.; all represent the darkest expressions of the sadistic and incestuous human unconscious, and all are analogous to the paranoid hatreds embodied within Lovecraft's own shoggoths, with their embedded Jewish, black, and feminine aspects. Indeed, that there is some psycho-sexual connection between the vulvic layout of the drain, the sadistic fantasies of local residents (doubtlessly teenaged boys) about the drain, and the graffiti upon the walls, cannot be doubted, any more than we can doubt a connection between Danforth's final horrific vision, Lovecraft's shoggoths, and Lovecraft's stalled and infantile sexuality. The racist graffiti here, in other words, is the unconscious equivalent of Lovecraft's excremental shoggoths; the darkness of the lurking feminine underworld in both instances corresponds, in the unconscious mind, to the primal, repressed sadism lurking within.

It is highly doubtful, of course, that any of these New Jerseyites were inspired by H. P. Lovecraft's weird fiction in their rumors about a subterranean lair filled with skulls and skeletons. Rather, both images ultimately derive from the same archetypal source: in this case, an image of the vagina as realm of death, and as a castrating force — an image often allied with the strangely common misogynistic idea, noted by H. R. Hays, that female sexual "fulfillment was a cannibal act committed upon the male."[150] And although Lovecraft's lifelong fascination with cannibalism doubtlessly derived from accounts of primitive rites of human sacrifice perpetuated in the early *Munsey* pulps, its significance to him probably derived, at least in part, from just such a belief: hence the connection in his mind between the castrative rites of Cybele and Atys on the one hand, and the cannibalistic rites of the Delapores one the other.

Lovecraft, of course, is by no means the only writer of the macabre to be interested in (not to say obsessed with) such feminine underworld imagery. Another example is, again, Beckford's *Vathek*, with its portrait of the devouring mother in the form of both the underworld itself and also Prince Vathek's dreaded mother Carathis, who is depicted as a sorceress who knows the secret subterranean passages and "mysterious recesses"[151] in Vathek's tower just as well as her depraved son. At the end of *Vathek*, too, mother Carathis demonstrates an astonishing familiarity with, and affinity for, the Satanic underworld, passing "by rapid descents, known only to Eblis [Satan] and his most favored potentates; and thus penetrat[ing] the very entrails of the earth, where breathes the sansar, or the icy wind of death."[152] None of these "appalled her dauntless soul" — language already suggestive of the dynamics of Lovecraft's later misty moon-ladder in *At the Mountains of Madness*.

This character of the Elementary Feminine as vessel, cave, and underworld is also embodied in the archetypal image of the woman as tomb, both the grave within the ground and the coffin (or crematory vessel) itself, which were often regarded as taking the dead into themselves like a womb or vagina, an image well-represented throughout culture and folklore. Psychologist Ernest Jones cites a tale in which a young man's restless corpse is rejected by the grave (i.e., Mother Earth) because he had committed the crime of maternal incest while alive.[153] This idea reflects that homeopathic principle of like-affecting-like, which governs so many primitive and infantile relationships (as well as governing, perhaps, the reason for the Outsider's similar restlessness in Lovecraft's story.) As Erich Neumann observes, "in the Rig-Veda the earth is invoked as the coverer who takes the dead man to herself: '*As a mother covers her son* with the hem of her cloak'"[154] (italics mine). Thus, in much the same way that the womb of Mother Earth was thought to give birth to all life, so too was it seen as taking this life back into her womb again. This psychological confusion between sex and death permeates Lovecraft's weird fiction just as much as it did Poe's. In "The Tomb," Jervas Dudley's coming-of-age takes the form of a night spent sleeping in an otherwise empty coffin; and the sickening fate of Edward Derby in "The Thing on the Doorstep" is that his soul is transferred into Asenath Waite's dead body, which was buried in the cellar.[155] Lovecraft here reflects this idea of the feminine body as coffin quite literally.

IV. Other Feminine Symbols

Above and beyond these more obvious and procreative feminine archetypes, there are also several other archetypes, more abstract but no less common, that populate the Lovecraftian canon. The moon, for example, as a symbol of the Feminine, has already been adequately discussed in chapter 4. Another common symbol is the association of the Feminine with bodies of water, large or small: this is expressed via the numerous goddesses of rivers, springs, and fountains; the nymphs of the sea; and the more sinister female powers of the dark and brooding swamp, and of deep and mysterious wells. (Thus do we find that the witches' Sabbath was required to "be held near a lake, stream, or water of some kind."[156]) Many of Lovecraft's weird entities, too, whether feminine or not, likewise take up residence in bodies of water: the flooded rivers in "The Whisperer in Darkness," the hidden lake in "The Call of Cthulhu," Cold Spring Glen in "The Dunwich Horror," and the Antarctic sea in *At the Mountains of Madness*. Lovecraft's only requirement in making such associations, of course, was his aversion to the sea; but it was an aversion that perhaps reflects an unconscious archetypal basis.

Wells especially, combining as they do water with the archetypal symbolism of both the underworld and the Feminine vessel, find frequent and sinister representation in Lovecraft's weird fiction. As Erich Neumann observes, "in the well the elementary character of the Feminine"[157] (i.e., the primordial mother of unformed chaos and the abyss) "is still evident — it is no accident that in fairy tales a well is often the gate to the underworld and specifically to the domain of the earth mother." Lovecraft mentions that "well too deep for dredging"[158] in "The Horror at Red Hook," and Thurber suggestively describes "'wells leading nowhere'"[159] in "Pickman's Model," which Lovecraft, of course, then goes on to associate with the activities of "'witches and what their spells summoned.'" In "The Colour Out of Space," as we have seen, Lovecraft's cosmic Colour takes up residence in what he calls "the *yawning black maw* of *an abandoned well*"[160] (italics mine) on the Gardner farm. Indeed, Lovecraft's use of a well in "Colour" may preserve both a feminine *and* a witch by connotation; Murray's *Witch-Cult* refers throughout to the worshipping at wells by witches,[161] and even cites a 1590 account that describes the Devil himself— or one of his familiars — as hiding in a well in the form of a dog (which suggests, perhaps, the later canine well-dwellers of Pickman), and nearly dragging a woman down into the well via his powers of hypnotism.[162] And significantly, it is only "after a visit to the well"[163] that Mrs. Gardner's son Thaddeus finally "went mad" in "Colour"— suggestive, perhaps, of some incestuous contact between mother and son; that is, if we are to take literally the symbolism suggested between the maw of the well and the entrance to the underworld of Mother Earth. Ironically too, the only solution to the feminine, cosmic contamination of the Gardner's farm in this story is provided by yet another feminine body of water, in the form of that lake shortly to be created by the Arkham reservoir project, which will flood the entire valley. The lake perhaps represents a final resurgence of the primordial feminine once again, a blanketing of localized chaos beneath the much larger and all-smothering chaos of maternal, universal darkness; an analogue, again, to that merciful (and ultimately intrauterine) new Dark Age for which Lovecraft so dubiously pleads at the beginning of "The Call of Cthulhu."

The watery environment of the swamp, too, finds numerous (and often feminine) expressions in Lovecraft's weird fiction, from settings to surnames,[164] from the swamp where Cthulhu's statue is found, to the dreary salt marshes outside Arkham where Walter Gilman is sent wandering by his nightmares about the witch Keziah Mason, to the suicide of Iranon in a marsh of quicksand; not to mention the eponymous bog in "The Moon-Bog," which proves to hide within its depths an entire realm of feminine and fairy wonders: dancing naiads, a temple of Artemis, and a bacchanalian feminine power that can reach directly from the depths of the swamp up to the heights of the moon. Swamps also figure incidentally in Lovecraft's "Polaris"[165] and "The Statement of Randolph Carter," associated in the latter story with a yet another typically pagan "gross luxuriance of ... unhealthy vegetation."[166] This forms the setting for what Carter calls "amorphous shadows"[167] engaging in "some blasphemous ceremonial procession," an image closely akin, perhaps, to those fatal hypnotic (and feminine) processions that Lovecraft often associated with the Terrible Mother (discussed further below).

Such swamps are often associated in myth with female powers. Erich Neumann, for example, writes of the legendary "water lady"[168] of the Germans, who was regarded as being "the primordial mother." Neumann goes so far as to suggest a linguistic connection between the Germanic words for *mother*, *marsh*, *moor*, and *maritime*, an etymological connection that bears a close resemblance to a similar, psychologically based etymological relation that Ernest Jones suggests between the feminine words for *marsh*, *mare* (female horse) and *mara* (the nocturnal hag of the *nightmare*). (Jones devotes an entire chapter of *On the Nightmare* to this revealing issue of the *M-R* root). Nor is it any coincidence, perhaps, that the evil mother Carathis in *Vathek*, as well as her sinister retinue of black female servants, should find themselves so much at home in the swamp: Carathis enjoys "whatever filled others with dread,"[169] and thus glories in the "pestilential blast" that blew in from an "extensive marsh." A similarly feculent odor, likewise associated with mud, also characterizes the vampires of medieval myth, as well as the primitive witches of tribal Melanesian legends, who according to H. R. Hays "are supposed to smell like excrement and are particularly dangerous to mariners"[170] (the archetypal feminine relation to the sea, again). All these ideas share a psychological origin with Lovecraft's own equally excremental, partly aquatic (and, as I shall argue below, partially feminine) shoggoths.

The common feminine archetype of the "mound or tumulus"[171] is also well known, being reflected in works as diverse as Aubrey Beardsley's pornographic *Under the Hill* and H. P. Lovecraft's collaborative story "The Mound," in which the mound in the title leads to an underworld, called K'n-yan, described as "a veritable Witches' Sabbath"[172] and characterized, as we have seen, by the bacchanalian worship of Shub-Niggurath (Astarte). Significantly too, K'n-yan's underworld society is also characterized by widespread sexual freedom for women in particular: Lovecraft describes how the "large affection groups"[173] of Tsathian society included "many noblewomen of the most extreme and art-enhanced beauty." It is in this sadistic, decadent society that the hero Zamacona finds female companionship in the form of the native woman "T'la-yub," a love that later proves disastrous, however, as her reanimated corpse seizes and captures him. As Lovecraft puts it, he is *"Seized by the will of K'n-yan in the headless body of T'la-yub"*[174] (italics Lovecraft's and Bishop's). Erich Neumann elsewhere refers to this as the capacity of the Terrible Mother for paralyzing and ensnaring the unwary male.[175] As with Edward Derby being transported into the rotting corpse of wife Asenath Waite, the female body is here presented as a vessel of death. Lovecraft's use of mound-symbolism in "The Mound" may also partially reflect his reading of Murray's *Witch-Cult*, in which her hypothetical race of prehistoric Devil-worshippers are described as "living as mound-dwellers"[176] on the European moors; although as early as "The Lurking Fear" (which was written before Lovecraft ever read Murray), the "isolated spawning, multiplication"[177] of the Martense family occurs beneath a series of sinister mounds. In "The Colour Out of Space," too, the crash site of the cosmic meteor is described as a "big brownish mound."[178]

One of the most subtle and unexpected expressions of the feminine archetype in Lovecraft's weird fiction is perhaps the symbol of the throne, whose shape is traced by Erich Neumann to the common maternal image of the child sitting in its mother's lap, as reflected throughout history in such things as the recurring religious art motif of Isis holding the child Horus, or the Virgin Mary holding the baby Jesus. (Both are reminiscent of those laps of the gigantic and mountainous gods in *The Dream-Quest of Unknown Kadath*, from which arise the hordes of sinister shantak-birds.) As Neumann explains, "The seated Great Mother is the original form of the 'enthroned Goddess,' and also of the throne itself,"[179] with the legs and thighs of the seated goddess becoming very the legs and seat of the chair. Neumann traces this idea through the widespread and often gigantic throne-cults found throughout ancient Anatolia and the Mediterranean, and also in the very name of the goddess Isis herself, which means literally "'the seat,' 'the throne,' the symbol of which she wears on her head."[180] (Not surprisingly, either, we also find occultist John Uri Lloyd invoking similar throne-imagery of the feminine in *Etidorhpa*; the eternal goddess of the underworld tells us that she is seated upon "the highest throne"[181] in heaven.) One notes a similar giganticism of thrones in Lovecraft's parodic collaboration "The Horror in the Museum" (1932), in which he describes "a curious throne whose proportion could have not been designed for a human occupant."[182] In the throne sits a thing whose giganticism matches that of its cyclopean surroundings, and whose worship is connected with what Lovecraft characteristically calls "'obscene legends.'"

Lovecraft will also visit this image of the throne throughout "The Horror at Red Hook," in which the she-demon Lilith is repeatedly depicted as squatting upon her throne[183] in a scatological and excremental inversion of Great Mother imagery. As discussed in my essay "Nightmare Imagery in the Writings of H. P. Lovecraft" (forthcoming), the recurrence of this "squatting" language with regard to evil entities throughout Lovecraft's weird fiction seems to reflect some joint primitive and excremental obsession; the fact that a female demon adopts such a posture in the traditional context of Feminine goddess worship further suggests a sadistic psychological connection between childbirth and defecation (which makes sense, considering Lovecraft's largely negative view of life), in which the mother gives birth not to life but only to dung (an essential component of fertility, vegetation, and farming). The depraved Marquis de Sade describes a similar such equation of birth with defecation in his sadistic, scatological novel *Justine*, in which Justine's defecation upon a priest's face is likened to a soft "'egg'"[184] that the woman lays. Lovecraft, however, further inverts such maternal imagery in this story by describing how Lilith's nude body is baptized in the blood of "stainless childhood"[185] by her followers, even as she unswaths the dead body of her sacrificial husband, Suydam, whose corpse is wrapped in "bedding"[186] much like that of a small baby. Lilith thus represents the lascivious and devouring obverse of motherhood, an Earth Mother of dung, reduced to a devouring, infanticidal whore. The throne of the Earth Goddess here becomes equated with the porcelain throne.

This throne imagery of the devouring goddess or priestess was pervasive throughout the early pulp and science-fantasy stories that Lovecraft devoured as a youth, particularly the tales of Edgar Rice Burroughs, whose villainesses routinely leer down upon the bound hero from a lofty bench or throne. (So too was the recurring Lovecraftian "squatting" language with regard to primitive people or bestial monsters; although it must be noted, again, that Lovecraft alone takes the added step of applying such language to the posture of a female priestess.) Lovecraft may also have been influenced in the curious imagery of blood, innocence, and vampires in "Red Hook" by Perley Poore Sheehan's *Judith of Babylon* (*All-Story*, 1915), in which a Babylonian magician named Cush — much like Lilith in Lovecraft's tale — attempts to take over New York City one block at a time, beginning with the slums. The sinister Cush at one point explains how the shedding of "innocent blood"[187] often attracts "vampires, larvae, elementals!" from the darkness, all glowing with "phosphorescence"; very much like the phosphorescent Lilith. Yet this still does nothing to explain Lovecraft's choice of this particular imagery, or why it should have found such resonance with his own imaginative conceptions regarding absolute evil.

And if, as I argue elsewhere, Lovecraft's often gigantic weird entities represent an inverted version of his recurring parental obsessions, then Lilith's throne perhaps represents yet another malevolent obverse of Lovecraft's recurring ejaculations of "God Save the King!" and "'God Save the Queen!'"[188] throughout his letters: the lascivious and sadistic Lilith perhaps symbolizes Lovecraft's ambivalent anxiety at ceding his mental and physical emancipation to his own maternal godhead, with the incestuous anxieties this naturally entailed. Indeed, Lovecraft's Lilith, in addition to being described in medieval Jewish lore as "a demon who ate children,"[189] was also described, tellingly (and much like Lovecraft's equally parental Old Ones), as "the mother of all things,"[190] the former idea doubtlessly being homeopathically rooted within the latter.

And although both kings and the paternal godhead later usurped this throne-symbol of the Great Mother (as Erich Neumann writes, the "goddess, as a feminine figure of wisdom, was *disenthroned* and repressed"),[191] the original symbolism of the throne itself as a seat of power still remains to this very day, although largely divested of its original, maternal meaning. In much the same way, too, I would argue, was Lilith's throne later usurped by Lovecraft's masculine Cthulhu, who in "The Call of Cthulhu" (written just a year after "Red Hook") is similarly described as having "squatted evilly on a rectangular block or pedestal."[192] The undead Cthulhu takes possession of the throne of Lilith, and in so doing also reclaims the throne for the equally undead and equally masculine Robert Suydam, who like the immortal Cthulhu lives on for a time even after the evil Lilith puts him to death.[193] There are a number of close similarities between the post-mortem Suydam and the undead Cthulhu, both of whom are masculine figures, and both of whom are described as being corpulent and jellyish.[194] A case could be made that the later dispossession of Lilith's throne by Cthulhu, or at least by the Masculine principle, is actually depicted, albeit symbolically, near the end of section 6 of "Red Hook," in which Suydham strains "every rotting muscle toward the carved golden pedestal"[195] and finally sends it careening down into the water, thus toppling Lilith's magical power (while also incidentally sending it deep into Cthulhu's own watery realm). As Lovecraft himself cryptically observes, this golden throne of Lilith's is of "primary occult importance"[196] in the story; and if Cthulhu's creation has any discernable point of psychological origin, then perhaps it lies here, in this toppling of the Feminine/matriarchal lordship principle. Lovecraft's invention of his famous figure of Cthulhu merely requires a shift of fictional focus from the maternal, wifely Lilith to the paternal, husbandly Suydham. The complexion of Cthulhu's worshippers, who, much like Lilith's earlier henchmen, are described as swarthy hybrids and mulattoes, likewise perpetuates an originally feminine constellation — in this case, Lovecraft's association of women with blacks (as discussed in Section 5 below.)

Ironically, given what Robert Waugh has noted concerning the aegis of "the Great Mother archetype"[197] in Dr. Margaret Murray's work, Murray herself may have also laid the groundwork for Lovecraft's usurpation of the Great Mother or Lilith by the masculine Cthulhu, in the form of that hypothetical masculine god that Murray theorized formed the idol of her witch-cult, and who combined, just like Cthulhu later on, anthropomorphic with theriomorphic characteristics.[198] According to Murray, and just as with Lovecraft's Lilith later on, this "worship of the male deity appears to have superseded that of the female."[199] On the other hand, Lovecraft may simply have found it more profitable — and more potent — from a fictional standpoint, to describe and explore the horror inherent in the active and male Chthonic serpent, rather than in the abyssal Great Mother, who in any case is mainly static and unconscious in her basic form, and retributive in terms of her actions (as seen via the revenge scheme of the feminine sea monster in "The Horror at Martin's Beach" or in the revenge scenario of the oceanic witch-lights in "The Temple"). That there may also be a connection between the throne imagery in these two stories, and Lovecraft's abortive romance with the Arcadian poetess Winifred Jackson, too, is suggested by his poem "On Receiving a Portraiture of Mrs. Berkeley, yᶜ Poetess" (1920), in which a thunderous Jove is depicted as granting the lovely Jackson an "exalted throne"[200] situated above goddesses like Pallas, the Muses and Venus alike. But as Lovecraft apparently later discovered to his dismay, Jackson, like Lilith, had her own train of dark-skinned lovers; and hence, perhaps, the later toppling of this throne into the river.

Lilith is not the only feminine prefigurement of Cthulhu in Lovecraft's writings. One thinks of the retributive moon-priestess Cleis in "The Moon-Bog," who, like Cthulhu lying beneath the sea, is said to lie "cold and silent"[201] in her buried grave beneath the Irish peat. (Just like Cthulhu, whose submerged temple rests upon "a single mountain-top"[202] of R'lyeh, Cleis' temple rests on the "high peak"[203] of a larger submerged mountain.) Critic Dennis Quinn, too, cites Stephen R. Wilk on the supposed parallels between Cthulhu and a description of the gorgon in Hesiod's *Shield of Hercules*.[204] The gorgon, although Quinn does not address this fact, just like Lilith, is yet another version of the negative feminine archetype of Terrible Mother (discussed further below). (In his collaborative story "Out of the Aeons," Lovecraft perhaps makes acknowledgement of this Medusean influence on his later Mythos entities: the presumably male alien entity Ghatanothoa[205] appropriates the Medusaean ability to turn its victims to stone; while the parodic entity in "The Horror in the Museum" is given "the traditional serpent-locks of Medusa."[206]) At the end of "The Rats in the Walls," there is what could perhaps be a tentative intimation of Cthulhu's name during Delapore's frenzied references to the Mother Goddess, which are followed by a sub-human, pre-human growl: "...*chchch*...,"[207] eerily suggestive of those guttural consonants in Cthulhu's name, and reflecting perhaps a Chthonic connection with that otherwise inexplicable "spotted snake" referenced earlier in Delapore's deranged rant. The very idea of a sea monster of the deep itself, as we have already seen via the maternal monster in "The Horror at Martin's Beach," is also an archetypally feminine conception, reflecting, again, a basic identification of the depths of the ocean (and its deep-sea denizens) with the abyssal and feminine unconscious. In the Mesopotamian myth of the maternal sea monster Tiamat, the creature's slain corpse gives rise to the structure of the universe[208]; in Lovecraft's mythos, however, Cthulhu is now Father Dagon, the undead husband to (a seemingly unseen) Mother Hydra, whose eclipse beneath the larger shadow of her consort corresponds to Cthulhu's more basic eclipse of the suboceanic Great Mother as a whole.

Several other, even more fragmentary or abstract, aspects of the archetypal Feminine occur in Lovecraft's weird writings. The cello or violin shape, for instance, typical of certain abstract Stone-Age feminine idols,[209] and interpreted by Erich Neumann as "an archaic 'abbreviation' of the Primordial Goddess,"[210] perhaps appears in the form of the viol in Lovecraft's "The Music of Erich Zann," played by Zann during his solitary (and seemingly autoerotic) revels in his room. The motif of the vulture, too — much like the winged sirens and harpies of the Greeks — was regarded by the Egyptians[211] (and perhaps also by the ancient Anatolians) as having feminine significance. And it is perhaps significant in this regard that Lovecraft goes on to reference the furies (calling them "loathsome Furies robbing / Night and noon of peace and rest")[212] in his poem "Despair" (1919), in the stanza immediately following his mention of vultures (referred to as "evil wings in ether beating; / Vultures at the spirit eating"), both of which he characteristically contrasts with the supposed paradise of (suicidal) oblivion: here called the "sweet oblivion" that is "waiting" beyond "abhorrent Life." (Tellingly, S. T. Joshi observes that this poem was written by Lovecraft "in response to the illness of his mother,"[213] an illness that was clearly more psychological than physiological in origin. It may be, then, that this poem is rooted less in Lovecraft's despair at his mother's illness than in his chafing under the symptoms of this illness itself, a chafing doubtlessly symbolized by the "clawing fiends"[214] that so trouble the poet in this poem. This image is later recapitulated in the "steel-like claws"[215] of the aged crone Keziah Mason in "Dreams in the Witch House," and also, as discussed below, in the phallic claws of the Terrible Mother.)

As we have already seen with regard to the connection between the feminine and Lovecraft's recurring night flight imagery, this (feminine?) image of the wings reappears throughout his weird writings: from the "black wings"[216] seen by Robert Blake at the end of "The Haunter of the Dark," which would seem to constitute a physical manifestation of the unseen (and, as discussed below, basically feminine) haunter of darkness in that story; to those "Black Winged Things"[217] that attend the ceremonies of Cthulhu's worshippers in "The Call of Cthulhu"; or, even more significantly, those "'wings'"[218] that Danforth sees at the end of *At the Mountains of Madness*, during his horrific vision of the cosmic primal scene. There is an explicitly feminine aspect to what Lovecraft calls that "legion of bat-winged devils"[219] spoken of in "The

Rats in the Walls," which, according to Lovecraft, "kept *Witches' Sabbath each night* at the priory" (italics mine). Delapore even (erroneously, however, as it turns out) associates these winged devils with the "vast gardens" of "coarse vegetables harvested" on the priory grounds; the language is highly suggestive, again, of the archetypal relation of the Feminine to the fruits of the earth, later cosmicized in "The Colour Out of Space."

The recurring eye imagery in H. P. Lovecraft's weird fiction represents yet another aspect of the Feminine archetype, an idea reflected in the staring eyes in such nightmare-derived feminine figures as the gorgon or Medusa, the Balinese demon-witch Rangda, or the infanticidal Lamia, the latter of whom who possessed the ability, according to Robert Graves, of alternately "plucking out and replacing her eyes at will."[220] (Erich Neumann reproduces several images of abstract prehistoric "Eye Idols,"[221] in which the goddess has been abbreviated to a stick decorated with glowing or staring eyes.) And although critic Robert Waugh is quick elsewhere to connect Lovecraft's various eye-covered entities with the Greek god Argus,[222] also known as "*Panoptes*, 'the all seeing,'"[223] Lovecraft's eye-imagery in such instances — much like his recurring nightmare-derived imagery elsewhere — shares a more visceral origin in the psycho-sexual contents of his own subconscious, rather than in his readings of classical mythology. Witness Lovecraft's instinctive reaction, described by Samuel Loveman, "when a young woman steadily 'gave him the eye'"[224] on the subway: "'My one desire,' he had confided to me ..., 'is to remain inconspicuous and unnoticed. If I could render myself invisible, I would gladly do so.'" Throughout Lovecraft's works, he associates eyes with sexuality in its most naked form: whether the stares of the men watching Marceline Bedard's sexy strip show in "Medusa's Coil,"[225] the "sheep's eyes"[226] made by Marceline herself while modeling nude in "Medusa's Coil"; or the mutual eyeing of Alfred Jermyn and his temperamental gorilla-friend in "Arthur Jermyn"[227]; all are synonymous with "the lover's leer"[228] denounced by the virginal Lovecraft in his irate letters to *The Argosy*.

We have already noted the large "single eye"[229] of the hypnotic, maternal sea monster in "The Horror at Martin's Beach." Similar images, by extension, occur in the "seemingly unmotivated stare"[230] directed toward Walter Gilman by the witch Keziah Mason in "The Dreams in the Witch-House"; or the serpentine gaze of the lycanthropic wife, Dame de Blois, in "Psychopompos," her eyes described as being "too bright by half"[231]; not to mention the sinister "leers and winks"[232] of the preternatural Asenath Waite in "The Thing on the Doorstep," which are allied with a power of genuine hypnotism. In "Medusa's Coil," too, we find the expected references to "the myth of the gorgon's glance,"[233] a myth that the narrator realizes too late is all too true. And it is significant that what I argue to be a feminine entity of primordial darkness in Lovecraft's "The Haunter of the Dark" is apprehensible at the end of the story only as what protagonist Robert Blake calls a "'three-lobed burning eye,'"[234] an image that curiously combines the vulvic and labial with the ocular. Of course, if Lovecraft had consciously intended an obvious feminine symbology in this tale, he would perhaps have been more explicit (although one certainly cannot discount the muting influence of Puritanism in such imagery); what we are detecting here, rather, are unconscious clues to Lovecraft's underlying motivations, particularly for some of the more obscure aspects of his works: particularly Danforth's cryptic "'eyes in darkness,'"[235] included along with the "'moon-ladder'" in his final vision in *At the Mountains of Madness*, an image simultaneously inverted in the same story into the multitudinous eyes of the equally dark shoggoths. And ultimately it is the idea of the all-seeing mother, whose reach is ineludible and whose power is unstoppable, that ultimately forms the origin for such figures as the all-seeing god Argus, and to which we must also in turn in search for the origin of Lovecraft's recoil from the all-seeing eye.

The symbol of the gate, doorway, or threshold, likewise partakes of this archetypal feminine imagery, being regarded in the ancient world as now (as in the marriage rites of newlywed couples) as the entrance into the womb of the Great Goddess,[236] at whose threshold libations and other seminal offerings were routinely spilled. Not surprisingly either, given this sexual symbology, we also find the witch-rituals cited by Murray often being closely associated with a gate.[237] Such archetypal imagery also commonly, as we have already seen in the New Jersey example, is twisted into such prevalent misogynistic ideas as the familiar "gates of hell." Thus too does Lovecraft, whose fiction displays a certain arrested development in this area, end "The Temple" with the evil Lt. Ehrenstein only *preparing* to enter the temple of witch-goddess beneath the sea (as he puts it, about to "walk boldly up the steps into that primal shrine"),[238] an attitude of fearful sexual anticipation similar to that of the narrator at the end of "The Shadow Over Innsmouth," or, as we have already seen, of Jervas Dudley trembling with excitement at, but never entering, the slightly ajar door of the Hydes' tomb. Similarly, Zamacona in "The Mound" is reduced forever to standing as a ghostly guard at the doorway to the feminine underworld, after being ensnared by his native bride. As Maurice Levy observes, in Lovecraft's works "all thresholds are, in essence, forbidden,"[239] and for Lovecraft, the forbidden, as his fascination with the unnamable and the unspeakable shows, is essentially rooted in issues related to sexual taboos and social proprieties.

V. The Terrible Mother

> The minute I saw it I understood what — she — was, and
> what part she played in the frightful secret that has come
> down from the days of Cthulhu and the Elder Ones.
> — H. P. Lovecraft and Zealia Bishop, "Medusa's Coil"[240]

Of all these archetypal symbols, however, the Terrible Mother is the most prominent manifestation of the feminine archetype in Lovecraft's weird fiction. The vast majority of his female villainesses — the Dame de Blois, Queen Nitokris, Lady Margaret Trevor in "The Rats in the Walls," the witch Keziah Mason, and the she-devil Asenath Waite — all conform to this particular aspect of the cosmic Feminine, an aspect that is considered so deadly precisely because she represents, in luscious human form, a tiny fragment of that larger feminine abyss of primordial chaos, set loose in an unwary world.

Standard mythological representations of this figure include Medusa, Lilith, Astarte, Hecate, the winged furies, and the Old Witch,[241] figures that, as we have already seen, are also not unknown in Lovecraft's weird fiction. (Indeed, as is usual with Lovecraft, in "Medusa's Coil" he even goes so far as to reverse history, by describing his own Marceline Bedard as being "the thing from which the first dim legends of Medusa and the Gorgons had sprung."[242] Lovecraft's inversions have the usual effect of subverting the purely psychological origins of such mythological imagery and supplanting them with a fictional cosmology of his own.) Such well-known literary femme fatales as Arthur Machen's Helen Vaughn in *The Great God Pan* (1895) and Frank Wedekind's Lulu in *Earth Spirit* (1895) likewise conform to this archetype; they are women who, as the celibate, racist, and anti–Semitic philosopher Otto Weininger complained in his book *Sex and Character* (1903), think only "of the pleasures of the world, of dancing, of dressing, of theatres and concerts, of pleasure-escorts,"[243] and who "flame through the world, making all its ways a *triumphant march for their beautiful bodies*" (italics mine). (Such femme fatales were also quite common in the *Munsey* magazines from Lovecraft's childhood, usually in the form of sadistic, sexually aggressive, and scantily-clad princesses, who provided the readers with titillation amid all their villainy. They include the nude priestess La in Edgar Rice Burroughs' *Tarzan and the Jewels of Opar*, the sensual but evil Kalamita in J. U. Giesy's *Palos of the Dog Star Pack*, and the homicidal courtesan-sorceress Queen Netokris in Perley Poore Sheehan's *The Woman of the Pyramid* [*All-Story*, 1914], who seems to have done much to influence Lovecraft's own later version of Nitokris.)

Lovecraft's portrait of the sexually devouring woman in "Medusa's Coil" closely conforms to this image of the societal demimonde or courtesan, in her more humble roles as chorus girl, artist's model, and Beardsleyan woman. The model, dancer and priestess Marceline dances naked, models nude, and later, after her marriage, displays a Beardsleyan interest in cosmetics, mirrors, and elaborate beauty rituals.[244] Such an overlapping of roles is typical of this archetype, as such women often blur the fine line between prostitute and priestess,[245] and, in turn, between priestess and goddess. The sultry chorus girls who are the preferred consorts for the bestial males in "Arthur Jermyn,"[246] as well as the cannibalistic artist's model depicted in "Pickman's Model," also represent this archetype of the femme fatale or prostitute, transformed, however, in the latter example, into something far more grotesque and sinister. Lovecraft conspicuously situates Lilith's Devil-worshipping cult in "The Horror at Red Hook" in what he calls a "dance-hall church,"[247] a mixture of the sacred and profane that underlines the Puritan orientation of his relation to the Feminine, such dance halls being a convenient front for prostitution during the 1920s and '30s. (Lovecraft was perhaps influenced in this dance hall–church imagery by Perley Poore Sheehan's *Judith of Babylon*, in which the populace, influenced by the pagan Cush's neo–Babylonian rites, begins "burning churches, turning the cathedrals into dance-halls."[248])

Lovecraft's Lilith herself is literally a scarlet woman: her glowing naked body, as we have seen, is anointed with children's blood by her followers in a clever inversion of the story of prostitute Mary Magdalene anointing the body of Jesus. All of this merely represents an occult version of Lovecraft's earlier fan letters to *The Argosy*, in which he attacks what he calls "the fallen public's ear."[249] "Fallen" here reflects the Judeo-Christian view of the "fallen" woman, and ultimately, the Fall of Mankind itself. Interestingly, Otto Weininger — whose views on Jews, blacks and women in *Sex and Character*, as we shall see, so closely parallel Lovecraft's own — similarly and feverishly denounces what he calls "this quite modern 'coitus-cult'"[250] with its "Dionysian view of the music hall." Weininger takes the added step, however, of attributing the masculine acceptance of this cult to "the influence of modern Judaism."

Frequently, the Terrible Mother is associated with powers of hypnotism, such as paralysis, control, transformation, and magic; anything that serves to symbolize the destruction of the (masculine) conscious mind and a regression into the unconscious, which is associated with both the Feminine and with death. Hence the archetypally feminine aspects of things such as the rites of Dionysus, whose rituals of dance, rhythm, chanting, and Astartean nudity all tend to destabilize and nullify the consciousness beneath drunkenness and orgiastic ecstasy. Hence too the largely feminine imagery of nepenthe in classical legends (which anthropologist Erich Neumann identifies as belonging exclusively "to the matriarchal sphere"),[251] such as the drug of forgetfulness administered to Odysseus by Circe for seven long years; or the nepenthe (in reality poison) offered to Theseus by the witch-woman and mother-surrogate Medea; or even the forgetfulness of Lovecraft's Outsider, while trapped in the subterranean womb of death with his nurse. Very often, too, as we have seen, the Terrible Mother is also a phallic woman, either carrying a knife (such as the sacrificial knife wielded by Keziah Mason), beclawed, or fanged and possessed of a devouring and toothed orifice, which threatens to castrate and cannibalize the unwary male (as with the rites of Atys that cause such horror to Delapore in "The Rats in the Walls"). Although most Lovecraftian critics are quick to point out that Lovecraft's Asenath Waite is actually a man, as if this invalidates her status as a female villain, such phallicism is in no way unusual for the Terrible Mother of ancient mythology, whose *vagina dentata* often takes the form of a phallic serpent or wolf's head lurking between her legs.

As we have seen, the hypnotic powers of the Terrible Mother are repeatedly evinced throughout Lovecraft's weird canon. We have already noted what Lovecraft and Greene call the "unknown powers"[252] displayed by the maternal monster in "The Horror at Martin's Beach," as well as the evil eyes of Asenath Waite, the Dame de Blois, and the cosmic entity in "The Haunter of the Dark," which, as a terrified Robert Blake complains, "'is taking hold of my mind.'"[253] As husband Denis de Russy laments about his Medusean wife in "Medusa's Coil": "*She had me hypnotized* so that I couldn't believe the plain facts"[254] (italics mine). And although Lovecraft does not specifically mention the Feminine in this tale, one also notes the joined ocular and hypnotic aspects of the Pole Star in Lovecraft's "Polaris," which is repeatedly described throughout the story as being "like an insane watching eye,"[255] and in human terms as "leering like a fiend and tempter." (This star also has a winged aspect; it is described as "fluttering as if alive.") As Lovecraft's narrator explains — although we are left in doubt as to his sanity — it was this star that once hypnotized him during a previous existence, making him fall asleep before a crucial battle (the female attribute of nepenthe once again, here called "a sweet forgetfulness"),[256] resulting in the destruction of his austere, grave (and seemingly entirely masculine) race.

It is here, too, in this control and dissolution of the masculine consciousness beneath the power of the Feminine, where we must locate the figurative (as well as sometimes quite literal) dissolution frequently experienced by Lovecraft's male protagonists: the madness of Delapore, the madness of Thomas Malone, the madness of Danforth in *At the Mountains of Madness*, and even the complete physical decay of Robert Suydam and Edward Derby — what critic Alex Houstoun calls the "total collapse of the self"[257] experienced by the typical Lovecraftian hero. Indeed, poor Lovecraft already had a ready-made example of such feminine-influenced dissolution, in the form of his father, who was essentially reduced to madness and death by sex, and the writings of Poe would have provided a literary framework within which Lovecraft could recognize and explore this basic fear. As Erich Neumann observes, often in myth and religion, overt contact with the feminine archetype results in "disintegration of the consciousness, and loss of the ego,"[258] especially for the weak or immature man, whose infantile ego is easily overwhelmed by the alluring power of the Feminine.

It is here too, under the hypnotic and ecstatic aegis of the Terrible Mother, that Erich Neumann locates the common mythological theme of the reduction of men into beasts by women,[259] such as in Ishtar's transformation of her male lovers into animals, or Circe's transformation of the crew of Odysseus into swine. This idea finds its echo in the animalistic Delapore's identification of his own cannibalistic desires with rats at the conclusion of "The Rats in the Walls," not to mention the evolutionary degeneration of the semi-human quadrupeds in the same story, all under the overarching aegis of the Magna Mater and her irresistible will. Similar to this is the transformation of the peasant laborers into frogs by an overpowering feminine will in "The Moon-Bog," and the animalistic postures and sounds of the cult-worshippers in "The Horror at Red Hook" and "Call of Cthulhu."

These elements of the Feminine, hypnotism, the bacchanalia, and paralysis, are all combined, as we have already seen, in Lovecraft's odd recurring image of feminine ceremonial processions throughout his writings, often leading to the deaths of its (male) participants: the "ceremonial procession"[260] "led" by Lilith in "The Horror at Red Hook"; the "mixed throng of swaying figures"[261] led to their doom by the naiads in "The Moon-Bog"; the long line of men who are led to their deaths by drowning via the "paralyzing influence"[262] in "The Horror at Martin's Beach"; the poet (a procession of one?) in the poem "Unda; or, The Bride of the Sea," led to his death via drowning by a moonlight-maiden; and those "amorphous shadows" engaging in "some blasphemous ceremonial procession"[263] in "The Statement of Randolph Carter," all images that seem to reflect some palpable masculine anxiety in Lovecraft's mind — and all of them, one notes, very far removed from any notion of the cosmic. Such archetypal feminine processions, of course, are by no means unknown elsewhere, particularly in macabre fiction. The sinister demon-mother Carathis, for instance, is pictured as marching at the head of various genii and other elemental demons during her attempt to dethrone one of the ancient pre–Adamite kings (in yet another instance of the female matriarchal principle vs. the triumphant masculine principle). "Thus marched she,"[264] Beckford writes, "in triumph, through a vapour of perfumes, amidst the acclamations of all the malignant spirits, with most of whom she formed a previous acquaintance." Lovecraft's procession imagery also owes much to the early *Munsey* magazines and their cognate publications, in whose pages such processions were also quite common: from the Oparian priestess, La, leading a procession of devolved and hybrid ape-men through the African jungles in Burroughs' *Tarzan and the Jewels of Opar*, to the treacherous and hypnotic sorceress Tigra, leading an army of devolved beast-men into battle in Lee Robinet's *The Bowl of Baal* (*All-Around*, Street and Smith, 1916–1917).

Lovecraft is also paralleled in this feminine procession imagery by proto-expressionist artist and writer Alfred Kubin, whose incestuous, suicidal devotion to his mother, perhaps not uncoincidentally, closely matches Lovecraft's own. (Kubin, who suffered from bouts of mental illness, once tried to kill himself on his mother's grave,[265] but failed when the gun proved too rusty to fire; a desire for incestuous oblivion that strangely echoes Lovecraft's similar sentiments at the time of his own mother's death, and that seems to correspond to what Erich Neumann calls the "uroboric incest of the death urge or ... madness"[266] that is common to "a certain type of creative man," who, like the 19th century Romantics, is dominated by the Terrible Mother archetype.) Kubin's eerie drawing "Our Universal Mother, the Earth" (1901–1902), reflects just such a hypnotic fascination, depicting a nude, pregnant, and apparently steatopygian fertility goddess leading a long procession of male heads or skulls in her wake, its line leading infinitely into the distance. This imagery strikingly prefigures the secret underground ossuaries at the end of Lovecraft's "The Rats in the Walls" and "The Dreams in the Witch House," not to mention the "bones and skeletons that strowed some of the stone crypts deep down among the foundations"[267] of the Outsider's maternal castle (imagery that is later incorporated into the skeletal body of Queen Nitkoris herself). Interestingly, Kubin's utilization of the pictorial medium enables him to go one better than Lovecraft in terms of symbolic concision: his depiction of heads or skulls, rather than full figures, allowing him to suggest beheading (symbolic castration), which is also to be found throughout Lovecraft's weird stories, such as the beheading of the Old Ones by the shoggoths, and the beheading of Herbert West by the legions of the undead. This imagery is suggestive of what Lovecraft saw as the undermining of legitimate authority by the unwashed masses, as well as the decapitation of the masculine intellect by the feminine unconscious.

In India, this Terrible Mother took the form of the goddess Kali, called by scholar Heinrich Zimmer the "'bone-wreathed Lady of the place of

Skulls.'"[268] Zimmer likens Kali's temple in India to "'a slaughterhouse'"[269]—language, once again, that suggests the final, bone-strewn landscape in "The Rats in the Walls." Like the earth goddess of the Meso-Americans, to whom thousands of people were sacrificed annually, and who was believed to "cry out in the night, demanding human hearts,'"[270] or the Greek goddess Artemis, also not unknown to Lovecraft (whose name Erich Neumann traces to the Greek word meaning "to slaughter"),[271] this Terrible Mother demands propitiation, even if that insatiable hunger that the ancients falsely believed to originate beneath the earth (and which the mad Delapore falsely attributes to the *rats* in Lovecraft's story) has its true origin in a homeopathic misunderstanding of the need for blood sacrifice, as well as in more basic, and sadistic, suppressed human desires. And when Delapore begins raving about the maiming of his son in World War I, by saying: "'The war *ate my boy*, damn them all'"[272] (italics mine), the cannibalistic language he uses to describe his son's invalidism is equally suggestive of the ravenous inner earth and of the *vagina dentata*. Indeed, as Lovecraft makes clear, the younger Delapore survived two years after the war, but only as a "maimed invalid,"[273] suggesting that if that war did eat him, it either ate him slowly, or it ate him in quite another fashion — one familiar from Hemingway's *The Sun Also Rises*— by eating his masculine sexual and generative capacity. Maiming or invalidism can have several meanings, as Lady Chatterley could attest, and in "The Thing on the Doorstep" it takes a particularly hideous form, in Edward Derby's symbolic castration via his switching of bodies with his wife Asenath. Whereas Samuel Loveman sang a somber song of what he saw as the decadent beauties of "The Hermaphrodite," Lovecraft writes of maternal emasculation.

Of course, as noted above, Lovecraft's use of such archetypal symbols derives quite a bit from the science-fantasy stories in the early pulp magazines, in which they are quite common. The woman as seer, as priestess, as sorceress; the woman with the hypnotic eyes of masculine fascination; the woman as all-mother, as provider of milk and honey, or as languorous feline lioness; the terrible mother enthroned, all-powerful and aged; and the phallic demoness of castration and sexual destruction, wielding her sinister sacrificial blade — all are prevalent in the early science-fantasy stories of Edgar Rice Burroughs, Lee Robinet, Victor Rousseau, and J. U. Giesy. Indeed, as noted above, Lovecraft's use of Queen Nitkoris in two of his stories — although sometimes believed to derive from the writings of Romantic poet Thomas Moore — seems to have derived even more from the Netokris of pulp writer Perley Poore Sheehan, whose nocturnal revels (as Sheehan explains, Nitokris reserves "the nights for her pleasures")[274] do much to explain the nature of the Outsider's nocturnal revels with this queen at the end of Lovecraft's story, and also to indicate the whorish and possibly adulterous contours of the Outsider's forgotten crime. (As Sheehan observes, "There wasn't a man in Memphis who wouldn't rather see the queen [Nitokris] than his own wife."[275])

Given Lovecraft's numerous representations of both the Great and Terrible Mother throughout his writings, however, it is also of interest to note what attributes of the feminine archetype are *not* included in his fiction. The spider, for instance — which is utilized almost universally as a symbol of voracious feminine evil[276] — is, aside perhaps from the spiders present in the womblike beginning of "The Outsider,"[277] seemingly nowhere to be found in his *oeuvre*, perhaps because he regarded the theme as overly familiar (Lovecraft himself wrote somewhat wearily of what he calls "'the familiar overgrownspider theme so frequently employed by weird fictionists'").[278] The common "feline image" of the Feminine, too — whose talons and fangs anthropologist H. R. Hays directly links "to the toothed vagina"[279] symbolism of the phallic woman — is likewise rare in Lovecraft's fiction, perhaps due to his fondness for cats; a fondness that I have elsewhere (in my essay "H. P. Lovecraft and Nightmare Imagery" [forthcoming]) linked with Lovecraft's love for his mother. In Lovecraft's collaborative "Medusa's Coil," however, Lovecraft will loosen up sufficiently to have husband Denis de Russy describe his Medusean wife as "that woman —*that leopardess*, or gorgon, or lamia, or whatever she was"[280] (italics mine). Marceline even gives her husband what he calls "a wild jungle beast look"[281] right before she "sprang for me with claws out like a leopard's" (again, much like Keziah Mason). Undoubtedly, large predatory cats were not on his mother's approved list, and were thus acceptable for use in his canon of feminine imagery.

Also largely missing from Lovecraft's weird fiction is the archetype of the celestial woman, the symbol of higher and heavenly wisdom: the Greek Sophia, or the Christian Virgin Mary; the goddess of heavenly ascents, and of initiation into the luminous, esoteric mysteries. True, Lovecraft's "Starry Wisdom"[282] sect in "The Haunter of the Dark" does, with its theosophical and mystical aspects, seem, at first, to fit into this category. Ultimately however, as Robert Blake discovers to his sorrow, this cult is but a cloak for a creature of pure cosmic darkness; the positive feminine manifestation of the Celestial Good Mother inevitably gives way, for Lovecraft, to the primal, maternal abyss of pure intrauterine darkness. As Erich Neumann observes of the goddess of wisdom, "As spirit mother, she is not, like the Great Mother of the lower phase, interested primarily in *the infant, the child, and the immature man*"[283] (italics mine), like most of the male heroes (and author surrogates) in Lovecraft's weird fiction. But this is not so for the primordial and elementary Feminine, whose relationship to mankind is essentially that of (the large) mother to (the tiny) infant, and whose overwhelming nocturnal consciousness eventually envelopes and destroys the mind of any tribal man (or Lovecraftian protagonist) unfortunate enough to become attached to it.

Another aspect of the negative feminine archetype strikingly absent from the Lovecraft canon is what anthropologist Erich Neumann identifies as the "seductive young witch,"[284] the negative analogue to the beautiful young ingénue or virgin, also glaringly missing from his fiction. This fact is also significant, reflecting as it does Lovecraft's lifelong immersion beneath, and lifelong adherence to, the womb of the mother, whether identified with his aunts, Mother England, or the familiar Mother Earth of his native Providence. As Neumann observes: "The more unconscious a man is, the more the anima figure"[285] of the archetypal woman "remains fused or connected with the mana figure *of the mother or of the old woman*" (italics mine) in his mind — a fact which, again, begs comparison with the various aged, old, or elder figures that manifest themselves throughout Lovecraft's weird fiction. Indeed, the process by which Lovecraft seems to have apparently transposed his mother Susan or his grandmother Rhoby into the various elder or aged figures in his stories eerily parallels the process described by Neumann, by which an "infantile ego"[286] can transform even the Good Mother into such negative figures as "the witch in the fairy tale of Hansel and Gretel, whose house, i.e. exterior, is made of gingerbread and candy, but who in reality eats little children." The latter idea recalls, once again, the strongly infanticidal themes of Lovecraft's stories, as well as his concern with the haunted houses of Etienne Roulet and Keziah Mason. Nor is it any coincidence, perhaps, to find that cannibalism in Lovecraft's fiction is also sometimes directly associated with the infantile image of eating candy: the ghoul in "Pickman's Model," for instance, is described as "gnawing at the head"[287] (the theme of beheading again) of a victim "as a child nibbles at a stick of candy." For Lovecraft, the maternal formed but a candy coating over a voracious and nightmarish inner sadism, which threatened to utterly destroy his masculine identity by eating it whole.

Again, it quickly becomes clear that Lovecraft did not eschew women in his fiction, as so many readers believe. But whereas the writers of the *Munsey* pulps presented a stark contrast between their virginal heroines on the one hand, and their sadistic and seductive femme fatales on the other, Lovecraft simply dwelled upon their malevolent or terrible aspects. And while it may be objected that such villainesses appear most often in Lovecraft's most commercial or least characteristic stories, such as "The Horror at Red Hook" or "Medusa's Coil," certainly such a criticism ignores the presence of Queen Nitokris at the end of "The Outsider," long considered one of Lovecraft's most personal and revealing tales.

VI. The Old Witch and the Ghouls

The figure of the Old Witch is perhaps the most familiar manifestation of the Terrible Mother to most people, being pictured even now in many popular storybooks, Halloween decorations, films, books, and cartoons. And she is also perhaps the most prevalent example of the Terrible Mother in H. P. Lovecraft's weird writings.

As critic Robert Waugh observes, Lovecraft was strongly influenced in his depiction of witches by his 1923 reading of Dr. Margaret S. Murray's *The Witch-Cult in Western Europe*.[288] And it is significant, given Lovecraft's own staunchly non-psychological and steadfastly mythological characterization of the weird phenomena in his own stories, that the primary mission of Murray's book was to rescue the witch-cult of history from its previous and purely psychological basis, and to instead study the late-medieval witch phenomenon from a purely anthropological point of view. Just like Lovecraft's own narrators, who repeatedly stress the reality of their occult experiences — often in the face of skeptical doctors or psychiatrists who deride them as mere hallucinations, or as evidence of mental illness — Dr. Murray vehemently objects throughout her book to the idea that "hysteria and hallucination were the foundation of the witches' confessions."[289] The merits and accuracy of Dr. Murray's thesis (which have been, and still are, the topic of much debate, and even censure, in anthropological circles) need not concern us here; suffice it to say that Lovecraft, for a number of years at least, seems to have believed it completely; more than that, her thesis left its mark on numerous weird tales that he went on to write, beginning, as Robert Waugh points out, with "The Festival," written in late 1923.

In addition to her non-psychological approach, Dr. Murray's thesis would also have recommended itself to Lovecraft for several other important reasons, which further diminish the supposed "irony"[290] that Robert Waugh detects in his usage of her matriarchal ideas. First, there is the role played by class in Murray's witch-cult, which was, she observes, made up "chiefly certain classes of the community,"[291] i.e., "the more ignorant or those in the less thickly inhabited parts of the country,"[292] or in other words the peasant masses of the pre-industrial period. As Murray goes on, "The so-called conversion of Britain [to Christianity] meant the conversion of the rulers only; the mass of the people continued to follow their ancient customs and belief with a veneer of Christian rites."[293] Elsewhere, too, Murray repeatedly speaks of the witch-cult as being representative of what she calls the "religions of *the Lower Culture*"[294] (italics mine), and although she never clearly defines this latter term, a later elaboration makes it clear that she regards "sexual ritual"[295] in particular as being common to "many religions of the Lower Culture." This fact, Murray goes on, "has always horrified members of the higher religions both in ancient and modern times" (a notion which both parallels, and serves to further clarify, Lovecraft's own idea of the horror aroused by the practices of the worldwide cults of Cthulhu, Yog-Sothoth, and the Deep Ones).[296] Even in the modern period, these same class-based ideas of Murray's have gone on to inform some of the misguided witch covens on the leftmost side of the political spectrum, who often see the witch as a representative of the poor and oppressed, and who view the witch "'as a revolutionary image for women.'"[297]

The concordances here with Lovecraft's own aristocratic values are clear; Lovecraft, as late as 1928, contrasted such things as the rural decay of "the gentry"[298] in New England — who he says still manage to "maintain a very high level of life and thought," despite their occasional lapses from decorum — with the decay of "a few of *the lower orders*" (italics mine) who have fallen into a "deep and insidious decay" characterized by "odd perversions." And it seems likely that Lovecraft's utilization of the witch also reflects a similar classist basis. Lovecraft may also have been influenced by another source cited in Murray's book, who delineates a three-level hierarchy of witches, rising from "hagges and witches, who are people of a sordid and base condition"[299] on the bottom rung, to "Magicians who are Gentlemen and people of a higher ranke [sic],'" inhabiting the third and topmost tier. This idea is perhaps loosely adhered to in "The Whisperer in Darkness," in which he presents a clear contrast between the rustic farmer Walter Brown who serves the malevolent Outer Ones, and their equally subservient and yet "cultivated"[300] and "fashionably dressed" ally from Boston, Mr. Noyes. In "The Horror at Red Hook," too, we find this lower class represented by the largely male Kurdish or Yezidee slum inhabitants, while this higher third class is represented by the gentlemanly but shabby aristocrat Robert Suydam.

Ultimately, this class-based structure of Murray's witch-cult seems to have provided Lovecraft with a general template through which to incorporate his own classist views into his weird fiction. And while, according to biographer L. Sprague de Camp, H. P. Lovecraft was influenced by Murray only insofar as her ideas had imaginative appeal and story potential,[301] it was a story potential that simultaneously provided him with a medium through which to convey an already existing socio-political polemic. Dr. Murray's witch-cult thesis laid the groundwork not only for his later Cthulhu Cult (in yet another instance of patriarchal usurpation of the feminine) but also for Lovecraft's larger, general idea of a mass movement of evil, largely lower-class or foreign, anarchistic political forces, beginning with "The Horror at Red Hook" and culminating in "The Shadow Over Innsmouth." (Indeed, much like the sub-human or hybrid Deep Ones of "Innsmouth," Murray's theory allowed Lovecraft the luxury of categorizing the witches themselves as members of a separate species.[302])

Consider Lovecraft's short story "The Street," composed around 1920 (years before his reading of Dr. Murray), whose Hogarth-like depiction of the unwashed masses closely prefigures the polemical views of Lovecraft's later weird fiction. Even so, this piece was followed in short order by Lovecraft's "The Moon-Bog" (1921), "The Lurking Fear" (1922), and "The Rats in the Walls" (1923), in all of which the peasant populations of the stories, although admittedly decayed and primitive, are still merely the innocent victims of mainly aristocratic evil. The peasant masses in "The Moon-Bog," for example, fear the bog of the fairies, and "refused to help"[303] with Denys Barry's attempts to drain the bog, instead fleeing the area, thereby requiring Barry to bring in new laborers "from the north." The terrified peasants in "The Lurking Fear," too, while decayed and inbred, are still basically sympathetic, and completely at the mercy of the evil and aristocratic forces of the Martense family line that beset them, as are the peasants in "The Rats in the Walls," who detest the aristocratic Delapores and oppose their return. Nor are the decayed peasants in "Beyond the Wall of Sleep" (1919) anything other than pathetic and helpless. By the time of the writing of "The Festival," however, Lovecraft had read Murray's *Witch-Cult* and was beginning his process of depicting the whole of a decadent rural population (what Murray repeatedly calls "the mass of the people")[304] as subversive, and as largely given over to perverse thaumaturgic practices. The way was thus being paved for the creation of "The Horror at Red Hook," in which collective evil has taken over an entire borough of New York City, and "The Call of Cthulhu," in which a cult threatens to destroy all of Western civilization. Murray's *Witch-Cult* thus paved the way for integrating Lovecraft's socio-political polemics within his weird fiction.

Lovecraft would have been further enamored of Dr. Murray's thesis, too, because of her linking of the latter-day witch-cult in England with the issue of sedition, a topic that was also very much on his mind throughout his lifetime, whether with regard to what he regarded as the unjust rebellion of the American colonies against Great Britain, the rebellion of satellite provinces against the Roman Empire, or even the actions of socialist, Bolshevist, or anarchist forces in the United States in the early 20th century. According to Murray, many witches were implicated in terrorist plots, including assassination attempts and sabotage, including a 1590 attempt to murder the king and queen,[305] the destruction of a bridge,[306] an assassination attempt by a witch upon "'the Laird of Park'" with a flint arrow, and the making of curse against the minister of Auldearne.[307] As Lovecraft observed in 1930, the witch-cult "fostered a spirit of seditious malignity aimed at all existing institutions"[308] that "would have virtually wrecked European civilization if left unopposed." Nor, one assumes, would these witches have joined with Lovecraft in his characteristic exclamation, "God Save the King!"; the Devil supposedly described the king of England to his witches as "'the greatest enemie hee hath in the world.'"[309]

This subversive complexion of the witch-cult continued on into the modern period, with some branches of the modern Wiccan movement finding allies and common cause with environmentalist, feminist, luddite, leftist, gay liberation, and other radical organizations. Indeed, given some of the dubious socio-political conclusions that practicing witch (and National Public Radio correspondent) Margot Adler draws in her book *Drawing Down the Moon*, Lovecraft was prescient to utilize this tincture of feminine archetypes, fertility rites, the bacchanalia, witches, and sedition to characterize his polemical antagonisms. Adler writes, for instance, of how

> in Gillo Pontecorvo's extraordinary film *The Battle of Algiers*, Algerian women confront the French by giving out an eerie yell, a high ululation that makes the flesh crawl. These women have a great sense of power and strength, perhaps the power of the maenads. After the film appeared I occasionally heard the same cry in the demonstrations of the late 1960s, but never in the way I have heard it more recently, in meetings of women. Amazons are coming into existence today. I have heard with them and joined with them. We have howled with the bears, the wolves, and the coyotes.[310]

And they have also "howled with" (unknowingly of course, and in caricatural, prophetic form) Lovecraft's bestial and equally animalistic followers of Cthulhu. Just as in Lovecraft's weird fiction, political radicalism is here allied with animalistic bacchanalianism and resurgent matriarchy. Clearly, what Robert Waugh terms the "implicit feminism"[311] of Dr. Margaret Murray's works was no impediment to Lovecraft's use of them to embody his polemical viewpoint; indeed, far from being ironic, it would have been a recommendation. And whereas for Robert Waugh, witchcraft for Lovecraft was partially "related to the repression of a narrow religiosity"[312] amongst the New England Puritans (a notion that is based mainly upon the incongruous anti–Puritan notions expressed in Lovecraft's earlier and more immature works), I think rather that for Lovecraft, witches actually represented merely one additional aspect of that sensual, pagan, and ultimately feminine decadence that he deplored, and which in his dark imagination was allied with an apocalyptic vision of the eventual downfall of civilization.

H. P. Lovecraft also follows Dr. Murray's book in more practical ways, adopting a number of the more obscure details from the witch trial accounts she cites.[313] In "Medusa's Coil," for instance, homicidal husband Denis de Russy frantically urges his father to destroy the portrait of his Medusaean wife Marceline, exclaiming: "'Oh, God — that thing! Don't ever look at it! Burn it with the hangings around it *and throw the ashes into the river!*"[314] (italics mine). This act parallels Murray's earlier description of "a common rite, in religions of the Lower Culture, after the sacrifice of the Incarnate God,"[315] in which "the ashes [of the deceased] were collected and thrown into running water." (Murray uses the fact that Joan of Arc's ashes were treated in such a manner to argue for her being a latter-day member of the pre–Christian witch-cult.) Thus Denis de Russy's exhortations in this instance serve to reinforce the divinity of the goddess Marceline in the story, and her identity, not only as a priestess, but also as the precursor of such divine feminine figures as Tanit and Isis.

The changeling plot of Lovecraft's "Pickman's Model," too — in which it is suggested that decadent artist Richard Upton Pickman is of the "changelings"[316] left behind by the "weird people" (i.e., the ghouls) "in cradles in exchange for the human babies they steal" — is prefigured by Murray's citation from Cunningham's *Traditional Tales of the English and Scottish Peasantry* (1874), which describes how the fairies are constrained to give one of their own children to the Devil every seven years, and how one devoted fairy mother, determined to avoid this, instead gave her offspring into human charge.[317] Indeed, Murray even goes so far as to suggest that an actual reality underlies such accounts, suggesting that a theoretical dwarf race in Europe once "stole children from the neighboring races and *brought them up to be victims*"[318] (italics mine). Lovecraft was perhaps impressed by the strongly maternal overtones of Cunningham's story of the loving fairy mother, overtones that are lacking in Lovecraft's Pickman story, although one can easily see the parallels with Lovecraft's later "The Shadow Over Innsmouth," in terms of the maternal alienage of the hero. Murray's observation, too, regarding the victimization and eventual sacrifice of such children, perhaps had some psychological resonance with Lovecraft's own unfortunate childhood experiences and with his (seemingly parental) belief in the cruel jests sometimes played by fate.

Lovecraft's description of the Sabbath in "The Horror at Red Hook," too, telling how "incubi and succubae howled praise to Hecate,"[319] seems to directly parallel a passage in Murray's book about the orgies that took place at the post-medieval Witches' Sabbath (although the Puritan Lovecraft carefully elides over the sexual content of the passage), which describes how "'the Incubus's [archaic spelling] in the shapes of proper men satisfy the desires of the Witches, and the Succubus's [archaic spelling] serve for whores to the

Wizards.'"[320] Nor does it take much imagination to connect what Dr. Murray calls the "joyous gaiety of the [witches'] meetings"[321] during the post-medieval period, and what Lovecraft similarly calls the "gaiety"[322] of "the unnamed feasts of Nitokris beneath the Great Pyramid" at the end of "The Outsider." Indeed, the clearly bacchanalian overtones of Murray's Sabbath accounts, which combine feasting,[323] alcohol,[324] nudity,[325] the sound of piping,[326] and reports of infanticide and/or cannibalism,[327] would have provided Lovecraft with the basic bacchanalian template for his later Cthulhu Cult, even without the classical accounts of Livy. (Perhaps it is stretching things a bit, too, to see a connection between that manifestation of pagan and feminine decadence called the "Black Mass" during the Middle Ages, and its antonym, in the form of that black mass called the shoggoth, in Lovecraft's writings.) It may also be that Lovecraft's description of Shub-Niggurath in his letters as a "hellish cloud-like entity"[328] was also directly influenced by Murray's *Witch-Cult*, in which the witches' familiars and devils are described as appearing "'sometimes in the likeness of a black cloud.'"[329]

H. P. Lovecraft's picture of the witch Keziah Mason, too, his most fully delineated and prominent witch character, was also highly influenced by the witch accounts cited by Dr. Murray; his repeated description of Mason as a "beldame,"[330] for example, closely parallels a lengthy 1645 account cited by Murray regarding "'the old beldame West,'"[331] in which she uses the phrase "'old beldame'" at least three times.[332] And it is perhaps significant in this regard that the various accounts cited by Dr. Murray repeatedly reveal the oddly maternal complexion of the witches' relationships with their rat-like familiars, a motherly relationship which further reinforces the analogously maternal and, consequently, incestual overtones of both Keziah Mason and the larger theme of old women as seen throughout Lovecraft's weird fiction. As one source cited in her book observes: "'and being asked, if she would not be afraid of her impes, the said Elizabeth answered, "What, do yee think I am afraid of my children?"'"[333] This maternal relation is further reinforced by the numerous instances of oral sadism associated with such creatures, in which the maternal power of nursing is transformed, via unconscious sadistic processes, into a vampiric sucking of blood from the witch for sustenance, either from a cut finger or from hidden teats located in various locations on the witch's body.[334] Keziah Mason's hybrid familiar Brown Jenkin, perhaps alone amongst Lovecraft's weird entities, is tiny in size, and equally suggestive, therefore, of a child. Does he, too, suckle at Keziah Mason's superfluous nipple(s), like the rat-like familiars described by Murray? And, if so, is Brown Jenkin thus a nightmarish caricature of Lovecraft's own repressed maternal, incestuous anxieties?

Murray's *Witch-Cult* would also have provided H. P. Lovecraft with numerous additional instances of male-female couples, there called "'Hagges and Sorcerers,'"[335] who were frequently associated with Sabbath rites, which closely correspond to the numerous malevolent and basically parental married couples also found in Lovecraft's weird fiction, including Keziah Mason and the Black Man of Arkham, who forms her apparent consort in Lovecraft's tale. Indeed, according to Murray, witches were believed to have sexual intercourse with the Devil at the Sabbath, an act that was regarded as a "'marriage vnto [sic] him.'"[336] Murray perceptively goes on to link this practice with the ancient pagan custom of sacred marriages to ensure fertility. In much the same way, as we have seen, Lovecraft, in "Pickman's Model," suggests a close (and doubtlessly sexual) relationship between his witches and his ghouls; Pickman thus, in addition to being a ghoul-changeling, also is the offspring, however distant, of a witch. Yet again, Lovecraft's use of the figure of the witch reveals its essentially maternal foundations.

Lovecraft strongly hints at these sexual rites of witches in "The Dreams in the Witch House," describing how "the old woman and the small furry thing"[337] (the woman's vulva?) advance toward Walter Gilman in his room at night, while the paralysis of the nightmare (the archetypal feminine powers of hypnotism, again) stifles all of Gilman's "attempts to cry out." The witch's mark given to Gilman plays a role in this sequence, since, as the case histories quoted by Murray describe, such witches' marks were typically said to be given to the initiate *after intercourse with the Devil in the shape of a woman*.[338] Nor is Keziah's great age any bar to such an interpretation in this instance: since, as Dr. Murray observes, it was believed that the Devil had sex with witches "of every class *and every age*, from just above puberty *to old women of over seventy*"[339] (italics mine). In a translation of Jules Michelet's *Satanism and Witchcraft*, too, published just two years after Lovecraft's death, the historian dilates at length upon the specifically incestuous aspects of the Witches' Sabbath, particularly between mother and son (as Michelet observes, Satan "made this particular crime into a virtue.")[340] Lovecraft's February 27, 1933, letter to Donald Wandrei confirms his own association of incest with the Witches' Sabbath. We should note, too, that symbolic triangular gulf into which Keziah Mason's sacrificial knife falls in his story, and which we later learn leads to an ossuary containing the bones of numerous sacrificed "small children"[341] (Lovecraft's infantile sense of scale, again). The mother's womb again (just as with Jervas Dudley) is reimagined as a tomb, which kills even as it gives life, symbolic of that larger uroboric infinity of the Great Mother and her endless (and, to Lovecraft, ultimately meaningless) cycle of life and death.

VII. The Primordial Feminine Abyss

Such figures as the Terrible Mother, the evil Old Witch who devours children, or the hypnotic siren of either the high seas or the brothel, however, are ultimately only localized variations of the real Magna Mater, the real Great Goddess; that hidden, irrational, and unknown mother of blackness, unconscious, placid, formless, unending, eternal, original; what Lovecraft possibly refers to, again, as the "'original, the eternal, the undying'"[342]; words that suggest nothing other than some infinite universal womb, beyond space and time, from which all after her originates. She exists like an egg, with every abstract potential already contained undifferentiated within her, however warring or contradictory; an idea that manifested itself in ancient myth as the image of the Cosmic Egg (sometimes held by the androgynous god Dionysus) or as the Uroboros (the circular and hermaphroditic snake of infinity, which devours its own tail).

It is this elementary, primordial Feminine, according to anthropologist Erich Neumann, that was seen as providing the "matter, the *materia*, from which all things arise,"[343] much in the same way, perhaps, that the "'primal white jelly'"[344] and the "'proto-shoggoths'" figure into the primal scene witnessed by Danforth in *At the Mountains of Madness*. In the Old Testament, she is seen as a primordial ocean of darkness from which the universe is later born, the water of gestation and birth. This is the ocean, Neumann writes, from which eventually rises the archetypal "primeval hill,"[345] also called by him "an 'island' in the sea"—an island that stands in the same relation to the larger ocean around it as the human consciousness does to the unconscious. Cthulhu's island R'lyeh rises from what Lovecraft suggestively calls "his black abyss"[346] at the bottom of the Pacific; the island in "Dagon" similarly rises from what he suggestively calls "an abyss which had yawned *at the bottom of the sea since the world was young*"[347] (italics mine) (Lovecraft's emphasis on maternal age, again)—the same maternal sea into which Olmstead plans to descend at the end of "The Shadow Over Innsmouth." In Lovecraft's fiction, however, the island never rises very far or for very long. Cthulhu brings the abyss up with him, and then descends, and mankind is left alone upon what he calls a "placid island of ignorance,"[348] forever lost amid much larger "black seas of infinity," which are both womb-like and threatening at the same time.

In "The Colour Out of Space," Lovecraft refers to this primal cosmic void in the plural, calling it: "*unformed realms* of infinity beyond all Nature as we know it"[349] (italics mine), and "black extra-cosmic gulfs ... whose mere existence stuns the brain and numbs us" (i.e., numbs or destroys the higher masculine consciousness). Lovecraft's Haunter of the dark, too, is presented as a creature of "the void'"[350] and thus either an extension of or a survival of the original, undivided, and chaotic Primordial Feminine; a creature that is only accessible, as we have seen, from within a transdimensional "egg-shaped ... object,"[351] which provides a view out into "an infinite gulf of darkness." And as one would expect of those contradictory forces that are united within the uroboric infinity of the feminine Cosmic Egg, we find the Haunter's otherworldly realm to be characterized by a union of warring opposites: doomed writer Robert Blake, in his final fragmentary notes, complains that "light is dark and dark is light"[352] and that "far is near and near is far," before concluding that he "must get out and unify the forces"—a unification that necessarily means his destruction within the larger, all-encompassing feminine whole. In "Under the Pyramids," meanwhile, we find a more localized version of this same abyss, here identified with the devouring maw of the underworld, and described as a hole with "so vast a surface that only by moving the eye could one trace its boundaries"[353] (parental giganticism again, as well as yet another transfer of the cosmic abyss into the subterranean world).

Here too, in this primordial abyss, we must also locate that primordial oblivion Lovecraft so misguidedly sought for so much of his life: what he calls the "safety of a new dark age"[354] in the preamble to "The Call of Cthulhu," and which closely corresponds to what Erich Neumann in *The Great Mother* calls the "irrational power of the primordial age,"[355] and which he identifies with "the nocturnal bliss of sleep in the unconscious" to be found upon a return to the maternal "original home."[356] As critic Maurice Levy similarly observes, in Lovecraft's weird fiction, the "irrational"[357] (what Erich Neumann would call the unconscious) "seems indissociable from the images of the depths," which are themselves merely a reflection of the larger cosmic abyss above; although Levy, once again, stops conspicuously short of making a connection between such abysms and the feminine.

Indeed, although one sees numerous intimations of this feminine orientation throughout Lovecraftian criticism, many critics stop short of making the obvious leap. In Peter Cannon's 1989 critical study of H. P. Lovecraft, Cannon accurately divides Lovecraft's weird fiction into horrors deriving from "'below,' 'beyond,' and 'the past,'"[358] but he stops short of identifying this "below" with the devouring feminine underworld, this "beyond" with the cosmic feminine abyss, and "the past" with an overwhelming maternal heredity. This feminine alignment of Lovecraft's cosmic void is especially brought home by T. S. Miller's essay "From Bodily Fear to Cosmic Horror (and Back Again): The Tentacle Monster from Primordial Chaos to Hello Cthulhu" (2011), although, again, Miller never makes Lovecraft's relation to the Feminine the centerpiece of his essay. And although Miller goes so far as to compare

Lovecraft's characteristic feeling of cosmic dread with that suicidal dread similarly experienced by Goethe's suicidal young Werther — called by Goethe "'an eternally *devouring, eternally regurgitating monster*'"[359] (italics mine), which is closely akin to "'the consuming power that lies hidden in the *Allness of nature*'"[360] (italics mine) — Miller nowhere suggests a connection with the archetypal image of the devouring Feminine, or that feminine uroboric infinity suggested by this image of endless consumption (although he does admittedly make note [without further comment] of the clear similarity with Lovecraft's own conception of "the grotesquely maternal Shub-Niggurath").[361]

Unwilling to delve into these markedly feminine aspects of Lovecraft's cosmic anxieties, T. S. Miller is forced to suggest, instead, that Lovecraft's "horror at ultimate reality ... arguably derives ... from his 'mechanistic materialism' and resultant atheism,"[362] rather than deriving it from Lovecraft's overwhelming maternal apprehensions, and a maternal ambivalence projected onto the cosmic scale. Indeed, Lovecraft's vaunted mechanistic materialism — however strictly he adhered to it, which is debatable — seems to have provided him with some level of comfort and control, in opposition to this idea of a fickle, uncontrollable, and (ultimately parental) feminine determinism and fate. Indeed, it is not for nothing that the Fates are most often represented by women, particularly old women, who are believed to weave the destinies of men: the Fates of the Greeks, the Norns of the North, the goddess Fortuna of both the Greeks and the Romans, and those Valkyries who decree death on the battlefield. I would suggest that Lovecraft's nihilism and pessimism, as reflected via his oft-declared belief that "nothing really amounts to anything,"[363] is rooted in a helpless reaction to an archetypal feminine conception of reality, in which Lovecraft's love for such things as his mother, the queen of England, and what he calls the Mistress of the World (i.e., Rome), essentially war with a simultaneous unease at being smothered by the might and weight of the very feminine that he adored, and that in his dreams yanked him up to the heights of heaven, only to just as quickly throw him down again.

As we have already seen, Lovecraft's cosmic beyond is not content to remain solely in the beyond. Instead, it returns to the earth, whether in the form of an unknown cosmic Colour or in the form of the shoggoths. And as we shall see below, many of the most common archetypal aspects of the Feminine mentioned by anthropologist Erich Neumann and others (giganticism, eyes, darkness, a relation to the subterranean underworld, and a characteristically feminine linking of subservience and passivity with a simultaneously essential role) are replicated in the form of the shoggoths.

VIII. Missy Tanit, Missy Isis, and Marse Clooloo: Blacks and Women in H. P. Lovecraft's Weird-Fiction

> It is not without reason that we associate wailing with women.
> — Otto Weininger, *Sex and Character*[364]

The strange linkage of blackness with feminine characteristics in the shoggoths is actually prefigured in various subtle ways throughout the Lovecraftian canon, often in ways so subtle that it suggests the linkage was an unconscious one in Lovecraft's mind rather than a matter of conscious reflection. As we have already seen, all of the various manifestations of the feminine in Lovecraft's writings, whether the cosmic abyss, the subterranean underworld, or the dark oceanic depths, all have darkness in common; a darkness that, as Erich Neumann asserts, ever stands in a parental relation to that consciousness that, childlike, is born from it.[365] Thus, even Lovecraft's fascination with the darkness reflects an essentially parental relation. But this larger darkness is a parent that breeds monsters, in the form of the restive demons of the repressed unconscious, whether racial or sexual.

As leftist psychologist Joel Kovel observes in his book *White Racism: A Psychohistory* (1970), there is a common identification of what he calls the id (the repressed and primitive portion of the mind) "as having the quality that comes from darkness; as being black. The id, then, is the referent of blackness within the personality; and the various partial trends within the id, all repressed, make themselves symbolically realized in the world as the forms of blackness embodied in the fantasies of race."[366] (Nor is this true only for whites, as poet Langston Hughes' identification of his own blackness with both the night and the depths makes clear.[367]) Indeed, as Margaret Murray's late-medieval witch accounts show, even before extensive European exploration and colonization of Africa, blackness had already been inextricably confounded with both evil (Satanism) and sexuality within the European imagination: the Devil repeatedly was described in the witch trials as being a tall or large "black man,"[368] who is often met by the female witch at night, and who often conspicuously carries a phallic wand or candle.[369] The Witches' Sabbath itself — in which the blackness of the Devil and the sexuality of women join inextricably together — inevitably came to be seen as a sexual theater of sorts, used for the carrying out of all the various repressed desires of the unconscious, whether oral, sadistic, incestuous, cannibalistic, or anal. Even now, this medieval "'Man in Black'"[370] still haunts our popular imagination in the form of those infamous "Men in Black" supposedly associated with the UFO phenomenon, and whose appearances even now are directly associated with the irrational impulses of the unconscious, via the sometimes odd and incongruous forms of behavior which supposedly occurs during so-called "MIB" encounters.

H. P. Lovecraft's ostensibly humorous statement in his 1929 Virginia travelogue (written just one year before the Satanic interracial marriage depicted in "Medusa's Coil") linking blacks and wives as joint "troubles": "In 1619, wives were sent out for the colonials, and in the same year the first cargo of African blacks arrived — proving that troubles never come singly."[371] As editor S. T. Joshi observes, "Yes, this is sexist and racist, but it is also funny"[372]; certainly, the statement is no worse than any of the humor seen every week on *Saturday Night Live.* And, to be fair to Lovecraft, he is not alone in his complaints regarding these women: according to historian Alden Vaughan, the early Virginia colony (much like Lovecraft's Old Ones, who had their own labor problems) suffered from an acute shortage of both labor and women, a problem, Vaughn writes, that "lay as much in the untimely arrival of the settlers as in *their poor quality*"[373] (italics mine). Some complained "that Sir Thomas had sent 'but few women thither & those corrupt.'"[374]

Lovecraft reflects this same, and seemingly incongruous, association of both women and blacks with cargo shipments in his earlier story "The Horror at Red Hook," in which the first reference to Lilith in the tale is immediately followed by the arrival of a mysterious steamer ship piloted by "a horde of swart, insolent ruffians,"[375] including a "Negroid"[376] leader, who swarm aboard Suydam's honeymoon cruise-ship and take charge of his murdered body — save that here Lovecraft strangely inverts the above image, so that instead of wives arriving, we instead find the body of a husband being carried away and later delivered to his demonic consort Lilith by the dark seamen. In both instances, however, we find blacks arriving by boat. This theme of importation is also associated with the shoggoths in both "The Shadow Over Innsmouth" (indeed, the furtive importation of shoggoths on the part of the Deep Ones is what Zadok Allen calls "'the reel [sic] horror'"[377] of his story) and *At the Mountains of Madness,* in which Lovecraft, as in his 1929 travelogue, speaks of the increasing "trouble"[378] of their management. Clearly, Lovecraft's joke about blacks and wives being joint troubles was not merely a purely flippant, playful comment, but rather a darkly revealing statement, representing a wider and more comprehensive socio-political worldview.

Lovecraft's connection of blacks with women also characterizes some of his earliest examples of published literary expression in 1913–1914. His attacks upon "erotic themes"[379] in the letter columns of *The Argosy* connect feminine eroticism, Africa, and blacks: Lovecraft writes of what he calls "the wanton waltzing of barbaric boors; / The shameful steps that all decorum lack; / The capers copy'd from the Afric black."[380] In his satirical poem "The Nymph's Reply to the Modern Business Man" (1917), too, we see a sexually experienced woman (she refers, for example, to her "seventh husband"[381]— not quite the thousand young of Shub-Niggurath, but she's getting there) make a barbed retort to a businessman's sexual overtures, observing: "But others have said things like that—/ And led me to a Harlem flat!" Later too, as we have seen, Keziah Mason's consort takes the form of a "Black Man"; and although Lovecraft makes a pretence of differentiating the Black Man of Arkham from African Americans,[382] later witnesses in the same story have no difficulty in identifying Arkham's Black Man as a Negro.[383]

Nor should Lovecraft's connections in this regard surprise us. As psychologist Joel Kovel observes, "A mountain of evidence has accumulated to document the basically sexualized nature of racist psychology. Yet it is doubtful whether the majority of educated people have any idea of the extent, organization, or intensity of such fantasies."[384] The frightening racist and sexual hallucinations experienced by Lovecraft's demented father, during which he believed an imaginary black man was assaulting his wife in a hotel room,[385] merely are one, admittedly more overt, example — an idea later culminating, once again, in Shub-Niggurath, with her thousand young. And although Lovecraft was certainly influenced in this association by the more open sexuality of the black jazz culture, his reaction to this culture of sex was determined by the subconscious contours of white psychology, which was shaped by the repressive attitudes of his New England upbringing.

In "The Rats in the Walls," too, we find blacks being juxtaposed with women, this time in relation to the destruction, by Northern soldiers, of the Delapore estate, which is accompanied by the image of "the women screaming, and the negroes howling and praying."[386] Later on in "Medusa's Coil," also in the context of an aristocratic Southern plantation family, Lovecraft refers to a similar black and feminine howling, here called a "distant howl and wail."[387] The "howling" in this case is that of the Zulu "witch-woman"[388] known as old Sophy, crying for the death of her serpentine priestess/goddess Marceline, and praying to her lord Cthulhu. Indeed, Lovecraft's combination of Cthulhu, Satanic, and feminine themes in this story is remarkable, and perhaps testifies to the degree to which the Cthulhu Cult is merely a gloss or veneer over this basic feminine/witch-cult conception. Later on, indeed, old Sophonisba prays in a remarkable and extraordinary passage, in which Lovecraft combines the purportedly alien language of his Cthulhu Cult with the African American literary patois of the late 19th century, such as he would have frequently encountered in the pages of the *Munsey* magazines of his youth: "*Ya, yo! N'gagi nebula bwana n'lolo! Ia! Shub-Niggurath!* She daid! Old Sophy know!'"[389] (italics Lovecraft's and Bishop's). That the entity, Shub-Niggurath, to whom Old Sophy prays in this passage is both feminine and black merely heightens the continuities of race and gender that we have been discussing here; never mind the irony of H. P. Lovecraft having a black woman apparently worshipping a caricature of her own degradation.

The blacks led in Dionysian procession by the demoness Lilith in "The Horror at Red Hook," too, in "Medusa's Coil" are absorbed into the very personage of wife Marceline Bedard herself, who is revealed at the end of the tale to have been, "though in deceitfully slight proportion, ... a negress."[390] This absorption of the feminine within the black (or the black within the feminine) eventually culminates in the amorphous feminine/black form of H. P. Lovecraft's shoggoths. And although critic Robert Waugh suggests elsewhere that "the casual description of blacks in 'Medusa's Coil' is a blotch on the work, for the miscegenation of the last paragraph is clearly tacked on, a mere appendage,"[391] it seems more likely that the racism in the story formed its original, indissoluble and central core, around which certain complementary additions (such as the Cthulhu Cult) later aggregated as a sort of veneer.

For instance, husband Denis de Russy's supposedly cosmic horror at the revelation of his wife's true bloodline manages to capture, at the same time, the semi-religious rhetorical tone of a white pro–Segregationist rally of the period; Denis complains (in terms that echo Lovecraft's own aversion to marriage) that Marceline "'"was a taint that wholesome human blood couldn't bear."'"[392] Lovecraft and Bishop later expand this language to the apocalyptic fervor of a lynching party: "'"I had to exterminate her — she was the devil — the summit and high-priestess of all evil — the spawn of the pit."'"[393] Much of Denis' horror at his wife's deception, as authors Lovecraft and Bishop establish at the very start of the story, derives from what the authors call his "high notions"[394] and "points of honor" regarding interracial affairs (or, as Lovecraft puts it more plainly, it was "no trouble at all to make him let the nigger wenches alone"). Unlike Arthur Jermyn's far more disreputable predecessors, with their penchant for chorus girls and the like, it is assured at the outset that Denis' gentlemanly code of "honor"[395] would "keep him out of the *most serious complications*" (italics mine) — what Lovecraft had just a year earlier called those twin "troubles" of blacks and wives; all of which is intended to make the revelation of Marceline's race at the end of the tale all the more significant.

Years later, Lovecraft continued to refer to similar acts of feminine and racial deceit in his writings. In "The Shadow Over Innsmouth," for instance, written just one year later, he writes of Olmstead's ancestor as having become married to a hybrid female Deep One "'by a trick.'"[396] He also twice suggested a similar plot involving a mysterious woman who seduces an unwary male to two of his friends and fellow writers: to E. Hoffman Price in 1932 (just two years later),[397] and to Reinhardt Kleiner as early as 1919[398] (in a story plot that sounds very similar to Sheehan's *The Woman of the Pyramid*). This fact, plus the close similarities, noted by S. T. Joshi,[399] between the revelation at the end of this tale and the earlier revelation at the conclusion of "Arthur Jermyn" (in which the true racial identity of a wife and mother is revealed) makes it clear that the disclosure at the climax to "Medusa's Coil" reflected a theme that was much on his mind. (Lovecraft may also have been influenced in his larger mythological associations with blacks and women in this story by the original Greek myth of Lamia, who according to legend was a former "African queen who lived only for her beauty"[400] but who was driven mad by Hera.)

Lovecraft may also have intended to indicate a parallel in "Medusa's Coil" with an actual and well-known mixed-race relationship in literary history: between decadent poet Charles Baudelaire and his muse, Jeanne Duval, who, like Marceline Bedard, was a light-skinned black woman with hypnotic eyes and luxurious dark hair, whose queenly grace was balanced by a dark, feral, and serpentine side. As Baudelaire's friend, the famed photographer Nadar observed, Jeanne Duval was "'a negress, a real negress, or at least a mulatto, incontestably; the packets of powdered chalk she had crushed over her face, neck and hands could not whiten their coppery hue.'"[401] Like Lovecraft's Marceline Bedard, Jeanne Duval was also an actress. And like Marceline, who is possessed of what Lovecraft and Bishop unflatteringly call a "hateful crinkly coil of serpent-hair,"[402] Duval was known for the "'wild luxuriance of her ink-black wavy mane.'"[403]

Baudelaire's relationship with Duval seems to have represented his profound sense of alienation from contemporary French-Catholic society as well as his perverse desire to shock and protest against small-minded proprieties. Even in his art criticism, Baudelaire could not resist hinting at forbidden interracial sexuality, once snidely suggesting in a review — and with a certain aura of authority — that Ingres' "unusual working methods"[404] included using "a negress as a model to emphasize more markedly certain bodily developments and attenuations." At least three times throughout the story, Lovecraft and Bishop compare decadent artist Frank Marsh, who has an abortive affair with Marceline, to Baudelaire,[405] even ending their tale with her hair "twining vampirically around"[406] Marsh's skeleton, a consciously and very Baudelairean image. Marsh's apparent powers of second sight — as evinced by his visionary ability to discern Marceline's twin Medusean and racial nature — also parallels that theory of symbolism and mystical correspondences evolved by Baudelaire, in which the poet was believed able to perceive hidden and secret spiritual truths in life and nature. All of which further suggests, again, that the racial aspect of the story was less an afterthought than a basic kernel, upon which Lovecraft later chose to expand and elaborate in various ways, thereby enabling him to delve deeper into his own problematic relationship with the decadent movement. (Lovecraft later seems to combine Frank Marsh and Marceline Bedard — both of whom are said to possess staring, dilated eyes — into a single personage, in the form of the staring-eyed, decadent, male/female Asenath Waite herself, perhaps in a satire, conscious or unconscious, of Samuel Loveman's decadent Hermaphrodite.)

"Medusa's Coil" finally ends with Lovecraft's narrator uncovering additional information about Denis and his wife Marceline in town: the townsfolk, it appears (much like the peasants in Lovecraft's poem "Psychopompos," who similarly objected to the sinister wife of the Sieur de Blois) "didn't like the looks of her [Marceline],"[407] thinking "she was a mighty odd sort." The townspeople, though, are unaware of the precise nature of Marceline's problem, and are unable to say precisely why she disturbed them. One townsperson, significantly, even asks Lovecraft's narrator: "What d'ye reckon was *the trouble* with that gal young Denis married? She kinder made everybody shiver and feel hateful, though ye couldn't never tell why" (italics mine). This word, "*trouble,*" is the same word that Lovecraft had used one year earlier to describe blacks and wives upon their arrival at the American colonies (and Marceline, as it will soon transpire, is both). Lovecraft and Bishop even go on to emphasize this point: the narrator tells the inquiring townsperson "that if anyone was to blame for *the trouble* at Riverside it was the woman, Marceline. She was not suited to Missouri ways, I said, and it was too bad that Denis had ever married her"[408] (italics mine).

We have already discussed, above, the possible role played by poetess Winifred Jackson in Lovecraft's caricatural inversion of Arcadia; and it may also be that the connection between blacks and women in Lovecraft's works, already present as early as his 1913 poetry, may have been further exacerbated by his abortive relationship with Jackson. As biographer S. T. Joshi observes, although the exact circumstances of Lovecraft's relationship with Jackson are obscure, several close sources have reported a romance of some sort between them[409]; and certainly Lovecraft's June 1921 letter to Jackson, written shortly after the death of his mother, constitutes an attempt at courtship. Jackson, however, had previously been married to Horace Jordan, a black man,[410] and was also involved in a relationship with William Stanley Braithwaite, a noted black poet and editor.[411] If Lovecraft had not known of such relationships before (and one can hardly imagine him becoming close to Jackson if he had), his eventual discovery of the circumstances of Jackson's affairs would certainly have come as a shock. Lovecraft himself ceased his literary collaborations with Jackson in 1921, and it was around this same time, with the writing of "Herbert West: Reanimator" (1921–1922), that the first hints of racism, already present in Lovecraft's juvenile poetry and amateur journalism, began in Lovecraft's fiction, in the form of his particularly venomous and caustic description of black boxer "Buck Robinson."

Certainly, Lovecraft and Bishop's description of Marceline Bedard's murder by her husband is particularly brutal. The authors describe Marceline's blood as being "spattered everywhere — on the walls, furniture and floor,"[412] and husband Denis de Russy even puts his foot on Marceline's back after he kills her, in the manner of a hunter with his quarry, so that her corpse "had the gory print of a shod human foot in the middle of [her] naked back." (As Denis explains, "I felt that I had fought the legions of Satan, and put my foot on the back of the thing I had annihilated."[413]) All of this testifies, certainly, to a certain lingering bitterness on Lovecraft's part, for whatever reason. Of course, as is typical of Lovecraft, the sympathies of artist Frank Marsh — who is aware of Marceline's black heritage — are reserved entirely for her (later murderous) husband; Marsh laments: "Poor Denis! My God, it's a shame!"[414] Dyer's later pity for the Old Ones, rather than their slaves, the shoggoths, in *At the Mountains of Madness*, merely perpetuates such misplaced sympathies.

This combination of black with feminine characteristics had certain precedents in weird fiction, of which Lovecraft was well aware. In Sheehan's *The Woman of the Pyramid*, for instance, Queen Nitokris is trained in the arts of black magic by the Ethiopian Kashta, her closest minister and adoptive father, whose "jet black"[415] and animalistic appearance is strikingly contrasted with that of the luscious and evil queen. Lovecraft's later depictions of this same Nitokris, as well as his picture of Lilith, were strongly influenced by such themes. In *Vathek*, too, as we have seen, Carathis is perpetually followed about by what William Beckford calls a "swarthy retinue"[416] of "fifty female negroes,"[417] who, much like the witches in Lovecraft's "Pickman's Model," are depicted as the loving consorts of Beckford's necrophilic ghouls, with whom they engage in an orgiastic bacchanalia amid the corpses of a cemetery. As Beckford observes (recording in detail what Lovecraft's Puritanism could only suggest, but not portray, in his description of the "gaiety" of the feasts of Queen Nitokris beneath the pyramid):

> The negresses, full of joy at the behests of their mistress, and promising themselves much pleasure from the society of the Ghoules, went with an air of conquest, and began their knockings at the tombs. As their strokes were repeated, a hollow noise was made in the earth; the surface hove up in heaps; and the

Ghoules, on all sides, protruded their noses to inhale the effluvia which the car-
casses of the woodmen began to emit.... Her negresses, who were forming tender
connexion with the Ghoules, importuned her, with all their fingers, to wait at
least till the dawn. But Carathis, being chastity in the abstract, and an implaca-
ble enemy to love intrigues and sloth, at once rejected their prayer.[418]

Lovecraft, of course, omits the black-on-ghoul love scenes, but the same general "connexion," one thinks, likewise underlies the general parameters of his
work, and his frequent invocation of blacks, and ghouls, and women in his
writings as symbols of degeneracy. It only remained for Lovecraft to combine
all these symbols into that ultimate embodiment of the "'thing that should
not be'"[419]: the shoggoths.

Lovecraft, of course, is not the only writer to invoke this connection
between blacks and women in the service of a social, political, or aesthetic
vision, on either side of the political spectrum. On the Left we find such
things as John Lennon and Yoko Ono's feminist pop song, "Woman Is the
Nigger of the World," or the feminist witches discussed by Margot Adler,
with their rather dubious campaign to, and I quote, "have the same rights
blacks have asked for: asking that 'Witch' like 'nigger' stop being a pejorative
term.'"[420] As conservative writer (and former leftist radical) David Horowitz
observes, in the extremely liberal academic world of today, in which the radical
rhetoric of the 1960s still has great currency, courses with "names like 'Black
Studies' and 'Women's Studies'"[421] often have "political subtexts and [are] really
devoted to Black Nationalism, feminism, and similar ideological programs."

Lovecraft's views, of course, represent the most extreme aspect of the
other side of this equation, his views having evolved very little from that of
the Democratic slavery supporters of the post–Civil War period, whose ostensibly political rhetoric involving "miscegenation" likewise preserved an underlying psycho-sexual obsession. In this, Lovecraft's vision is uncannily similar
to that of Otto Weininger, who in his seminal volume *Sex and Character* combined Judaism, feminism, and blackness into a single plasticine whole, all as
part of what writer Ray Monk calls Weininger's peculiarly "Viennese preoc-
cupation with the decay of modern times."[422] As Weininger (who, like Lovecraft, believed that the emancipation of black slaves in the United States was
a mistake) observed:

The emancipation of woman is analogous to the emancipation of Jews and
negroes. Undoubtedly the principal reason why these people have been treated as
slaves and inferiors is to be found in their servile dispositions; their desire for
freedom is not nearly so strong as that of the Indo-Germans.[423]

Already, with such sentiments, we find ourselves in the same rancid realm as
Lovecraft's near-contemporaneous poem "De Triumpho Naturae" (1905), with

its defense of slavery, as well as his later fascist essay "Cats and Dogs" (1926), with its idea of an innate servile or collective slave mentality among certain peoples. We note here, too, Weininger's easy transition from gender to race, in a way that also suggests some of the later feminine and transformative aspects of Lovecraft's amorphous shoggoths.

IX. Triumvirate of "Trouble": Women, Blacks and Jews

> Some men are fond of dogs and detest cats; others are devoted to cats and dislike dogs. Inquiring minds have delighted to ask in such cases, Why are cats attractive to one person, dogs to another? Why? I do not think that this is the most fruitful way of stating the problem. I believe it to be more important to ask in what other respects lovers of dogs and cats differ from one another.
> — Otto Weininger, *Sex and Character*[424]

A combination of the black, the Jewish, and the feminine can already be discerned in the very name of Lovecraft's shoggoths, which, I argue, is basically nothing more than a contraction of the equally feminine, Astartean, and black *Shub-Niggurath*. (A similar process of contraction, from *Shub-Niggurath* [first mentioned in 1927] to *shoggoth* [1929–1930], can also be seen in Lovecraft's shortening of *Yog-Sothoth* [1927] to *Yuggoth* [1929–1930] around this same time period.) Lovecraft was certainly not averse to such contractions: elsewhere he transforms the cat name "Nigger-Man" in "The Rats in the Walls" into the slightly (because it is both regional and archaic) more innocuous "Nig,"[425] found in both *The Case of Charles Dexter Ward* and "Cats and Dogs." (Lovecraft would have been conscious of the possibilities inherent in such contractions from his earlier reading of Murray's *Witch-Cult*, in which she presents such contractions as being typical of the late-medieval witch religion, such as the use of "'Naip' for Barbara Napier"[426] or "Mary" for "Marion."[427])

And although critic Robert M. Price does not specifically discuss the word "shoggoth" in his essay "Mythos Names and How to Say Them" (1987), (except to refer to its "obvious" "Semitic basis"[428]), he does discuss the name of its obvious etymological precursor, "Shub-Niggurath," observing that its double "g" and "-ath" ending also reflect Semitic features.[429] Early biographer L. Sprague de Camp concurred, tracing Lovecraft's "habit of ending made-up names in -ath and -oth"[430] to fantasy writer Lord Dunsany, who himself in turn probably "got it from the Bible and similar sources, for *-oth* is a common feminine plural ending in Hebrew." (Significantly perhaps, we also find Lovecraft, around 1934, advising correspondent Duane Rimel to adjust the title of his fantasy poem "Dreams of Yid" to "Dreams of Yith." Lovecraft suggested, as Robert M. Price explains, "that 'Yid' had an unfortunate 'slang connotation,'"[431] thereby suggesting some sort of veiled equivalency between the *-th* ending and the Hebraic in Lovecraft's mind.)

In addition to this Semitic element, however, as Price observes, Lovecraft also adds an additional black element to the name, one that transforms Dunsany's Judaic "Sheol-Nugganoth" via the addition of "the syllable 'nig,'" from "the Latin niger, 'black,'"[432] most likely in the service of Lovecraft's ongoing racist polemic. (Personally I think it much more likely that Lovecraft simply ignored the Latin completely, and merely inserted "Nig" from the nickname for his cat into the word, just as elsewhere he seems to have inserted the surname of the Marquis de Sade into the names of his entities Os*sada*gowah and its offspring *Sado*gowah.[433]) At any rate, here, as with the shoggoths later on, we can see Lovecraft suggesting a connection between the feminine and the black, reinforced with the addition of a Semitic or Hebraic context. And if this is true of Shub-Niggurath, then it could also be argued that Lovecraft's retention of many of these same features in the word "shoggoth," including the double-*g* from "niggur" and the Hebraic *-th* ending, preserves these larger connotations.

And while some Lovecraft readers have suggested a link between the shoggoths and those barbaric Visigoths who were associated with the decline and fall of the Roman Empire, such a simple meaning as *shoggoths = Ostrogoths* does nothing to explain the other peculiarly specific attributes of the shoggoths: their imitativeness, their plasticity, their status as slaves, their subterranean origin, their blackness, their multiple eyes, their luminosity, their giganticism, and their association with Palmyrene decay, all of which reflect specifically black, Jewish, and feminine aspects, and forming a triumvirate, if not of evil, then at least of those "troubles" that "do not come singly" ... at least within the corridors of Lovecraft's mind.

X. *The Characteristics of the Shoggoths*

Admittedly, the ever-shifting properties of Lovecraft's shoggoths are wide enough to suggest any number of symbolic, unconscious, and polemical meanings; anything that, for Lovecraft, "'should not be.'" Lovecraft manages to combine nearly all of his various antagonisms within a single, excremental body, which is able to change its shape endlessly. As psychologist Joel Kovel observes in *White Racism*, "the white striving for moral purity is fused in the unconscious mind with the flight from the black, excremental body"[434]; a flight that also results in what critic Robert Waugh similarly calls "the untransformed excremental images"[435] of the shoggoths. And there are a number of additional structural properties of the shoggoths that also possess demonstrable polemical parallels with Lovecraft's larger socio-political and aesthetic concerns.

First, the shoggoths are collective entities, possessing no individual personality or identity whatsoever. Their name is lowercase in Lovecraft's stories. As Lovecraft takes pains to point out, their every action is a feeble echo of their former masters; and when their masters were alive, they gladly molded their bodies and their actions to suit their masters' hypnotic will. As Robert Waugh observes in his essay "The Subway and the Shoggoth," "a shoggoth may not be individual — it is legion."[436] The shoggoths thereby form the perfect plastic medium by which not only to embody many different meanings simultaneously, but also to form a caricatural embodiment of an entire race of people, or of many different peoples.

In this, of course, Lovecraft's shoggoths closely mirror the familiar racial vituperations found throughout his correspondence regarding the immigrant crowds in New York City and Providence. Lovecraft, like the unabashed collectivist that he was, admitted that he found himself unable to discern the "individual grotesque"[437] amid what he calls "the collectively devastating" image of this larger "morbid soul of disintegration and decay." In Lovecraft's 1926 description of a walk through a Providence slum, he describes what he calls certain "slug-like beings (half Jew and half Negro, apparently),"[438] which he discerned amid the other "shapeless forms of organic entity," a combination of the black and the Jewish that mirrors that coalescing of Jewish and Irish characteristics already mentioned in the introduction, and which will, again, later go on to characterize the eternally malleable shoggoths.

Second, as Robert Waugh observes, the "shoggoths are pointedly black."[439] One immediately obvious reason for this is Lovecraft's racism, although that merely skims the surface; Lovecraft here reveals a more artful, and more fundamental, psychological identification of the loathed object with dirt, and of dirt, in turn, with the repressed fantasies of the unconscious. We have already noted this with regard to the Western European creation of the *Homme Noir* during the Middle Ages, a process likewise operative in the creation of such diverse products of fantasy as the folkloric association of vampires with odorous, feculent mud,[440] not to mention Lovecraft's own recurring nightmares and dream imagery involving "hellish black"[441] mires, "knee-deep ... filth,"[442] and "deep mud,"[443] into which he literally felt himself being sucked down.

The customs of Africa, such as cannibalism, nudism, and tribalism (savage from the perspective of the medieval European), would have further cemented this connection between blackness, evil, and the unconscious fantasies of the European mind: an identification that found its echo in their own furtive and repressed desires for savagery, nudism, and indeed, sometimes even cannibalism. As Joel Kovel observes, "scarcely anyone grows up without exposure to the myth of African cannibalism: grinning black devils with bones stuck through their nostrils dancing about the simmering pot containing the hapless missionary. *What child has not contemplated this scene in one form or another?*"[444] [italics mine]. Setting aside the issue of whether African cannibalism was, as Kovel seems to assert, merely a "myth": Kovel's description of a child contemplating this scene is suggestive of that infantile "tickle"[445] felt by the old man in "The Picture in the House," by which Lovecraft attempts to convey something of the sexual, sadistic stimulation aroused within him by a woodcut image of African cannibalism; certainly, in the case of this preternaturally ancient old man, this infantile cannibalistic interest has lasted quite awhile. (Lovecraft himself would have been introduced to such images as Kovel describes from his reading of the *Munsey* magazines, especially Edgar Rice Burroughs' *Tarzan* stories, in which the image of the "savage African cannibal"[446] is quite common, and is repeatedly depicted as the extreme antithesis of humanity and civilized society.)

The shoggoths will be further linked directly with the black (in the sense of the African American) via Lovecraft's designating them as former slaves, whose creation and breeding by the Old Ones he laments in much the same manner as he earlier lamented the importation of African slaves into the Jamestown colony. As H. P. Lovecraft emphasizes, the shoggoths were regarded as "beasts of burden"[447] and as "ideal slaves," using unique plasmatic and shape-shifting abilities to "lift prodigious weights"[448] in order to construct the Old Ones' stone cities (but only, one notes, under the Old Ones' hypnotic direction.) And, much like the slaves in the American South, who engaged in numerous plots and uprisings, both individually and collectively,[449] in order to regain their freedom, at times the shoggoths also became "particularly intractable"[450] during certain periods, eventually requiring what Lovecraft calls (in echo of the U.S. Civil War) a virtual "war of re-subjugation" to regain control over them.

Indeed, although he compares the way in which the shoggoths were "tamed and broken" by their masters to the way in which "wild horses ... were tamed by cowboys" in the Wild West, a closer parallel is to be found in the disciplining techniques exercised by men like Lovecraft's favorite Southern gentleman, to whom he refers enthusiastically in his 1929 travelogue as "the great landed proprietor, poet, and cavalier William Byrd, Gent.,"[451] a slave-owner who, by his own account, "'had several people whipped'"[452] in September 1811, who placed "'a branding iron on the place'" a slave complained of when he "'pretend[ed] to be sick'" in January 1811, who "forced [a slave] to wear the bit for 24 hours" in January 1810, when the slave claimed to be injured, and who wrote in his diary in August 1810, "'I had a severe quarrel with little Jenny and beat her too much for which I was sorry.'" As an Arkansas slaveholder observed, writing in 1860, "'it is like 'casting pearls before swine' to try to persuade a negro to work. He must be *made* to work, and should always be given to understand that if he fails to perform his duty he will be punished for it.'"[453] In the fascist utopia of Lovecraft's Old Ones, however, such pearl-like methods of persuasion — in the form of the Old Ones' powers of hypnosis — do in fact suffice (at least for a time) in controlling their unwilling charges; but only so long as the shoggoths do not possess (and this is a significant conceit) any minds of their own.

Lovecraft may have been influenced in this fanciful idea of hypnotic slavery by his voluminous reading of the *Munsey* pulp magazines during his youth, in which this idea of the hypnotic domination of a less powerful will by a stronger one was a recurring theme. In Don Mark Lemon's "The Gorilla" (*All-Story*, 1905), a story that Lovecraft later described as "the prize-winner with me"[454] when he first read it at age fifteen, a humanlike ape has "been unwillingly subdued by its master's superior intellect."[455] (Significantly, this ape is at first mistaken by the narrator for "a negro servant.") In *The Abyss of Wonders* by Perley Poore Sheehan (whose works Lovecraft strongly praised elsewhere[456]), Sheehan depicts the black, apelike servants of a mysterious and decadent Great Race in the Gobi Desert as being mindless machines or puppets; as the hero of the story disgustedly observes: "Servility! No will of their own! Trained apes!"[457] Sheehan even suggests something of the shoggoths' later protoplasmic flexibility by describing how these apelike servitors are "subservient to his will, yet marvelously elastic, as if their tireless muscles were his own."[458] The early pulp writers seem to have been strangely fascinated with this dark fantasy of domination and subjugation, an image of black powerlessness that psychologist Joel Kovel describes as being highly characteristic of the Northern white imagination.

This *powerlessness* of this black body is the key: "the aversive Northerner,"[459] Kovel writes, requires "a powerless object with which to play out the symbolic game." As Lovecraft explains, the shoggoths are "slaves of suggestion,"[460] "given life, thought, and plastic organ patterns solely by the Old Ones" and possessing "no language save" that of the Old Ones and "*likewise no voice save the imitated accents of their bygone masters*"[461] (italics Lovecraft's).

Only then is the black body finally able to become, as Kovel puts it, "the double negative of anality, the fantasy of a fantasy,"[462] in the Northern aversive imagination — i.e., H. P. Lovecraft's "thing that should not be." Hence too, Kovel writes, the peculiar transformations of this black body within the white averse mind: a body reduced, as Kovel writes, to "phallus, vagina, anus, mouth, breast, all available and ordained to be without inhibition because they were without guiding self,"[463] a "magical excremental body ... black, warm, odorous, undifferentiated," just like Lovecraft's shoggoths, who are capable, he writes, of magically "moulding their tissues into all sorts of temporary organs under hypnotic influence" and whose bodies are essentially undifferentiated and embryonic, being composed of endlessly multiplying "multicellular protoplasmic masses."[464]

Indeed, while Lovecraft's general picture in *At the Mountains of Madness* generally mirrors the Southern slave-system, of which Lovecraft strongly approved, the means he used to embody this parable are peculiarly Northern in complexion, having their origin in that aversive racism which psychologist Joel Kovel associates mainly with the North, and which, unlike the more overt institutionalized and "dominative"[465] racism of the American South, was far more furtive and psychologically murky. As Kovel observes: "Northerners, right from the start, were more secretive and guilty about all aspects of their sexual behavior toward blacks, and locked within the darktowns of their minds what was openly acted upon in the South,"[466] developing instead "a reaction of aversion, and even of horror, toward blacks without any personal experience with them."[467] Indeed, Kovel's description of the psychological aspects of Northern aversive racism reads almost like a case-study of H. P. Lovecraft himself, whose own "darktown of the mind" eventually took the outward form of shadow-haunted Innsmouth.

There is a similarly aversive picture of collective and bestial African American evil in George Allan England's *Darkness and Dawn* trilogy (1912–1913), one of Lovecraft's favorite science fantasy stories as a young man.[468] The ape-like descendants of present-day blacks inspire what England revealingly calls "an almost irresistible repugnance, a compelling aversion, more of the spirit than of the flesh"[469] in his hero Allan Stern, so much so that "the temptation lay strong upon him to get rid of at least a dozen or a score"[470] with his firearm. Stern later, in a moment of genocidal anger, goes so far as to declare that "his life work was to include a total slaughter of the Anthropoids."[471] England, one notes, although born in Nebraska, later moved to Boston with his family and was educated at Harvard,[472] which perhaps accounts for the peculiarly Northern virulence of his hatred, a hatred later shared by Lovecraft's weird fiction, with its similar and undeniable lynch-mob mentality, as demonstrated by such things as the sailor Johansen's slaughter of the Polynesian crew of the *Alert*, whose "destruction seem[ed] almost a duty."[473] Lovecraft, interestingly, maintained a brief but friendly correspondence with England in later life,[474] and one wonders whether England was aware of the thematic debt that the younger author owed to him.

According to Joel Kovel, such vehemently aversive attitudes have their origin in the peculiarly Northern renunciation of the body, which, along with its allied and Puritan socio-political system of prohibitions, transformed the desired black body into "a taboo,"[475] the temptation of which was "to be obeyed henceforth by aversion." Thus confronted with the rejected world in the form of the black body, Kovel explains, "the best the North could do within the terms of its symbolic matrix was to express hatred and rage against the black body," resulting in what Kovel calls "an obscure yet violent hatred for Negroes."[476] This hatred has "rarely examined because of its intensity," and manifests itself, in Lovecraft's writings, in the tortured and hallucinatory rhetoric of his letters, as well as in the eternally shifting body of the equally taboo and hated shoggoths. Indeed, as Kovel goes on (and as the numerous fantastic permutations discernable in Lovecraft's weird fiction amply show), this Northern aversion has a "rich symbolic content of its own."[477]

Ironically, of course, these shoggoths that Lovecraft so deplored had no origin other than in the tormented recesses of his own mind and in the Puritan processes of white aversive racism. The creators who dared so unwisely to breed the shoggoths on this planet were not the Old Ones, but rather Lovecraft himself.

XI. "'The eyes in darkness'"[478]

> It has been exhaustively proved that the female is soulless
> and possesses neither ego nor individuality, personality
> nor freedom, character nor will.
> — Otto Weininger, *Sex and Character*[479]

The shoggoths are not merely black, however, but also iridescent, their luminous glow deriving from those multiple eyes (described by Lovecraft as "a shapeless congeries of protoplasmic bubbles, faintly self-luminous, and with myriads of temporary eyes forming and unforming"[480]) that conglomerate within their bodies — eyes that we earlier, in section 4 of this chapter, identified with both the archetypal feminine and the leeringly sexual. (Even this luminosity of the shoggoths suggests resonances with the Feminine, mirroring as it does the earlier luminosity of Lilith, Mrs. Gardner, and the cosmic

Colour from space that lands on the Gardner farm.) Witch Keziah Mason, too, in "The Dreams in the Witch House," is repeatedly described, in her trans-dimensional state, as resembling an "iridescent bubble congeries,"[481] a description that sounds very much like the eye component of the shoggoths, which has subsequently been separated out into its purely ocular or feminine component. (And, much like those earlier immaterial psychic projections of the undead seen in "He" and "The Unnamable," Lovecraft specifically identifies these congeries in "Witch House" as being "projections of life-forms from our planet,"[482] i.e., human beings.) This feminine component of their makeup may also explain why the shoggoths are so at home in the suboceanic abysses situated beneath the Old Ones' Antarctic city, and also why they are so at home in the caves and tunnels of the surrounding mountains: both are symbols, as discussed above, of the archetypal Feminine.

It may also be, too, that the very shape-shifting capabilities of the shoggoths, as well as their impressionable, imitative, and hypnotizable nature, were also (at least for some writers during the early 20th century) characteristic of the Feminine. Lovecraft already shows an acquaintance with this constellation of ideas in his summary of Arthur Machen's *The Great God Pan* in his essay "Supernatural Horror in Literature," in which, as he recounts, the femme fatale Helen Vaughn "is put to death amidst *horrible transmutations of form* involving *changes of sex* and *a descent to the most primal manifestations of the life-principle*"[483] (italics mine)—what Machen himself similarly describes, in markedly feminine and hermaphroditic language, as a descent into "the abyss of all being,"[484] after which she dissolves into "the principle of life, which makes organism" (all things later witnessed by Danforth during the hermaphroditic primal scene at the end of *At the Mountains of Madness*). Significantly, Lovecraft's Asenath Waite, like a shoggoth in miniature, is also later possessed of this same Feminine or sexual transformative ability, albeit to a lesser degree: she confines herself to those horrific "changes of sex" that Lovecraft earlier noted with regard to Arthur Machen's story, although her corpse later also decays into a pile of slime.

The allied transformative and hypnotizable aspects of Lovecraft's shoggoths are closely mirrored by philosopher Otto Weininger's characterization of the feminine principle in his seminal book *Sex and Character*, whose racist and anti–Semitic rhetoric is, as already noted above, eerily similar to Lovecraft's own, suggesting either that Lovecraft had read or perhaps heard of Weininger (which is unlikely, given their widely separated milieus), or, what is more likely, that Lovecraft was strongly influenced by the same reigning ideas (and prejudices) as Weininger. Indeed, in reading Weininger's works, it almost seems that he, much like H. P. Lovecraft, was simply searching for the perfect embodiment or image of negation — the ultimate example of that "thing which should not be" — and, so, simply stumbled upon an image that happened to parallel Lovecraft's own. As such, Weininger's writings may provide a guide to the way in which Lovecraft's own polemical concerns coalesced with the radical ferments within his mind, in order to produce his various later weird entities.

Like Lovecraft, Weininger was overtly concerned with the supposed decay of modern times; and, much like Lovecraft, with his aristocratic pose and anti-capitalistic ethos, Weininger, according to writer Ray Monk, "attributes this decay to the rise of science and business and the decline of art and music, and characterizes it, in an essentially aristocratic manner, as the triumph of pettiness over greatness."[485] As Weininger observes in his chapter on Judaism in *Sex and Character* (Weininger characterized as "Jewish" whatever he happened to dislike in modern life): "The decision must be made between Judaism and Christianity, between business and culture, between male and female."[486] Like the gentlemanly Lovecraft, one of Weininger's main complaints is that "what is meant by the word 'gentleman' does not exist amongst the Jews."[487] Weininger further complained that "there is no Jewish nobility,"[488] a specious method of argument later resumed in Lovecraft's pro-fascist essay "Cats and Dogs," in which he contrasts the supposedly aristocratic qualities of cats with the supposedly plebian and lower-class qualities of dogs. Indeed, Weininger's repeated references to the supposedly "slavish"[489] and "servile"[490] dispositions of both Jews and women closely mirror Lovecraft's own denunciations, in "Cats and Dogs," of what he calls the "boorish slaves of eastern darkness"[491] during the Middle Ages, as well as his more general attacks upon effeminacy elsewhere. Nor is it any coincidence to find Weininger — much like Lovecraft, with his fastidious attacks upon dogs' overtly tactile displays of affection — characterizing his polemical opposition to the Feminine in both canine and tactile terms: describing the vaunted quality of female loyalty and faithfulness, for instance, as "a condition of actual slavery, dog-like, attentive, full of instinctive tenacious attachment, comparable with that necessity for actual contact which marks female sympathy."[492]

Weininger, much like the Puritan Lovecraft, was both venomously anti-sexual in his writings, and sexually celibate in his personal life. As Weininger observed, prefiguring both the later sentiments of Lovecraft, and also the horror experienced by Danforth during his final glance to the west: "Every form of fecundity is loathsome, and no one who is honest with himself feels bound to provide for the continuity of the human race."[493] And, much like Lovecraft, with his venomous letters regarding nude artist's models[494] and his poems chastising the "erotic themes"[495] prevailing in our new and "vulgar age,"

Weininger deplored what he saw as the prevailing sexuality of the modern era; a sexuality that he traced chiefly to the combined influence of women and Jews, declaring, "It is the Jew and the woman who are the apostles of pairing to bring guilt on humanity."[496] Weininger's strange combination of feminine and Jewish characteristics throughout his work is very like the continuity and integration of all of Lovecraft's own polemical antagonisms, which, in the shoggoths, finally merged and mixed into one single, plasmid form.

XII. Hypnotism

For Otto Weininger, Woman possesses no "free will."[497] Like the shoggoths, who "had always been controlled through the hypnotic suggestions of the Old Ones"[498] and were entirely dependent upon their masters' powers for any ideas or thoughts or actions they might take, Weininger saw women as being entirely dependent on their male betters to guide, mold, and influence them. "All women can be hypnotized and like being hypnotized,"[499] Weininger goes on; "Woman is not a free agent; she is altogether subject to her desire to be under man's influence."[500] Indeed, those views that Woman most naturally accepts, Weininger writes, are those of Man. Woman acquires, thereby, Weininger asserts (much like the shoggoths via the Old Ones, or those worms devouring the bodies of dead magicians in H. P. Lovecraft's "The Festival," which afterward learn to walk and not to crawl), "a second nature, without even guessing that it is not her real one."[501] And just as Robert Waugh observes that the "essential development of this figure"[502] of the shoggoth in Lovecraft's weird fiction "lies in its history and its explicit ability to imitate and supplant its masters," it is Weininger's chief worry that Woman, having adapted Man's nature as her own, with then attempt to supplant him.

For the time being, however, and much like the mindless, brainless shoggoths, Woman is a blank, protoplasmic slate. "Mind cannot be predicated of her at all"[503]; Weininger writes, "she is mindless." And, as Weininger goes on, in terms that already suggest a pre–shoggoth-like plasticity: "Woman is nothing; therefore, and only, therefore, *she can become anything*" (italics mine). Man alone possesses the ability to mold *"her formless nature"*[504] (italics mine) into any shape he chooses. Already, we are in the shoggothian realm of beings with pronounced "modeling powers,"[505] which are seen by Lovecraft as "infinitely plastic and ductile"[506] and as possessed of "a constantly shifting shape and volume."[507] There are traces here, too, of anthropologist Erich Neumann's primal feminine abyss; that primal, unformed, and undifferentiated matter that contains all forms embryonically within it, and that gives birth, in turn, to all of the endlessly changing shapes of life and mutability. Indeed, as Weininger goes on in shoggoth-like language that suggests Neumann's Primordial Feminine: "Women are matter, *which can assume any shape*"[508] (italics mine), able to become "all without being anything."[509]

Otto Weininger also writes of what he calls the "plasticity"[510] of Woman, who, like the similar "formless protoplasm"[511] of the shoggoths, merely exists as what others "make her."[512] Woman thus, Weininger goes on — and much like the "amorphous"[513] shoggoths, who have the ability to absorb and then cover their victims with a hideous coating of "slime"[514] — has an "absorbing and absorbable nature."[515] And just as critic Robert Waugh observes of the shoggoths, "it seems striking how absolutely Lovecraft insists that a shoggoth is no individual,"[516] for Weininger, too, the chief flaw of Woman is that she "does not recognise her own entity," and instead exists in "an indistinct state of fusion with others,"[517] thus existing, like the shoggoths, in a purely collective state, closely akin to that which Lovecraft attributed to the immigrant hordes oozing around him. "The woman is always living in a condition of fusion with all the human beings she knows, even when she is alone," Weininger complains elsewhere; "Women have no definite individual limits."[518]

Thus, as Weininger goes on, "The supremest moment in a woman's life" occurs only when this eternally changeable feminine plasticity achieves sexual union, for it is at this time, and at this time only, Weininger explains, that Woman finally reaches "the greatest joy of passivity, stronger even than the contented feeling of a hypnotized person, the desire of matter which has just been formed, and wishes to keep that form forever."[519] Much like Machen's Helen Vaughn, who eventually dissolves into nothing but shapeless protoplasm, or Lovecraft's Asenath Waite, whose body is reduced to a "mostly liquescent horror,"[520] for Otto Weininger, Woman is in constant danger of disintegrating into formlessness throughout her lifetime. "The absolute female is capable of sub-division,"[521] Weininger asserts; "the female is composite, and so can be dissociated and cleft." (Hence, Weininger intriguingly suggests, the well-known phenomenon, mainly among women, of "authenticated cases of double or multiple personality."[522]) True, it is usually Lovecraft's *male* characters who occasionally dissolve into protoplasm, but aside from Dr. Munoz in "Cool Air" or the Dutch gentleman in "He," they usually do so under the disintegrative auspices of the overpowering and Terrible Feminine, such as Robert Suydam or Edward Derby.

However, Otto Weininger warns us that — much like those troublesome shoggoths, who sometimes, as Dyer worriedly observes, "developed a semi-stable brain whose separate and occasionally stubborn volition echoed the will of the Old Ones without always obeying it"[523] — women are sometimes

able to break out of the mindless mold into which soulless feminine malleability has congenitally consigned them. But even here, Weininger notes
that (just as with the imitative shoggoths, who never possess a true personality
of their own, even after their liberation) Woman is only able to rebel insofar
as she herself is as Masculine as her masters. As Weininger puts it, it is "not
the wish for outward equality with man, but what is of real importance in
the woman question, the deep-seated craving to acquire man's character, to
attain his mental and moral freedom, to reach his real interests and his creative
power. I maintain that the real female element has neither the desire nor the
capacity for emancipation in this sense."[524] This is also the same sense in
which H. P. Lovecraft's she-devil Asenath Waite goes about pursuing her
goals — her ultimate aim being to reverse her current, and lamentable, feminine state, and inhabit the body of a male (in this case, that of her husband).
As Lovecraft famously puts it, Asenath Waite's "crowning rage ... was that she
was not a man; since she believed a male brain had certain unique and far-
reaching cosmic powers. Given a man's brain, she declared, she could not
only equal but surpass her father in mastery of unknown forces."[525] For both
Asenath Waite and Weininger's rebellious woman, the desire is not for women's
emancipation as such, but rather the mental and bodily assumption of a male
identity: a desire that, as Weininger writes, again in shoggothlike terms, is
strongly facilitated by women's "undoubted imitative powers."[526]

Weininger is quick to identify the heroes of the women's rights movement
with what he calls "sexually intermediate forms"[527] — language that at first
seems redolent of the terminology of sexual pathology, but that also recalls
the sexual indeterminacy of the dying Helen Vaughn, as well as the troubling
physical malleability of both Asenath Waite and the shoggoths. That such
mannish or "hybrid" women during Lovecraft's era included such figures as
occultist H. P. Blavatsky (Weininger specifically cites Blavatsky as an example
of the mannish-type woman),[528] or Mabel Doge Luhan, a leftist, modernist,
and radical — both of them diametrically opposed to Lovecraft on various
polemical issues — further underlines the broad sweep (so to speak) of Lovecraft's conservative critique. Did H. P. Lovecraft intend a satire of H. P.
Blavatsky in his depiction of the (secretly masculine) occultist Asenath Waite?
As Weininger observes, alluding to what he saw as the markedly feminine
aspects of Theosophy: wherever "a weak and vague sentimentality can be
expressed with little effort, as ... in pseudo-mysticism and theosophy, women
have sought and found a suitable field for their efforts."[529] This feminine
aspect of theosophy may have constituted yet another aspect of Lovecraft's
critique of Blavatsky's movement, and caused his inclusion of it amid the
larger picture of apocalyptic corruption in "The Call of Cthulhu," in addition

to the anti–Imperialist, interracial, and cross-cultural aspects of this philosophy that would have likewise drawn his ire.

XIII. Jews, Palmyra, and Art

"The Roman people," says Aurelian, in an original letter, "speak
with contempt of the war which I am waging against a woman.
They are ignorant of both the character and the power of Zenobia."
— Edward Gibbon, *The Decline and Fall of the Roman Empire*[530]

Much in the same way that H. P. Lovecraft compulsively and collectively linked blacks with women, Otto Weininger linked Jews and women inextricably in his mind. As Weininger writes, "Judaism is saturated with femininity."[531] "The homology of Jew and woman,"[532] Weininger later declares, becomes "closer the further examination goes." And much like Lovecraft's plasmatic shoggoths, as well as Weininger's equally plasticine women, for Weininger Jews exist only collectively, "in the same mould, the whole forming as it were *a continuous plasmodium*"[533] (italics mine), which tends "to adhere together," rather than interacting as "free independent individuals."[534] More troublingly, Weininger further locates what he calls "the congruity between Jews and women"[535] in what he calls "the extreme adaptability of the Jews," who "can become everything." This again bears a marked resemblance to Lovecraft's adaptive shoggoths, which have the ability, so troubling to the Old Ones (and later to Dyer himself) to adapt to any environment, however hot, wet, or cold,[536] all of which eerily prefigures the methods and rhetoric later employed by Nazis to test and somehow counter this supposed Jewish adaptability: whether the ghettos, the boxcars, or later, the concentration camps.

As one would expect, Weininger (like H. P. Lovecraft after him) is not content merely to apply such noxious ideas to the biological or sociological realm, but must also apply them to the world of aesthetics as well. Indeed, just like Lovecraft — with his repeated railing against what he saw as the rootless, amorphous, and autochthonous artistic productions of the modern age — we find Weininger railing against formlessness in modern art. Weininger, however, takes the added step of explicitly identifying this formlessness with the feminine. "There is no art without form,"[537] Weininger writes, "no artistic beauty which does not conform to the laws of art"; and "male thought is fundamentally different from female thought in its craving for definite form, and all art that consists of moods is essentially a formless art."[538] Thus, and much like the imitative shoggoths, whose powers merely "echoed the will of their masters,"[539] so too do the artistic works of both women and Jews require some larger guiding force or influence, Weininger writes, of which their work is ultimately but a pale imitation or parody. Indeed, this supposedly imitative quality of Jewish achievements is a staple of anti–Semitic rhetoric, figuring even in the writings of the arch anti–Semite Adolf Hitler himself, for whom "what they [the Jews] do accomplish in the field of art is either patchwork or intellectual theft ... [which] can be seen from the fact that he is mostly found in the art which seems to require least original invention, the art of acting. But even here, in reality, he is only a 'juggler,' or rather an ape."[540]

This same quality of imitation likewise characterizes the Palmyrene bas-reliefs and murals of the Old Ones' so-called decadent period — what Lovecraft calls "degenerate murals *aping and mocking* the things they had superseded"[541] (italics mine), so much so that they seemed "more *like a parody* than a per-petuation of"[542] (italics mine) the previous tradition. This language also suggests Love-craft's later description of Asenath Waite's own femi-nine and "mostly liquescent body"[543] as a "foul, *stunted parody.*"[544] It seems, too, that Lovecraft intends, in his description of the Old Ones' mocking sculptures, a clear connection between the way the shoggoths themselves are "able *to mock and reflect* all forms and organs and pro-cesses."[545] Indeed, what Love-craft ultimately seems to be suggesting is that the increas-ingly independent shoggoths themselves, having learned, as we have seen, to mimic their masters (and like those "assimilated" Jews, such as Samuel Loveman, of whom Lovecraft wrote in his letters), have eventually gone on to become a part of Old Ones'

One of Palmrya's "ungainly and hybrid" sculp-tures? Note the great size of the mother, as com-pared to the smallness of the child: the Great Mother archetype, once again. *Funerary Bust of Tibnan*, Palmyra, Syria, 2nd century CE. Lime-stone, 56 × 45 cm. A01998. Photograph Herve Lewandowski. Louvre, Paris, France. Réunion des Musees Nationaux / Art Resource, NY.

society and culture, thereby introducing into their artwork what Lovecraft tellingly calls "some subtly but profoundly alien element ... to the aesthetic feeling behind the technique."[546]

Lovecraft also adds a further, and explicitly Semitic, element to this picture of decay in *At the Mountains of Madness*, when he describes the latter-day Old Ones' sculptures as being closely akin to "such hybrid things as the *ungainly Palmyrene sculptures* fashioned in the Roman manner"[547] (italics mine), a sentiment that critic Robert Waugh suggests he derived from his reading of George Albert Cooke's article on the Syrian city of Palmyra in the *Encyclopædia Britannica*.[548] There is also a hint here of Oswald Spengler's similarly apocalyptic anti–Eastern polemic in *Decline of the West*, in which Palmyra is mentioned at least three times[549] in the context of what Spengler describes as an influx of mystical and religious ideas from the East: where, as Spengler sadly observed, "a whole new form-world grew up. Under a mask of Graeco-Roman conventions, it filled even Rome itself. The master-masons of the Pantheon and the Imperial Fora were *Syrians*"[550] (italics Spengler's).

Modern classical scholars are far less negative in their assessments of both this new Eastern world and Palmyra's achievements than either Lovecraft or their predecessors. As scholar G. W. Bowersock observes, classical scholars are now looking "father and farther afield, from the centers of power (Rome, Athens, Byzantium, Jerusalem) to the remote peripheries in search of indigenous cultures and their interactions with traditional classical cultures."[551] At the same time, Bowersock observes, "late antiquity"[552] itself "has emerged not as a decadent afterglow of the classical past but as a vibrant world all its own," thus calling "into question the entire concept of decline and fall." Scholar Jaś Elsner observes simply that "Palmyrene art asserted the particularly Palmyrene identity within the empire."[553] Palmyra belonged, Elsner writes, to "a world of cosmopolitan cities ... whose wealth, amenities, and architectural splendor proclaimed the triumph of Roman ways of life, yet whose syncretistic and eastern-oriented religions, whose styles of art and whose languages affirmed a deeply held identity in their own cultural ways."[554]

But there was a method to Lovecraft's madness. As Robert Waugh observes, "the fact that Palmyra is an Arabic, a Semitic city, is probably not without force in Lovecraft's passage."[555] Nineteenth-century scholar William Smith identifies Palmyra in his classical dictionary with the Hebrew city of Tadmor, founded by King Solomon, and further describing its later population, after the Islamic conquest, as consisting "chiefly of Jews."[556] Thus too were the imitative and Judaic aspects of both the Old Ones' sculptures and the imitative shoggoths themselves, closely linked in Lovecraft's mind. Nor, as in the works of Weininger, were women absent from Lovecraft's imitative picture.

For Palmyra was also ruled for a time by a beauteous black queen, Zenobia, a reputed descendant of Cleopatra who led an abortive revolt against Roman rule, attempting to create an independent empire that would form a check on Roman power; a factor that surely also figured in Lovecraft's choice of comparisons. (Lovecraft seems to directly allude to Zenobia's splinter kingdoms in "Out of the Aeons," in which he speaks of "the forgotten Semite empires of Africa"[557] and what he sees as their close [and doubtlessly feminine] connection to the witch-cult of the Middle Ages, as well as to his own fictional, and Medusean, cult of Ghatanothoa.) As William Smith recounts, Zenobia "sought to include all Syria, Asia, and Egypt within the limits of her sway, and to make good the title which she claimed of Queen of the East. By this rash ambition she lost both her kingdom and her liberty."[558] Surely none of this was beneath Lovecraft's notice, especially given his jealous affection for the empire of Rome, even during its decadent phases. That the agent of this sedition was a Queen Nitokris–like femme fatale in the Cleopatra mode, who was simultaneously black, feminine, and Semitic, would likewise either have confirmed (or instigated) Lovecraft's ire. As Edward Gibbon recounted, in terms that again recall Lovecraft's hated Marceline Bedard: "She [Zenobia] was of dark complexion (for in speaking of a lady, these trifles become important). Her teeth were of a pearly whiteness and her large black eyes sparkled with uncommon fire, tempered by the most attractive sweetness."[559] And, much like Lovecraft's Lilith and the naiads of "The Moon-Bog," we find Queen Zenobia figuring at the head of a procession: Gibbon observed how Zenobia "sometimes marched several miles on foot at the head of the troops,"[560] thereby animating her "armies by her presence."[561]

Did this description of Zenobia in any way influence Lovecraft's picture of Marceline Bedard, or Queen Nitkoris? And did the legends (largely untrue, as it now turns out)[562] of Zenobia's supposed affair with the brilliant Greek scholar Longinus suggest a parallel with his own apparent entrapment by the overpowering, "Junoesque,"[563] and predatory Sonia Greene? If so, the lessons he took from this story were tendentious in the extreme. And whereas Lovecraft presents us with a picture of the slow and Palmyrene decay of Old Ones' society under the influence of the shoggoths, history tells instead of a defeated Zenobia brought helpless in chains to Rome, where she eventually was given a villa, and lived out her days, as Gibbon observes, as a traditional "Roman matron,"[564] completely assimilated into the society she once opposed. Palmyra, however, never returned to its former glory: its temples becoming ruins, amid which its decimated population pitched their tents, destroyed by the retributive legions of Rome. In real life, the Palmyrene shoggoths lost.

XIV. Conclusions

There is, of course, a world of difference between Weininger and Lovecraft. And whereas Weininger's work betrays a long immersion in the rarified Germanic world of Kant, Beethoven and Wagner, Lovecraft's betrays a peculiarly American immersion in the world of pulp magazines, mother-worship, Puritanism, and Temperance lectures. And whereas Weininger could contemptuously declare that "the Jew is of all persons the least perturbed by mechanical, materialistic theories of the world; he is readily beguiled by Darwinism and the ridiculous notion that men are derived from monkeys,"[565] Lovecraft, at least, had absorbed Darwin and Huxley, even if his own racial notions still remained as infantile as Weininger's. Obviously, Otto Weininger could not even have begun to conceive of such a complex person as the simultaneously aristocratic, materialistic, and Darwinian H. P. Lovecraft.

Both of them, however, remain alike in their wrestling with what they saw as a fallen modern world; a world corrupted, for Lovecraft, by some unnamable and unspeakable "cosmic sin,"[566] and corrupted for Weininger by a collective Jewish-feminine philosophy. "For matter itself is nothing,"[567] Weininger writes, attacking the very primal feminine *materia* out of which all existence is born; "it can only obtain existence through form. The fall of 'form' is the corruption that takes place when form endeavors to relapse into the formless." This too, for Lovecraft, is the ultimate horror of the liquescent shoggoths, who are, as Lovecraft tells us, our biological cousins, and who, like the rest of Lovecraft's amorphous cosmic entities, all too soon relapse into liquescence. Ultimately, for both men, this relapse into formlessness is equivalent to the supposed crime of sexuality, and what scholar J. J. Bachofen, paraphrased by anthropologist Erich Neumann, calls that materialistic "matriarchal world,"[568] which is "merely that of the lower level, of earthly transience and darkness."[569]

Lovecraft could transform or veil or depict this Earth Mother in any number of unflattering ways, but at the same time, he could never escape from the totality of her power or influence. Indeed, part of the horror of his weird fiction derives from the very totality of this cosmic power, a power that swelled to gigantic proportions beneath Lovecraft's infantile pen. Thus, for Lovecraft, writing in one of his more bitter moods, "the only cosmic reality is mindless, undeviating fate — automatic, unmoral, uncalculating inevitability,"[570] a fate identical with the dreaming and mindless Earth Mother, insensible of her copulation; that principle of the eternal undying Feminine, constantly multiplying and giving birth to new forms that are just as constantly relapsing back into formlessness, like the proto-shoggoths and primal jelly

mentioned at the end of *At the Mountains of Madness*, or the partially immaterial Cthulhu-spawn; every form containing within itself a trace of that feminine nothingness from which it was born. The fate that Lovecraft so
pessimistically and resignedly accepted was the same fate that had given him
madmen for parents, forever laboring under the prohibitive pall of the unnamable; nature playing a "hellish jest"[571] on him, just as it did on the Outsider,
and just as it did on the Old Ones.

According to anthropologist Erich Neumann, images representing the
Great Mother are some of the "earliest cult works and works of art known to
us."[572] Perhaps it is not surprising, then, given the oddly tribal and primeval
texture of Lovecraft's own imagination, as well as his ostensible concern with
the ancient, primordial past, that he too should have fastened upon this figure
in his writings. Lovecraft is different from most other male writers in their
engagement with the eternal Feminine, however, in that, unlike the overtly
misogynistic Strindberg or Huysmans, for example, his Puritanism has a curious muting effect on his delineation of the Feminine. Even so, that Unnamable
which Lovecraft so struggled to depict surely had a feminine component,
rooted as it was in both his father's unspeakable illness, as well as his own
semi-incestuous connection with his mother, both of which were quite beyond
the social pale. On the one side, there was the ravening sexuality of his father,
and on the other, the frigid and devouring mother, with Lovecraft as the
small child trapped between these dueling Old Ones.

Either one would account for Lovecraft's lifelong and obsessive immersion in issues of the unnamable and the forbidden. At the same time, the
Puritan Lovecraft was forced to veil his conceptions of the Feminine; causing
them, like the shape-shifting shoggoths themselves, to assume ever new and
varied forms, and to multiply like the Goat with a Thousand Young beneath
his cautious and Puritan pen. And although such revisionary collaborations
as "The Mound" and "Medusa's Coil" enabled him to "let his hair down" (so
to speak) in his depiction of his feminine weird entities, in his canonical
fiction they nearly always appear draped, just like the nude artist's models
should have been in the story published by his friend W. Paul Cook.

As I argued above, it seems that Lovecraft's civilized anxiety with regard
to the ancient bacchanalia was basically rooted in this antipathy toward the
Feminine — as was, ultimately, Lovecraft's opposition to ancient Greece, which
Lovecraft, as we have seen, characterized as effeminate and unmanly using
the same language found in his pro–Allied World War I poetry. Lovecraft's
other antipathies, too, including dancing, nudity, and eyeing or leering, also
display a similarly Feminine origin. Yet even this does not fully explain Lovecraft's concurrent fascination with such overtly familial issues as maternal

heredity, domination, paralysis and control, unless one also recognizes that embedded in Lovecraft's feminine antipathy there is also ambivalence — an ambivalence ultimately rooted in the maternal bond and parental love. Like the Gorgon and the Rangda of ancient mythology, and all those other examples of the Terrible Mother throughout history, Lovecraft's weird entities are born from the dark half of the Great Mother, whose love devours and smothers even as it nourishes, and whose mother's milk is rooted in that primal white jelly of creation that also drives the sensitive Danforth mad.

When I first began my analysis of Lovecraft's weird fiction, several years ago, I was immediately struck by the clear disparity between Lovecraft's cosmic intentions as propounded in his letters on the one hand, and the overwhelmingly mundane and sadistic nature of the majority of his weird stories on the other, in which the cosmic was applied mainly as a thin veneer over a larger, overarching anti-bacchanalian polemic. I quickly discerned a satirical, pro-Roman, and anti–Greek critique underlying Lovecraft's Arkham cycle of stories. But this still did nothing to explain the basic connection (which Lovecraft quite evidently saw) between cosmicism and sadism: the connection that existed between the supposed cosmicism of Cthulhu on the one hand and the sadism of both Cthulhu and his followers on the other, at least in his own imagination. The contradiction seemed unanswerable. What was the connection?

The answer is to be found, I now believe, in Lovecraft's basic relation to the Feminine and to the maternal. For it is in Lovecraft's engagement with the unending Feminine that we find both the root of Lovecraft's conception of and fascination with cosmicism, and the origin of that anxiety-reaction embedded within Lovecraft's depiction of it; a reaction that manifests itself in the nightmare imagery characteristic of his weird fiction. The Great Mother thus underlies Lovecraft's vision of the cosmic abyss, while her more threatening and terrible aspects define his reaction to it. Both exist hand in hand; and both were ultimately defined by his ambivalent maternal relationship, in which love and hate, devotion and repulsion, were so equally and detrimentally intermixed. Thus, too, did Lovecraft's ambivalence towards his own mother become a larger ambivalence toward life itself, resulting in a passive, almost suicidal sort of nihilism and pessimism, which he only afterward attempted to connect with ideas of aristocratic and gentlemanly fortitude, and with classical ideas about stoicism and indifference with regard to fate. (Witness, for example, the young Lovecraft's chiding of a hapless acquaintance who made the mistake of calling Lovecraft's "mother 'Ma'am' — I said that a future scientist should not talk like a servant!"[573] Lovecraft's forged aristocratic identity thus acted as a buffer against maternal endearment and encroachment.) It is most striking, too, that Lovecraft's fantasy stories, in which the anxiety-reaction characteristic of his weird fiction is almost completely absent, are likewise stories with strongly masculine or paternal features: "Celephais," for example, deals with Kuranes' attempt to regain his lost kingship in the world of dreams; while *The Dream-Quest of Unknown Kadath* is basically a nostalgic homage to the Burroughsian (and extremely masculine) pulps of Lovecraft's youth, with warring armies, picturesque allies, clever stratagems, and tricky escapes. True, "The Quest of Iranon" deals in part with Prince Iranon's quest for the lost love of his mother, but here there is no anxiety, only an infantile nostalgia for the nights when she would sing to him in the moonlight.

According to Neumann in *The Great Mother*, "Fate may appear *as a maternal old woman*, presiding over the past and the future, or in a young fascinating form, as the soul"[574] (italics mine). For Lovecraft, the archetypal old woman — whether appearing as the aged nurse, or the aged priestess, or the aged witch — was the prevailing image. Nor are such archetypal manifestations of the Feminine a mere accident. Rather, they reflect a basic conception of the woman as the determiner and controller of life. Lovecraft's basic conception of his Old, Elder, or Great Ones reflects such a basically determinist perspective: an infantile despair at ever creating or building anything new, anything large or cyclopean enough to compare with the parental constructs in terms of grandeur or eldritch scale. Lovecraft's mother was Great: but she was also Terrible.

Caught between the *liebestod* sexual corruption of the father, and the viselike grip of maternal love, it is no wonder that Lovecraft should have chosen a third, non-sexual, Puritan alternative, in order to achieve some measure of emancipation and self-identity, even if the consequent repression he experienced also led to nightmares — nightmares that, adopting the example of Poe and the *Munsey* science-fantasy magazines, he was eminently successful in channeling into his weird fiction. Lovecraft's horror stories can thus be seen as an attempt to come to terms with this overriding and all-controlling maternal force. Although he, in the long run, acknowledged his defeat, unlike writers like Charles Baudelaire or Hart Crane, who eventually consumed themselves and their talent in a fruitless struggle against the bonds of the maternal Feminine, he was ultimately able to find peace in this pessimistic acknowledgement, and did not, like Baudelaire or Crane, or any of the other suicidal, self-destructive decadents who also pursued and investigated such themes, finally choose the course of actual suicide, drug addiction, and death. Lovecraft's aristocratic pose, with its allied 18th century persona, however unrealistic or atavistic, at least preserved him from that.

Appendix —
Empires in the Air

Sir Arthur Conan Doyle is not the only possible precursor to Lovecraft's fascination with the mysterious arcana of the higher atmosphere. Indeed, such upper-air imagery was also highly popular in the pulp magazines throughout the era when H. P. Lovecraft was writing — an interest possibly stimulated by Conan Doyle's story. From George Allan England's *The Empire in the Air* (*All-Story*, 1914) — published just one year after Doyle's — to Frank Orndorff's "The Terrors of the Upper Air" (*Amazing Stories Quarterly*, 1928) to "The Thing That Walked on the Wind" (*Strange Tales*, 1933) by August Derleth, the mysteries of the upper atmosphere were as stimulating to the early 20th-century imagination as the deepest oceans or the blackest jungles. Indeed, science fiction publisher Hugo Gernsback devoted an entire magazine to this topic: *Air Wonder Stories* (July 1929–May 1930).

England's *The Empire in the Air* had an especially strong influence on Lovecraft. From its apocalyptic atmosphere of alien invasion, and its eerie depiction of the sudden dissolution of human civilization, to the cold, cosmic malevolence of its alien invaders — even the idea that the *date* of the alien invasion is dependent on the configuration of the stars — all have their direct and unmistakable echoes in Lovecraft's later fiction. England's sinister description of the semi-immaterial yet tentacled aliens, too — whose merest touch has the ability to chill its victim with the cold void of deepest space — has its direct echo in Lovecraft's polypous Elder Things and semi-material Cthulhu spawn.

Like the hero-pilot in Conan Doyle's "The Horror of the Heights," England's story begins with protagonist Paul Kramer inexplicably vanishing while attempting to attain a new world's altitude record in a plane. Later, a strange, semi-gaseous yet tentacled alien suddenly appears before a gathering of astronomers and scientists — and just as quickly vanishes. It is discovered, however, that where the alien was hovering just moments before, some *human handwriting* has been scratched upon the tabletop — handwriting *which proves to be that of the missing Paul Kramer!* (an idea which prefigures the awesome climax of Lovecraft's later "The Shadow out of Time"). It turns out that Kramer is now trapped in the fourth dimension, where (just as for Robert Blake in "The Haunter of the Dark"), the concepts of space, size, and direction no longer exist. Indeed, this new trans-dimensional state gives England's hero a feeling of omnipotence (a feeling later echoed by the narrator's friend in Lovecraft's "Hypnos," during their own bodiless transgressions in other dimensions.) Kramer warns his friends that aliens from outside our galaxy are planning an invasion of the earth, intending to reduce our planet to a semi-immaterial state, mirroring their own. (Indeed, Kramer explains, the supernovae which astronomers sometimes see in the heavens are revealed to actually be the result of these 4-D entities' depredations of other worlds! — an idea later used by Lovecraft in his conclusion to "Beyond the Wall of Sleep," in which a supernova is seen as evidence of interstellar combat.)

The aliens are finally defeated by a layer of dust particles suspended in the upper atmosphere of the earth, left over from the volcanic eruption of Krakatoa in 1883. According to Kramer, these particles now exist partly in the fourth dimension, having been sublimated into a higher form of matter which makes them dangerous to the alien invaders. There then follows a final, desperate battle at the zenith of the earth, as Kramer's allies attempt to detonate the charged particles, in order to hurt the aliens. Later, when the particles explode in the zenith, the detonation is described (just like the glow at the end of Lovecraft's "The Colour Out of Space") as resembling *a glow of St. Elmo's fire*, while a rain of ash falls down to the earth, withering all the vegetation that it touches (again, just like the blasted heath in "Colour.") After their decisive defeat, all the 4-D aliens flee the earth — including numerous hidden aliens, lurking (like Lovecraft's later alien entities) amid groves and ruins in obscure corners of the globe.

Clearly, England's story had a huge influence on Lovecraft's later fiction. England's idea especially, that *dust from Krakatoa* still exists at the zenith of the sky in a higher-dimensional state, may perhaps serve to explain Lovecraft's curious images in *Mountains of Madness*, in which a *mirage of an alien city* is seen hovering in the sky, high above the Old Ones' ruined city. According to Lovecraft's cosmology, one recalls, our moon was torn free from the South Pacific during a terrific prehistoric explosion, in which a land mass simultaneously arose from the inner earth beneath the oceans. I would suggest that this *strange vaporous mirage* seen at the zenith of the sky throughout Lovecraft's story is somehow related to this *ancient explosion* which created the moon: and that this image of an *alien city* is actually ghost city from some original continent which existed before the moon, and which still exists in some higher dimensional state (just like the dust from Krakatoa.) An alien city, whose ghostly inhabitants still make the transit from the inner earth to the moon via the moon-ladder.

Pulp-author George Allan England seems to have had a particular penchant for this idea of immaterial creatures and higher-dimensional realms. In *The Flying Legion* (1919), for example, England delves into the idea of different vibratory rates of matter and light — and new sensory organs which evolve to perceive them — in a way which strongly prefigures Lovecraft's later "From Beyond" (1920), as well as the moon-ladder scene from "The Shadow out of Time." Indeed, the scene in which England's protagonist, The Master, holds a French soldier captive by using a higher-dimensional ray, which excites his matter to a different wavelength — all the while The Master offers the reader a lengthy disquisition on the limited nature of human senses and human perceptions — could very easily, with very little alteration, have been inserted into Lovecraft's story of Crawford Tillinghast and his unnamed victim. The only thing that George Allan England's work lacks, is the extreme *compression* and *concentration* of a Lovecraft tale: an obsessive concern with atmosphere and mood, to the exclusion of all superfluous details of romance or adventure, which makes all of HPL's work so distinctive and unforgettable.

Chapter Notes

All quotations from H. P. Lovecraft's standard works in this book are cited according to the nomenclature established by *Lovecraft Studies* and the *Lovecraft Annual*: *AT*: *The Ancient Track* (2001, edited by S. T. Joshi, Night Shade); *CE* 1–5: *Collected Essays* (2004–2006, edited by S. T. Joshi, 5 vols., Hippocampus); *D*: *Dagon and Other Macabre Tales* (1986, edited by S. T. Joshi, Arkham House); *DH*: *The Dunwich Horror and Others* (1984, edited by S. T. Joshi, Arkham House); *HM*: *The Horror in the Museum and Other Revisions* (1989, edited by S. T. Joshi, Arkham House); *MM*: *At the Mountains of Madness and Other Novels* (1985, edited by S. T. Joshi, Arkham House); *MW*: *Miscellaneous Writings* (1995, edited by S. T. Joshi, Arkham House); *SL* 1–5: *Selected Letters* (1965–76; 5 vols., edited by August Derleth, Donald Wandrei, and James Turner, Arkham House); *SOT*: *The Shadow Out of Time* (2003, edited by S. T. Joshi and David E. Schultz, Hippocampus).

Introduction

1. Allen A. Debus, "Children of the Night! Before the Wolf-man," *Scary Monsters Magazine* 51 (June 2004), 51–57.
2. In the introduction to his early edition of Lovecraft's verse, *A Winter Wish*, for example, editor Tom Collins writes of how "as Ezra Pound repented his anti-Semitism in the end, so Lovecraft overcame his prejudice, too. And as with Pound's, it ultimately is irrelevant" (Chapel Hill, NC: Whispers, 1977), 2.
3. Will Brooker, *Batman Unmasked, Analyzing a Cultural Icon* (New York: Continuum, 2000), 12.
4. *DH* 399.
5. Fritz Leiber's essay "A Literary Copernicus," cited by Peter Cannon, *H. P. Lovecraft*, Twayne's United States Authors Series (Boston: Twayne, 1989), 65; Cannon later calls Leiber's essay

"the finest general critical essay on Lovecraft" (133).
6. *DH* 122.
7. Peter Cannon, *H. P. Lovecraft*, op. cit., 130, citing S. T. Joshi's essay "Lovecraft and the Regnum Congo," *Crypt of Cthulhu* 4.
8. S. T. Joshi, explanatory notes for "The Picture in the House," in H. P. Lovecraft, *The Call of Cthulhu and Other Weird Stories* (Penguin, 1999), 373. Significantly, too, both Huxley's original description and Lovecraft's later redactions of the Pigafetta illustrations call attention to the "imagination" involved in their creation: "'It may be that these apes are as much figments of the *imagination* of the ingenious brothers as the winged, two-legged, crocodile-headed *dragon* which adorns the same plate'" (Thomas Huxley, quoted in Joshi's notes, Lovecraft, *Call* [1999], op. cit., 372–373) (italics mine); "The engravings were indeed interest-

ing, drawn wholly from *imagination*" (*DH* 119) (italics mine); "If I say that my somewhat extravagant *imagination* yielded simultaneous pictures of an octopus, a *dragon*, and a human caricature, I shall not be unfaithful to the spirit of the thing" (*DH* 127) (italics mine).
9. *DH* 127.
10. *DH* 134.
11. *DH* 138.
12. Lorenso Mastropierro, "The Theme of Distance in the Tales of H. P. Lovecraft," in *Lovecraft Annual* No. 3 (New York: Hippocampus, 2009), 80.
13. *DH* 137.
14. Lovecraft further reinforces this African aspect of Cthulhu in his racist collaborative story "Medusa's Coil," in which the crocodile from both Thomas Huxley and "The Picture in the House" is invoked in relation to the voodoo rites of the African Zulu priestess, old Sophy, who worships

an entity she calls "'Marse Clooloo'" (*HM* 189, 190) (i.e., Cthulhu) via bacchanalian rites that involve dancing "in de moonshine roun' de crocodile-stone" (*HM* 190).

15. S. T. Joshi, *H. P. Lovecraft: A Life* (West Warwick, RI: Necronomicon, 2004), 491.

16. *MM* 95–96.

17. L. Sprague de Camp, *Lovecraft: A Biography*, abridged ed. (New York: Ballantine, 1976), 366.

18. Justin Taylor, "The Crawling Chaos," review of Michel Houellebecq's *H. P. Lovecraft: Against the World, Against Life* (http:www.counterpunch.org/taylor04302005.html, accessed November 5, 2005).

19. Peter Cannon, editor, *Lovecraft Remembered* (Sauk City, WI: Arkham House, 1998), 399.

20. Cannon, *H. P. Lovecraft*, op. cit., 102.

21. Fritz Leiber, "Through Hyperspace with Brown Jenkin: Lovecraft's Contribution to Speculative Fiction," reprinted in Cannon, *Lovecraft Remembered*, op. cit., 481.

22. For more on Lovecraft's *At the Mountains of Madness* as an argument, see David A. Oakes, "A Warning to the World: The Deliberative Argument of *At the Mountains of Madness*," *Lovecraft Studies* 39 (Summer 1998), 21–25, in which Oakes suggests the potency of Dyer's argument derives from the clear "similarities between the society of the Old Ones and human civilization" (Oakes, 23), although Oakes stops short of seeing *At the Mountains of Madness*, as I do, as a deliberate parable.

23. The title of a 1676 sermon (by a Puritan moderate!) named William Hubbard, quoted in Perry Miller, ed., *The American Puritans: Their Prose and Poetry* (Garden City, NY: Anchor, Doubleday, 1956), 116.

24. Joshi, *H. P. Lovecraft*, op. cit., 491.

25. Interview with Guillermo del Toro, quoted in Andrew Migliore and John Strysil's *Lurker in the Lobby: A Guide to the Cinema of H. P. Lovecraft* (Portland, San Francisco: Night Shade, 2006), 215.

26. *D* 146.

27. S. T. Joshi, explanatory notes to "Herbert West: Reanimator," in Lovecraft, *Call of Cthulhu*, op. cit., 377.

28. *SL* I:99.

29. *MW* 44.

30. Maurice Levy, *Lovecraft: A Study in the Fantastic*, trans. S. T. Joshi (Detroit: Wayne State University Press, 1988), 62; Kevin Dole, review of Michel Houellebecq's *H. P. Lovecraft: Against the World, Against Life*, in *Lovecraft Annual* No. 1, ed. S. T. Joshi (New York: Hippocampus, 2007), 149.

31. *SL* II:51.

32. Peter Cannon, "The Adventure of the Three Anglo-American Authors" (1994), in *The Lovecraft Papers* (Guild America, n.d.), 134.

33. Rheinhart Kleiner, "Discourse on H. P. Lovecraft" (1951), in Cannon, ed., *Lovecraft Remembered*, op. cit., 158.

34. Wilfred B. Talman, "The Normal Lovecraft" (1973), in *Lovecraft Remembered*, ed. Cannon, op. cit., 213.

35. Levy, *Lovecraft*, op. cit., 108.

36. Ibid., 12.

Chapter One

1. *DH* 154.

2. Richard Ellmann, *Oscar Wilde* (New York: Alfred A. Knopf, 1988), 28.

3. David Sox, *Bachelors of Art: Edward Perry Warren and the Lewes House Brotherhood* (London: Fourth Estate, 1991), 94.

4. W. H. Auden, "The Fall of Rome," quoted in G. W. Bowersock, *From Gibbon to Auden: Essays on the Classical Tradition* (Oxford University Press, 2009), 199, 203.

5. Simone Petrément, *Simone Weil* (New York: Schocken, 1988), 350.

6. Bliss Carman, *Echoes from Vagabondia* (Boston: Small, Maynard, 1912; accessed at http://books.google.com), 12.

7. *SL* IV:333 (italics Lovecraft's).

8. Gerald Messadie, *A History of the Devil*, trans. Mare Romano (New York: Kodansha America, 1993), 152.

9. See *SL* IV:333, and Frank

Belknap Long, *Howard Phillips Lovecraft: Dreamer on the Nightside* (Sauk City, WI: Arkham House, 1975), 88.

10. *SL* IV:57.

11. L. Sprague de Camp, *Lovecraft: A Biography*, abridged ed. (New York: Ballantine, 1976), 361.

12. See Peter Cannon, *H. P. Lovecraft*, Twayne's United States Authors Series (Boston: Twayne, 1989), 2; and S. T. Joshi, *H. P. Lovecraft: A Life* (West Warwick, RI: Necronomicon, 2004), 17.

13. Joshi, *H. P. Lovecraft*, op. cit., 16.

14. *AT* 404.

15. *MW* 253.

16. *SL* II:188–189.

17. *MM* 322.

18. *MM* 347.

19. *MM* 346.

20. *MM* 324.

21. *MM* 348.

22. *MM* 347 (italics mine).

23. Ibid. (italics mine).

24. William Smith, *A Classical Dictionary of Biography, Mythology, and Geography* (Albemarle Street: John Murray, 1881), 157.

25. *SL* IV:333.

26. Long, *Howard Phillips Lovecraft*, op. cit., 90.

27. Frank Belknap Long also refers to this difference between H. P. Lovecraft's Roman classicism and Samuel Loveman's decadent classicism, writing: "Howard [Lovecraft] never quite shared the childlike wonder and wild surmise in the presence of the ancient gods and human heroes that Samuel Loveman did, simply because even as a very young child he was capable of imagining more terrible entities buried in the depths of the sea and beyond the universe of stars" (Long, *Howard Phillips Lovecraft*, op. cit., 90). The larger social, political, and aesthetic differences between Lovecraft's and Loveman's respective uses of classicism are here unaddressed, although Long does acknowledge the origins of the Lovecraft Mythos in this very contrast between them.

28. In his notes to Lovecraft's stories, scholar S. T. Joshi suggests that Lovecraft's name for the fictional "Arkham" probably derives the New England towns

of "Oakham" or "Arkwright" (Joshi, note in H. P. Lovecraft, *The Call of Cthulhu and Other Weird Stories* [Penguin, 1999], 372); but I would guess that, given Lovecraft's obsession with classical references and ancient history, the mystical pagan Arcadia was, at least unconsciously, also prominent in his mind — especially given the overwhelmingly Arcadian turn of much of Lovecraft's earlier, pastoral poetry. And if it be objected that Arcadia is a rural backwater in Hellas, while Arkham is a city in Massachusetts, it must be noted that the phrase "Arkham country" (*DH* 80) — encompassing both the witch-haunted Arkham *and* its wilder, wooded environs to the west — is also utilized by Lovecraft as a term for his larger, sinister fictional world.

29. AT 113.
30. *DH* 80.
31. Messadie, *History of the Devil*, op. cit., 150.
32. See the hints of human-teratological copulation in *D* 203–204, *D* 264, and *DH* 172.
33. Messadie, *History of the Devil,* op. cit., 150.
34. *DH* 13–14.
35. J. W. Mackail, *An Introduction to Virgil's Aeneid*, abridged from the author's edition of the Aeneid, privately printed for the Virgil Society (Glasgow: University Press, 1946), 17.
36. Mark Schorer, *Pieces of Life* (New York: Farrar, Straus and Giroux, 1977), 135.
37. Mackail, *Introduction to Virgil's Aeneid*, op. cit., 17.
38. Rheinhart Kleiner, "Bards and Bibliophiles" (1951), reproduced in Peter Cannon, ed., *Lovecraft Remembered* (Sauk City, WI: Arkham House, 1998), 157–158.
39. Ibid., 158.
40. *MW* 212.
41. Long, *Howard Phillips Lovecraft*, op. cit., 210.
42. *SL* I:136.
43. De Camp, *Lovecraft*, op. cit., 34.
44. Maurice Levy, *Lovecraft: A Study in the Fantastic*, trans. S. T. Joshi (Detroit: Wayne State University Press, 1988), 74.
45. Edgar Allan Poe, *The Unabridged Edgar Allan Poe* (Phila-delphia, PA: Running Press, 1983), 66.
46. Long, *Howard Phillips Lovecraft*, op. cit., 237.
47. Joshi, *H. P. Lovecraft*, op. cit., 272.
48. *SL* I:20.
49. *CE* 2:22.
50. Arthur Machen, "The Letter of Advice," in *The Great God Pan and the Inmost Light* (Boston: Roberts Bros., 1895; accessed at http://books.google.com), 66.
51. Levy, *Lovecraft*, op. cit., 59.
52. *SL* I:27 (italics mine).
53. *MW* 111 (italics mine).
54. Cannon, *H. P. Lovecraft*, op. cit., 31.
55. Ibid., 129.
56. *AT* 137.
57. *AT* 279.
58. *SL* I:7.
59. Mary Warner Blanchard, *Oscar Wilde's America* (New Haven, CT: Yale University Press, 1998), 132.
60. *MW* 535.
61. *D* 10.
62. *MW* 534–535.
63. *DH* 116.
64. *MW* 534.
65. *AT* 138.
66. *DH* 192.
67. *DH* 192.
68. *DH* 35.
69. Stringfellow Barr, *The Will of Zeus: A History of Greece from the Origins of Hellenic Culture to the Death of Alexander* (Philadelphia: J. B. Lippincott, 1961), 11.
70. Ibid., 12.
71. *DH* 247.
72. *DH* 179.
73. *DH* 57.
74. Barr, *The Will of Zeus*, op. cit., 12.
75. *D* 260.
76. *D* 215.
77. *MW* 295.
78. *DH* 57.
79. *D* 119.
80. *DH* 116.
81. Smith, *Classical Dictionary*, op. cit., 137.
82. Ibid., 262.
83. Ibid., 379.
84. Ibid., 210.
85. *AT* 473.
86. *AT* 270.
87. *AT* 271.
88. *AT* 267.
89. *AT* 279.
90. *AT* 281.
91. *AT* 277.
92. *AT* 291.
93. *AT* 292.
94. *DH* 55.
95. *CE* 2:22.
96. *MW* 295.
97. *DH* 53.
98. *DH* 61.
99. *DH* 55.
100. *DH* 154.
101. *AT* 297.
102. *SL* I:138.
103. Smith, *Classical Dictionary*, op. cit., 518.
104. Ibid.
105. *HM* 216.
106. *AT* 242.
107. See Bliss Carman, *The Pipes of Pan*, vol. 1, *From the Book of Myths* (Albemarle Street: John Murray, 1903; accessed at http://books.google.com), 56.
108. H. R. Hays, *The Dangerous Sex: The Myth of Feminine Evil* (New York: G. P. Putnam's Sons, 1964), 68.
109. *DH* 116.
110. Robert M. Price, "Mythos Names and How to Say Them," *Lovecraft Studies* 15, vol. 6, no. 2 (Fall 1987), 52.
111. Smith, *Classical Dictionary*, op. cit., 518.
112. There are the "attitudes of panic fear" (*DH* 41) displayed by the skeletons in "The Rats in the Walls"; the "eldritch panic" (*D* 179) experienced in "The Lurking Fear"; the attacks of "panic" (*DH* 181) in "The Dunwich Horror"; the "panic fear" (*D* 123) experienced by the narrator in "The Moon-Bog," among other instances.
113. Alexander S. Murray, *Manual of Mythology*, ed. William H. Klapp (New York: Tudor, 1936), 150.
114. *DH* 170.
115. *AT* 27.
116. *DH* 104.
117. E. A. Edkins, "Idiosyncrasies of H.P.L." (1940), reproduced in Cannon, ed., *Lovecraft Remembered*, op. cit., 95.
118. *DH* 174–175.
119. Cannon, *H. P. Lovecraft*, op. cit., 87.
120. Smith, *Classical Dictionary*, op. cit., 247.
121. August Derleth, "Lovecraft's Sensitivity" (1949), reproduced in Cannon, ed., *Lovecraft Remembered*, op. cit., 34.

122. Murray, *Manual of Mythology*, op. cit., 150.

123. See scholar and occult-writer Montague Summers: "The ceremonies and lore of the Arcadian mountains were closely connected with a number of legends concerning werewolves" that "preserve the memory of the immolation of human victims" (*The Vampire in Europe* [New Hyde Park, NY: University Books, 1968], 19); and also scholar Sabine Baring-Gould: "It is to be observed that the chief seat of Lycanthropy was Arcadia" (*The Book of Werewolves* [London: Senate Studio Editions, 1995], 13).

124. *AT* 12.

125. *D* 51.

126. *D* 50.

127. Robert Eisler, *Man Into Wolf: An Anthropological Interpretation of Sadism, Masochism and Lycanthropy* (London: Spring, n.d.), 265.

128. *MW* 206–207.

129. *MW* 269.

130. *MW* 207.

131. Jaś Elsner, *Imperial Rome and Christian Triumph: The Art of the Roman Empire AD 100–450*, Oxford History of Art (Oxford University Press, 1998), 183.

132. Cannon, *H. P. Lovecraft*, op. cit., 86.

133. *D* 4.

134. *D* 7.

135. *D* 4.

136. De Camp, *Lovecraft*, op. cit., 208.

137. *D* 5.

138. *DH* 175.

139. *D* 7.

140. *D* 6.

141. *D* 5.

142. *D* 11.

143. *D* 6.

144. *DH* 170.

145. *SOT* 62.

146. *AT* 416.

147. Ibid.

148. *DH* 68.

149. *HM* 8.

150. *HM* 4 (italics Lovecraft's/Jackson's).

151. *HM* 7.

152. *HM* 5.

153. A. Merritt, "The People of the Pit," in *The People of the Pit and Other Early Horrors from the Munsey Pulps* (Normal, IL: Black Dog, 2010), 17.

154. *HM* 5.

155. *HM* 8.

156. Lovecraft may also have been influenced in this image by Cotton Mather's *The Wonders of the Invisible World* (1692), in which Mather speaks of a "Green Meadow" mentioned in Swedish witch accounts, where the witches "gave themselves unto" the Devil (*Cotton Mather on Witchcraft: Being The Wonders of the Invisible World, First Published at Boston in October 1692 and Now Reprinted, with Additional Matter and Old Wood-Cuts, for the Library of the Fantastic and Curious* [New York: Dorset, 1991], 137).

157. *AT* 137.

158. *AT* 136.

159. *D* 199.

160. *AT* 137.

161. *DH* 154.

162. *AT* 137.

163. Charles Seltman, *The Twelve Olympians* (New York: Thomas Y. Crowell, 1960), 76.

164. Smith, *Classical Dictionary*, op. cit., 518.

165. *DH* 195.

166. Joshi, *H. P. Lovecraft*, op. cit., 237.

167. De Camp, *Lovecraft*, op. cit., 143.

168. *D* 355.

169. *D* 351.

170. *D* 350.

171. *D* 351.

172. *D* 349.

173. *D* 351 (italics mine).

174. *DH* 136.

175. *SOT* 64.

176. *DH* 141.

177. *D* 351 (italics mine).

178. *D* 351–352.

179. *DH* 153.

180. *DH* 154.

181. *D* 352.

182. *D* 72.

183. *D* 65.

184. *D* 70.

185. *D* 69.

186. *D* 70.

187. Smith, *Classical Dictionary*, op. cit., 227.

188. *D* 66.

189. *D* 67.

190. *HM* 193.

191. *D* 69.

192. *HM* 12.

193. Joshi, *H. P. Lovecraft*, op. cit., 242.

194. *HM* 13.

195. *D* 354.

196. *HM* 14.

197. Ibid.

198. *DH* 154.

199. *DH* 46.

200. *MW* 534.

201. Joshi, *H. P. Lovecraft*, op. cit., 251.

202. De Camp, *Lovecraft*, op. cit., 161.

203. *D* 125.

204. *D* 120.

205. Smith, *Classical Dictionary*, op. cit., 703.

206. *D* 122.

207. *D* 119.

208. *DH* 212.

209. Smith, *Classical Dictionary*, op. cit., 94.

210. *D* 125.

211. *D* 120.

212. *D* 121.

213. *DH* 279.

214. Joel Pace, "Queer Tales? Sexuality, Race, and Architecture in 'The Thing on the Doorstep,'" *Lovecraft Annual* No. 2, ed. S. T. Joshi (West Warwick, RI: Necronomicon, 2008), 110.

215. See what Lovecraft calls the "wilder hymn" (*AT* 137) of Pan in "The Voice"; the "unspeakable grossness and wildness of the erratic" poet (*MW* 423), Walt Whitman; the "wild dances" (*D* 4) of the dryads in "The Tomb"; the "wild harmony" (*D* 350) heard in "Poetry and the Gods"; "The wild hills" (*MW* 294) in Lovecraft's 1927 Vermont travelogue; and the "wild yet beautiful" (*D* 70) bacchanalian chant overheard in Lovecraft's "The Temple," culminating in "Those wild hills" (*DH* 264) in "The Whisperer in Darkness"; sylvan hills that are now, however, described as "surely the outpost of a frightful cosmic race" (*DH* 264). The name of Lovecraft's erotic "Sir Wilful *Wildrake*" (italics mine) (*AT* 241), too, has his origin here, in this decadent/sylvan language of wildness.

216. *D* 348.

217. *MM* 30.

218. *D* 124.

219. Lovecraft, quoted in De Camp, *Lovecraft*, op. cit., 27.

220. *D* 196 (italics mine).

221. What Lovecraft calls "black and blasphemous alliances" (*MM*

35) between "life and death, space and time."

222. *D* 189.
223. *D* 196.
224. *D* 182.
225. *D* 183.
226. *D* 180.
227. *D* 190.
228. *D* 197.
229. *D* 260.
230. Cannon, *H. P. Lovecraft*, op. cit., 83.
231. *DH* 53.
232. DH 54.
233. Levy, *Lovecraft*, op. cit., 37.
234. *DH* 54.
235. Cannon, *H. P. Lovecraft*, op. cit., 85.
236. *DH* 55 (italics mine).
237. W. Paul Cook, "In Memoriam: Howard Phillips Lovecraft: Recollections, Appreciations, Estimates" (1941), reproduced in Cannon, ed., *Lovecraft Remembered*, op. cit., 112.
238. *DH* 60.
239. *DH* 63.
240. Lovecraft's evocative description of the "chromatic perversion" (*DH* 63) of the Gardner's crops, and of the "sinister menace" (63) in the colors of "the bloodroots" (63), also recalls a similar tale from actual New England folklore, of which Lovecraft may have been aware, regarding the so-called "'Bloody' Apples" on a farm in Franklin, Connecticut. According to the story, an apple tree on the farm of Micah Rood began producing apples with blood-red spots inside, after farmer Rood supposedly murdered a peddler visiting his property in the early 1700s (Joseph A. Owens, "Franklin's 'Bloody' Apples," *Mysterious New England,* ed. Austin N. Stevens [Dublin, New Hampshire: Yankee, 1971], 156–158).
241. *DH* 95.
242. *DH* 96.
243. *DH* 95.
244. *DH* 63.
245. *DH* 62.
246. *DH* 64.
247. D 199.
248. See Bliss Carman's poem "Spring Song": "Make me over Mother April, / When the sap begins to stir!" (Bliss Carman and Richard Hovey, *Songs from Vagabondia* [Boston: Small, Maynard,

1894], 10); and "Earth's Lyric": "April. You harken, my fellow? / Old slumberer down in my heart? / ... The sap feels a start" (Bliss Carman and Richard Hovey, *More Songs from Vagabondia* [Boston: Copeland and Day, 1896], 5). Both books accessed at http://books.google.com.
249. *AT* 136.
250. *AT* 271.
251. *DH* 76.
252. *DH* 157.
253. *DH* 170.
254. *DH* 172.
255. *DH* 170–171.
256. *DH* 170.
257. *DH* 159.
258. *DH* 156.
259. *DH* 157.
260. *DH* 156.
261. See the poem "June Night in Washington," in Carman and Hovey, *More Songs,* op. cit., 37; and poems 13 and 14 in Bliss Carman, *Pipes of Pan Number Three: Songs of the Sea Children* (Boston: L. C. Page, 1903; accessed at http://books.google.com), 22, 25.
262. *DH* 196.
263. *DH* 231.
264. *DH* 214.
265. *D* 50.
266. *DH* 214.
267. *DH* 228.
268. *MM* 291.
269. *DH* 210.
270. *DH* 222.
271. MW 293.
272. Isaiah 34:14.
273. Aleister Crowley, *Liber Liberi vel Lapidis Lazuli: Adumbratio Kabbalae Aegyptorum, Sub Figura VII* (Fairfax, CA: Ordo Templi Orientis, 1989), ch. 4, line 17 (n.p.).
274. *D* 353.
275. Douglass Shand-Tucci, *Boston Bohemia, 1881–1900,* vol. 1, *Ralph Adams Cram: Life and Architecture* (Amherst: University of Massachusetts Press, 1995), 139.
276. Edward Carpenter, *Toward Democracy* (London: John Heywood, 1883; accessed at http://books.google.com), 22.
277. *CE* 5:69.
278. *MW* 557.
279. Carman and Hovey, *More Songs,* op. cit., 6.
280. Carman, *Pipes of Pan Number Three,* op. cit., 11; Carman, *The Pipes of Pan,* vol. 1, *From the*

Book of Myths, op. cit., 27, 56 and 86.
281. Carman and Hovey, *More Songs,* op. cit., 5, 27; Carman, *Pipes of Pan Number Three,* op. cit., 127; Bliss Carman, *Echoes from Vagabondia* (Boston: Small, Maynard, 1912), 1.
282. Carman, *Echoes,* op. cit., 16.
283. Carman, *The Pipes of Pan,* vol. 1, *From the Book of Myths,* op. cit., 87.
284. Carman and Hovey, *Songs from Vagabondia,* op. cit., 27; Carman, *Pipes of Pan Number Three,* op. cit., 12.
285. Bliss Carman and Richard Hovey, *Last Songs from Vagabondia* (Boston: Small, Maynard, 1900; accessed at http://books.google.com), 41.
286. Ibid., 14.
287. Carman, *The Pipes of Pan,* vol. 1, *From the Book of Myths,* op. cit., 71.
288. Carman, *Pipes of Pan Number Three,* op. cit., 14.
289. Carman and Hovey, *Last Songs,* op. cit., 41.
290. Carman, *The Pipes of Pan,* vol. 1, *From the Book of Myths,* op. cit., 96.
291. Ibid., 79.
292. Carman and Hovey, *More Songs,* op. cit., 43.
293. Roger Austen, *Genteel Pagan, The Double Life of Charles Warren Stoddard,* ed. John Crowley (Amherst: University of Massachusetts Press, 1991), 138.
294. Carman and Hovey, *Songs from Vagabondia,* op. cit., 1.
295. *MW* 423.
296. Walt Whitman, "From Pent-Up Aching Rivers," *Leaves of Grass* (Philadelphia: David McKay, 1894), 80.
297. Paul Zweig, *Walt Whitman: The Making of a Poet* (New York: Basic, 1984), 164.
298. Carman and Hovey, *Songs from Vagabondia,* op. cit., 15.
299. Ibid., 14.
300. Ibid., 15.
301. Aleister Crowley, *Magick in Theory and Practice* (Secaucus, NJ: Castle, 1991), 14.
302. *SL* I:31–32.
303. Carman and Hovey, *Last Songs,* op. cit., 57.
304. Carman and Hovey, *More Songs,* op. cit., 3.
305. *D* 9.

306. *AT* 202.
307. *DH* 138.
308. *D* 204.
309. Carman, *Echoes*, op. cit., 16.
310. Ibid., 15.
311. Shand-Tucci, *Boston Bohemia*, op. cit., 380.
312. Douglass Shand-Tucci, *The Crimson Letter: Harvard, Homosexuality, and the Shaping of American Culture* (New York: St. Martin's, 2003), 88.
313. Shand-Tucci, *Boston Bohemia*, op. cit., 390; Carman and Hovey, *Last Songs,* op. cit., 64, 66.
314. Ellmann, *Oscar Wilde*, op. cit., 142.
315. Oscar Wilde, *The Complete Works of Oscar Wilde* (New York: Harper and Row, 1989), 813.
316. Jean Overton Fuller, *The Magical Dilemma of Victor Neuburg,* rev. ed. (Oxford, UK: Mandrake, 1990), 145.
317. Crowley, *Magick,* op. cit., v.
318. Margot Adler, *Drawing Down the Moon: Witches, Druids, Goddess-Worshippers, and Other Pagans in America Today* (Boston: Beacon, 1979), 407.
319. Ibid., 404.
320. Ibid., 405.
321. Philip A. Shreffler, *The H. P. Lovecraft Companion* (Westport, CT: Greenwood, 1977), 107.
322. George E. Mylonas, *Eleusis and the Eleusinian Mysteries* (Princeton, NJ: Princeton University Press, 1961), 308.
323. *MW* 442.
324. Long, *Howard Phillips Lovecraft*, op. cit., 92.
325. Cannon, *H. P. Lovecraft*, op. cit., 31.
326. *DH* 143–144.
327. *HM* 175.
328. Lovecraft, quoted in S. T. Joshi, "Lovecraft's Aesthetic Development: From Classicism to Decadence," *Lovecraft Studies* 31 (Fall 1994), 29.
329. *CE* I:310.
330. *SL* II:225.
331. Estelle Jussim, *Slave to Beauty: The Eccentric Life and Controversial Career of F. Holland Day, Photographer, Publisher, Aesthete* (Boston: David R. Godine, 1981), 112.
332. Ibid., 109.
333. *CE* 2:23.
334. *SL* II:118–119.
335. *SL* II:168.

336. *DH* 128.
337. *HM* 175.
338. *D* 78.
339. *DH* 17.
340. Blanchard, *Oscar Wilde's America,* op. cit., 33.
341. Ibid., 32.
342. Joshi, *H. P. Lovecraft*, op. cit., 185.
343. *DH* 143.
344. *D* 155.
345. Ellmann, *Oscar Wilde*, op. cit., 422.
346. *SL* II:91.
347. *SL* II:50.
348. S. T. Joshi, notes for "The Hound," in Lovecraft, *Call of Cthulhu*, op. cit., 378.
349. *D* 166.
350. *D* 170.
351. Smith, *Classical Dictionary*, op. cit., 457.
352. *D* 165.
353. *D* 170.
354. *MM* 73 and 74.
355. *DH* 278.
356. *DH* 131.
357. Shand-Tucci, *Boston Bohemia*, op. cit., 52.
358. *DH* 226.
359. *DH* 227.
360. *DH* 260.
361. *DH* 261.
362. *DH* 254.
363. *DH* 265–266.
364. *DH* 224.
365. *DH* 239.
366. *DH* 256.
367. *DH* 306.
368. Marion L. Starkey, *The Devil in Massachusetts: A Modern Inquiry into the Salem Witch Trials* (New York: Alfred A. Knopf, 1950), ch. 2, section 2, 26.
369. Jean Gibran and Kahlil Gibran, *Kahlil Gibran: His Life and His World* (New York: Interlink, 1991), 41.
370. Ibid., 53.
371. Jussim, *Slave to Beauty,* op. cit., 14.
372. Shand-Tucci, *Boston Bohemia*, op. cit., 96, 407.
373. Carman, *Echoes*, op. cit., 21.
374. *DH* 225.
375. *DH* 227.
376. *DH* 232.
377. Shand-Tucci, *Boston Bohemia*, op. cit., 373.
378. *DH* 266.
379. *DH* 132.
380. *MW* 253.
381. *DH* 132.

382. Sylvia Cranston, *The Extraordinary Life and Influence of Helena Blavatsky, Founder of the Modern Theosophical Movement* (New York: G. P. Putnam's Sons, 1994), 196.
383. Ibid., 194.
384. *DH* 132.
385. E. Hoffman Price, *Book of the Dead, Friends of Yesteryear: Fictioneers and Others (Memories of the Pulp Fiction Era),* ed. Peter Ruber (Sauk City, WI: Arkham House, 2001), 61.
386. Ibid.; *DH* 126.
387. Robert M. Price, "HPL and HPB, Lovecraft's Use of Theosophy," *Crypt of Cthulhu* vol. 1, no. 5 (Roodmas 1982), 9.
388. Gibran and Gibran, *Kahlil Gibran,* op. cit., 126.
389. Shand-Tucci, *Boston Bohemia*, op. cit., 381.
390. Jussim, *Slave to Beauty,* op. cit., 48.
391. Shand-Tucci, *Boston Bohemia*, op. cit., 122.
392. Jonathan Fryer, *Robbie Ross: Oscar Wilde's Devoted Friend* (New York, Carroll and Graf, 2000), 95.
393. *D* 268.
394. *DH* 260.
395. *DH* 263.
396. Mather, *The Wonders of the Invisible World,* op. cit., 157.
397. M. I. Rostovtzeff, "The Decay of the Ancient World and Its Economic Explanations," in *The Fall of Rome, Can It Be Explained?* ed. Mortimer Chambers, 2nd ed., European Problem Studies (Holt, Rinehart and Winston, 1970), 60.

Chapter Two

1. Otto Weininger, *Sex and Character*, trans. from the 6th German ed. (New York: G. P. Putnam's Sons, reprinted by Kessinger, n.d.), 290–291.
2. J. J. Bachofen, quoted in Erich Neumann, *The Great Mother: An Analysis of the Archetype,* trans. Ralph Manheim, Bollingen series 47 (Princeton, NJ: Princeton University Press, 1983), 265.
3. Bachofen, quoted in Neumann, *Great Mother,* op. cit., 267.
4. Margaret S. Murray, *The Witch-Cult in Western Europe*

(New York: Barnes and Noble, 1996), 231.

5. Ibid., 234.

6. Samuel Rosenberg, *Naked Is the Best Disguise: The Death and Resurrection of Sherlock Holmes* (Indianapolis, IN: Bobbs-Merrill, 1974), 64.

7. H. R. Hays, *The Dangerous Sex: The Myth of Feminine Evil* (New York, G. P. Putnam's Sons, 1964), 8.

8. H. C. Bunner, *Airs from Arcady and Elsewhere* (New York: Charles Scribner's Sons, 1884), 3.

9. Ibid., 8.

10. Bliss Carman, *Pipes of Pan Number Three: Songs of the Sea Children* (Boston: L. C. Page, 1903), 24.

11. Ibid., 75.

12. Ralph Adams Cram, *Spirits Black and White* (West Warwick, RI: Necronomicon, 1993), 20.

13. Mary Warner Blanchard, *Oscar Wilde's America* (New Haven, CT: Yale University Press, 1998), 219–220.

14. *AT* 270.

15. *AT* 295.

16. *AT* 147.

17. *D* 50.

18. *DH* 131.

19. *DH* 143.

20. *D* 52.

21. *AT* 224 (italics mine).

22. *AT* 492.

23. *HM* 367.

24. Ibid.

25. *DH* 63–64.

26. *DH* 76.

27. *DH* 77.

28. *DH* 188.

29. *DH* 226.

30. *DH* 213.

31. *DH* 265.

32. *DH* 227.

33. *DH* 352.

34. *DH* 336, 363.

35. *D* 256.

36. Maurice Levy, *Lovecraft: A Study in the Fantastic,* trans. S. T. Joshi (Detroit: Wayne State University Press, 1988), 61.

37. See what Lovecraft calls the "swarming movements" (*SL* I: 181) of immigrant hordes; as well as his description of Jews, who, he says, "always swarm where money is to be had" (*MW* 325).

38. *SL* I:181.

39. *CE* I:172.

40. Lovecraft to *The Argosy*

(1914), quoted in Samuel Moskowitz, *Under the Moons of Mars: A History and Anthology of the "Scientific Romance" in the Munsey Magazines, 1912–1920* (New York: Holt, Rinehart, and Winston, 1970), 375.

41. George Allan England, *The Vacant World* (Boston: Small, Maynard, 1914; accessed at http://books.google.com), ch. 19, 105.

42. England, *Vacant World,* op. cit., ch. 16, 92.

43. L. Sprague de Camp, *Lovecraft: A Biography,* abridged ed. (New York: Ballantine, 1976), 67.

44. Victor Rousseau (as by H. M. Egbert), *The Sea Demons,* Classics of Science Fiction reprint series (Westport, CT: Hyperion, 1976), 100.

45. Ibid., 131.

46. *DH* 332.

47. *MM* 55.

48. *DH* 20.

49. *D* 197.

50. *D* 197.

51. *DH* 20.

52. William Beckford, *Vathek,* in *Three Gothic Novels,* ed. Peter Fairclough (Middlesex, England: Penguin, 1972), 188.

53. Neumann, *Great Mother,* op. cit., 265.

54. Ibid., 266.

55. Rosenberg, *Naked Is the Best Disguise,* op. cit., 64–65.

56. Neumann, *Great Mother,* op. cit., 266.

57. *DH* 47, *D* 85, *DH* 277.

58. Neumann, *Great Mother,* op. cit., 267.

59. William Fulwiler, "E.R.B. and H.P.L.," *ERB-dom* 80 (Feb. 1975), 41 and 44.

60. Edgar Rice Burroughs, *At the Earth's Core* (New York: Grosset and Dunlap, 1922), ch. 5, 93.

61. *MW* 89.

62. *SOT* 56, 57.

63. Lovecraft to Barlow (1935), quoted in *SOT* 111.

64. Frank Belknap Long, "The Great Cold" (1935), in *The Rim of the Unknown* (New York: Condor, 1978), 230.

65. Ibid., 229.

66. Ibid., 227.

67. *SL* V:28.

Chapter Three

1. Lucilla Burn, *The Greek*

Myths (Austin: University of Texas Press, 1992), 24.

2. William Smith, *A Classical Dictionary of Biography, Mythology, and Geography* (Albemarle Street: John Murray, 1881), 766.

3. *DH* 198.

4. *MM* 155.

5. *D* 194.

6. *DH* 330.

7. Smith, *Classical Dictionary,* op. cit., 766.

8. H. P. Lovecraft, *H. P. Lovecraft in the Argosy: Collected Correspondence from the Munsey Magazines,* ed. S. T. Joshi (West Warwick, RI: Necronomicon, 1994), 15.

9. Despite his overriding nihilism and pessimism, one can catch an occasional glimmer of the heroic in Lovecraft's fiction: such as in the theme of escape from or revenge upon one's parents, which animates the ghoul in "The Outsider" and the young boys in "The Cats of Ulthar"; and in the notorious good-vs.-evil scenarios that animate the plots of "The Shunned House," "The Horror at Red Hook," "The Dunwich Horror," and *The Case of Charles Dexter Ward,* which seems to represent a legacy of Lovecraft's childhood reading of the Sherlock Holmes mysteries, just as the heroic aspects of *The Dream-Quest of Unknown Kadath* seem to represent a retention of the heroic themes from Lovecraft's youthful reading of Edgar Rice Burroughs' pulp fiction stories. For critic Peter Cannon, act of writing itself in Lovecraft's fiction often "assumes heroic proportions" (Peter Cannon, *H. P. Lovecraft,* Twayne's United States Authors Series [Boston: Twayne, 1989], 119). Lovecraft's protagonists, like Robert Blake in "The Haunter of the Dark," often write up until the moment of death, much like Lovecraft himself in real life.

10. Victoria Nelson, *The Secret Life of Puppets* (Cambridge, MA: Harvard University Press, 2001), 117.

11. S. T. Joshi, *H. P. Lovecraft: A Life* (West Warwick, RI: Necronomicon, 2004), 13–17. As Joshi observes, Lovecraft lost his father Winfield Lovecraft to

syphilis at around age eight, after a long and terrifying illness. Winfield's first confinement began in 1893, when Lovecraft was almost three.

12. Significantly, it is not solely in Lovecraft's fiction that this concern with paternal or patriarchal legacies was located: Lovecraft's own personal "magical inheritance" from his father including some paternal clothing (Joshi, *H. P. Lovecraft*, op. cit., 17), which Lovecraft himself later wore until they wore out (L. Sprague de Camp, *Lovecraft: A Biography*, abridged ed. [New York: Ballantine, 1976], 74), as well as a "paternal watch" (*SL* I:124), about which Lovecraft wrote effusively to his mother in 1921 shortly before her death.

13. Lovecraft's life and fiction also parallels the Theseus myth in another fashion, however; as witness the Greek tradition that Theseus was forced to leave his wife Ariadne behind "because he was ashamed to bring a foreign wife to Athens" (Smith, *Classical Dictionary*, op. cit., 78). In Lovecraft's life and fiction, too, the most catastrophic results adhere to the violation of this common exogamic taboo. Peter Cannon notes a similarity between Theseus' use of Ariadne's thread in the maze of the Minotaur, and Danforth and Dyer's later use of pieces of paper to mark their journey through the Old Ones' city in *Mountains of Madness* (Cannon, *H. P. Lovecraft*, op. cit., 104).

14. See my essays "More on H. P. Lovecraft and Sherlock Homes" and "A Reprehensible Habit: H. P. Lovecraft and the Munsey Magazines" (forthcoming).

15. Maurice Levy, *Lovecraft: A Study in the Fantastic*, trans. S. T. Joshi (Detroit: Wayne State University Press, 1988), 96.

16. Smith, *Classical Dictionary*, op. cit., 100.

17. Levy, *Lovecraft*, op. cit., 18.

18. Burn, *Greek Myths*, op. cit., 27.

19. Smith, *Classical Dictionary*, op. cit., 616.

20. *HM* 344.

21. *DH* 262.

22. *DH* 344.

23. *DH* 122.

24. Ernest Jones, *On the Nightmare* (New York: Liveright, 1951), 269.

25. Ibid., 270.

26. Ibid., 289.

27. *MM* 417; also called a "carved oak box of archaic wonder" (*MM* 414); similar to these are the "puzzling" (*DH* 126) box that proves to contain all the grand-uncle's notes and clippings in "The Call of Cthulhu," and the "rotting chest" (*D* 8) that Jervas Dudley believes holds a key to the tomb.

28. *SL* I:71.

29. *MM* 419.

30. *MM* 415 (italics mine).

31. *MM* 418.

32. *MM* 415.

33. *D* 7.

34. *D* 111.

35. Cannon, *H. P. Lovecraft*, op. cit., 71.

36. *DH* 305.

37. *D* 8.

38. *MM* 239.

39. *DH* 28.

40. Cannon, *H. P. Lovecraft*, op. cit., 60.

41. *MM* 414.

42. Levy, *Lovecraft*, op. cit., 43.

43. Robert M. Price, "HPL and HPB, Lovecraft's Use of Theosophy," *Crypt of Cthulhu* vol. 1, no. 5 (Roodmas, 1982), 9.

44. *D* 256.

45. *D* 257.

46. *DH* 282–283.

47. Levy, *Lovecraft*, op. cit., 91.

48. Sherwood Anderson, "Departure," in *Winesburg, Ohio* (New York: Viking, 1960), 247.

49. *MW* 508.

50. S. T. Joshi, notes for "Arthur Jermyn," in H. P. Lovecraft, *The Call of Cthulhu and Other Weird Stories* (Penguin, 1999), 365–366.

51. *D* 6.

52. Ibid.

53. *D* 7.

54. Charles Kingsley, *The Heroes, or Greek Fairy Tales for My Children* (New York: Thomas Y. Crowell, 1900), 201.

55. *D* 7.

56. *D* 4.

57. *D* 5–6.

58. *D* 6.

59. Dudley's necrophilic sleeping within this coffin likewise

suggests a paternal basis, in the form of that ancient practice of incubation, associated with the serpent god, Aesculapius, practiced during the classical period, during which people slept upon graves in order to promote healing. Psychologist Ernest Jones suggests a direct connection between this process of incubation and ancestor worship, as well as a between the phallic power of the father or ancestors and the symbol of the snake (Jones, *Nightmare,* op. cit., 92–95). Lovecraft himself recapitulates this idea throughout his weird fiction, for example "that spotted snake" (*DH* 45) invoked as Delapore descends into the depths of ancestral memory at the end of "The Rats in the Walls," and the already-mentioned snake-den associated with Randolph Carter's ancestors in "The Silver Key." Hallucinatory visions are associated with the paternal horrors in "The Lurking Fear"; Lovecraft's narrator raves of "snakes and dead men's skulls swelled to gigantic proportions" (*D* 180), snakes and heads being symbols of the phallic and paternal, as well as of parental giganticism.

60. *D* 11 (italics Lovecraft's).

61. Ibid.

62. *D* 6.

63. *D* 12.

64. Ibid.

65. *MM* 343–344.

66. *MM* 342.

67. *DH* 22.

68. *DH* 24.

69. *DH* 39.

70. *DH* 40.

71. *DH* 48.

72. *HM* 119.

73. *HM* 150.

74. *HM* 162.

75. *D* 282.

76. *D* 281.

77. *D* 282.

78. *HM* 220.

79. *HM* 277.

80. *MM* 201.

81. *MM* 168.

82. *D* 6.

83. *MM* 228.

84. *D* 333.

85. *D* 334.

86. *D* 336.

87. Oswald Spengler, *Decline of the West,* vol. 1, *Form and Actuality,*

trans. Charles Francis Atkinson (New York: Alfred A. Knopf, 1930), 341.

88. *AT* 13.
89. *HM* 236–237.
90. *DH* 106.
91. *DH* 109.
92. *D* 248.
93. Joshi, *H. P. Lovecraft*, op. cit., 15.
94. *MM* 116.
95. *MM* 117.
96. *MM* 116.
97. *MM* 147.
98. *MM* 116.
99. *D* 204.
100. *AT* 47.
101. *DH* 106.
102. Kingsley, *The Heroes*, op. cit., 243.
103. *MW* 99.
104. *D* 330.
105. *D* 6.
106. *DH* 27.
107. *DH* 30.
108. *MM* 417.
109. Vyvyan Holland, *Son of Oscar Wilde*, rev. ed., ed. Merlin Holland (London: Robinson, 1999), 170.
110. Ibid., 85–86.
111. Ibid., 171.
112. *DH* 326.
113. *DH* 335 (italics mine).
114. *D* 6.
115. *SL* I:305 (italics mine).
116. *D* 330.
117. *SL* IV:126.
118. Joshi, *H. P. Lovecraft*, op. cit., 69.
119. *DH* 45.
120. *D* 248.
121. Cannon, *H. P. Lovecraft*, op. cit., 51.
122. *DH* 28 (italics mine).
123. *SOT* 97.
124. *MM* 107.
125. *MM* 111.
126. Philip Rieff, *Freud: The Mind of the Moralist* (New York: Viking, 1959), 132.
127. Ibid., 126.
128. *MM* 188.
129. *MM* 244, 247.
130. *DH* 14.
131. *D* 31 (italics mine).
132. *D* 29.
133. Rousseau's intern protagonist, like Lovecraft's, describes himself as having "been working too hard" (Victor Rousseau, *Draft of Eternity*, ed. Brian Earl Brown [Detroit, MI: Beb, n.d.], 5), and

as being "utterly weary of everything" (4), a fact his fatherly boss, Dr. Moreland, attempts to remedy by inviting him to a party to meet his daughter.

134. *D* 6.
135. *SOT* 71.
136. *SOT* 85.
137. *SOT* 72.
138. *SOT* 97.
139. *SOT* 18.
140. *MM* 177.
141. *MM* 170.
142. *MM* 193.
143. *MM* 181.
144. Lovecraft, quoted in Joshi, *H. P. Lovecraft*, op. cit., 16 (italics mine).
145. *HM* 8.
146. *D* 282 (italics mine).
147. *D* 117.
148. A similar intermixture of young with old was found in the classical myths, such as the story of the autochthonous Etruscan god Tages, depicted as a white-haired young "boy with the wisdom of an old man," who "suddenly rose out of the ground" (Smith, *Classical Dictionary*, op. cit., 741). Lovecraft reverses this slightly in "The Crawling Chaos," in which a young sylvan divinity suddenly drops *down* from a tree.) In Charles Kingsley's retelling of the myth of Perseus, the great height of Perseus while still just a teenager is taken as evidence that he is a son of Zeus (Kingsley, *The Heroes*, op. cit., 30).
149. *HM* 168.
150. *HM* 169.
151. *D* 330.
152. *D* 331.
153. *D* 332.
154. Levy, *Lovecraft*, op. cit., 78.
155. *D* 335.
156. *DH* 332.
157. Lovecraft, it is true, may also have been influenced in his depiction of the possession of both immortality and gold by the le Sorciers and the Deep Ones by the early science fiction magazines, in which the two themes of the elixir of life and the creation of gold were perennial motifs of the genre (R. Jere Black, quoted in Mike Ashley and Robert A. W. Lowndes, *The Gernsback Days: A Study of the Evolution of Modern Science Fiction from 1911 to 1936*

[Holicong, PA: Wildside, 2004], 169–170).
158. *MM* 138.
159. De Camp, *Lovecraft*, op. cit., 13.
160. *MM* 149.
161. Holland, *Son of Oscar Wilde*, op. cit., 156.
162. *D* 11.
163. *DH* 54.
164. *D* 11.
165. *DH* 56.
166. *DH* 47.
167. *DH* 48.
168. *DH* 50.
169. *MM* 338.
170. *MM* 342.
171. *MM* 310.
172. *DH* 52.
173. *DH* 58.
174. Robert Waugh, "'Cool Air,' 'The Apartment Above Us,' and Other Stories," *Lovecraft Annual* No. 5 (2011), 235.
175. *DH* 51.
176. *AT* 243.
177. *DH* 46.
178. Jones, *Nightmare*, op. cit., 68.
179. Ibid., 65.
180. Denton Welch, *In Youth Is Pleasure* (New York: E. P. Dutton, 1985), 4–5.
181. Levy, *Lovecraft*, op. cit., 88, 114.
182. Stuart Gordon, commentary track, *H. P. Lovecraft's Re-Animator*, Millennium Edition (Elite Entertainment, 2002; DVD).
183. *DH* 82.
184. *MM* 413.
185. *MM* 414.
186. *AT* 21 (italics mine).
187. James Goho, "What Is 'the Unnamable'? H. P. Lovecraft and the Problem of Evil," in *Lovecraft Annual* No. 3, ed. S. T. Joshi (New York: Hippocampus, 2009), 23.
188. *D* 125.
189. Jones, *Nightmare*, op. cit., 63.
190. Ibid., 346.
191. Lafcadio Hearn, quoted in Erdman Palmore and Daisaku Maeda, *The Honorable Elders Revisited: A Revised Cross-Cultural Analysis of Aging in Japan* (Durham: Duke University Press, 1985), 19.
192. Levy, *Lovecraft*, op. cit., 101.
193. Edward Gibbon, excerpt

from "Decline and Fall of the Roman Empire," reproduced in *The Fall of Rome: Can It Be Explained?*, ed. Mortimer Chambers, 2nd ed. (New York: Holt, Rinehart and Winston, 1970), 7.

194. Keith Hopkins, *Death and Renewal: Sociological Studies in Roman History*, vol. 2 (Cambridge, U.K.: Cambridge University Press, 1985), 227.

195. Levy, *Lovecraft,* op. cit., 103.

196. *DH* 302.

197. *D* 6.

198. Levy, *Lovecraft,* op. cit., 40.

199. Leontine Young, *Life Among the Giants: A Child's Eye View of the Grown-Up World* (New York: McGraw-Hill, 1965), 71–73.

200. *HM* 194.

201. *D* 109.

202. *D* 11.

203. *DH* 129, *DH* 131, *DH* 132.

204. *MM* 414 (italics mine).

205. *DH* 141.

206. *DH* 139 (italics mine).

207. Cannon, *H. P. Lovecraft,* op. cit., 67.

208. Jones, *Nightmare,* op. cit., 100.

209. Levy, *Lovecraft,* op. cit., 112.

210. *MM* 413.

211. Jones, *Nightmare,* op. cit., 99.

212. *D* 205.

213. *MM* 363 (italics mine).

214. *SL* 1:141.

215. *MM* 311.

216. *MM* 314.

217. *MM* 96.

218. *DH* 151.

219. *D* 99.

220. John Salonia, "Cosmic Maenads and the Music of Madness: Lovecraft's Borrowings from the Greeks," *Lovecraft Annual* No. 5, ed. S. T. Joshi (New York: Hippocampus, 2011), 101 (italics mine).

221. Robert Waugh, "Dr. Margaret Murray and H. P. Lovecraft: The Witch-Cult in New England," *Lovecraft Studies* 31 (Fall 1994), 31.

222. Will Murray, "More Lovecraft in the Comics," *Crypt of Cthulhu* #75, vol. 9, no. 8 (Michaelmas 1990), 25.

223. *HM* 118.

224. *DH* 46.

225. *MM* 22 (italics mine).

226. *D* 79.

227. *D* 80.

228. *DH* 333.

229. *D* 7.

230. *D* 31.

231. *D* 161.

232. *D* 139–140 (italics mine).

233. *D* 134.

234. *MM* 414 (italics mine).

235. Jones, *Nightmare,* op. cit., 168.

236. *MM* 367.

237. *MM* 261.

238. Cannon, *H. P. Lovecraft,* op. cit., 133.

239. Ibid., 64.

240. Young, *Life Among the Giants,* op. cit., 59.

241. *DH* 141.

242. Alex Houstoun, "Lovecraft and the Sublime: A Reinterpretation," in *Lovecraft Annual* No. 5, ed. S. T. Joshi (New York: Hippocampus, 2011), 179.

243. *SOT* 55.

244. *SOT* 94.

245. *SOT* 64.

246. *D* 191.

247. *D* 180.

248. *MW* 38.

249. Erich Neumann, *The Great Mother: An Analysis of the Archetype*, trans. Ralph Manheim, Bollingen series 47 (Princeton, NJ: Princeton University Press, 1983), 212n2.

250. *D* 104.

251. *AT* 400.

252. *D* 114.

253. *D* 117.

254. Margaret Mahler, "A Psychoanalytic Evaluation of Tic in Psychopathology of Children: Symptomatic Tic and Tic Syndrome," in *The Selected Papers of Margaret S. Mahler: Vol. One: Infantile Psychosis and Early Contributions; Vol. Two: Separation-Individuation,* intro. Marjorie Hartley and Annemarie Weil (New York: Jason Aronson, 1982), 65.

255. *DH* 32.

256. *MW* 323.

257. *D* 76.

258. Cannon, *H. P. Lovecraft,* op. cit., 63.

259. *D* 140.

260. *D* 139–140.

261. *MM* 410.

262. *MM* 217.

263. *D* 285.

264. *D* 142.

265. *D* 143.

266. Jones, *Nightmare,* op. cit., 156.

267. Ibid., 168.

268. Nathaniel Hawthorne, *The Scarlet Letter* (Leipzig: Bernhard Tauchnitz, 1852; accessed at http://books.google.com), ch. 16, 220.

269. *MM* 281.

270. *MM* 289.

271. *DH* 300.

272. *DH* 135.

273. Jones, *Nightmare,* op. cit., 168.

274. Ibid., 168–169.

275. *MM* 342.

276. *HM* 145.

277. *D* 87.

278. *D* 100.

279. In his 1918 essay "At the Root," Lovecraft uses similar imagery to describe civilization itself as a mere coverlet over the more basic bestial or savage tendencies of mankind (*CE* 5:29). His association of an ogre with such imagery thus reinforces the unfortunate convergence of the bestial with the parental in his mind.

280. Jones, *Nightmare,* op. cit., 81.

281. Hesiod, quoted in H. R. Hays, *The Dangerous Sex: The Myth of Feminine Evil* (New York: G. P. Putnam's Sons, 1964), 80, 83.

282. *D* 353.

283. Hesiod, quoted in Hays, *The Dangerous Sex,* op. cit., 80.

284. Hays, *The Dangerous Sex,* op. cit., 86.

285. Ibid.

286. Ibid., 77.

287. *DH* 196 (italics mine).

288. *D* 334.

289. *D* 279.

290. *D* 283.

291. *DH* 124.

292. *D* 5.

293. *D* 11.

294. *D* 182.

295. *D* 179.

296. *D* 180–181.

297. *D* 199.

298. *D* 186.

299. *D* 183.

300. *D* 10.

301. *DH* 109.

302. *DH* 281.

303. *MM* 168.

304. *MM* 167.

305. *D* 131.

306. Jones, *Nightmare,* op. cit., 185.

307. Ibid., 167.

308. *DH* 177 (italics mine).

309. *DH* 112.
310. Jones, *Nightmare*, op. cit., 310.
311. Neumann, *Great Mother*, op. cit., 294.
312. Jones, *Nightmare*, op. cit., 307–308.
313. Ibid., 308.
314. *D* 182.
315. *MM* 244.
316. *HM* 158.
317. *SOT* 62 (italics Lovecraft's).
318. Perley Poore Sheehan, *The Abyss of Wonders*, ed. Brian Earl Brown (Detroit, MI: Beb, n.d.), ch. 15, 30.
319. *SOT* 62.
320. *D* 99.
321. *D* 101.
322. *D* 109.
323. *DH* 52.
324. *D* 102.
325. *D* 107.
326. *D* 110.
327. "persistent rage" *MM* 27, "malignant rage" *D* 109.
328. *MM* 43.
329. *MM* 33.
330. *D* 104.
331. *D* 106.
332. *HM* 307.
333. *HM* 309 (italics mine).
334. *D* 243.
335. Lovecraft, quoted in Joshi, *H. P. Lovecraft*, op. cit., 16.
336. William Lumley, "The Diary of Alonzo Typer," in *Ashes and Others*, by H. P. Lovecraft and Divers Hands, aka *Crypt of Cthulhu* 10, vol. 2, no. 2 (Bloomfield, NJ: Miskatonic University Press, Yuletide 1982), 22.
337. Ibid., 21.
338. *DH* 336–337 (italics mine).
339. De Camp, *Lovecraft*, op. cit., 73.
340. *SL* II:224.
341. William Arrowsmith, notes to Petronius, *The Satyricon* (New York: New American Library, 1959), 170.
342. Edmund Wilson, *Memoirs of Hecate County*, afterword by John Updike (New York: Farrar, Straus and Giroux, 1995), 321.
343. *MM* 179.
344. Joshi, notes to "The Picture in the House," in Lovecraft, *Call of Cthulhu*, op. cit., 372.
345. George Allan England, *The Vacant World* (Boston: Small, Maynard, 1914; accessed at http://books.google.com), ch. 12, 27.

346. *AT* 269.
347. *D* 347.
348. *DH* 326.
349. *SOT* 97.
350. *SL* V:374.
351. *DH* 272–273.
352. *MM* 291.
353. *D* 265.
354. *D* 114.
355. *DH* 19.
356. *D* 56.
357. *D* 58.
358. *D* 57.
359. Levy, *Lovecraft*, op. cit., 25.
360. Mel Gordon, *Expressionist Texts* (New York: PAJ, 1986), 96.
361. Wilson, *Memoirs of Hecate County*, op. cit., 29.
362. Jones, *Nightmare*, op. cit., 129.
363. Ibid., 346.
364. *HM* 322.

Chapter Four

1. Edgar Lee Masters, *Spoon River Anthology* (New York: Collier, 1962), 262.
2. Robert H. Barlow, *On Lovecraft and Life*, intro. S. T. Joshi (West Warwick, RI: Necronomicon, 1992), 17.
3. S. T. Joshi, quoted in Matt Cardin, "The Master's Eyes Shining with Secrets: H. P. Lovecraft's Influence on Thomas Ligotti," in *Lovecraft Annual* No. 1, ed. S. T. Joshi (New York: Hippocampus, 2007), 101.
4. S. T. Joshi, *H. P. Lovecraft: A Life* (West Warwick, RI: Necronomicon, 2004), 164.
5. *HM* 6.
6. *MM* 106.
7. Ibid.
8. T. R. Livesey, "Dispatches from the Providence Observatory: Astronomical Motifs and Sources in the Writings of H. P. Lovecraft," in *Lovecraft Annual* No. 2, ed. S. T. Joshi (New York: Hippocampus, 2008), 4.
9. *MM* 106.
10. *DH* 170.
11. Virgil, *Virgil's Eclogues and Georgics*, ed. Horace Andrews, M.A., 2nd ed. (Boston: Crocker and Brewster, 1866; accessed at http://books.google.com), eclogue 8, 26.
12. Robert Waugh, "The Subway and the Shoggoth (Part II)," *Lovecraft Studies* 40 (1998), 27.

13. *MM* 106.
14. *AT* 11.
15. *AT* 146 (italics mine).
16. *AT* 44–45 (italics mine).
17. *DH* 281.
18. *SOT* 88.
19. *MM* 281.
20. *DH* 86.
21. *DH* 86.
22. *AT* 213 (italics mine).
23. *MW* 33.
24. *D* 124.
25. *D* 125.
26. *D* 126.
27. Cotton Mather, *Cotton Mather on Witchcraft: Being the Wonders of the Invisible World, First Published at Boston in October 1692 and Now Reprinted, with Additional Matter and Old Wood-Cuts, for the Library of the Fantastic and Curious* (New York: Dorset, 1991), 140.
28. *DH* 315.
29. Nathaniel Hawthorne, *The Scarlet Letter* (Leipzig: Bernhard Tauchnitz, 1852; accessed at http://books.google.com), 285.
30. Maurice Levy, *Lovecraft: A Study in the Fantastic* (Detroit: Wayne State University Press, 1988), 14.
31. Ibid., 50.
32. In a 1923 letter Lovecraft discusses his great admiration for the New England Puritans, who despite what he calls a few "aesthetic and intellectual fallacies" (*SL* I:275) still managed to apply a "refreshing technique" of "artificial values" to "shifting humanity," thereby developing "a simple standard of life and conduct," which, while at times "extravagant," was also "healthy and practical." He especially admired the fact that the Puritans "hated life and scorned the platitude that it is worth living." Lovecraft concludes, "I am myself very partial to it [Puritanism] — it is so quaint and wholesome" (*SL* I:276).
33. Mather, *The Wonders of the Invisible World*, op. cit., 85.
34. Ibid., 51.
35. *MM* 335.
36. *DH* 195.
37. Mather, *The Wonders of the Invisible World*, op. cit., 14.
38. *HM* 325.
39. Joshi, *H. P. Lovecraft*, op. cit., 277.
40. *HM* 326–27 (italics mine).

41. *HM* 327 (italics mine).

42. *HM* 330.

43. *HM* 328.

44. *HM* 329.

45. As described by James Joyce in his December 3, 1909, Dublin letter to Nora in Zurich (Richard Ellmann, *Selected Letters of James Joyce* [London: Faber, 1975]). Cf. Juvenal's description in one of his satires of a sexually loose Roman matron, who "'would puke on her spouse, but now feeds with the sailors, / Wanders all over the ship, *has fun pulling the handropes'*" (quoted in H. R. Hays, *The Dangerous Sex: The Myth of Feminine Evil* [New York: G. P. Putnam's Sons, 1964], 99); italics mine.

46. Joshi, *H. P. Lovecraft*, op. cit., 276.

47. *D* 124.

48. *HM* 329.

49. Edgar Rice Burroughs, *At the Earth's Core* (New York: Grosset and Dunlap, 1922), ch. 8, 138.

50. *HM* 144.

51. Frank Savile, *Beyond the Great South Wall: The Secret of the Antarctic*, illus. Robert L. Mason (New York: Grosset and Dunlap, 1901; accessed at http://books. google.com), 57.

52. Ibid., 186.

53. Ibid., 185.

54. Burroughs, *At the Earth's Core*, op. cit., 202.

55. *HM* 330.

56. *HM* 329.

57. Joshi, *H. P. Lovecraft*, op. cit., 278.

58. *HM* 330 (italics mine).

59. England calls it "some cosmic cataclysm" (George Allan England, *Beyond the Great Oblivion* [Boston: Small, Maynard, 1914], 296), that occurred when "an enormous mass" "split bodily off from the earth" (305), thereby forming a new moon.

60. *MM* 71.

61. *MM* 103.

62. *MM* 66.

63. Charles Stilson, *Minos of Sardanes*, ed. Brian Earl Brown (Detroit, MI: Beb, n.d.), 56.

64. *MM* 71.

65. *MM* 335.

66. Charles Stilson, *Polaris of the Snows*, ed. Brian Earl Brown (Detroit, MI: Beb, n.d.), 25; and Robert Ames Bennet (pen name Lee Robinet), *Thyra, A Romance*

of the Polar Pit (eBook No.: 0900 541.txt, Project Gutenberg Australia, accessed at http://guten berg.net.au/ebooks09/0900541h .html), ch. 3, unpaginated.

67. *MM* 43; *MM* 104.

68. A. Merritt, "The People of the Pit," in *The People of the Pit and Other Early Horrors from the Munsey Pulps* (Normal, IL: Black Dog, 2010), 15.

69. *MM* 103.

70. *MM* 43.

71. *SOT* 81.

72. *MM* 87.

73. *D* 112.

74. *DH* 195.

75. *DH* 196.

76. Robert Waugh, "'Cool Air,' 'The Apartment Above Us,' and Other Stories," *Lovecraft Annual* No. 5 (2011), 235.

77. Levy, *Lovecraft*, op. cit., 70.

78. Ibid., 102.

79. Ibid., 70.

80. *DH* 158 (italics mine).

81. *DH* 154.

82. Ernest Jones, *On the Nightmare* (New York: Liveright, 1951), 258.

83. John Webster, *The Duchess of Malfi*, in *John Webster and Cyril Tourneur, Four Plays*, intro. and ed. John Addington Symonds, series ed. Eric Bentley (New York: Hill and Wang, 1956), act II, scene 5, 157.

84. *D* 85.

85. *MM* 286.

86. *D* 215.

87. *MM* 106.

88. Jones, *Nightmare*, op. cit., 266.

89. *D* 178.

90. Jones, *Nightmare*, op. cit., 259.

91. Ibid., 204.

92. Leontine Young, *Life Among the Giants: A Child's Eye View of the Grown-Up World* (New York: McGraw-Hill, 1965), 118.

93. *DH* 122.

94. *SOT* 88.

95. Levy, *Lovecraft*, op. cit., 103.

96. Joshi, *H. P. Lovecraft*, op. cit., 285.

97. William Beckford, *Vathek*, in *Three Gothic Novels*, ed. Peter Fairclough (Middlesex, England: Penguin, 1972), 224.

98. Ibid., 231.

99. *D* 166 (italics mine).

100. *D* 230.

101. *D* 229.

102. *MM* 90.

103. *D* 229–230.

104. *MM* 104.

105. George Allan England, *Beyond the Great Oblivion* (Boston: Small, Maynard, 1914), 315–316.

106. *DH* 339.

107. *MM* 188.

108. *MM* 78; *MM* 81.

109. Dorothy C. Walter, "Three Hours with H. P. Lovecraft," in Cannon, ed., *Lovecraft Remembered*, op. cit., 45.

110. William Smith, *A Classical Dictionary of Biography, Mythology, and Geography* (Albemarle Street: John Murray, 1881), 299.

111. Margot Adler, *Drawing Down the Moon: Witches, Druids, Goddess-Worshippers, and Other Pagans in America Today* (Boston: Beacon, 1979), 107.

112. Ibid., 19.

113. *D* 255.

114. T. R. Livesay, "Dispatches from the Providence Observatory," in *Lovecraft Annual* No. 2, ed. S. T. Joshi (New York: Hippocampus, 2008), 36.

115. Ibid.

116. *HM* 181.

117. *SL* IV:328.

118. Oscar Wilde, *The Complete Works of Oscar Wilde* (New York: Harper and Row, 1989), 982.

119. Garrett P. Serviss, *The Moon Metal*, ed. Suzanne L. Shell and Joris Van Dael (e-text, http: //www.booksshouldbefree.com/ download/text/Moon-Metal-by-Garrett-P-Serviss.txt, n.d.), ch. 12.

120. Lovecraft, quoted in Samuel Moskowitz, *Under the Moons of Mars: A History and Anthology of the "Scientific Romance" in the Munsey Magazines, 1912–1920* (New York: Holt, Rinehart, and Winston, 1970), 374.

121. *CE* 3:15.

122. Serviss, *Moon Metal*, op. cit., ch. 14, n.p.

123. Victor Rousseau (as by H. M. Egbert), *The Sea Demons*, Classics of Science Fiction reprint series (Westport, CT: Hyperion, 1976), 32.

124. *CE* 2:223.

125. A. Merritt, "The Moon Pool," in Moskowitz, *Under the Moons*, op. cit., 144 (italics mine).

126. Ibid., 144–145 (italics mine).
127. Ibid., 140.
128. Ibid., 152.
129. Ibid., 154.
130. Ibid., 145.
131. Ibid., 143.
132. Ibid., 145.
133. MM 106.
134. *SOT* 89.
135. Merritt, "Moon Pool," op. cit., 145 (italics mine).
136. J. U. Giesy, *Palos of the Dog Star Pack*, ed. Brian Earl Brown (Detroit, MI: Beb, n.d.), 13–14.
137. *DH* 104.
138. *D* 259–260.
139. *MM* 404.
140. John Salonia, "Cosmic Maenads and the Music of Madness: Lovecraft's Borrowings from the Greeks," *Lovecraft Annual* No. 5, ed. S. T. Joshi (New York: Hippocampus, 2011), 93.
141. Levy, *Lovecraft*, op. cit., 34.
142. Ibid., 49.
143. *MW* 317.
144. John Uri Lloyd (as communicated to Llewelyn Drury), *Etidorhpa; or, The End of Earth*, 5th ed. (Cincinnati: Robert Clarke, 1896, reproduced in Mokelumne Hill, CA: Health Research, 1966; accessed at http://books.google.com), 300.
145. *DH* 44.
146. *HM* 141.
147. *MM* 43.
148. *MM* 104.
149. *MM* 103.
150. *SOT* 88.
151. Sir Arthur Conan Doyle, "The Horror of the Heights," in *Tales of Terror and Mystery* (Project Gutenberg E-text #537, 2008; accessed at http://www.gutenberg.org/5/3/537/), unpaginated.
152. *AT* 137.
153. *DH* 170.
154. *DH* 158.
155. *DH* 185.
156. Lloyd, *Etidorhpa*, op. cit., 76.
157. Ibid., 335.
158. *DH* 170.
159. *MM* 66.
160. *SOT* 62.
161. *SOT* 61.
162. *DH* 223.
163. *HM* 144 and *DH* 226 — there called "Him Who is not to be Named."

164. *SOT* 62.
165. Victor Rousseau, *Draft of Eternity*, ed. Brian Earl Brown (Detroit, MI: Beb, n.d.), 69.
166. *SOT* 88.
167. *SOT* 89.
168. *MM* 106.
169. *SOT* 89.
170. Erich Neumann, *The Great Mother: An Analysis of the Archetype*, trans. Ralph Manheim, Bollingen series 47 (Princeton, NJ: Princeton University Press, 1983), 256–257 (italics mine).
171. *MM* 104 (italics mine).
172. *MM* 102.
173. *MM* 89.
174. *D* 230.
175. *MM* 90.
176. George Kirk, quoted by Mara Kirk Hart, "Walkers in the City, George Willard Kirk and Howard Phillips Lovecraft in New York City, 1924–1926," in Cannon, ed., *Lovecraft Remembered*, op. cit., 236.
177. *MM* 92.
178. *MM* 98.

Chapter Five

1. *AT* 434.
2. S. T. Joshi, *H. P. Lovecraft: A Life* (West Warwick, RI: Necronomicon, 2004), 499.
3. Ibid., 501.
4. L. Sprague de Camp, *Lovecraft: A Biography*, abridged ed. (New York: Ballantine, 1976), 377.
5. Joshi, *H. P. Lovecraft*, op. cit., 500.
6. Bruce Lord, "The Genetics of Horror: Sex and Racism in H. P. Lovecraft's Fiction," *Contrasoma*, 2004, http://www.contrasoma.com/writing/lovecraft.html, accessed November 6, 2005.
7. Scott Connors, letter, *Nyctalops* 14 (March 1978), 50.
8. *AT* 139.
9. *DH* 330.
10. *AT* 213.
11. *AT* 138.
12. *MW* 36.
13. *AT* 138.
14. Maurice Levy, *Lovecraft: A Study in the Fantastic*, trans. S. T. Joshi (Detroit: Wayne State University Press, 1988), 32.
15. See *D* 19; *D* 331; *D* 335; *DH* 287; *DH* 365; and *MM* 413.
16. Lovecraft, quoted in Joshi, *H. P. Lovecraft*, op. cit., 325; and

De Camp, *Lovecraft*, op. cit., 213.
17. Joshi, *H. P. Lovecraft*, op. cit., 388.
18. Ibid., 60.
19. *SL* IV:358.
20. *MW* 38.
21. *MW* 89.
22. Lovecraft, quoted in Joshi, *H. P. Lovecraft*, op. cit., 256 (interpolations mine).
23. *DH* 364.
24. *AT* 139.
25. *AT* 138.
26. *SL* IV:358.
27. *MW* 36.
28. *DH* 321.
29. R. Jere Black, quoted in Mike Ashley and Robert A. W. Lowndes, *The Gernsback Days: A Study of the Evolution of Modern Science Fiction from 1911 to 1936* (Holicong, PA: Wildside, 2004), 170.
30. *DH* 367.
31. Alexander S. Murray, *Manual of Mythology*, ed. William H. Klapp (New York: Tudor, 1936), 165.
32. William Smith, *A Classical Dictionary of Biography, Mythology, and Geography* (Albemarle Street: John Murray, 1881), 100.
33. Ibid., 512.
34. *DH* 366–367 (italics mine).
35. *HM* 193.
36. Charles Stilson, *Polaris and the Goddess Glorian*, ed. Brian Earl Brown (Detroit, MI: Beb, n.d.), 5 (italics Stilson's).
37. *DH* 150 (italics mine).
38. *DH* 364.
39. *DH* 367 (italics mine).
40. Joshi, *H. P. Lovecraft*, op. cit., 147.
41. *SL* I:236–237.
42. De Camp, *Lovecraft*, op. cit., 65.
43. H. P. Lovecraft, *Letters to Alfred Galpin*, ed. S. T. Joshi and David E. Schultz (New York: Hippocampus, 2003), 53.
44. Frank Belknap Long, *Howard Phillips Lovecraft: Dreamer on the Nightside* (Sauk City, WI: Arkham House, 1975), 31.
45. August Derleth, interestingly, in his clever Lovecraftian pastiche "The Survivor" (1954), gives the invalid antiquarian friend of the narrator the name of "Gamwell." As Derleth's narrator observes: "Poor fellow, [he]

was even then on his deathbed, though neither of us knew it" (August Derleth [as by H. P. Lovecraft and August Derleth], *The Survivor and Others* [New York: Ballantine, 1971], 9).

46. *AT* 434.

47. Smith, *Classical Dictionary,* op. cit., 332.

48. Ibid., 10.

49. *DH* 277.

50. See W. Paul Cook, "In Memoriam: Howard Phillips Lovecraft, Recollections, Appreciations, Estimates," reproduced in Peter Canon, ed., *Lovecraft Remembered* (Sauk City, WI: Arkham House, 1998), 112–113.

51. *DH* 66.

52. *MM* 241.

53. *MM* 242.

54. *DH* 367.

55. *MM* 243.

56. *MM* 241.

57. *DH* 366.

58. Frank Belknap Long, *It Was the Day of the Robot* (New York City: Belmont, 1963), 24.

59. John Munder Ross, *The Sadomasochism of Everyday Life: Why We Hurt Ourselves — and Others — and How to Stop* (New York: Simon and Shuster, 1997), 142.

60. Eugene O'Neil, quoted in H. R. Hays, *The Dangerous Sex: The Myth of Feminine Evil* (New York: G. P. Putnam's Sons, 1964), 264.

61. Levy, *Lovecraft,* op. cit., 23.

62. Ibid., 74.

63. *SL* II:177.

64. Erich Neumann, *The Great Mother: An Analysis of the Archetype,* trans. Ralph Manheim, Bollingen series 47 (Princeton, NJ: Princeton University Press, 1983), 12.

65. *DH* 366.

66. Neumann, *Great Mother,* op. cit., 30.

67. *AT* 42 (italics mine).

68. *DH* 366.

69. Ibid.

70. Neumann, *Great Mother,* op. cit., 291.

71. Ibid., 292.

72. Hays, *The Dangerous Sex,* op. cit., 94–95 (interpolation mine).

73. Tony Kelly, "Pagan Musings," quoted in Margot Adler, *Drawing Down the Moon: Witches,* *Druids, Goddess-Worshippers, and Other Pagans in America Today* (Boston: Beacon, 1979), 407.

Chapter Six

1. E. Hoffmann Price, *Book of the Dead, Friends of Yesteryear: Fictioneers and Others,* ed. Peter Ruber (Sauk City, WI: Arkham House, 2001), 66 (italics Price's).

2. Barbara Hambly, "The Man Who Loved His Craft: A Guidebook to the Mountains of Madness," intro. to H. P. Lovecraft, *The Transition of H. P. Lovecraft: The Road to Madness* (New York: Ballantine, 1996), ix.

3. Peter Cannon, *H. P. Lovecraft,* Twayne's United States Authors Series, series ed. Warren French (Boston: Twayne, 1989), 4.

4. Stuart Gordon, commentary track, *H. P. Lovecraft's Re-Animator,* Millennium Edition (Elite Entertainment, 2002; DVD); and Stuart Gordon, commentary track, *H. P. Lovecraft's from Beyond* (MGM, 2007; DVD).

5. Critic Dennis Quinn, for example, observes how "Lovecraft seldom makes any allusions to sex in his writings. He rarely even has a woman in his stories at all" (Quinn, "Endless Bacchanal: Rome, Livy, and Lovecraft's Cthulhu Cult," in *Lovecraft Annual* No. 5, ed. S. T. Joshi [New York: Hippocampus, 2011], 205). This is despite Quinn's earlier observations regarding 1) the prominence of the bacchanalia in Lovecraft's weird writings, 2) Livy's numerous references to the importance of women in this cult (197, 202) and 3) Quinn's observations regarding Lovecraft's consultation and utilization of the accounts of Livy in his fiction. Obviously, we can regard the bacchanalia itself, much like the witch-cult phenomena also represented throughout Lovecraft's writings, as an example of the presence of women in Lovecraft's fiction, although obviously in transmuted and veiled form.

6. H. P. Lovecraft, *H. P. Lovecraft in the Argosy: Collected Correspondence from Munsey Magazines,* ed. S. T. Joshi (West Warwick, RI: Necronomicon, 1994), 9.

7. *DH* 30.

8. *DH* 277.

9. *D* 210 (italics mine).

10. *DH* 19.

11. *CE* 5:244.

12. *HM* 276.

13. *HM* 273.

14. *HM* 144–145.

15. *DH* 243.

16. *DH* 226.

17. *MW* 336.

18. *AT* 112.

19. *DH* 365.

20. Erich Neumann, *The Great Mother: An Analysis of the Archetype,* trans. Ralph Manheim, Bollingen series 47 (Princeton, NJ: Princeton University Press, 1983), 270.

21. *AT* 37.

22. *D* 265.

23. Margaret S. Murray, *The Witch-Cult in Western Europe* (New York: Barnes and Noble, 1996), 225.

24. Ibid., 133, 135, 141, 151, 152, 155, among others.

25. *HM* 174.

26. Neumann, *Great Mother,* op. cit., 68.

27. S. T. Joshi, *Lovecraft: A Life* (West Warwick, RI: Necronomicon, 2004), 252.

28. Neumann, *Great Mother,* op. cit., 184.

29. Ibid., 212.

30. *DH* 47.

31. H. R. Hays, *The Dangerous Sex: The Myth of Feminine Evil* (New York: G. P. Putnam's Sons, 1964), 158.

32. *CE* 5:253.

33. Neumann, *Great Mother,* op. cit., 178.

34. Hays, *The Dangerous Sex,* op. cit., 64.

35. Ibid., 65.

36. *DH* 47.

37. *D* 121.

38. *AT* 42.

39. *MM* 59 (italics mine).

40. Neumann, *Great Mother,* op. cit., 214 (italics mine).

41. *MM* 66 (italics mine).

42. Hays, *The Dangerous Sex,* op. cit., 35–36 (italics mine).

43. *HM* 14.

44. John Munder Ross, *The Sadomasochism of Every Life: Why We Hurt Ourselves — and Others — and How to Stop* (New York: Simon and Shuster, 1997), 169–170 (italics mine).

45. Hays, *The Dangerous Sex,* op. cit., 28.
46. *MM* 292 (italics mine).
47. *D* 6.
48. Murray, *Witch-Cult,* op. cit., 146, 180, among others.
49. *MM* 281.
50. *DH* 301.
51. Neumann, *Great Mother,* op. cit., 129.
52. *MM* 103.
53. Donald R. Burleson, "A Note on 'The Book,'" *Lovecraft Studies* 42–43 (Autumn 2001), 53.
54. *MM* 367.
55. *MM* 391.
56. Neumann, *Great Mother,* op. cit., 43.
57. Ibid., 204.
58. *IIM* 321.
59. Charles Seltman, *The Twelve Olympians* (New York: Thomas Y. Crowell, 1960), 37.
60. Ibid., 69.
61. Neumann, *Great Mother,* op. cit., 325.
62. Hays, *The Dangerous Sex,* op. cit., 102.
63. William Smith, *A Classical Dictionary of Biography, Mythology, and Geography* (Albemarle Street: John Murray, 1881), 220.
64. *HM* 273.
65. Neumann, *Great Mother,* op. cit., 43.
66. Hays, *The Dangerous Sex,* op. cit., 42.
67. Murray, *Witch-Cult,* op. cit., 24.
68. Ibid., 158.
69. *D* 259, *D* 148, *MM* 288, and others.
70. Hays, *The Dangerous Sex,* op. cit., 155 (italics mine).
71. Murray, *Witch-Cult,* op. cit., 124, 169 (italics mine).
72. *DH* 55 (italics mine).
73. Murray, *Witch-Cult,* op. cit., 169.
74. Ibid., 245.
75. Maurice Levy, *Lovecraft: A Study in the Fantastic,* trans. S. T. Joshi (Detroit: Wayne State University Press, 1988), 70.
76. *HM* 178.
77. *HM* 179.
78. Hays, *The Dangerous Sex,* op. cit., 142 (italics mine).
79. Neumann, *Great Mother,* op. cit., 296.
80. Margot Adler, *Drawing Down the Moon: Witches, Druids, Goddess-Worshippers, and Other*

Pagans in America Today (Boston: Beacon, 1979), 351.
81. Neumann, *Great Mother,* op. cit., 299–301.
82. *D* 370.
83. *AT* 42 (capitals Lovecraft's).
84. Ibid.
85. *SL* I:333.
86. *CE* 5:247 (italics mine).
87. *MM* 62, *MM* 75, and *MM* 95.
88. Neumann, *Great Mother,* op. cit., 118.
89. *D* 199.
90. *MW* 38.
91. *MW* 89.
92. *DH* 47.
93. Neumann, *Great Mother,* op. cit., 233 (italics mine).
94. According to J.-M. Rajala, the various reported sightings of this work over the years have never been confirmed (Rajala, "Locked Dimensions Out of Reach: The Lost Stories of H. P. Lovecraft," in *Lovecraft Annual* No. 5, ed. S. T. Joshi [New York: Hippocampus, 2011], 21–22).
95. *HM* 187.
96. Hays, *The Dangerous Sex,* op. cit., 35–36; and John Munder Ross, *The Sadomasochism of Everyday Life: Why We Hurt Ourselves—and Others—and How to Stop* (New York: Simon and Shuster, 1997), 144–145.
97. Hays, *The Dangerous Sex,* op. cit., 27.
98. *MM* 106.
99. *D* 199 (italics mine).
100. Levy, *Lovecraft,* op. cit., 110.
101. Mircea Eliade, quoted in Levy, *Lovecraft,* op. cit., 110.
102. Levy, *Lovecraft,* op. cit., 113.
103. Ibid., 111.
104. *MM* 359 (italics mine).
105. *D* 57.
106. *D* 56.
107. *MM* 106.
108. Carl Jung, paraphrased by Neumann, *Great Mother,* op. cit., 221.
109. Neumann, *Great Mother,* op. cit., 182.
110. Ibid., 183 (italics mine).
111. *MM* 106.
112. Sir Wallis Budge, quoted by Neumann, *Great Mother,* op. cit., 221.
113. *MM* 106.
114. *MM* 83.
115. Neumann, *Great Mother,* op. cit., 317.

116. Ibid., 310.
117. Ibid., 317.
118. *HM* 14.
119. Neumann, *Great Mother,* op. cit., 289.
120. Hays, *The Dangerous Sex,* op. cit., 84.
121. Ibid., 86.
122. *MM* 106.
123. *DH* 106.
124. *D* 364 (italics mine).
125. Robert Waugh, "The Subway and the Shoggoth, Part II," *Lovecraft Studies* 40 (Fall 1998), 27.
126. Neumann, *Great Mother,* op. cit., 296.
127. Murray, *Witch-Cult,* op. cit., 100.
128. *D* 156.
129. Murray, *Witch-Cult,* op. cit., 209, 211.
130. Neumann, *Great Mother,* op. cit., 191.
131. Ibid., 288.
132. *MM* 291.
133. *MM* 297.
134. Neumann, *Great Mother,* op. cit., 191.
135. Murray, *Witch-Cult,* op. cit., 157.
136. Neumann, *Great Mother,* op. cit., 44.
137. *D* 75.
138. Neumann, *Great Mother,* op. cit., 170.
139. *AT* 41.
140. *AT* 42.
141. Neumann, *Great Mother,* op. cit., 189.
142. Ibid., 149.
143. *HM* 15.
144. Hays, *The Dangerous Sex,* op. cit., 74.
145. Ibid., 77.
146. *MM* 105.
147. *DH* 94.
148. *Weird N.J. Video Adventures,* narr. R. Stevie Moore, post prod. by Alexander Hartenstine, 30 min. (Bloomfield, NJ: Weird N.J., 1999) (videocassette).
149. Hays, *The Dangerous Sex,* op. cit., 56, 61, 70.
150. Ibid., 291.
151. William Beckford, *Vathek,* in *Three Gothic Novels,* ed. Peter Fairclough (Middlesex, England: Penguin, 1972), 177.
152. Ibid., 253.
153. Ernest Jones, *On the Nightmare* (New York: Liveright, 1951), 104.

154. Neumann, *Great Mother,* op. cit., 223 (italics mine).
155. *DH* 302.
156. De Lancre, quoted in Murray, *Witch-Cult,* op. cit., 107.
157. Neumann, *Great Mother,* op. cit., 48.
158. *D* 264.
159. *DH* 16.
160. *DH* 55 (italics mine).
161. Murray, *Witch-Cult,* op. cit., 22–23, 39.
162. Ibid., 206–207.
163. *DH* 66.
164. The name "Marsh" is a favored Lovecraftian surname in both "The Shadow Over Innsmouth" and "Medusa's Coil." Lovecraft perhaps follows Margaret Murray here, who in her *Witch-Cult* cites the name "Marsh of Dunstable," who was said to be the "'head of the whole Colledge [sic] of Witches'" in the Dunstable area in 1649 (Murray, *Witch-Cult,* op. cit., 48).
165. *D* 20, 24.
166. *MM* 301.
167. *MM* 303.
168. Neumann, *Great Mother,* op. cit., 260.
169. Beckford, *Vathek,* op. cit., 228.
170. Hays, *The Dangerous Sex,* op. cit., 142.
171. Neumann, *Great Mother,* op. cit., 46.
172. *HM* 147.
173. *HM* 146.
174. *HM* 163.
175. Neumann, *Great Mother,* op. cit., 65.
176. Murray, *Witch-Cult,* op. cit., 14.
177. *D* 199 (italics mine).
178. *DH* 57.
179. Neumann, *Great Mother,* op. cit., 98.
180. Ibid., 99.
181. John Uri Lloyd (as communicated to Llewelyn Drury), *Etidorhpa; or, The End of Earth,* 5th ed. (Cincinnati: Robert Clarke, 1896, reproduced in Mokelumne Hill, CA: Health Research, 1966; accessed at http: //books.google.com), 257.
182. *HM* 222.
183. *D* 260, 261.
184. Marquis de Sade, quoted in Ross, *Sadomasochism,* op. cit., 122.
185. *D* 260.

186. *D* 261.
187. Perley Poore Sheehan, *Judith of Babylon,* ed. Brian Earl brown (Detroit, MI: Beb, n.d.), 84.
188. *SL* 1:34.
189. Hays, *The Dangerous Sex,* op. cit., 144.
190. Ibid., 145.
191. Neumann, *Great Mother,* op. cit., 331.
192. *DH* 134.
193. True, in early 1921, long before the writing of "Red Hook," Lovecraft had already contemplated writing of a pilgrimage to the throne of Azathoth, an entity whom Lovecraft elsewhere identifies as male (*DH* 110); but even so, Lovecraft never actually utilized this image until 1926–1927, around the time of the writing of *The Dream-Quest of Unknown Kadath*; and in any case, there seems to be a close similarity between Lovecraft's conception of Azathoth as an all-devouring entity of cosmic chaos, and that archetypal conception of the primordial and all-devouring Great Round or Great Abyss, which identifies the primal darkness of unformed chaos with the maternal Feminine.
194. Cthulhu is "of a somewhat bloated corpulence" (*DH* 134) and like a "jelly" (*DH* 153); while Suydam is both "jellyish" (*D* 262) and "corpulent" (*D* 261, 262).
195. *D* 262.
196. *D* 264.
197. Robert Waugh, "Dr. Margaret Murray and H. P. Lovecraft: The Witch-Cult in New England," *Lovecraft Studies* 31 (Fall 1994), 5.
198. Murray, *Witch-Cult,* op. cit., 12.
199. Ibid., 13.
200. *AT* 143.
201. *D* 121.
202. *DH* 150.
203. *D* 121.
204. Dennis Quinn, "Endless Bacchanal: Rome, Livy, and Lovecraft's Cthulhu Cult," in *Lovecraft Annual* No. 5, ed. S. T. Joshi (New York: Hippocampus, 2011), 191.
205. Robert M. Price, for example, perhaps following Lovecraft's description of him as a

"patron demon," refers to Ghatanothoa as a "him" (Price, "Monsters of Mu: The Lost Continents in the Cthulhu Mythos," *Crypt of Cthulhu* vol. 1 no. 5, [1982], 12).
206. *HM* 225.
207. *DH* 45.
208. Neumann, *Great Mother,* op. cit., 214.
209. Ibid., 113, and plate 157a.
210. Ibid., 306.
211. Ibid., 141.
212. *AT* 43.
213. *AT* 476.
214. *AT* 43.
215. *MM* 292.
216. *DH* 115.
217. *DH* 140.
218. *MM* 106.
219. *DH* 31 (italics mine).
220. Robert Graves, *The Greek Myths,* vol. 1 (New York: Penguin, 1955), 205.
221. Neumann, *Great Mother,* op. cit., 111.
222. Robert Waugh, "'Cool Air,' 'The Apartment Above Us,' and Other Stories," in *Lovecraft Annual* No. 5, ed. S. T. Joshi (New York: Hippocampus, 2011), 225.
223. Smith, *Classical Dictionary,* op. cit., 77.
224. Samuel Loveman, "Lovecraft as Conversationalist," in *Out of the Immortal Night: Selected Works of Samuel Loveman,* ed. S. T. Joshi and David E. Schultz (NY: Hippocampus, 2004), 224.
225. *HM* 181.
226. *HM* 186.
227. *D* 77.
228. Lovecraft, *H. P. Lovecraft in the Argosy,* op. cit., 14.
229. *HM* 330.
230. *MM* 268.
231. *AT* 31.
232. *DH* 115.
233. *HM* 196.
234. *DH* 115.
235. *MM* 106.
236. Neumann, *Great Mother,* op. cit., 158.
237. Murray, *Witch-Cult,* op. cit., 126, 168, 108, 119, and others.
238. *D* 72.
239. Levy, *Lovecraft,* op. cit., 39.
240. *HM* 187.
241. Neumann, *Great Mother,* op. cit., 83.
242. *HM* 193.
243. Otto Weininger, *Sex and Character,* trans. from the 6th

German ed. (New York: G. P. Putnam's Sons, reprinted by Kessinger, n.d.), 233 (italics mine).
244. *HM* 177.
245. *HM* 193.
246. *D* 76–78 passim.
247. *D* 255, 263.
248. Sheehan, *Judith of Babylon*, op. cit., 82.
249. Lovecraft, *H. P. Lovecraft in the Argosy*, op. cit., 14.
250. Weininger, *Sex and Character*, op. cit., 332.
251. Neumann, *Great Mother*, op. cit., 300.
252. *HM* 329.
253. *DH* 114.
254. *HM* 187 (italics mine).
255. *D* 20.
256. *D* 23.
257. Alex Houstoun, "Lovecraft and the Sublime," in *Lovecraft Annual* No. 5, ed. S. T. Joshi (New York: Hippocampus, 2011), 161.
258. Neumann, *Great Mother*, op. cit., 75.
259. Ibid., 271.
260. *D* 261.
261. *D* 122.
262. *HM* 329.
263. *MM* 303.
264. Beckford, *Vathek*, op. cit., 253.
265. Michael Gibson, *Symbolism* (Taschen, 2006), 139, 235.
266. Neumann, *Great Mother*, op. cit., 34n18.
267. *DH* 47.
268. Neumann, *Great Mother*, op. cit., 150.
269. Ibid., 152.
270. Ibid., 183.
271. Ibid., 276.
272. *DH* 44 (italics mine).
273. *DH* 28.
274. Perley Poore Sheehan, *The Woman of the Pyramid*, ed. Brian Earl Brown (Detroit, MI: Beb, n.d.), 19.
275. Ibid., 17.
276. Neumann, *Great Mother*, op. cit., 177, 233. See also Hanns Heinz Ewers, "The Spider," in *Strange Tales*, intro. Stephen E. Flowers, foreword Don Webb, 105–120 (Smithville, TX: Runa-Raven, 2000).
277. *DH* 47.
278. *CE* 2:99.
279. Hays, *The Dangerous Sex*, op. cit., 291.
280. *HM* 187 (italics mine).

281. *HM* 188.
282. *DH* 93, 103.
283. Neumann, *Great Mother*, op. cit., 331 (italics mine).
284. Ibid., 75.
285. Ibid., 295 (italics and editorial interpolation mine).
286. Ibid., 38.
287. *DH* 22.
288. Robert Waugh, "Dr. Margaret Murray and H. P. Lovecraft: The Witch-Cult in New England," *Lovecraft Studies* 31 (Fall 1994), 2–10.
289. Murray, *Witch-Cult*, op. cit., 205.
290. Waugh, "Dr. Margaret Murray," op. cit., 9.
291. Murray, *Witch-Cult*, op. cit., 19.
292. Ibid., 12.
293. Ibid., 19.
294. Ibid., 169 (italics mine).
295. Ibid., 175.
296. On the other hand, although she never weaves this fact into her larger, classist thesis, Murray also notes numerous seemingly isolated examples of aristocrats, local magistrates, and gentlemen who were also implicated in the witch trials (Murray, *Witch-Cult*, op. cit., 40, 48, 50, 154, 161–162, 170–171, 191, 201, 203). And although Robert Waugh suggests that Lovecraft had not yet read Murray's book before his writing of "The Rats in the Walls" in the autumn of 1923 (Waugh suggested instead that the various similarities between Lovecraft's story and Murray's thesis "simply [show] how receptive he was to Murray's hypothesis" [Waugh, "Dr. Margaret Murray," op. cit., 6]), it is hard not to detect a similarity between Lovecraft's picture of decadent aristocratic evil in this story and Murray's own discussion of how some converted English kings sometimes forsook Christianity to return to their old gods, including one "Redwald, King of the East Saxons, who 'in the same temple had an altar to sacrifice to Christ, and another small one to offer victims to devils'" (Murray, *Witch-Cult*, op. cit., 20–21).
297. Feminist witch leaflet (1968), quoted in Adler, *Drawing Down the Moon*, op. cit., 202.
298. *MW* 304 (italics mine).

299. Murray, *Witch-Cult*, op. cit., 129.
300. *DH* 245.
301. According to de Camp, Lovecraft admired her book "as stimuli for the writing of weird fiction" (De Camp, *Lovecraft*, op. cit., 238).
302. *SL* III:178.
303. *D* 119.
304. Murray, *Witch-Cult*, op. cit., 20.
305. Ibid., 50, 167.
306. Ibid., 117.
307. Ibid., 116.
308. *SL* III:180.
309. Murray, *Witch-Cult*, op. cit., 52.
310. Adler, *Drawing Down the Moon*, op. cit., 186.
311. Waugh, "Dr. Margaret Murray," op. cit., 5.
312. Ibid., 4.
313. It is also interesting to note, however, one area in which H. P. Lovecraft does *not* follow Murray, and that is in the *names* of the witches. Murray notes the curious fact that there are no Old Testament names among the witches in the trial records she examined (Murray, *Witch-Cult*, op. cit., 255). Lovecraft however, perhaps following New England custom, does not hesitate to give his evil sorcerers and witches such Biblical names as Asenath, Ephraim, and Keziah.
314. *HM* 187 (italics mine).
315. Murray, *Witch-Cult*, op. cit., 276.
316. *DH* 19.
317. Murray, *Witch-Cult*, op. cit., 246.
318. Ibid., 238 (italics mine).
319. *D* 260.
320. Murray, *Witch-Cult*, op. cit., 126.
321. Ibid., 97.
322. *DH* 52.
323. Murray, *Witch-Cult*, op. cit., 124.
324. Ibid., 140, 141, 142, among others.
325. Ibid., 150, 173.
326. Ibid., 133, 134, 136, 140.
327. Ibid., 123, 143, 150, 152.
328. *SL* V:303.
329. Murray, *Witch-Cult*, op. cit., 208.
330. *MM* 281, 286, 292.
331. Murray, *Witch-Cult*, op. cit., 214.

332. Ibid., 224.
333. Ibid., 214.
334. Ibid., 210, 217, among others.
335. Ibid., 138.
336. Ibid., 176.
337. *MM* 286.
338. Murray, *Witch-Cult*, op. cit., 46 (italics mine).
339. Ibid., 177 (italics mine).
340. Jules Michelet, *Satanism and Witchcraft: A Study in Medieval Superstition*, trans. A. R. Allinson (NY: Citadel, 1939), 115.
341. *MM* 298.
342. *MM* 106.
343. Neumann, *Great Mother*, op. cit., 49.
344. *MM* 106.
345. Neumann, *Great Mother*, op. cit., 240.
346. *DH* 154.
347. *D* 17 (italics mine).
348. *DH* 125.
349. *DH* 83 (italics mine).
350. *DH* 114.
351. *DH* 101.
352. *DH* 115.
353. *D* 241.
354. *DH* 125.
355. Neumann, *Great Mother*, op. cit., 214.
356. Ibid., 68.
357. Levy, *Lovecraft*, op. cit., 64.
358. Cannon, *H. P. Lovecraft*, op. cit., 15.
359. T. S. Miller, "From Bodily Fear to Cosmic Horror (and Back Again): The Tentacle Monster from Primordial Chaos to Hello Cthulhu," in *Lovecraft Annual No. 5*, ed. S. T. Joshi (New York: Hippocampus, 2011), 121.
360. Ibid., 127.
361. Ibid., 128.
362. Ibid., 136.
363. *SL* I:284.
364. Weininger, *Sex and Character*, op. cit., 199.
365. Neumann, *Great Mother*, op. cit., 212.
366. Joel Kovel, *White Racism: A Psychohistory* (New York: Random House, 1970), 66.
367. See Hughes' poem "The Negro": "I am a Negro: / Black as the night is black, / Black like the depths of my Africa" (Langston Hughes, "The Negro," in *Anthology of the World's Best Poems*, vol. 2, ed. Edwin Markham, Memorial Edition [New York: Wm. H. Wise, 1948], 803).

368. Murray, *Witch-Cult*, op. cit., 29, 33, 35, 36, 37, 38, 39, 41, 42, 50, 53, 55, 62, 63.
369. Ibid., 35, 36, 37, 57.
370. Ibid., 147.
371. *MW* 336.
372. *MW* 290.
373. Alden T. Vaughan, *American Genesis: Captain John Smith and the Founding of Virginia*, ed. Oscar Handlin, Library of American Biography (Boston: Little Brown, 1975), 130 (italics mine).
374. Ibid., 133.
375. *D* 257.
376. *D* 258.
377. *DH* 339.
378. *MM* 68.
379. Lovecraft, *H. P. Lovecraft in the Argosy*, op. cit., 14.
380. Ibid., 39.
381. *AT* 224.
382. *MM* 281.
383. *MM* 289.
384. Kovel, *White Racism*, op. cit., 67.
385. S. T. Joshi, *H. P. Lovecraft: A Life* (West Warwick, RI: Necronomicon, 2004), 14.
386. *DH* 27.
387. *HM* 185.
388. *HM* 189.
389. *HM* 190 (italics Lovecraft's/Bishop's).
390. *HM* 200.
391. Robert Waugh, "The Subway and the Shoggoth, Part I," *Lovecraft Studies* 39 (Summer 1998), 27.
392. *HM* 188.
393. *HM* 186.
394. Thus; *HM* 170.
395. *HM* 171 (italics mine).
396. *DH* 338.
397. E. Hoffmann Price, *Book of the Dead*, op. cit., 47.
398. *SL* I:98.
399. S. T. Joshi, "What Happens in 'Arthur Jermyn,'" *Crypt of Cthulhu* #75, vol. 9, no. 8 (Michaelmas 1990), 28.
400. Hays, *The Dangerous Sex*, op. cit., 145.
401. F. W. J. Hemmings, *Baudelaire the Damned* (New York: Charles Scribner's Sons, 1982), 50.
402. *HM* 200.
403. Hemmings, *Baudelaire*, op. cit., 51.
404. Charles Baudelaire, *Art in Paris 1845–1862*, ed. and trans. Jonathan Mayne, Landmarks in

Art History series, 2nd ed. (Oxford: Phaidon, 1981), 38.
405. *HM* 170, 175, 192.
406. *HM* 200.
407. *HM* 199 (italics mine).
408. *HM* 200 (italics mine).
409. Joshi, *H. P. Lovecraft*, op. cit., 200, 201.
410. Ibid., 199.
411. Ibid., 200.
412. *HM* 184.
413. *HM* 188.
414. *HM* 181.
415. Sheehan, *Woman of the Pyramid*, op. cit., 19.
416. Beckford, *Vathek*, op. cit., 233.
417. Ibid., 177.
418. Ibid., 230–231.
419. *MM* 101.
420. Adler, *Drawing Down the Moon*, op. cit., 378.
421. David Horowitz, *The Professors: The 101 Most Dangerous Academics in America* (Washington, D.C.: Regnery, 2006), x.
422. Ray Monk, *Ludwig Wittgenstein: The Duty of Genius* (New York: Penguin, 1991), 20.
423. Weininger, *Sex and Character*, op. cit., 338.
424. Weininger, *Sex and Character*, op. cit., 61.
425. *MM* 166, *MW* 553.
426. Murray, *Witch-Cult*, op. cit., 85.
427. Ibid., 255.
428. Robert M. Price, "Mythos Names and How to Say Them," *Lovecraft Studies* 15, vol. 6, no. 2 (Fall 1987), 49.
429. Ibid., 51.
430. L. Sprague de Camp, *Lovecraft: A Biography*, abridged ed. (New York: Ballantine, 1976), 350.
431. Robert M. Price, Introduction, in *Ashes and Others*, by H. P. Lovecraft and Divers Hands, aka *Crypt of Cthulhu* 10, vol. 2, no. 2 (Bloomfield, NJ: Miskatonic University Press, Yuletide 1982), 2.
432. Price, "Mythos Names," op. cit., 51.
433. *CE* 5:253.
434. Kovel, *White Racism*, op. cit., 200.
435. Robert Waugh, "The Subway and the Shoggoth, Part II," *Lovecraft Studies* 40 (Fall 1998), 27.
436. Ibid., 16.
437. *SL* I:334.
438. *SL* II:44.

439. Waugh, "The Subway, Part II," op. cit., 17.

440. Jones, *Nightmare,* op. cit., 122.

441. *D* 15.

442. *DH* 35.

443. *MM* 286.

444. Kovel, *White Racism,* op. cit., 66 (italics mine).

445. *DH* 112.

446. Edgar Rice Burroughs, *The Beasts of Tarzan,* illus. J. Allen St. John (New York: A. L. Burt, 1916), 79.

447. *MM* 65.

448. *MM* 62.

449. Kenneth M. Stampp, *The Peculiar Institution: Slavery in the Ante-Bellum South* (New York: Random House, 1956), 89; and Herbert Aptheker, *The Colonial Era,* 2nd ed. (New York: International, 1979), 44.

450. *MM* 67.

451. *MW* 326.

452. Aptheker, *Colonial Era,* op. cit., 42–43.

453. Arkansas slaveholder, quoted in Kenneth Stampp, *Peculiar Institution,* op. cit., 1/1.

454. H. P. Lovecraft, *O Fortunate Floridian,* ed. and intro. S. T. Joshi and David E. Schultz (Tampa, FL: University of Tampa Press, 2007), 36.

455. Don Mark Lemon, "The Gorilla," in George Dodds' *The Ape-Man: His Kith and Kin, A Collection of Texts Which Prepared the Advent of Tarzan of the Apes by Edgar Rice Burroughs,* n.d., ERBzine, http://www.erbzine.com/mag18gorilla.htm.

456. Lovecraft to *The Argosy* in 1914: "'I strongly hope that you have added Perley Poore Sheehan permanently to your staff, for in him may be recognized an extremely powerful writer'" (Lovecraft, quoted in Samuel Moskowitz, *Under the Moons of Mars: A History and Anthology of the "Scientific Romance" in the Munsey Magazines, 1912–1920* [New York: Holt, Rinehart, and Winston, 1970], 374.).

457. Perley Poore Sheehan, *The Abyss of Wonders,* ed. Brian Earl Brown (Detroit, MI: Beb, n.d.), 39.

458. Ibid., ch. 30, 57.

459. Kovel, *White Racism,* op. cit., 194–195.

460. *MM* 95.

461. *MM* 101 (italics Lovecraft's).

462. Kovel, *White Racism,* op. cit., 194–195.

463. Ibid., 193.

464. *MM* 62.

465. Kovel, *White Racism,* op. cit., 33.

466. Ibid., 68.

467. Ibid., 33.

468. Lovecraft to *The Argosy* (1914): England is "'one of the three supreme literary artists of the house of Munsey'" (quoted in Moskowitz, *Under the Moons,* op. cit., 374).

469. George Allan England, *The Vacant World* (Boston: Small, Maynard, 1914; accessed at http://books.google.com), 105.

470. Ibid., 106.

471. George Allan England, *The After Glow* (Boston: Small, Maynard, 1914), 528.

472. Moskowitz, *Under the Moons,* op. cit., 53.

473. *DH* 150.

474. *CE* 5:267.

475. Kovel, *White Racism,* op. cit., 193.

476. Ibid., 194.

477. Ibid., 195.

478. *MM* 106.

479. Weininger, *Sex and Character,* op. cit., 207.

480. *MM* 101.

481. *MM* 276.

482. *MM* 273.

483. *D* 423 (italics mine).

484. Arthur Machen, *The Great God Pan and the Inmost Light* (Boston: Roberts Brothers, 1895; accessed at http://books.google.com), 100.

485. Ray Monk, *Ludwig Wittgenstein: The Duty of Genius* (New York: Penguin, 1991), 20.

486. Weininger, *Sex and Character,* op. cit., 330.

487. Ibid., 308.

488. Ibid.

489. Ibid., 313.

490. Ibid., 272.

491. *MW* 548.

492. Weininger, *Sex and Character,* op. cit., 221.

493. Ibid., 346.

494. W. Paul Cook, "In Memoriam: Howard Phillips Lovecraft: Recollections, Appreciations, Estimates" (1941), reproduced in Cannon, ed., *Lovecraft Remem-* bered (Sauk City, WI: Arkham House, 1998), 114–115.

495. Lovecraft, *H. P. Lovecraft in the Argosy,* op. cit., 14.

496. Weininger, *Sex and Character,* op. cit., 329.

497. Weininger, *Sex and Character,* op. cit., 250.

498. *MM* 67.

499. Weininger, *Sex and Character,* op. cit., 270.

500. Ibid., 278.

501. Ibid., 264.

502. Waugh, "The Subway, Part II," op. cit., 17.

503. Weininger, *Sex and Character,* op. cit., 253.

504. Ibid., 294 (italics mine).

505. *MM* 67.

506. *MM* 95.

507. *MM* 67.

508. Weininger, *Sex and Character,* op. cit., 293–294 (italics mine).

509. Ibid., 295.

510. Ibid., 280.

511. *MM* 95.

512. Weininger, *Sex and Character,* op. cit., 280.

513. *MM* 76.

514. *MM* 95.

515. Weininger, *Sex and Character,* op. cit., 288.

516. Waugh, "The Subway, Part II," op. cit., 18.

517. Weininger, *Sex and Character,* op. cit., 287.

518. Ibid., 198.

519. Ibid., 296.

520. *DH* 302.

521. Weininger, *Sex and Character,* op. cit., 211.

522. Ibid.

523. *MM* 67.

524. Weininger, *Sex and Character,* op. cit., 65.

525. *DH* 281.

526. Weininger, *Sex and Character,* op. cit., 70.

527. Ibid., 65.

528. Ibid., 68.

529. Ibid., 119.

530. Edward Gibbon, *The History of the Decline and Fall of the Roman Empire,* vol. 1, ed. the Rev. H. H. Milman (New York: Harper and Bros., 1841; accessed at http://books.google.com), ch. 11, 173.

531. Weininger, *Sex and Character,* op. cit., 306.

532. Ibid., 309.

533. Ibid., 310 (italics mine).

534. Ibid., 308.
535. Ibid., 320.
536. *MM* 67, 76.
537. Weininger, *Sex and Character,* op. cit., 246.
538. Ibid., 191.
539. *MM* 67.
540. Adolf Hitler, *Mein Kampf,* trans. Ralph Manheim (Boston: Houghton Mifflin, 1971), 303 (italics mine).
541. *MM* 94 (italics mine).
542. *MM* 92 (italics mine).
543. *DH* 302.
544. *DH* 301.
545. *MM* 95 (italics mine).
546. *MM* 92.
547. Ibid. (italics mine).
548. Waugh, "The Subway, Part II," op. cit., 24.
549. Oswald Spengler, *Decline of the West,* vol. 1, *Form and Actuality,* trans. Charles Francis Atkinson (New York: Alfred A. Knopf, 1930), 209n, 406; and Oswald Spengler, *Decline of the West,* vol. 2, *Perspectives of World History,* trans. and ed. Charles Francis Atkinson (New York: Alfred A. Knopf, 1930), 206.
550. Spengler, *Decline* vol. 2, op. cit, 208 (italics Spengler's).
551. G. W. Bowersock, *From Gibbon to Auden: Essays on the Classical Tradition* (Oxford University Press, 2009), 134–135.
552. Ibid., 134.
553. Jaś Elsner, *Imperial Rome and Christian Triumph: The Art of the Roman Empire AD 100–450,* Oxford History of Art (Oxford University Press, 1998), 125.
554. Ibid., 115.
555. Waugh, "The Subway, Part II," op. cit., 24.
556. Smith, *Classical Dictionary,* op. cit., 516.
557. *HM* 276.
558. Smith, *Classical Dictionary,* op. cit., 274.
559. Gibbon, *Decline,* vol. 1, op. cit., ch. 11, 170–171.
560. Ibid., 171.
561. Ibid., 172.
562. H. J. Rose, *A Handbook of Greek Literature, from Homer to the Age of Lucian* (New York, E. P. Dutton, 1960), 400.
563. De Camp, *Lovecraft,* op. cit., 173.
564. Gibbon, *Decline,* vol. 1, op. cit., ch. 11, 176.
565. Weininger, *Sex and Character,* op. cit., 314–315.
566. *D* 260.
567. Weininger, *Sex and Character,* op. cit., 299.
568. J. J. Bachofen, paraphrased by Neumann, *Great Mother,* op. cit., 61.
569. Bachofen, paraphrased by Neumann, *Great Mother,* op. cit., 62.
570. *CE* 5:70.
571. *MM* 95.
572. Neumann, *Great Mother,* op. cit., 94.
573. De Camp, *Lovecraft,* op. cit., 52.
574. Neumann, *Great Mother,* op. cit., 304 (italics mine).

Bibliography

I. Works by H. P. Lovecraft

The Ancient Track. Ed. S. T. Joshi. San Francisco: Night Shade, 2001.

At the Mountains of Madness and Other Novels. Ed. S. T. Joshi. Sauk City, WI: Arkham House, 1985.

The Call of Cthulhu and Other Weird Stories. Ed. S. T. Joshi. Penguin, 1999.

Collected Essays, 5 vols. Ed. S. T. Joshi. New York: Hippocampus, 2004–2006.

Dagon and Other Macabre Tales. Ed. S. T. Joshi. Sauk City, WI: Arkham House, 1986.

The Dunwich Horror and Others. Ed. S. T. Joshi. Sauk City, WI: Arkham House, 1984.

The Horror in the Museum and Other Revisions. Ed. S. T. Joshi. Sauk City, WI: Arkham House, 1989.

H. P. Lovecraft in the Argosy: Collected Correspondence from the Munsey Magazines. Ed. S. T. Joshi. West Warwick, RI: Necronomicon, 1994.

Letters to Alfred Galpin. Ed. S. T. Joshi and David E. Schultz. New York: Hippocampus, 2003.

Miscellaneous Writings. Ed. S. T. Joshi. Sauk City, WI: Arkham House, 1995.

O Fortunate Floridian. Ed. and introduction by S. T. Joshi and David E. Schultz. Tampa, FL: University of Tampa Press, 2007.

Selected Letters. 5 vols. Ed. August Derleth, Donald Wandrei, and James Turner. Sauk City, WI: Arkham House, 1965–1976.

The Shadow Out of Time. Ed. S. T. Joshi and David E. Schultz. New York: Hippocampus, 2003.

A Winter Wish. Ed. Tom Collins. Chapel Hill, NC: Whispers, 1977.

II. Lovecraft Studies

Barlow, Robert H. *On Lovecraft and Life*. Introduction by S. T. Joshi. West Warwick, RI: Necronomicon, 1992.

Burleson, Donald R., PhD. "A Note on 'The Book.'" *Lovecraft Studies* 42–43 (Autumn 2001), 52–54.

Cannon, Peter. *H. P. Lovecraft*. Twayne's United States Authors Series. Boston: Twayne, 1989.

———. *The Lovecraft Papers*. N.p.: Guild America, n.d.

Cannon, Peter, ed. *Lovecraft Remembered*. Sauk City, WI: Arkham House, 1998.

Cardin, Matt. "The Master's Eyes Shining with Secrets: H. P. Lovecraft's Influence on Thomas Ligotti." In *Lovecraft Annual* No. 1, ed. S. T. Joshi, 94–125. New York: Hippocampus, 2007.

De Camp, L. Sprague. *Lovecraft: A Biography*. Abridged ed. New York: Ballantine, 1976.

Derleth, August (as by H. P. Lovecraft and August Derleth). *The Survivor and Others*. New York: Ballantine, 1971.

Dole, Kevin. Review of Michel Houellebecq's *H. P. Lovecraft: Against the World, Against Life*. In *Lovecraft Annual* No. 1, ed. S. T. Joshi, 145–149. New York: Hippocampus, 2007.

Fulwiler, William. "E.R.B. and H.P.L." *ERBdom* 80 (Feb. 1975), 41 and 44.

Goho, James. "What Is 'the Unnamable'? H. P. Lovecraft and the Problem of Evil." In *Lovecraft Annual* No. 3, ed. S. T. Joshi, 10–52. New York: Hippocampus, 2009.

Houstoun, Alex. "Lovecraft and the Sublime: A Reinterpretation." In *Lovecraft Annual* No. 5, ed. S. T. Joshi, 160–180. New York: Hippocampus, 2011.

Joshi, S. T. *H. P. Lovecraft: A Life*. West Warwick, RI: Necronomicon, 2004.

_____. "What Happens in 'Arthur Jermyn.'" *Crypt of Cthulhu* #75, vol. 9, no. 8 (Michaelmas 1990), 27–28.

Levy, Maurice. *Lovecraft: A Study in the Fantastic*. Trans. S. T. Joshi. Detroit: Wayne State University Press, 1988.

Livesey, T. R. "Dispatches from the Providence Observatory: Astronomical Motifs and Sources in the Writings of H. P. Lovecraft." In *Lovecraft Annual* No. 2, ed. S. T. Joshi, 3–87. New York: Hippocampus, 2008.

Long, Frank Belknap. *Howard Phillips Lovecraft: Dreamer on the Nightside*. Sauk City, WI: Arkham House, 1975.

Lord, Bruce. "The Genetics of Horror: Sex and Racism in H. P. Lovecraft's Fiction." 2004. Unpaginated. http://www.contrasoma.com/writing/lovecraft.html. Accessed 11/6/05.

Loveman, Samuel. *Out of the Immortal Night: Selected Works of Samuel Loveman*. Ed. S. T. Joshi and David E. Schultz. NY: Hippocampus, 2004.

Mastropierro, Lorenso. "The Theme of Distance in the Tales of H. P. Lovecraft." In *Lovecraft Annual* No. 3, ed. S. T. Joshi, 67–95. New York: Hippocampus, 2009.

Migliore, Andrew, and John Strysil. *Lurker in the Lobby: A Guide to the Cinema of H. P. Lovecraft*. San Francisco: Night Shade, 2006.

Miller, T. S. "From Bodily Fear to Cosmic Horror (and Back Again): The Tentacle Monster from Primordial Chaos to Hello Cthulhu." In *Lovecraft Annual* No. 5, ed. S. T. Joshi, 121–154. New York: Hippocampus, 2011.

Murray, Will. "More Lovecraft in the Comics." *Crypt of Cthulhu* #75, vol. 9, no. 8 (Michaelmas 1990). 22–26. Ed. Robert M. Price. Upper Montclair, NJ: Cryptic Publications.

Nelson, Victoria. *The Secret life of Puppets*. Cambridge, MA: Harvard University Press, 2001.

Oakes, David A. "A Warning to the World: The Deliberative Argument of *At the Mountains of Madness*." *Lovecraft Studies* 39 (Summer 1998), 21–25.

Pace, Joel. "Queer Tales? Sexuality, Race, and Architecture in 'The Thing on the Doorstep.'" In *Lovecraft Annual* No. 2, ed. S. T. Joshi, 104–137. West Warwick, RI: Necronomicon, 2008.

Price, E. Hoffman. *Book of the Dead, Friends of Yesteryear: Fictioneers and Others (Memories of the Pulp Fiction Era*. Ed. Peter Ruber, intro. Jack Williamson. Sauk City, WI: Arkham House, 2001.

Price, Robert M. "HPL and HPB, Lovecraft's Use of Theosophy." *Crypt of Cthulhu* vol. 1, no. 5 (Roodmas 1982), 3–9. Ed. Robert M. Price. Upper Montclair, NJ: Cryptic.

_____. "Monsters of Mu: The Lost Continents in the Cthulhu Mythos." *Crypt of Cthulhu* vol. 1 no. 5, (1982), 10–14.

_____. "Mythos Names and How to Say Them." *Lovecraft Studies* 15, vol. 6, no. 2 (Fall 1987), 47–53. Ed. S. T. Joshi. West Warwick, RI: Necronomicon.

Quinn, Dennis. "Endless Bacchanal: Rome, Livy, and Lovecraft's Cthulhu Cult." In *Lovecraft Annual* No. 5, ed. S. T. Joshi, 188–215. West Warwick, RI: Necronomicon, 2011.

Rajala, J.-M. "Locked Dimensions Out of Reach: The Lost Stories of H. P. Lovecraft." In *Lovecraft Annual* No. 5, ed. S. T. Joshi, 3–90. West Warwick, RI: Necronomicon, 2011.

Salonia, John. "Cosmic Maenads and the Music of Madness: Lovecraft's Borrowings from the Greeks." In *Lovecraft Annual* No. 5, ed. S. T. Joshi, 91–101. West Warwick, RI: Necronomicon, 2011.

Schorer, Mark. *Pieces of Life*. New York: Farrar, Straus and Giroux, 1977.

Shreffler, Philip A. *The H. P. Lovecraft Companion*. Westport, CT: Greenwood, 1977.

Taylor, Justin. "The Crawling Chaos," review of Michel Houellebecq's *H. P. Lovecraft: Against the World, Against Life*. www.counterpunch.org. http:www.cou nterpunch.org/taylor04302005.html. Accessed November 5, 2005.

Waugh, Robert. "'Cool Air,' 'The Apartment Above Us,' and Other Stories." In *Lovecraft Annual* No. 5, ed. S. T. Joshi, 216–239. West Warwick, RI: Necronomicon, 2011.

_____. "Dr. Margaret Murray and H. P. Lovecraft: The Witch-Cult in New England." *Lovecraft Studies* 31 (Fall 1994), 2–10. Ed. S. T. Joshi. West Warwick, RI: Necronomicon.

_____. "The Subway and the Shoggoth, Part I." *Lovecraft Studies* 39 (Summer 1998), 25–34.

_____. "The Subway and the Shoggoth, Part II." *Lovecraft Studies* 40 (1998), 16–28. Ed. S. T. Joshi. West Warwick, RI: Necronomicon.

III. Classical Studies

Barr, Stringfellow. *The Will of Zeus: A History of Greece from the Origins of Hellenic Culture to the Death of Alexander.* Philadelphia and New York: J. B. Lippincott, 1961.

Bowersock, G. W. *From Gibbon to Auden: Essays on the Classical Tradition.* Oxford University Press, 2009.

Burn, Lucilla. *The Greek Myths.* Austin: University of Texas Press, British Museum Publications, 1992.

Elsner, Jaś. *Imperial Rome and Christian Triumph: The Art of the Roman Empire AD 100–450.* Oxford History of Art. Oxford University Press, 1998.

Gibbon, Edward, Esq. *The History of the Decline and Fall of the Roman Empire,* vol. 1. Ed. the Rev. H. H. Milman. New York: Harper, 1841. Accessed at http://books.google.com on 9/13/12.

Graves, Robert. *The Greek Myths,* vol. 1. New York: Penguin, 1955.

Hopkins, Keith. *Death and Renewal: Sociological Studies in Roman History,* vol. 2. Cambridge, U.K.: Cambridge University Press, 1985.

Kingsley, Charles. *The Heroes, or Greek Fairy Tales for My Children.* New York: Thomas Y. Crowell, 1900.

Mackail, J. W. *An Introduction to Virgil's Aeneid.* Abridged from the author's edition of *The Aeneid,* privately printed for The Virgil Society. Glasgow: University Press, 1946.

Murray, Alexander S. *Manual of Mythology.* Ed. William H. Klapp. New York: Tudor, 1936.

Mylonas, George E. *Eleusis and the Eleusinian Mysteries.* Princeton, NJ: Princeton University Press, 1961.

Petronius. *The Satyricon.* Ed. William Arrowsmith. New York: Mentor, New American Library, 1959.

Rostovtzeff, M. I. "The Decay of the Ancient World and Its Economic Explanations." In *The Fall of Rome: Can It Be Explained?* Ed. Mortimer Chambers. 2nd ed. European Problem Studies. New York: Holt, Rinehart and Winston, 1970.

Seltman, Charles. *The Twelve Olympians.* New York: Thomas Y. Crowell, 1960.

Smith, William. *A Classical Dictionary of Biography, Mythology, and Geography.* Albemarle Street: John Murray, 1881.

Virgil. *Virgil's Eclogues and Georgics.* Ed. Horace Andrews. 2nd ed. Boston: Crocker and Brewster, 1866. Accessed at http://books.google.com/ on 9/13/12.

IV. Anthropology and Psychology

Baring-Gould, Sabine. *The Book of Werewolves.* Introduction by Nigel Suckling. London: Senate Studio Editions, 1995.

Eisler, Robert. *Man Into Wolf: An Anthropological Interpretation of Sadism, Masochism and Lycanthropy.* Introduction by Sir David K. Henderson. London: Spring, n.d.

Hays, H. R. *The Dangerous Sex: The Myth of Feminine Evil.* New York: G. P. Putnam's Sons, 1964.

Jones, Ernest, M.D. *On the Nightmare.* New York: Liveright, 1951.

Kovel, Joel. *White Racism: A Psychohistory.* New York: Pantheon, 1970.

Mahler, Margaret. "A Psychoanalytic Evaluation of Tic in Psychopathology of Children: Symptomatic Tic and Tic Syndrome." In *The Selected Papers of Margaret S. Mahler: Volume One: Infantile Psychosis and Early Contributions; Volume Two: Separation-Individuation.* Introduction by Marjorie Hartley and Annemarie Weil. New York: Jason Aronson, 1982.

Messadie, Gerald. *A History of the Devil.* Trans. Mare Romano. Kodansha America, 1993.

Murray, Margaret S. *The Witch-Cult in Western Europe.* New York: Barnes and Noble, 1996.

Neumann, Erich. *The Great Mother: An Analysis of the Archetype.* Trans. Ralph Manheim. Bollingen Series 47. Princeton, NJ: Princeton University Press, 1974.

Palmore, Erdman, and Daisaku Maeda. *The Honorable Elders Revisited: A Revised Cross-Cultural Analysis of Aging in Japan.* Durham: Duke University Press, 1985.

Rieff, Philip. *Freud: The Mind of the Moralist.* New York: Viking, 1959.

Rose, H. J. *A Handbook of Greek Literature, from Homer to the Age of Lucian.* New York: E. P. Dutton, 1960.

Ross, John Munder. *The Sadomasochism of Everyday Life: Why We Hurt Ourselves — and Others — and How to Stop.* New York: Simon and Shuster, 1997.

Spengler, Oswald. *Decline of the West.* Vol. 1: *Form and Actuality.* Trans. and notes by Charles Francis Atkinson. New York: Alfred A. Knopf, 1930.

_____. *Decline of the West.* Vol. 2: *Perspectives of World History.* Trans. and ed. Charles Francis Atkinson. New York: Alfred A. Knopf, 1930.

Summers, Montague. *The Vampire in Europe.* New Hyde Park, NY: University Books, 1968.

Weininger, Otto. *Sex and Character.* Trans. from the 6th German edition. New York: G. P. Putnam's Sons, reprinted by Kessinger, n.d.

Young, Leontine. *Life Among the Giants: A Child's Eye View of the Grown-Up World.* New York: McGraw-Hill, 1965.

V. Historical

Aptheker, Herbert. *The Colonial Era.* 2nd ed. New York: International, 1979.

Mather, Cotton. *Cotton Mather on Witchcraft: Being the Wonders of the Invisible World, First Published at Boston in Oct.ᴿ 1692 and Now Reprinted, with Additional Matter and Old Wood-Cuts, for the Library of the Fantastic and Curious.* New York: Dorset, 1991.

Miller, Perry, ed. *The American Puritans: Their Prose and Poetry.* Garden City, New York: Anchor, Doubleday, 1956.

Owens, Joseph A. "Franklin's 'Bloody' Apples." In *Mysterious New England,* ed. Austin N. Stevens, pp. 156–15. Dublin, New Hampshire: Yankee, 1971.

Stampp, Kenneth M. *The Peculiar Institution: Slavery in the Ante-Bellum South.* New York: Vintage, 1956.

Starkey, Marion L. *The Devil in Massachusetts: A Modern Inquiry into the Salem Witch Trials.* New York: Alfred A. Knopf, 1950.

Vaughan, Alden T. *American Genesis: Captain John Smith and the Founding of Virginia.* Ed. Oscar Handlin. The Library of American Biography. Boston: Little Brown, 1975.

VI. Decadence and Vagabondia

Austen, Roger. *Genteel Pagan: The Double Life of Charles Warren Stoddard.* Ed. John Crowley. Amherst: University of Massachusetts Press, 1991.

Baudelaire, Charles. *Art in Paris 1845–1862: Salons and Other Exhibitions Reviewed by Charles Baudelaire.* Ed. and trans. Jonathan Mayne. Landmarks in Art History series. 2nd ed. Oxford: Phaidon, 1981.

Blanchard, Mary Warner. *Oscar Wilde's America.* New Haven, CT: Yale University Press, 1998.

Carman, Bliss. *Echoes from Vagabondia.* Boston: Small, Maynard, 1912. Accessed at http://books.google.com on 6/28/11.

_____. *The Pipes of Pan,* vol. 1. *From the Book of Myths.* Albemarle Street: John Murray, 1903. Accessed at http://books. google.com on 3/4/12.

_____. *Pipes of Pan Number Three: Songs of the Sea Children.* Boston: L. C. Page, 1903. Accessed at http://books.google.com on 3/4/12.

Carman, Bliss, and Richard Hovey. *Last Songs from Vagabondia.* Boston: Small, Maynard, 1900. Accessed at http://books.google.com on 6/28/12.

_____. *More Songs from Vagabondia.* Illus. Tom B. Meteyard. Boston: Copeland and Day, 1896. Accessed at http://books.google. com on 3/4/12.

_____. *Songs from Vagabondia.* Boston: Small, Maynard, 1894. Accessed at http://books. google.com on 3/4/12.

Carpenter, Edward. *Toward Democracy.* London: John Heywood, 1883. Accessed at http://books.google.com on 6/28/12.

Cram, Ralph Adams. *Spirits Black and White.* West Warwick, RI: Necronomicon, 1993.

Ellmann, Richard. *Oscar Wilde.* New York: Alfred A. Knopf, 1988.

Fryer, Jonathan. *Robbie Ross, Oscar Wilde's Devoted Friend.* New York: Carroll and Graf, 2000.

Gibran, Jean, and Kahlil Gibran. *Kahlil Gibran: His Life and His World.* New York: Interlink, 1991.

Hemmings, F. W. J. *Baudelaire the Damned.* New York: Charles Scribner's Sons, 1982.

Holland, Vyvyan. *Son of Oscar Wilde.* Rev. ed. Ed. Merlin Holland. London: Robinson, 1999.

Jussim, Estelle. *Slave to Beauty: The Eccentric Life and Controversial Career of F. Holland Day, Photographer, Publisher, Aesthete.* Boston: David R. Godine, 1981.

Shand-Tucci, Douglass. *Boston Bohemia, 1881–1900.* Vol. 1, *Ralph Adams Cram: Life and Architecture.* Amherst: University of Massachusetts Press, 1995.

_____. *The Crimson Letter: Harvard, Homosexuality, and the Shaping of American Culture.* New York: St. Martin's, 2003.

Sox, David. *Bachelors of Art: Edward Perry Warren and the Lewes House Brotherhood.* London: Fourth Estate, 1991.

Whitman, Walt. *Leaves of Grass*. Philadelphia: David McKay, 1894.

Wilde, Oscar. *The Complete Works of Oscar Wilde*. New York: Perennial Library, Harper and Row, 1989.

Zweig, Paul. *Walt Whitman: The Making of a Poet*. New York: Basic, 1984.

VII. Science Fiction, the Pulps and the Macabre

Ashley, Mike, and Robert A. W. Lowndes. *The Gernsback Days: A Study of the Evolution of Modern Science Fiction from 1911 to 1936*. Holicong, PA: Wildside, 2004.

Beckford, William. *Vathek*. In *Three Gothic Novels*, ed. Peter Fairclough, intro. Mario Praz. Middlesex, England: Penguin, 1972.

Bennet, Robert Ames (pseud. Lee Robinet). *Thyra, A Romance of the Polar Pit*. Prod. Robert D. Cody. Project Gutenberg Australia. Accessed at http://gutenberg.net.au/ebooks09/0900541h.html on 6/10/12.

Burroughs, Edgar Rice. *At the Earth's Core*. Illus. J. Allen St. John. New York: Grosset and Dunlap, 1922.

_____. *The Beasts of Tarzan*. Illus. J. Allen St. John. New York: A. L. Burt, 1916.

Doyle, Arthur Conan. "The Horror of the Heights." In *Tales of Terror and Mystery*. Project Gutenberg Etext #537, 2008. Accessed at http://www.gutenberg.org/5/3/537/ on 4/25/12.

England, George Allan. *Darkness and Dawn*. Boston: Small, Maynard, 1914. Accessed at http://books.google.com on 6/12/12.

Giesy, J. U. *Palos of the Dog Star Pack*. Ed. Brian Earl Brown. Detroit, MI: Beb, n.d.

Lemon, Don Mark. "The Gorilla." In George Dodds' *The Ape-Man: His Kith and Kin, A Collection of Texts Which Prepared the Advent of Tarzan of the Apes by Edgar Rice Burroughs*. N.d., unpaginated. *ERBzine*. Accessed at http:// www.erbzine.com/mag18 gorilla.htm on June 12, 2012.

Long, Frank Belknap. *It Was the Day of the Robot*. New York: Belmont, 1963.

_____. *The Rim of the Unknown*. New York: Condor, 1978.

Lumley, William. "The Diary of Alonzo Typer." In *Ashes and Others*, by H. P. Lovecraft and Divers Hands, aka *Crypt of Cthulhu* 10, vol. 2, no. 2 (Yuletide 1982), 21–25. Bloomfield, NJ: Miskatonic University Press.

Machen, Arthur. *The Great God Pan and the Inmost Light*. Boston: Roberts Bros., 1895. Accessed at http://books.google.com on 1/15/12.

Merritt, A. "The People of the Pit." In *The People of the Pit and Other Early Horrors from the Munsey Pulps*. Normal, IL: Black Dog, 2010.

Moskowitz, Samuel. *Under the Moons of Mars: A History and Anthology of the "Scientific Romance" in the Munsey Magazines, 1912–1920*. New York: Holt, Rinehart, and Winston, 1970.

Poe, Edgar Allan. *The Unabridged Edgar Allan Poe*. Philadelphia, PA: Running Press, 1983.

Rousseau, Victor. *Draft of Eternity*. Ed. Brian Earl Brown. Detroit, MI: Beb, n.d.

_____ (pseud. H. M. Egbert). *The Sea Demons*. Classics of Science Fiction reprint series. Westport, CT: Hyperion, 1976.

Savile, Frank. *Beyond the Great South Wall: The Secret of the Antarctic*. Illus. Robert L. Mason. New York: Grosset and Dunlap, 1901. Accessed at http://books. google.com on 6/12/12.

Serviss, Garrett P. *The Moon Metal*. Ed. Suzanne L. Shell, Joris Van Dael, and the Online Distributed Proofreading Team, n.d. Ch. 12, unpaginated. Accessed at http://www.booksshouldbefree.com on 5/21/12.

Sheehan, Perley Poore. *The Abyss of Wonders*. Ed. Brian Earl Brown. Detroit, MI: Beb, n.d.

_____. *Judith of Babylon*. Ed. Brian Earl Brown (Detroit, MI: Beb, n.d.

_____. *The Woman of the Pyramid*. Ed. Brian Earl Brown. Detroit, MI: Beb, n.d.

Stilson, Charles. *Polaris and the Goddess Glorian*. Ed. Brian Earl Brown. Detroit, MI: Beb, n.d.

_____. *Polaris—of the Snows*. Ed. Brian Earl Brown. Detroit, MI: Beb, n.d.

_____. *Minos of Sardanes*. Ed. Brian Earl Brown. Detroit, MI: Beb, n.d.

VIII. Occultism

Adler, Margot. *Drawing Down the Moon: Witches, Druids, Goddess-Worshippers, and Other Pagans in America Today*. Boston: Beacon, 1979.

Cranston, Sylvia. *The Extraordinary Life and Influence of Helena Blavatsky, Founder of the Modern Theosophical Movement*. New York: G. P. Putnam's Sons, 1994.

Crowley, Aleister. *Liber Liberi vel Lapidis Lazuli: Adumbratio Kabbalae Aegyptorum,*

Sub Figura VII. Fairfax, CA: Ordo Templi Orientis, 1989.

_____. *Magick in Theory and Practice*. Secaucus, NJ: Castle, 1991.

Fuller, Jean Overton. *The Magical Dilemma of Victor Neuburg*. Rev. ed. Oxford, UK: Mandrake, 1990.

Lloyd, John Uri (pseud. Llewelyn Drury). *Etidorhpa; or, The End of Earth*. 5th ed. Illus. J. Augustus Knapp. Cincinnati: Robert Clarke, 1896. Reprint Mokelumne Hill, CA: Health Research, 1966. Accessed at http://books.google.com on 4/24/12.

Michelet, Jules. *Satanism and Witchcraft: A Study in Medieval Superstition*. Trans. A. R. Allinson. NY: Citadel, 1939.

IX. Other Media

Gordon, Stuart. Commentary track. *H. P. Lovecraft's from Beyond*. MGM, 2007. DVD.

_____. Commentary track. *H. P. Lovecraft's Re-Animator*. Millennium ed. Elite Entertainment, 2002. DVD.

Weird N.J. Video Adventures. Narr. R. Stevie Moore, post-production Alexander Hartenstine. 30 min. Bloomfield, NJ: Weird N.J., 1999. Videocassette.

Index

Numbers in **_bold italics_** indicate pages with photographs.

Cram, Ralph Adams 32, 42, 45, 50, 52–54, 55, 60, 266
Crane, Hart 48, 241
Crowley, Aleister 42, 44, 46, 58, 267–268
Cthulhu: call of 26, 96; as father-figure 104; as undead/revenant 9
Cybele 161; and castration 74, 170, 184, 185; as Mother Goddess 171; see also Great Goddess
cyclopean 113, 129, 148; and Devil 108–109; and parental giganticism 80, 100, 118, 169, 170, 241

Danforth 33, 35, 51, 109, 122, 123, 126, 129, 131, 133, 136, 138, 139, 141, 142, 143, 168, 175–180, 184, 193, 195, 198, 211, 229, 230, 240, 250n13
Day, Fred Holland 43, 45, 48, 50, *51*, 53–56, 60
de Blois, Dame 161, 164, 196; hypnotic powers of 194, 198
decadence *3*, 15, 16, 22, 32, 35, 36, 39, 40, 42–56 *passim*, 60, 159, 218, 219, 241, 246n215
De Camp, L. Sprague 4, 30, 34, 64, 90, 116, 205, 222, 259n301, 263
Demeter 34, 59, 171; see also Great Goddess
De Palma, Brain: *Body Double* 183
Derleth, August 127, 139, 147, 153, 255n45
De Sade, Marquis 190, 223
the Devil 19, 53, 56, 62, 88, 108, 111, 126, 127, 164, 187, 207, 208, 210, 214, 217, 246n156, 259n296; see also Black Man of Arkham
Diana 35, 124, 131, 136; see also moon goddess
Dionysus 31, 59, 65, 197, 211; see also Bacchus
dryads 18, 20, 22, 24–26, 28, 34, 39, 40, 42, 44, 46, 163, 164, 246n215
Dunsany, Lord 17, 222, 223
Dyer, Prof. William 4, 14, 51, 114, 123, 126, 130, 131, 135, 141, 144, 145, 175, 179, 220, 232, 234, 244n22, 250n13

Eddy, Clifford M. 62, 70, 79
Edkins, E. A. (Ernest Arthur) 23, 40
Elagabalus 49
Elder Things 99, 112, 113, 141, 143; see also Old Ones
Elsner, Jaś X 25, 236, 265
England, George Allan 2, 45, 261n468; *Darkness and Dawn* trilogy 33, 116, 227, 254n59; *The Empire in the Air* 243; *The Flying Legion* 245
eye 51, 67, 176, 194, 228, 229; see also feminine archetypal ideas

Fate 75, 99, 124, 150, 167, 168, 171, 178, 208, 213, 238, 239, 240, 241
fauns 13, 17, 18, 20, 22–24, 28, 30, 33, 35, 37, 39, 40, 42–44, 56, 66; see also Faunus, Pan; sylvan deities
Faunus 19
feminine archetypal ideas 136, 172, 174, 184, 186, 199, 202, 207; celestial goddess 61, 136,

144, 179, 182, 202; eye goddess 194–195 (*see also* eye); gate/threshold symbolism 9, 78, 149, 184, 186, 195; marshes/swamps 29, 62, 72, 103, 145, 186, 187, 188, 258n164; moon imagery see moon; mound 37, 71, 165, 188, 189; mountain imagery 169–170; nepenthe 197; old woman 161, 169, 203, 209, 210, 213, 241; priestess 34, 59, 125, 136, 138, 166, 167, 173–174, 181, 190, 192, 196, 197, 200, 201, 208, 216, 217, 241, 243n14; throne 189–192, 199, 201, 258n193; vessel imagery 156, 157, 179–181, 185, 188; vulture 112, 193; water imagery 19, 125–128, 149, 151, 155, 157, 186, 187, 188; well imagery 186–187; young woman 203; witch see witches; see also Great Goddess; hypnotism; Terrible Mother
fertility 21, 25, 35–38, 40, 50, 52, 59, 60, 63, 65, 89, 112, 114, 161, 162, 172, 173, 174, 177, 180, 190, 200, 207, 210 see also Great Goddess, sylvan deities
Fitzgerald, Edward: *Rubaiyat of Omar Khayyam* 42
Fortune, Dion 17
Frazer, Sir J. G.: *The Golden Bough* 93
Freud, Sigmund 70, 85, 177, 265
Fulwiler, William 65, 166, 263
furies 135, 193, 196

Galpin, Alfred 61, 124, 126, 153, 263
ghouls 2, *3*, 13, 23, 24, 45, 50, 64, 77, 85, 87, 90–93, 96, 97, 99, 113, 118, 135, 151, 156, 161, 163, 203, 204, 208, 210, 220–221, 249n9
Gibbon, Edward: *Decline and Fall of the Roman Empire* 95, 234, 237, 265
Gibran, Kahlil 54, 55, 266
Giesy, J. U.: *Palos of the Dog Star Pack* 86, 139, 196, 201, 267
giganticism 37, 45, 66, 110, 112, 266; of parents 100, 101, 102, 103, 104, 108; see also cyclopean
"God Save the King!" 104, 190, 207
Goethe, Johann Wolfgang von: *The Sorrows of Young Werther* 213
Goho, James 94, 263
Gordon, Stuart: *Re-Animator* 93, 160, 268
gorgon 164, 192, 194, 240; see also Terrible Mother
Graves, Robert 194, 265
Great Goddess 9, 169, 171, 172, 176, 180, 189, 191, 193, 195, 202, 210, **235**, 239, 240; and the primordial abyss/void 178, 192, 211
Great Mother see Great Goddess
Great Old Ones 8, 98, 99, 101, 105; see also Old Ones
Greece, Ancient see Lovecraft, H.P.
Greene, Sonia 26, 127, 128, 145, 149, 237
Griffith, D. W. (David Wark): *The Avenging Conscience* 17

Hambly, Barbara 160
Hasenclever, Walter: *The Son* 119
Hawthorne, Nathaniel 17; *The Scarlet Letter* 108, 126